Market Place

Market Place:
Food Quarters, Design
and Urban Renewal in London

By

Susan Parham

CAMBRIDGE
SCHOLARS

PUBLISHING

Market Place: Food Quarters, Design and Urban Renewal in London,
by Susan Parham

This book first published 2012

Cambridge Scholars Publishing

12 Back Chapman Street, Newcastle upon Tyne, NE6 2XX, UK

British Library Cataloguing in Publication Data
A catalogue record for this book is available from the British Library

Copyright © 2012 by Susan Parham

All rights for this book reserved. No part of this book may be reproduced, stored in a retrieval system,
or transmitted, in any form or by any means, electronic, mechanical, photocopying, recording or
otherwise, without the prior permission of the copyright owner.

ISBN (10): 1-4438-4172-2, ISBN (13): 978-1-4438-4172-6

For my father, Anthony, and in memory of my mother, Joy

Contents

Preface ix

Acknowledgements x

List of Illustrations xi

Part 1: Situating the Food Quarters

Chapter One 3
Designing for Food

Chapter Two 31
Framing the Research

Part 2: Exploring the Food Quarters

Chapter Three 75
Food-Centred Space

Chapter Four 118
Designed Renewal at Borough Market

Chapter Five 154
Renewal 'From Below' at Broadway Market

Chapter Six 186
Renewal of a Different Kind at Exmouth Market

Part 3: Summing Up the Food Quarters

Chapter Seven 221
Food-Led Renewal in Review

Chapter Eight 247
Food Quarters for the Future?

Appendix 1 270
Interview Matrix

Bibliography 272

Index 310

Preface

I first started writing about food and urban design in the late 1980s as I began to bring together my thinking about how food interconnects with the spatiality and political economy of cities. In *The Table In Space: A Planning Perspective* (1990) I set out a range of food and place making concerns from the scale of the shared table outward, and advocated for returning food to its central role in shaping public and private space. Since then I have continued to explore the fascinating and complicated interplay between urban development, design and planning on the one side and sustainable food systems and cultures on the other. This has always been an applied concern: from identifying gastronomic strategies for cities, researching possibilities for more food-centred, convivial green space, and protecting productive landscapes to avoid sprawl. I have looked at gastronomic architecture and townscapes and written about the healthy cities design paradox of gastronomically rich 'fat cities' where people are thin and long-lived.

This book arose out of these research preoccupations and examines in depth a fast changing area of food and city design. It is focused on primary research into the renewal of food-centred space in areas around moribund food markets in contemporary London. The research findings suggest that what are conceptualised as 'food quarters' have emerged, in which new forms of interconnection between physical design and social processes are being modelled, with food at the heart. The book explores how traditional city design and spatiality has informed the making of a richer, healthier, more food-centred everyday life around Borough, Broadway and Exmouth Markets, while producing places that have also became the loci for food led-gentrification. It frames this paradoxical experience within more spatially dominant approaches to urbanism that have produced 'obesegenic' environments and closed off convivial food options that would support a more satisfying and sustainable urban life. The book draws some conclusions about the complexities of designing and planning for food-led renewal that might apply more broadly to other places in London and potentially to other cities in future.

Acknowledgements

In completing this book, heartfelt gratitude goes to Matthew Hardy, my inspiration over many years, for his wisdom and enduring support, and to my sisters, Felicity, Jennifer and Christabel, for putting up with an apparently endless obsession with food and cities. I want also to acknowledge the excellent contribution of Fran Tonkiss, whose wit, good humour and incisive criticism made the research process far less painful than it might have been. A thank you is also due to Leslie Sklair for his kindness in providing academic support, and to Ricardo Vasconcelos, Iliana Ortega-Alcazar, Alasdair Jones, Eva Neitzert, Roberto Timpano and Lita Khazaka for the friendship and good company that helped in the research and writing of this book.

To the very kind and highly knowledgeable Louise Breward, a special thank you for her many insights and great generosity in spending time discussing Broadway Market and reviewing the draft chapters related to Broadway. Similar gratitude is due to George Nicholson and Ken Grieg in relation to Borough Market. To all those others interviewed I would like to also acknowledge my appreciation of your thoughtful observations about the nature of London's burgeoning food quarters.

A thank you is also owed to the staff of the London Guildhall Library and to Mr Jeremy Smith of the City of London, London Metropolitan Archives for kind assistance as I delved into the fascinating maps record, for permission to reproduce map details, and for allowing me to view the beautiful original lithographs of Edward Bawden's London market series. Thank you also to Dominic Honeysett for producing the three walkability diagrams of the case study areas on open source mapping bases.

Finally, a very grateful acknowledgement to The Estate of Edward Bawden and the Trustees of the Higgins Art Gallery, Bedford, England for their kind permission to use a reproduction of Bawden's 1967 lithograph, Borough Market, as a splendid element of the cover of this book.

LIST OF ILLUSTRATIONS

Figure 3.1: *Borough study area walkability radius*
Figure 3.2: *Rocque's map of 1746, detail*
Figure 3.3: *Horwood's map of 1792-1799, detail*
Figure 3.4: *Stanford's map of London and its suburbs, 1862 (detail)*
Figure 3.5: *Ordnance Survey map of Bermondsey and Wapping of 1894*
Figure 3.6: *Market stalls under the railway viaducts across Bedale Street*
Figure 3.7: *Broadway Market study area walkability radius*
Figure 3.8: *Rocque's map of London and the Country 10 Miles Round, 1746*
Figure 3.9: *Ordnance Survey map of Dalston of 1870*
Figure 3.10: *Ordnance Survey map of Dalston of 1913*
Figure 3.11: *Housing blocks to north of Broadway Market*
Figure 3.12: *Broadway Market streetscape*
Figure 3.13: *Broadway's market in action*
Figure 3.14: *Exmouth Market study area walkability radius*
Figure 3.15: *Detail of Horwood's 1792 map*
Figure 3.16: *Horwood's 1819 map (detail)*
Figure 3.17: *Stanford's map of 1862 (detail)*
Figure 3.18: *Ordnance Survey 1894 map of Exmouth area*
Figure 3.19: *Ordnance Survey 1914 map of Exmouth area*
Figure 3.20: *Exmouth Market view looking north-east*
Figure 4.1: *Key to Borough Market Food Uses Map*
Figure 4.2: *Borough Market Food Map*
Figure 4.3: *Borough Market Food Cluster Map*
Figure 5.1: *Broadway Market newspapers*
Figure 5.2: *Graffiti on the market street*
Figure 5.3: *Broadway Food Map Key*
Figure 5.4: *Broadway Market Food Shops and Land Uses*
Figure 5.5: *Broadway Market Food Stalls*
Figure 6.1: *Key to Exmouth Market Food Map*
Figure 6.2: *Food Map of Exmouth Market*

PART 1:

SITUATING THE FOOD QUARTERS

Chapter One

Designing For Food

Designing for Food

This book is about designing for food. It explores ways that food production, distribution, and consumption arrangements have been played out in three fast transforming urban sites in London in the period 2005 to 2008. It suggests that what are conceptualised here as 'food quarters' emerged during this timeframe, centred on Borough Market, Broadway Market and Exmouth Market, with each place modelling new forms of interconnection between physical design and social processes in which food was at the heart.

Using case study research, focused on these three previously run-down market places within London's traditional urban fabric, the book explores how compact city design informed the making of everyday life, increased the richness of experience of food and eating, and contributed to urban sustainability in these posited food quarters. It frames this experience within more spatially dominant approaches to city design, which seem to close off convivial food options and choices that would support a more satisfying urban life.

But what is a food quarter? The food quarter as explored and defined in this book is understood to be a 'fuzzy edged' food-centred area of an urban settlement, predicated on human scaled, highly mixed, walkable and fine grained urbanism that reflects the European City Model (Clos, 2005). The food quarter thus conceptualised is generally located in traditional urban fabric but its elements are capable of being retrofitted into more sprawling locations and built into new areas too. The market at the centre of the food quarter is not necessarily a farmers' market – and its operation challenges the easy stereotypes that situate traditional markets and farmers' markets as a clear cut duality – nor is it only servicing elite consumption needs. It is likely to be supported by a diverse range of food-related land uses including cafes and restaurants and its users may be visiting its market and food businesses as part of a mix of food consumption techniques including online methods.

In physical design terms, the food quarter features a strong design interplay between traditional built fabric and human scaled public spaces (Madanipour, 1996, 2003). Its physical features act as a frame for emergent forms of socio-spatial practice that reflect increased conviviality in everyday life (Maitland, 2007) and support economic and environmental renewal, but may also be marked by food led gentrification (Warde, 1991; Smith, 1996; Atkinson, 2000; Bridge, 2006), while its governance has been mostly 'from below' rather than predominantly the result of top-down regeneration processes.

Research into three such places in London shows that designing for food led renewal has not been a straightforward process. The research identified some paradoxical relationships in the rise of these food quarters, between sustainability, urban design and sociability focused on food on the one side, and food led gentrification and exclusion on the other. It found that relationships between the physical and the social in the three food quarters made a contribution to developing sustainable cities, by supporting and nurturing convivial food spaces and practices.

At the same time, the rise of new kinds of food spaces and practices at each food quarter also supported and underpinned gentrifying tendencies, by providing a setting for some individuals to play out a 'habitus' (Bourdieu, 1984) that was socially exclusive. The overall conclusion of the book is that although food quarters like the three studied in London can act as gentrifying sites in which to display taste and model distinction, these spaces also suggest consciously designing for food is broadly a good thing for sustainable cities, producing authentic places important for experiencing food led conviviality in everyday life.

This matters because the backdrop to the food quarters' renewal is urban development in which conviviality and sustainability are increasingly compromised (Brotchie and Batty et al, 1995; Frey, 1999; Haughton and Hunter, 2003). Research on the fat city (Parham, 1998; Sui, 2006), the growth of obesegenic environments (Lake and Townshend, 2006, 2008), the argued prevalence of food deserts and food insecurity (Wrigley, 2002; Shaw, 2006), and a crisis of obesity in children (Ebbeling et al 2002; Lobstein, Baur, and Uauy, 2004) reflect how food often interconnects with city form in negative ways, when undertaken within a context of conventional design approaches to urban growth and renewal (Whelan, Wrigley, Warm and Cannings, 2002; Neal, 2006). Yet certain urban experience also offers more positive examples of the intersection of food and cities (Parham, 1990, 1992, 1996, 2005, 2008); places where walkable, compact, food market centred quarters remain - or are being renewed and reconfigured - despite the dominant model presented by the development of sprawling urban conurbations.

Theorists have used the term 'fat city' to describe connections perceived between decisions about spatial form that contribute to sprawl and those that create the conditions for obesity (Sui, 2003; Marvin and Webb, 2007) although causality has been challenged (Eid et al, 2008). By focusing on the way food quarters are developing in London, the notion of fat cities is employed somewhat differently. Drawing on previous research (Parham, 1996, 1998) that predates the more recent, negative use of the term, the book explores the paradox of places that are at once 'fat' in the sense of relying on rich seasonal and regional food resources, yet support forms of place-based sociability that challenge dominant obesegenic spatial modes. At the core of this paradox are traditional quarters of the city characterised by highly walkable food-centred spaces, supported by convivial cultural traditions that stress moderation and balance in food consumption and a strongly developed focus on high quality food sourced from the peri-urban region around the city (Parham, 1998). In combination these elements appear to be important in producing healthful spaces and citizens, an apparent contradiction this book explores through the food quarter research.

Food and cities in context

This book investigates just one aspect of a wider set of research preoccupations that have helped to frame and contextualise its primary focus. Since the early 1990s, when this writer began to study the many roles food plays in urban life (Parham, 1990, 1992, 1993) the study of food and cities has moved from the margins to become a much more central concern in a range of academic disciplines: in sociology, geography, political economy, environmental science and related sustainability policy development, and within urban design theory and practice.

Increasingly, there is research interest in the "gastronomic possibilities" of urban space (Parham, 1992, p.1) focusing on how food can offer positive support to making sustainable and convivial places. Moreover, it has become clear that changes in one food sphere have results in others. Supermarket based consumption, for example, has many ripple effects along the food chain by shaping the agriculture that supports it and the food consumption patterns it in part determines (Bowlby, 2000; Eisenhauer, 2001). These consumption patterns in turn have profound effects on the spatiality they help configure (Lang and Heasman, 2004).

From the scale of the shared table outwards, food has transforming roles in both social and design terms, in both the private and public realms. Food affects the way we make and use kitchens, dining rooms, gardens, streets, neighbourhoods, town centres, suburbs and burgeoning urban conurbations. In the meantime, the issues associated with designing for food have become more acute. There are complex sustainability issues associated with the outdoor room of the food street, and the wider public realm of food markets, cafes, so called foodatainment places (Finkelstein, 1999), foodscapes (Yasmeen: 2006; Sobal and Wansink, 2007), and the gastronomic townscape (Parham, 1992), of which food quarters are argued here to be an important element.

On the productive city side, relevant concerns relate to green spaces in cities connected with food, including market gardens, allotments, community orchards, street trees, and productive urban peripheries (Parham, 1992; Hinchliffe and Whatmore, 2006). The recent revival of interest in urban farming is symptomatic of an increasing concern for food localism, quality, security and resilience that combats the rise of placeless foodscapes (Morgan, Marsden and Murdoch, 2006).

Meanwhile, at a broader spatial scale, new forms of food production, exchange and consumption are associated with the fast expanding post urban realm developing around cities, which tends to undermine the more traditional food approaches of the sustainable bio-region (Parham, 1996; Sonnino, 2009). All these spatial scales fit within the even wider global context of grossly unequal food relationships between the north and south, exacerbated by a largely unsustainable modern food system (Tansey and Worsley, 1995; Parham, 1996; Patel, 2007). In this way the study of the food quarter should be understood as a small part of a much bigger research field (Bell and Valentine, 1997) while acknowledging the impossibility of bringing all these research concerns about designing for food in an urban context together in one book.

Why look at food and design together?

Within sociology, studying food and eating has been until recent times at best a marginal area of enquiry (Mennell, 1991; Germov and Williams, 1999) and the relative neglect of food-related issues can be explained by a number of factors including its invisibility to sociologists as an apparently routine, everyday activity that is taken for granted (Beardsworth and Keil, 2004, p.2). Equally, this historic lack of interest reflects the fact that sociologists have tended not to see food production and distribution processes at work (ibid). This apparent marginality is also gendered, with food strongly associated with the mundane world of female domestic labour and thus holding "little intellectual appeal to the male researchers and theorists who have historically dominated the profession" (ibid).

Over the last twenty years though these marginalising perspectives on food studies in sociology have begun to shift, with research on food and eating no longer seen as frivolous (Mennell, 1996) but legitimately focusing on the "meanings, beliefs and social structures giving shape to food practices in western societies" (Lupton, 1996, p.1). The sociology of food and eating has become recognised not just as a valid sub-discipline, but central to the way boundaries between nature and culture are being rethought (Atkins and Bowler, 2001, p.ix). Additionally, food studies have benefited from the overall cultural turn experienced in sociology and sister disciplines in the 1990s (Ashley et al, 2004) and from renewed interest in both everyday life (Zukin, 1992, 1995, 2004; Stevenson 2003) and the body (Featherstone, 1991; Lupton, 1996).

There has been some, albeit limited, focus on the spatial planning and design aspects of food in cities and this is explored in some detail in the next chapter. Sharon Zukin's (1982, 1992) influential analysis of the parallel, connected, rise of gastronomy and gentrification in New York set the tone for much of the academic debate that followed (Amin and Graham, 1997; Bell, 2007). Zukin (1982) arguing that vernacular tradition and innovation were being combined in both food and architecture to produce gentrified spaces in declining urban areas which drew on a narrow range of design elements to serially reproduce marketable quarters for loft living. Discussion of gentrification - and its connections to food - cannot be avoided when exploring the way food quarters have developed, or in designing for food more generally.

At the same time, the examples presented in this book, and recent theoretical work cited below, demonstrate divergent perspectives on these transformations. For instance, work on spaces of consumption (Bell and Valentine, 1997), and specifically on the spatial and economic role of food market centred areas as potential models for 21st century urbanism (Parham, 1992, 2005, 2008; Esperdy, 2002), suggest more positive possibilities. Likewise, work on convivial spatiality (Mayer and Knox, 2006; Hinchcliffe and Whatmore, 2006; Bell, 2007), in part typified through Slow Food and Slow Cities (città slow) movements and theorising (Beatley, 2004; Mayer and Knox, 2006) brings a more nuanced analysis to processes of urban change in relation to food, that is discussed later in this chapter and the next.

Food and urban sustainability

Urban sustainability is a critical factor in looking at spatial design for food. This is because how food is grown, transported, bought, cooked and eaten presents issues with central material effects on creating a sustainable urban future. So, for this book, a critical framing element is the sharply increasing level of unsustainability of urban development and the ways this is reflected in food production, distribution and consumption in and around cities (Stren, White and Whitney, 1992; Hough, 1994; Haughton and Hunter, 2003). In particular, the food issues associated with climate change provide a context for the research into specific food places and practices in London (Taylor, Madrick and Collin, 2005).

Theorists of sustainable cities argue that in environmental terms a negative feedback loop has grown up in western post industrial cities whereby over consumption of resources including food is matched by overproduction of waste (Rudlin and Falk, 2001). Linked back to food production and forward to food consumption, this presents a problem for continued global sustainability in a context of massive urbanisation (Hough, 1984, 1995; Patel, 2007). Urban sprawl poses particular difficulties for food in a spatial sense: using up valued natural habitats, "whilst cities also pass on their impacts, making intensive demands on the environmental resources of their hinterland areas" (Haughton and Hunter, 2003, p.12). More compact approaches to urban development have been argued to slow resource use and lower impacts (Barton et al, 2003), and are discussed in later chapters where they offer insights into the design and social functioning of the food quarters.

Sustainability theorists point out that ways of conceptualising urban sustainability need to transcend the limitations of a purely environmental agenda, to bring in and give sufficient weight to social and economic factors (Jarvis, Pratt and Cheng-Chong Wu, 2001; Evans, Joas, Sundback and Theobald, 2005). Thus, the trefoil diagram commonly used to describe how sustainability reflects and interconnects these aspects is not about trading off "social, economic and environmental priorities, but the need to find solutions that marry all three" (Barton et al, 2003, p.5). A holistic approach to sustainability is argued for, in which there should be a triple bottom line, as, for example, in the London Sustainable Development Commission definition of sustainable development (Entec, 2006). The analysis of the food quarters reflects this understanding by encompassing the three interconnected and mutually supporting aspects of sustainability: social, economic and environmental, and applying such a sustainability based analysis to the particular conditions of the food-centred spaces.

Climate change impacts are accentuating the food-related concerns that are explored in this book. At the production end of the modern food system, while industrialised agriculture and its attendant high food miles are thought to be exacerbating climate change, the situation is not straightforward. Recent work suggests that food miles are a poor indicator of the environmental and ethical impacts of food production (Edwards-Jones et al, 2008) and that shifts in food preferences towards a less meat intensive diet may be likely to yield more significant results than lowering food miles in certain circumstances (Weber and Matthews, 2008). At the same time, climate change effects on productivity are sharpening food security and resilience concerns and predominant food distribution and consumption arrangements in urban areas, as largely organised by supermarkets, have a specific and largely negative influence on urban sustainability (Sustainable Development Commission, 2008; UK Cabinet Office, 2008).

Food chains account for a fifth of emissions associated with the climate change effects of households' food consumption in the United Kingdom (Sustainable Development Commission, 2008). Meat and dairy products, glasshouse vegetables, airfreighted produce, heavily processed foods and refrigeration are the main hotspots with disproportionately high levels of greenhouse gas emissions (Sustainable Development Commission, 2008, p.42). Moreover, in terms of social sustainability, these modern consumption arrangements are a key contributor to "obesity and diet-related disease including cancer, diabetes, heart disease and stroke" (op cit, p.68). There is growing evidence that

> "a healthy and seasonal diet, rich in fruit and vegetables, and containing less processed food and meat is also better for the planet, leading to lower greenhouse gas emissions and less impact on ecosystems" (ibid).

All this suggests that ease of access, in a spatial, social and economic sense, to sustainable sources of these foodstuffs is important at individual and systemic levels, yet many urban dwellers do not enjoy such access. Rather, within an increasingly complex geography of social exclusion in cities (Harvey, 1989; Sassen, 1991; Madanipour, Cars and Allen, 1998; Andersen and Van Kempen, 2000; Musterd, Murie and Kesteloot, 2006) adverse health effects associated with the modern food system are played out unevenly among individual city dwellers. These include rising levels of adult and childhood obesity (Sui, 2003; Lopez, 2004; Marvin and Wedd, 2006) alongside increasing levels of stigmatisation (Sobal, in Germov and Williams, 1999).

Likewise, the sustainability effects of these food processes are far from spatially uniform. In the United Kingdom, national sustainability policies, for example, have not been able to check the spatially uneven distribution of food effects caused by dominant trends in urban expansion and renewal (Batchelor and Patterson, 2007; Lang, Barling and Caraher, 2009). Climate change mitigation policies, which are aimed to reduce emissions from supermarket operations, have failed to sufficiently take transport issues into account. They would need to include the effects of transporting goods and the impact of planning laws on the use of cars by supermarket customers (Sustainable Development Commission, 2008). Nor have they succeeded in instituting a low carbon economy in relation to food (ibid).

Therefore a proposition considered in this book is that the richly food focused, compact, walkable, liveable food quarter may assist in avoiding, or at least mitigating, some of the unsustainable effects of the way food relationships are played out in urban space. In exploring this proposition, the focus is on places that demonstrate vernacular and traditional urban forms, as these broadly support a compact city model (De Roo and Miller, 2000; Jenks, 2000; Clos, 2005). This is because, despite arguments to the contrary (Bruegmann, 2005), the weight of evidence suggests such places demonstrate greater capacity to meet urban sustainability requirements than do urban forms derived from modernist traditions (Barnett, 1987; Holston, 1989; Aldous, 1992; Jenks, Burton, and Williams, 1996; Moughtin, 1996; Barton et al, 2000).

In particular, as explained in Chapter 3, food quarters appear better configured in physical design terms than are low density, car dependent places, to deal with the need for adaptation to the climate change effects that are already apparent in London. Given the fundamental nature of urban sustainability as an organising frame for the research, Chapters 4 to 6 are then structured around groupings of economic, environmental and social research material in relation to each food quarter. In Chapters 7 and 8, these three linked areas of research and analysis are drawn together more fully, to highlight insights that have emerged from the findings, in an integrated way.

Food and convivial cities

A second framing element for this book is the notion of the convivial city (Parham, 1992, 1993; Miles, 1998; Peattie, 1998). The use of the term is derived from Ivan Illich (1973) whose ideas about conviviality are particularly relevant to food. Sharing food together allows for a daily physical and social re-creation of the self that is also fundamental to the sense of human connection to others, and conviviality has been described as "the very nourishment of civil society itself" (Peattie, 1998, p.250). As Peattie (op cit, after Illich 1980, p.11) argues, conviviality encompasses feasting, drinking and good company and also

> "the opposite of industrial productivity ...to mean autonomous and creative intercourse among persons, and the intercourse of persons with their environment, and this in contrast with the conditioned response of persons to the demands made upon them by others, and by a man-made environment".

A central feature of convivial cities is the recognition of sociable pleasure taken in many purposeful activities (ibid). In the case of this book, these are sociable activities focused on food, directly connecting the use of the term to conviviality's etymological origins. Another way that conviviality links to the research is in the evanescent nature of the social energy that emerges in food-related practices in the food quarters. These create special occasions out of "the mundane materials of life" (ibid, p.247); events as simple as buying food at the market, sharing a coffee, or enjoying a meal together.

Eating and drinking together is at the heart of the notion of conviviality, and this has spatial design implications, which in turn affect the nature of social life and the formation of social groups. Such social groups are established "by eating together conviviality, and by particular forms and settings of conviviality" (Peattie, 1998, p.248). These design dimensions matter because, as argued previously

> "the physical design of cities can determine the richness of experiences of food and eating; working for or against the expression of conviviality by the way space is shaped and urban development approached...Proximity to the cafes, restaurants and markets of the centre, and the densities of people the centre attracts, allows for more chance encounters and a diversity of food and conversation. If the process of sharing food and drink excites the intellect, as well as satisfying the cravings of the body, it is little wonder that cafes have often been the sites of polemical debate and political agitation" (Parham, 1992, p.3).

Expressions of conviviality also tend to be everyday in nature, reflecting the quotidian, and thus the book's preoccupation with the making of everyday life in ways that go beyond instrumental, economic exchange. Much of the expression of this conviviality takes place in everyday "third places" (Oldenburg, 1989; Rosenbaum, 2006) between work and home, of cafes, bars, and coffee shops, which are so prevalent in the three food quarters. Both the design (about place) and the everyday (about time) facets of conviviality are explored in sections below.

It should also be recognised that conviviality has a strong, and at times ambivalent, relationship to economic activity. Notions of conviviality have been linked to forms of commercialisation and place marketing, with an attendant risk perceived that conviviality becomes increasingly "vestigial and episodic" through this relationship (Banerjee, 2004, p.15). For instance, place marketers may show a "propensity to service conviviality needs in the form of a growing number of third places in invented streets and spaces" (Banerjee, ibid) that act to co-opt and mystify their consumers. The intriguing spatial aspects of this argument are explored later in this chapter. Bell (2007), meanwhile, is less than sanguine about the processes of developing conviviality, theorising the use of commercialised hospitality to brand places as destinations, and arguing

> "urban regeneration, place promotion and civic boosterism are using food and drink hospitality spaces as public, social sites for the production and reproduction of ways of living in and visiting cities and neighbourhoods" (p.7).

As noted at the start of this introductory chapter, these arguments reflect work that suggests places to eat and drink are connected to the development of new forms of city living that gentrify previously run down urban areas (Zukin, 1991), as well as with 'gastro-tourism' (Parham, 1996; Boniface, 2003). Yet these arguments only go some way in explaining the research findings from the three food quarters and similar sites elsewhere. Bell (2007, p.19), for example, points out that the forms of hospitality that are being produced in such hospitable spaces are not confined solely to economic exchange, but create a kind of "hybrid hospitality" that is more authentically convivial than mere commercial transactions would allow (op cit).

It is also worth noting that the development of such convivial spaces has not necessarily pushed out existing food-related uses to replace them with more commodified ones. Instead, as in a Manchester case studied by Bell and Binnie (2005), a convivial ecology has been developed in the food quarters that mixes and combines traditional food spaces such as 'cafs' and eel and pie shops and newer food-related uses, including slow food inspired market stalls, restaurants and delis. These are sites for what Thrift (2005) calls lighter touch forms of sociality, that allow time for the mundane moments of togetherness that pattern everyday life (Morrill *et al.*, 2005).

The conviviality of food quarters in London also shows interesting parallels to the Slow Food and related Slow Cities (città slow) movements emanating from northern Italy. While città slow stresses sustainable urbanism and alternative economic strategies for local places based on food "territories" (Knox and Mayer, 2006, p.322), Slow Food promotes conviviality around food, with its proponents organising themselves into local convivia (Pink, 2008) focused on "countering the loss of local distinctiveness as it relates to food, conviviality, sense of place, and hospitality" (Knox and Mayer, 2006, p.322).

Slow Cities (città slow), meanwhile, has grown from Slow Food to focus in on the spatial expression of these convivial qualities within villages and towns. While 'official' Slow City status is conferred only up to a maximum population of fifty thousand people, it is recognised that distinct spatial areas within larger cities could also exhibit similar qualities. Slow Cities makes explicit the linkages between convivial places and sustainability, conceptualising these connections as about economy, environment and equity, and arguing for local economic strategies that reflect the connections between food and place. At least one of the food quarters studied in this book (Borough) has formed direct links to the Slow Food movement, while a design strategy reminiscent of Slow Cities can be argued for in each food quarter, and is discussed later in this chapter.

In London, primary research is yielding positive results about the development of convivial locations that place branding arguments do not entirely explain (Maitland, 2008). Relevant work has focused on the way that emerging tourism areas do not (in contrast to previous mainstream practice) rest upon flagship development providing special attractions. Instead these sites rely on the qualities of place, in particular their conviviality, which attracts visitors to previously 'undiscovered' urban areas within a polycentric city form (ibid). The three food quarters explored in this book are clearly examples of this process of grounding renewal on the qualities of place, and in these areas tourism has developed not as part of flagship sites but within wider processes of urban regeneration and gentrification (Maitland and Newman, 2004).

For so-called post tourists (Lash and Urry, 1994; Judd, 2008), or new tourists (Poon, 1993), the appeal of such places is founded on conviviality that is relatively unmediated. This can be contrasted with the artful yet repetitive reproduction of planned tourist spaces, and reflects a more sophisticated approach which links to the pleasures of the everyday. As Maitland (2007, p.18) says of his fieldwork subjects:

"For some of them, the exotic may be found in a move away from traditional tourist beats, and the opportunity to experience 'ordinary everyday life' rather than an extraordinary attraction or event that constitutes a 'tourism experience' in a tourist bubble".

Maitland's fieldwork results were based in part on primary research in Islington and Southwark (boroughs where two of the three food quarters are also located) and found strong connections between everyday life and a sense of enjoying a convivial event:

> "For most interviewees, getting to know the city was a convivial experience—local people and local places to drink coffee or shop were important. The emphasis is on the everyday and an appreciation of the conviviality of the ordinary" (2007, p.23).

Conviviality has also sometimes been connected up with political activity and social activism, particularly at the human scale of the local neighbourhood (Parham, 1992; Peattie, 1998). Again, this is no coincidence. Conviviality tends to occur between people who like being together, often 'bounded' in small groupings. As Peattie (ibid, p.251) says, conviviality's "natural habitat…is the bounded terrain of the likeminded". As the food quarters' research findings demonstrated, these places became sites for political expression and action. This was often directly about food as the subject of activity, or because the foodscape of the quarter was found to be a sympathetic environment in which to operate. Banerjee (2004, p.17) also reports from recent US experience of 'bottom-up' conviviality, that not-for-profit groups are emerging to run

> "community improvements - from affordable housing to small business development - and thus infusing conviviality and creating third places even in poorer neighborhoods that the conventional market sees as too risky for investment".

The findings from Broadway Market in particular, but also to some extent from both Borough and Exmouth Markets, demonstrated a similar process underway, in which charities and small and medium sized community based organisations and enterprises took the lead in food led renewal. Bell (2007, p.12) points to the emergence of "an ethics of conviviality that revitalizes urban living", based he argues on the potentially productive "ways of relating that are practised in bars, cafés, restaurants, clubs and pubs" (ibid). In design terms, what has been most notable in the revitalisation process this book focuses on are ways of relating convivially in the *public space* of the street and market space of the food quarters.

If the research was founded on a purely sociological approach, this book might identify issues about making convivial places, but not prescribe action. It is notable in cited work on conviviality, however, how many theorists conclude by making proposals for implementing public policies in support of more convivial places. This book similarly goes further than would a purely sociological one, proposing that spatial design for food can make an important contribution to convivial and sustainable cities. The final chapter offers some proposals for ways forward to better design for food in a fast changing urban world suffering from increasingly severe sustainability effects. Proposed action is grounded in the reflection that

> "opportunities for conviviality in the city rely upon an extended set of gastronomic possibilities. And these possibilities can be widely conceived in city planning and design. They relate as much to kitchen layout as to market gardening, to the psychology of the cafe as to policy for metropolitan growth (Parham, 1992, p.1).

A conclusion from the research is that such opportunities for conviviality could be enhanced by urban design choices that support gastronomic strategies for cities (Parham, 1992). As Peattie (1998, p.248) notes in this regard, conviviality cannot be forced but

> "it can be encouraged by the right rules, the right props, and the right places and spaces. These are in the realm of planning".

The research findings from this book appear to show that conviviality expressed through a hybrid form of hospitality (Bell, 2007) has developed in the food-centred space of the food quarters, and this may act as a useful frame for both theorising about and making more convivial places in future.

Food and everyday life

This book is a study of everyday life. It explores the interconnectedness of social and physical aspects of the everyday, as they have been played out in particular places through relationships to food. At the same time, food is more than simply a language or a sign of something else: it is a fundamental, material part of urban culture, which is judged to be in itself a legitimate field for study (Simmel, 1903). The book is similarly preoccupied with the interconnection between time, space and everyday life (Lefebvre, 1974, 1991) in that it considers the primary research in the light of the notion that recurrent material practices shape space-time.

Just as De Certeau, Giard and Mayol (1998) describe and analyse spatial practices with reference to food in their study of the Croix-Rousse neighbourhood in Lyon, the socio-spatial practices of place users in the Borough, Broadway and Exmouth Market areas have been closely studied to explore how that shaping of space over time has taken place though food relationships. This is, says Luce Giard (1998, p.xxxv), about "the creative activity of those in the practice of the ordinary" and encompasses the aesthetic experience of the food market, with its capacity for sight, touch and smell. The book's findings suggest that food has both shaped place and been shaped by it.

The work of Henri Lefebvre has been useful to this writer in bringing an acknowledgement of the role of consumption and a sense of the spatial to the study of everyday life. Lefebvre argues for places where human interaction is not solely predicated on money-based exchange, and the three food quarters reflect Lefebvre's insights by creating more than just a "simple material product" (1991, p.101). Rather than functioning only as spaces for consumption, they have provided room for meeting social needs (ibid). The food quarters may also have helped to expose the mystification operating in much of everyday life, in which apparent food plenitude, represented by increasing consumption, and obfuscating environmental costs and economic inequalities, is mistaken for real human richness (ibid). Consumption certainly occurs at the food quarters, but these sites have also worked as what Lefebvre calls "places of simultaneity and encounters, places where exchange would not go through exchange value" (ibid).

Meanwhile, Bourdieu's (1984) notion of the habitus, discussed at length in the next chapter, helps frame the way individual behaviour has supported the food quarters' day-to-day life. It also opens up areas that are more problematic, especially those relating to gentrification. Mennell (1992) has argued that Bourdieu's theoretical framework may be too static and fixed a concept to be entirely effective in explaining the dynamism evident in the practices of everyday life in relation to food. More recently, scholars working in a range of sociological areas relating to, for example, health and gastronomy have employed Bourdieu's theoretical constructs, including the habitus, to negotiate a theoretical path between the fixed and the transformative in relation to food (Lindelof et al, 2010; Gomez, 2011; Wills, 2011).

An approach that reflects both Bourdieu's strengths, and poststructuralist insights that emphasise "contingency over structure in explaining outcomes" (Fainstein, 2000, p.145), has helped to map the way spatial practices in everyday life shift over time and space. While the food quarters showed evidence of the playing out of an individual habitus that claimed distinction by differentiating and excluding, as found in work on "foodies" by Johnston and Baumann (2010), they also provided a number of examples of identification between very different people, based on shared aims and values in relation to food and sociability. Linking ideas about taste and distinction to the notion of conviviality, Bell (2007, p.19) points out that, in fact

> "commensality is not always a disguise for competitions over taste and status; it can also be about social *identification*, the sharing not only of food and drink but of world-views and patterns of living".

Research in the food quarters demonstrated a range of socio-spatial practices being undertaken in which food played a central or substantial part: practices based in the routine encounters and shared experiences of the small urban spaces (Whyte, 1980; Gehl, 1996) that are of particular interest in enlivening cities. Practices observed include walking, browsing, shopping, eating, talking, making art, doing community politics and tourist visiting. They both reflected the structured patterns of a number of individuals' habitus', yet some showed examples of dynamism and change. At each food quarter this was especially clear in the development of new forms of socio-spatial practice in relation to food distribution and consumption.

Equally clearly, not everyone was experiencing the food quarters in the same way. While not wishing to overplay, or make rigid demarcations, along the lines of race, class and gender, it was evident that issues in relation to class, in particular, were being played out in the food quarters, often directly expressed through food. At each quarter, the study of socio-spatial practices raised these issues broadly in the context of regeneration and gentrification, and of tradition and modernity, with food an area of sometimes-explicit class contestation. Studying socio-spatial practices in relation to food acted as a way in to understanding each quarter as a regenerating space. And while regeneration is a paradoxical process, giving rise to both positive and negative results in the three food quarters as social spaces, the research findings suggested that positive effects on everyday life predominated.

Social space, physical space and food

Another way of looking at the everyday in relation to food is through the design of place, and the book crosses discipline boundaries in order to make connections between social and physical space, in part through urban design and morphological analysis. This is because a central concern is whether, and if so, how, the design of physical form may shape the social construction of space in relation to food. So, as well as reflecting theoretical areas that fall within mainstream sociology, the book draws on theory and research methods from urban design, including identification of design elements (Lynch, 1961, 1985; Alexander et al, 1977; Bacon, 1982; Bentley et al., 1985; Broadbent, 1990; Hayward and McGlynn, 1993; Jacobs, 1993; Carmona, 2003; Moughtin, 2003) and master planning analysis (Urban Design Compendium, 2000, 2007). Urban design characteristics and elements of space are described in Chapter 2, and design based methods discussed in Chapter 3, while these form the basis for design findings and analysis of the food quarters in Chapters 4 to 8.

As pointed out earlier in this chapter, the study of the food quarters has a very distinct spatial design backdrop at the broad level of the city region; one of rapid and largely unsustainable development, expansion and renewal of urban space (Gillham, 2002; Waldheim, 2006; Cohen and Rustin, 2008; Gordon and Travers, 2010; Klemek, 2011) This is, in the main, within a design idiom of separation of land uses, and in a context of relatively low density, car dependent growth (Garreau, 1991; Dreier, Mollenkopf and Swanstrom, 2004; Hayden, 2004; Dunham Jones, 2011), in which commodified malls and shopping centres are the predominant foodscapes (Knox, 1992).

Meanwhile, as noted earlier, it is argued that fat city and Slow City inflected design, instead assists in creating ordinary places in keeping with the European City Model (Clos, 2005; Parham, 2006). This in turn presents both a distinct break with post war urban design experience, and a challenge to the dominant modernist mode of city shaping, bringing some of its shortcomings into stark relief. Also as noted at the beginning of this chapter, the food quarter's location is generally found in traditional urban fabric and is based on human-scaled, highly mixed, walkable and fine-grained urbanism, but its elements are capable of retrofitting sprawl and being built into new areas too.

At the same time, developments in the UK suggest that the food quarter itself could be reconfigured to increase its capacity to offer a sustainable approach to city design. The increasing focus on urban agriculture and food growing, for instance, demonstrates interesting potentialities in design terms for reshaping cities (Edwards and Mercer, 2010; Duany, 2011) that could be built into the food quarter's design mix. It does seem evident though that food quarters, including those studied, appear currently to be unique in connecting traditional urban fabric design to an alternative socio-spatiality which reflects pressing sustainability issues and opportunities for increased conviviality at the distribution and consumption end of the food chain.

But how conscious are food quarter users about the design attributes of these spaces? While urban designers and architects referenced in Chapter 3 were aware to varying degrees of the significant role urban design plays in the food quarters, place users referred to in Chapters 4 to 6 tended to describe physical design or form in much vaguer terms. Understandably, they mostly focused on how places felt or looked rather than seeking to analyse what design qualities the food quarters may have which would be instrumental in creating that atmosphere. However, the many observations and interviews undertaken as part of the research demonstrated that place users' socio-spatial practices in the food quarters were closely tied to the physical shape of these everyday spaces.

As explained above, an important backdrop to this book is recent work that has coalesced around the design of "ordinary places" (Knox, 2005, p.1). It appears that ordinary settings like those found at the three food quarters, can help develop slow places in a fast changing world (Mayer and Knox, 2006; Knox, 2005) by giving attention to design "strategies for local economic vitality that contribute to more equality and community stability" (Knox, 2005, p.1) and this, in turn, relates to their role as food places. Through these attributes, the three food quarter demonstrate a strong sense of place, and, as Knox (ibid) suggests

> "Central to good urban design is the capacity of the built environment to foster a positive sense of place in the ordinary places that provide the settings for people's daily lives. Sense of place is always socially constructed, but in ordinary places—physical settings that do not have important landmarks or major symbolic structures—the social construction of place is especially important".

How the research has been approached

The methodological basis for this research has been by way of a case study approach because this was judged as best suited to the nature of the research area being studied. It has comprised a collective case study (Stake, 1995, p.3-4), investigated through primary research in three food quarter sites located in London. These food quarters were chosen from a long list of potentially suitable sites in London and elsewhere and the set refined to focus in depth on three sites with considerable areas of similarity. All three sites were based on urban neighbourhoods centred on traditional food markets that have been regenerated into a new food market form.

The methodologies used to study the food quarters and to collect relevant research material, have been drawn from both sociology and urban design. The sociological methods comprise unstructured observation and semi-structured interviewing with experts and place-users (Bryman, 2001) undertaken within and supported by the case study approach (Yin, 1994, 1993). The emphasis on unstructured observation and semi-structured interviewing also supported shorter-term (rather than longer immersion) visits to the food quarters, using intensive interviewing to collect research material.

For this element of the research, over the course of the fieldwork period a number of semi-structured interviews were organised, conducted, written up and analysed. These interviews fell into two categories. The first set of interviews was with five experts identified in areas pertinent to the research topic selected from a long list of sixteen potential interviewees, chosen because they demonstrate substantial expertise in, variously, food policy, urban policy, urban sustainability, urban design, urbanism and architecture, and knowledge of these areas in relation to London. Some had specific expertise or detailed knowledge about particular food quarters while others had a broad grasp of some important framing issues and ideas which contextualise the quarters and the book topic.

Various themes were explored using a pro forma developed for the interviews. These included the theorised relationship of food and the design of urban space and specific urban design issues relevant to food such as connectivity, legibility, robustness, variety, visual richness, grain, and scale. There was also a focus on issues emerging from food markets and surrounding areas and catchments - using examples in London and elsewhere – as well as issues in retrofitting existing food spaces. Other pro forma topics were issues in building new food-centred urban fabric - design and sustainability related - and possible differences and similarities perceived between UK and mainland European experience.

The second set of interviews was more specific to each of the food quarters. These interviews were undertaken with twenty-five individuals who comprised a variety of place-users at each site, including shoppers, stallholders, food shop staff, café staff and owners, and restaurateurs. Each potential interviewee was approached and given a sheet with details about the research project and either interviewed straight away or at an agreed follow-up time. For the first pilot tranche of interviews, detailed notes were taken at the time, while the main body of interviews was recorded and transcribed.

The interviews explored themes encompassing local food consumption practices, such as shopping, eating and drinking; and any food issues perceived in (or relevant to) the area, such as food poverty, food miles and other aspects of sustainability. Interviews also dealt with views place-users held about local spatiality: design features they were aware of, their likes and dislikes and any improvements they would want to see in local built form, public space, or other design or social aspects. The spread of interviews, and a short description of each interview subject, are provided in Appendix 1.

Over three years the case study process included a substantial number of unstructured observations which varied from brief snapshots of activity at each site to prolonged visits and production of detailed notes about behaviours observed there. Some way into the process it seemed useful to undertake head counts of place-users' behaviours, literally counting up place-users observed undertaking different activities. The intention was to improve understanding about the range of practices being undertaken and the balance between them over time. The observations were undertaken from a central vantage point at each quarter and different kinds of activities observed and recorded over an hour of market operation on up to three days for each food market. The observational categories included walking, sitting, eating, drinking, conversing, shopping, and taking photographs. This series of head counts was used to distinguish various socio-spatial practices on each day of three days trading over a typical Thursday to Saturday trading period, as a schematic frame for thinking more closely about different kinds of behaviour in those spaces.

While findings about the interplay between physical and social space were predominantly based on direct fieldwork observations, mapping and interviews, primary source data has been augmented in Chapters 4 to 6 by local place users', activists' and artists' commentaries, drawn from online sites. These secondary sources are supported by a small amount of other material, gathered from journal articles and press reports, where these help contextualise the primary material.

Three methodological techniques have also been drawn from outside mainstream sociology: morphological analysis, master planning informed investigations and gastronomic mapping, all reflecting insights borrowed from urban design. The use of these methods has reflected the nature of the research concerns and the early judgement that sociological approaches alone could not yield all the kinds of material needed in order to adequately explore the book's themes. Given that the research has been substantially concerned with investigating urban design issues from a sociological perspective, and visual analysis is central to urban design theory and practice, it therefore seemed appropriate and necessary to collect visual data and to employ visually based techniques in both analysis and reporting.

This is not unheralded in sociological work as there has been growing interest within sociology (and related disciplines including anthropology) in representation theory and visual methodologies (Rose, 2001; Knowles and Sweetman, 2004; Paul Pink, Kurti And Alfonso, 2004). As Rose (2001) points out, researching visual methods must be mindful of the existence of scopic regimes, in that what is seen and how it is seen is culturally constructed. Visual methods in this context might be defined as "concerned with the complex processes through which people produce, circulate and read information about the world" (Pearson and Warburton, in Somekh and Lewin, 2005, p.164) with

> "theories of representation allow[ing] researchers to explore how people produce and consume images about themselves and the world they inhabit" (ibid, p.164).

This sociological approach to visual analysis seemed promising when developing the book methods, but a review of visual sociology and visual culture references suggested that its methodological repertoire was not an exact fit with the focus of the research. Visual methods used by sociologists and anthropologists tend to be concerned with how images such as photographs, film, and other visual representations of social practices can be analysed (Hockings, 1995; Kress and van Leeuwen, 1996; Hall, 1997; Prosser, 1998; Sturken and Cartwright, 2001; Rose, 2001; Van Leeuwen and Jewitt, 2001; Stanczak, 2007) rather than more directly analysing spatially based practices themselves. Space appears sometimes to be used metaphorically as an immaterial context within which content or discourse analysis can take place.

Certain studies have noted, for instance, how spaces and spatial practices have impacts on the construction of individual and group identity (Carson, Johnson, Mangat and Tupper, 2005), and techniques used by researchers to collect data on spatial practices have included interviews and photographic recording of spaces by their users in the context of collaborative research programmes (ibid). However, even in spatially based examples such as those cited above it is the responses to the photographic evidence that are reported as forming the central component of the research investigations and analysis rather than responses to practices in real spaces. Thus, although some of the research examples found within the visual sociology field do explicitly concern themselves with spatial practices, their capacity to deal with questions about socio-spatial behaviour in real, physical places appears to be somewhat lacking.

The difficulty in using the accepted approaches coalesced into two problems in the context of this research. Firstly, visual sociology appeared too narrowly focused on photographic images and graphics rather than actual experiences, and secondly it seemed too concerned with semiotics-based analysis of such images. Taken in combination, these features appeared to limit its capacity to provide a suitable research approach for the spatial data collection and analysis in this book. It is worth restating that this research is concerned with studying space, not as a metaphor for something else, but in a material way (Lefebvre, 1991) in order to better understand its social construction and dynamics. Methods used therefore needed to be able to feed into the analysis of space itself rather than of its representations through photographic or other images. In developing methodologies, asserting a material basis for studying space and socio-spatial practice suggested a requirement to extend or reshape the use of visual forms of representation and analysis sociologically.

So for the purposes of this research, in the apparent absence of sufficient sociological techniques for exploring space visually, methods have been borrowed from urban design, as another discipline not only concerned with social processes in urban space but also providing a wealth of techniques to capture data on spatiality. As Tonkiss (2008) notes, approaches within visual sociology are broadly interpretative, whereas urban design offers techniques for visual and spatial analysis that are more structured, systematic and comparative. The urban design techniques used in the spatial aspect of the research are discussed in the next section.

Applying methods from urban design

A number of methods used in the research are drawn from an urban design research repertoire as this was thought to be broadly appropriate for studying the spatial aspects of the food quarters. This is despite awareness that these methods tend to be structured in the form of guidance unreflexively directed towards shaping space (Madanipour, 2003). The normative nature of much urban design methodology means that in adapting such techniques to a sociological context it has been important to be systematic about the process; taking an open stance towards the research material and process, including the research setting, findings, data selection, collection, analysis and write-up (Tonkiss, p.260, in Seale 2001). Equally it was important to recognise that although urban design guidance has taken a pragmatic path it is not necessarily simplistic. Rather, it can be seen as capable of a nuanced, complex and subtle response to urban conditions and issues, if the depth of its sources is acknowledged.

Although such guidance does not in most cases sufficiently cite its sources to meet academic conventions, urban design advice does have a basis in substantial evidence from diverse disciplines such as environmental science, social psychology, visual perception, building design, architecture and transport planning. This may not be evident in a context where primary sources have become obscured or are inadequately referenced. For the purposes of this book, urban design techniques commonly used in master planning processes to understand the background and context to regeneration sites (Cowan, 2002) have been employed to explore each food quarter's urban armature: its spatial structure, define its movement patterns and investigate its existing and remnant built form and streetscape design details. The structuring of a master planning guidance document like the *Urban Design Compendium* (Llewelyn-Davies, 2007) has provided a basis for developing the kinds of design methods suitable for use at each site.

Another source for these aspects, *Shaping Neighbourhoods* (2003) covers some of the same urban design territory as the *Compendium*. Of particular interest is an explicit focus on food, which this master planning guidance places in the 'resources' category of design guidance and considers in relation to healthy lifestyles, healthy economies, allotments and orchards, local shops and markets, and city farms. Within the urban design synthesis category of *Shaping Neighbourhoods* (2003) for instance a number of urban design advice areas with a direct bearing on issues in this research are also specifically touched on, including neighbourhood character, key structuring elements, town shaping and designing places.

However, in this research, the intention has not been to undertake a complete master planning process using the entire repertoire of techniques. Instead, the research incorporates certain master planning analysis methods, which have assisted in defining existing urban conditions within the fieldwork sites, especially as they relate to food. The aim has been to gain a greater understanding of each neighbourhood's physical character, by identifying key structuring elements and exploring the detailed design of the public realm, especially of density nodes and connectivity, and the approach draws on the techniques of character appraisal and environmental appraisal (Urban Design Compendium, 2000, pp.24-27). The urban design findings from this work are described and analysed in most detail in Chapter 3, and have provided framing evidence for the other fieldwork material explored in Chapters 4 to 6.

As part of the master planning informed work, figure-ground studies were developed as a useful way of representing and analysing urban space (Koetter and Rowe, 1978; Hillier and Hanson, 1984) and to identify what kind of block configuration, scale and level of enclosure was evident in each food quarter, by sharply differentiating built form from the open space of streets and squares. This aspect of the research work also included a limited morphological study, which demonstrated how food-related land uses developed and changed over time at each site (Hanson, 1989; Whitehand and Larkham, 1992; Lane, 1993). Morphological analysis based on these food quarter investigations was used in particular to explore whether, and if so, how, compactness and walkability had impacts on the nature of food spaces and processes within the food quarters. Questions explored through morphological methods included how food-related land uses, such as shops, markets and cafes shifted spatially within the urban quarter over time, and which food-related land uses had appeared, disappeared or been maintained.

These visually based investigations were underpinned by a movement assessment which aimed to help document and explain the access patterns, permeability, legibility and walkability level of the sites being studied. Originally it was intended to use space syntax methods (Hillier, 1996) but these proved beyond the research resources. The movement assessment nevertheless was able to explore "the pattern or arrangement of development blocks, streets, buildings, open space and landscape" (Urban Design Compendium, 2000, p.33) and therefore formed the basis for understanding the connectivity of each food quarter's streets, which in turn helped define which were the most heavily used by pedestrians. The results of the movement assessment have been linked to the book's theoretical underpinnings (explored in Chapter 2) where walkability is posited as crucial to richer food relationships.

Meanwhile, catchment analysis, based on the approach advocated in *Towards an Urban Renaissance* (1999) assisted in defining the physical catchment at each quarter in terms of the distance that is normally travelled to access different kinds of land uses. In the fieldwork research, the technique was specifically employed in defining likely walking distances for food-related urban places, services and infrastructure such as shops, cafes, and food markets. It helped in developing a picture of the kind of catchments scales that a food quarter could expect to serve in food terms.

Part of the catchment analysis was the development of "ped-sheds" (Newman and Kenworthy, 2006, p.43) for each of the food quarters. These ped-sheds were defined to show walkable catchments for services and facilities, and demonstrated that a highly permeable street grid, as in the three sites, could be favourably compared with a hierarchical, dendritic (Hebbert, 2005) street layout imposing longer than necessary pedestrian journeys. By defining typical pedestrian catchments or 'ped-sheds' it was possible to understand how the urban layouts in each food quarter contributed to, or made pedestrian access to food facilities and services at the centre of the quarter more or less possible. Following this method, a range of ped-sheds was developed based on evidence gained through observations, interviews and gastronomic mapping as discussed below. The ped shed or walkability radius for each of the food quarters is shown in Chapter 3.

Bringing together the social and the spatial

A fundamental aim of the research has been to explore the relationship between social and spatial processes centred on food, in urban spaces of a particular design configuration. On that basis it seemed fruitful to explore techniques that had the potential to bring together both spatial and social elements of the research programme through combined methods. To go back to first principles, a central argument is that spatial design processes may have impacts on social, food-related relationships played out in that space; and vice-versa, that socio-spatial practices may also have impacts on physical space. It follows that methods that could capture aspects of this interconnectedness would have utility in the research programme. Thus, to bring together analytically the spatial, 'places' facets of the work with the social, or 'people' features, the research methods built on previous urban design-based mapping techniques (Lynch, 1961, 1985). Working on issues of urban identity, Kevin Lynch pioneered a technique of mapping space with participants who developed mental maps of city space and described their journeys, to define particular urban elements of paths, edges, nodes, districts and landmarks. More recently, Zukin (1992) has also noted the importance of mapping to understand transformations in urban space.

Adapted from Kevin Lynch's approach to mapping urban space, a process of 'gastronomic mapping' (Parham, 1993) was previously developed by the author in order to explore food-related elements in the design of local space, and the behaviour of place-users in relation to those elements, and there are now references to similar techniques reported (Marte, 2007). A modified form of gastronomic mapping seemed a valuable input into the data set, and annotated food maps were developed and produced for each of the three sites, based on two data sources. These were unstructured observation results, which generated information about place user behaviour in relation to food, and analysis of food-related design elements apparent in each food quarter. The mapping results provided useful material which helped explore both spatial design in relation to food, and the social behaviours evident in the use of the food quarter spaces. The food quarter maps and analysis are found in Chapters 4 to 8.

Finally, in relation to methods it is worth noting that the work has been undertaken in a way that explicitly linked each stage of the research to a coherent methodological framework. The methodological approach was designed to make the research process as focused, transparent and reflexive as possible. The gathering, reporting, interrogation and analysis of research material was primarily text-based but is supported in Chapters 2 to 8 by a range of visual material. The overall methodological intention was to generate relevant research material that helped in exploring the research topic from a number of different angles in a grounded, narrative, and visual way.

The book's structure

This book is made up of three parts and divided into eight chapters. Part 1 situates the research into food quarters, theoretically, methodologically and spatially. It comprises this introductory chapter, which sets out framing and methodological elements for the research, and Chapter 2, which explores the book's theoretical underpinnings. Part 2 then goes on to explore the three theorised food quarters; first in design and morphological terms, and then as in depth case studies that look at the interplay between physical form and social processes centred on food. Finally, Part 3 brings together findings and analysis in two related chapters that reach conclusions about the nature and possible future of such food-centred space.

Chapter 2 starts by clearing the decks: briefly dealing with the inadequacies of normative socio-biological and nutritional approaches to food. It then moves to look at perspectives on city form and food practices from social anthropology, geography, and the growing field of food sociology. Within urban sociology, meanwhile, it explores the limitations of functionalism and structuralism in relation to the research area but argues for retaining some structuralist perspectives. Chapter 2 also begins to draw on urban design theory, suggesting that while design constructs tend to be applied as a set of qualities or elements to be unreflexively achieved in urban space, urban design practice may, when well implemented, reflect insights into the physical shaping of cities that can be linked back to empirical research and thus retain validity in exploring socio-spatial practices in relation to food. Likewise, perspectives from political economy focusing on regeneration and gentrification are drawn upon to enrich the analysis of food quarters as transforming urban spaces.

Chapters 3 to 6 present the research material and analysis from the case study research, first covering morphological and urban design findings, and then moving on to consider the food quarters site by site. Chapter 3 deals primarily with the spatiality of the food quarters and thus incorporates the master planning methods and morphological investigations made into each of the food quarters. Together the data from these investigations helps delineate the three quarters, and underpins the analysis of their physical conditions. The chapter also acts as a foundation for exploring and analysing the relationship between physical design and social practices within each of the quarters, which is then presented in Chapters 4 to 6. Data sources for Chapter 3 include visual records based on site observations, and research material from relevant map and archival collections at the British Library, the City of London Guildhall Library and the London Metropolitan Archives. The bulk of Chapter 3 provides space to work through a design analysis with reference to each of the sites in turn: Borough, Broadway and Exmouth Markets and their surrounding areas and catchments. Chapter 3 concludes with a short section drawing out findings from each of the site analyses, and where appropriate, makes comparisons between quarters and research themes. Particular emphasis is given to the relationship between physical and social space that is explored in the subsequent chapters.

Chapter 4 focuses on the results from primary research conducted at Borough Market and its surroundings. Of the three food quarters under study, it is suggested that the Borough Market area constitutes the most fully realised urban food quarter. As set out in Chapter 1, the case study work of Chapters 4 to 6 is refracted through the lens of the sustainable city. Thus in Chapter 4 the data are structured around the economic, environmental and social roles of the Borough Market quarter as it experienced food-led renewal. The findings and initial conclusions in Chapter 4 rely on a number of research data collection methods, explained in Chapter 3. In summary, these methods comprise semi-structured interviews, of varying lengths, with experts and place users - architects, market trustees, food traders and visitors. Second, there are field notes and photographs taken from informal observational visits over a three-year period up to June 2008. Third, as a subset of the second method, there are a series of 'head counts' used to distinguish various social practices over a typical Thursday to Saturday trading period, in September 2007. Fourth, there is material from food mapping of the market and surrounding spaces, undertaken in June 2008. The substantive sections begin with consideration of the food quarter as an economic space, then its exploration in environmental terms, and finally interrogation as a space for socio-spatial practice. For each section, the chapter begins to connect findings to relevant framing theories. The end-of-chapter analysis and tentative conclusions prefigure the lengthier discussions in Chapters 7 and 8, where all three sites are considered together, and their connections to relevant theory further analysed.

Chapter 5 explores aspects of the relationship between economic, social, and environmental practices and physical space design, this time at the Broadway Market quarter. Broadway Market appeared poised between the fully realised food quarter of Borough (the subject of Chapter 4) and the emergent quarter of Exmouth, discussed in the next chapter (Chapter 6). Again, the fieldwork data are presented with the political economy of the quarter examined first, followed by discussion of its urban design character, the environmental aspects of its operation as a market, and then observed socio-spatial practices. While material about the interplay between physical and social space is predominantly taken from direct fieldwork observations, mapping and interviews, as noted above, local place users', activists' and artists' commentaries drawn from online sites add additional depth. There is also a small amount of other material, from recent journal articles and press reports, where it is judged that these help contextualise the primary data. Unlike the last chapter, there is no comparative 'head count' data, as Broadway only operated as a market on Saturdays at the time of the fieldwork process.

Chapter 6 explores food-related aspects of the economic, environmental and social life of the Exmouth Market quarter, providing a comparable range of research material to Chapters 4 (on Borough) and 5 (on Broadway), and following a broadly similar structure for its presentation and analysis. The discussion again draws on fieldwork interviews, informal observations and mapping, augmented by online commentary and press reports. As in the other fieldwork chapters, the material is refracted through a sustainability prism. While the social and economic aspects of sustainability receive substantial attention, there is little direct data gathered about Exmouth's environmental performance. Interviewees tend not to explicitly refer to these issues at Exmouth, but environmental concerns are implicit in many of their views.

As in the previous two chapters, the narrative of decline and food led regeneration is a major theme. The Exmouth Market quarter has been regenerated as a food space even more recently than the two other quarters, and demonstrates many similarities, including the urban design qualities of a particular kind of traditional city form. As at Borough, Exmouth has become a food space based on artisanal foods of high quality. As at Broadway, the communities of interest within the site's catchment are quite diverse and there are some examples of conflict between long-term working class residents and newer, more middle class arrivals. Unlike either Borough or Broadway, Exmouth's revived market has become predominantly a 'slow food' food court rather than a fully-fledged street market. Like Broadway Market, food based uses are a focus for some contention.

Chapters 7 and 8 draw together and review the findings from the case study and design based research, with conclusions explored in the light of the book's research propositions as defined in Chapter 1 and the theoretical framework in Chapter 2. It will be remembered that the book focuses on what is argued to be the development of food-centred place design and regeneration, leading to the emergence of urban food quarters. These quarters are based on existing food spaces, but represent a break from the past, as they seem to show the interplay of distinctively new combinations of socio-spatial practices with largely pre-existing physical design features. Their development is situated theoretically and materially as in distinct contrast to obesegenic sprawl and food deserts that are associated with the spatiality of much urban development elsewhere. Each is some way to becoming a fully realised food quarter, with Borough furthest along this trajectory. Chapter 7 reviews the paradoxical nature of the quarters as at once gentrifying and socially enabling spaces, while Chapter 8 considers the potential for food quarter development in future as more convivial, gastronomically rich and sustainable places for making everyday life.

CHAPTER TWO

FRAMING THE RESEARCH

Theorising food space

This chapter looks at theories that underpin the food quarter research. Setting out a framework for the empirical work at three food quarters in London, it sets the scene for later chapters where the relationship between city form and food practices is investigated through primary research. Beginning by briefly dealing with socio-biological and nutritional approaches to food that have gained currency in recent years, it then moves on to consider pertinent theories about both city form and food practices from social anthropology, geography, the growing field of food sociology, and urban sociology. Within sociology, it explores some of the limitations of functionalism and structuralism, while retaining some structuralist perspectives.

The research seeks to apply spatial thinking (Soja, 1989; 2000) to the study of food and city form, with particular reference to real places in London. It identifies a theoretical gap between food sociology on the one hand and urban sociology on the other, with the latter seen to be somewhat aspatial insofar as it touches on material, physical design for food. It concludes that not only can more be done to connect food and urban space in meaningful theoretical and empirical ways, but that this can be done at a variety of scales, from the wide reach of the city region to the very fine grain of the local area, in this case through the study of market-centred spaces as loci for the food system. In so doing, the notion of socio-spatial practices, as explored by Lefebvre (1974, 1991), Soja (1989, 1993, 2000) and de Certeau (1984, 1998), provides a useful theoretical construct through which to review the food quarter research findings. Equally Bourdieu's (1984) concept of the habitus provides a helpful frame for examining the nature of individual behaviour at the food quarters as spaces of consumption while Elias's (1978, 1982) work on civilising appetites also helps to situate that food-related behaviour in individual terms. Additionally, insights from Butler (2006, 2007), Butler with Robson (2001), and Webber (2007) are all valuable in connecting the habitus to spatialised aspects of gentrification.

Perspectives are drawn from urban sociology, insofar as they deal with the transformations in city space, especially since the second half of the 20th century. These are explored as a basis for the focus on urban spaces defined as food quarters in Chapter 1. Arguing that food practices have at least contributed to the shaping of the spatiality of the city, the chapter then connects food and urban sociological approaches with those from urban design and political economy. The role of urban design elements in the design of urban quarters is explored, with arguments made that food quarters share various design qualities with the traditional European urban quarter (Bell and Jayne, 2004; Clos, 2005; Parham, 2005). These urban design qualities – in part embodied in the European City Model – not only provide a context for socio-spatial practices in relation to food that in turn contribute to conviviality and sustainability, they may also influence those practices in significant ways. As noted in Chapter 1, while urban design theory tends to be applied unreflexively (Hayward and McGlynn, 2002), it does have an empirical basis which gives it value in exploring food practices. Likewise, perspectives from sociology and political economy, focusing on regeneration, gentrification and spaces of consumption (Butler and Robson, 2001; Ashley, Hollows, Jones and Taylor, 2004; Atkinson, 2004; Bridge, 2007) are drawn upon to enrich the analysis of food quarters as transforming urban spaces.

Relevant approaches to food and eating

This book primarily focuses on sociological and design theory approaches because these directly inform relevant arguments about designing for food. At the same time a brief review of dominant theoretical perspectives on food, from nutrition and socio-biology, seems worthwhile as these have strongly shaped understanding of food and eating. They act as a supposedly common sense view of food that can stand in the way of a more rigorous, empirically based theoretical framework. Nutritional or socio-biological perspectives have traditionally dominated research into eating practices (Lupton, 1996). These take a highly instrumental view that relates food habits and preferences to the anatomical functioning of the body. Sociobiologists argue that humans are naturally programmed to prefer foods that are physiologically good for us; and this programming is largely based on genetic predispositions (Falk, 1991). Nutritionists, meanwhile, are concerned with food in terms of its physiological effects on the body, defining the perfect diet for optimum health, and providing prescriptions to that end (Khare, 1980). Indeed, nutritional approaches have increasingly influenced food manufacturing and common understandings of the nature of food in recent years, and we have seen the related rise of functional foods and 'nutraceuticals' (Lang 1997, 2003; Pollan, 2008).

For both disciplines, food preferences, tastes and cultural habits are of secondary or marginal concern. However, even in such an apparently biologically based understanding of what is edible and what inedible, what is *culturally* determined as edible or inedible is not simply determined by, or a function of, the wisdom of the body based on metabolic processes and nutritional efficiency (Falk, 1991). In fact, as Beardsworth and Keil (1997, p.51) point out,

> "any given culture will typically reject as unacceptable a whole range of potentially nutritious items or substances while often including other items of dubious nutritional value".

Nutritional and sociobiological approaches appear unable to deal sufficiently rigorously with the dynamic nature of food tastes, preferences and habits over time. Moreover, they have difficulty in coming to grips with the implied issues relating to differences in demonstrated preferences between cultures, ethnicities, genders, ages, classes, and, for the purposes of this book, *places* in terms of food. A number of disciplines have noted the weakness of these approaches in conveying aspects of meaning in relation to food and eating, and perspectives from anthropology are first considered in this respect. Durkheim and Spencer appear to be the earliest social theorists to look seriously at food, and some of their preoccupations were taken up by anthropology (Germov and Williams, 1999). Anthropologists recognise the role of biological needs but share considerable territory with sociologists in that they are primarily concerned with the symbolic nature of food and eating practices. They acknowledge the role played by biological needs and food availability, but by elucidating the effect of cultural mores, demonstrate that food practices are "far more complex than a simple nutritional or biological perspective would allow" (Lupton, 1996, p.7). It is not surprising that food is a central concern for social anthropologists given their preoccupation with studying small scale, local social systems, often in traditional societies. A key point, given the book's preoccupation with the ordinary and everyday, is that food is understood as central to framing everyday life:

> "Looking at traditional society in this holistic fashion virtually demands that some attention be paid to the processes involved in producing, distributing, preparing and consuming food since these make up a complex

of activities which provides the whole framework of life on a daily and a seasonal basis" (Beardsworth and Keil, 2004, p.3).

In reviewing relevant approaches to food, three theoretical loci have been identified for this book. The first is the understanding of food as a socio-cultural context in which the logic and principles of different cultural systems is illuminated. The second loci shows food's role in the societies' mediation of material and moral systems. The third loci reflects the way that food as a set of nutriments represents both biological and cultural systems in human societies (Khare, 1980, p.525). Anthropological focus on food has famously treated food practices as a language that exemplifies sets of binary oppositions between nature and culture, raw and cooked, and food and non-food in human life, with particular attention to the transformations argued to be occurring from nature to culture through cooking (Lévi-Strauss, 1958; 1969). While Lévi-Strauss recognised that taste is culturally shaped and socially controlled, as with other structuralist theorists, he was weaker when it came to changes in taste over time. The notion of food loci, though, remains interesting and theorised in a more spatialised manner, is considered later in this chapter.

Social geography and cultural studies, meanwhile, have been more recent entrants in the field of food studies and have introduced aspects of the study of identity, consumption and place to the discussion of food and eating. Again, the nutritional aspects of food and eating are deemed inadequate to explain the social, cultural and symbolic meanings of food. Rather, as Bell and Valentine (1997, p.3) so nicely express the point, "In a world in which self-identity and place-identity are woven through webs of consumption, what we eat (and where, and why) signals…who we are". Equally, food is understood in relation to a range of important cultural processes, including those of food production and regulation, as well as identity and consumption (Ashley, Hollows, Jones, and Taylor, 2004, preface). Food is conceptualised as having a life story that is in turn defined as a cultural phenomenon. Food's life story thus represents "a circuit of culture" in which the above named cultural processes all play a part (Johnson, 1986; Jackson, 1992). At least implicitly, there is a spatial character to this theorising of food, with consideration of shopping, eating in, and eating out, among other activities, but tantalisingly this is not developed or elucidated in a fully spatialised way.

A critical point to be drawn from this brief survey is that understanding of food cannot be successfully reduced to simply its nutrient or biological role: food has strong cultural meanings that can change over time and place. Food is central to everyday life and increasingly to the construction of human identity (Fischler, 1988; Warde, 1997) as well as to attitudes to the body (Lupton, 1996). It is also evident that food and eating have become progressively more an interdisciplinary concern. Recent interest in food seems to be what Ashley, Hollows, Jones, and Taylor (2004, preface, n.p.n.) have described as "the product of a particular cultural enthusiasm" that cuts across disciplinary boundaries, a theoretical phenomenon commonly known as the cultural turn. This book likewise reflects food's interdisciplinary vitality as it traverses aspects of sociological, geographical, political economic and urban design theory.

Food and sociological research

It is from sociological perspectives on food that some of the central arguments relevant to this book are drawn, yet the starting point for this examination is that greater attention has been paid to food within anthropology, social geography and cultural studies, than has been evident within sociological literature until recent times, when it has moved closer to the sociological mainstream (Warde, 1997; Warde and Martens, 2000; Ward, Coveney and Henderson, 2010; Murcott, 2011). It is possible to speculate that the take up and study of food-related issues by other professions and academic disciplines might have reinforced sociology's comparative lack of interest in the area (Beardsworth and Keil, 2004, p.2). Notwithstanding this, sociologists, like anthropologists and geographers, conceptualise food in quite distinct and more convincing ways than either nutritionists or sociobiologists insofar that they attempt to place food within the social relations that produce it.

Within sociology food has become a legitimate area for enquiry in which at least two major traditions can be discerned. Growing in part out of functionalist anthropological and from linguistic perspectives, the structuralist approaches of sociologists including Bourdieu (1984), and the semiologist Barthes (1972), have influenced more recent work on taste, dining out (Finkelstein, 1989; Warde and Martens, 1998) and the way they interconnect with consumption (Warde; 1997). Meanwhile, historical sociologists (Mennell, 1996; 1992; Symons, 1998; 1982) have built on Norbert Elias's (1978, 1982) legacy to pursue a materialist approach to food, while others (Visser, 1986, 1993, 1997; Valentine, 1998) reflect Elias's civilising arguments by exploring aspects of eating including table manners, food customs, and eating in the street. It seems that there are broadly two routes through which food-related issues have made their way into mainstream sociology. The first is through the analysis of food production and (especially) consumption in order to deal with issues of differentiation. These tend to "illuminate existing sociological preoccupations....Thus the analysis of patterns of food allocation and consumption has been used very effectively to illustrate the ways in which the underlying dimensions of social differentiation (gender, age and class, for example) manifest themselves in the experiences of everyday life" (Beardsworth and Keil, 1997, p.5).

The second route demonstrates food-based topics becoming ends in themselves, with specific questions being asked about how food is obtained, selected, shared, and eaten, and sociological methods then applied to these questions. This book encompasses both, as it explores aspects of social differentiation, as well as specific food questions related to production, distribution and consumption. From these sociological bases, themes explored include the interconnections with the physical shaping of space, and various dimensions of social differentiation as manifest through food practices observed at sites in London. As Beardsworth and Keil (1997, p.6) point out, buying, selling and eating food is at an intersection point between a range of processes that are

"physiological, psychological, ecological, economic, political, social, and cultural...[and] such intersections present social science with some of their most intriguing questions and challenges".

Thus the research has required that boundary crossing occur within sociology as a discipline, as well as borders between sociology and other disciplines. Food-related research findings from historical sociology (Elias, 1994; Mennell, 1996) are used to enrich insights gained from urban sociology (Gottdeiner, 1994; Savage, Warde and Ward, 2003) while theoretical perspectives from urban design, geography and political economy add to both the food and the urban sides of the book's research preoccupations. These more urban aspects of theory are considered later in this chapter.

It is difficult to study food issues sociologically without reviewing relevant functionalist and structuralist theories, as they have had a powerful influence on the way both sociology, and its sister discipline social anthropology have approached food analysis (Goody, 1982; Mennell, Murcott and Van Otterloo, 1992). Sociologists and anthropologists who take a structuralist perspective reflect structuralism's roots in linguistics whereby the deep structure or form of language is of more interest than its content (de Saussure, 1916; Ashley, Hollows, Jones, and Taylor, 2004). Thus, as Lupton (1996, p.8) explains, structuralists "tend to view food practices and habits as if they were linguistic texts with inherent rules to be exposed. The aim of such research is predominantly to explore the uses to which food is put as part of social life".

A second major influence on the development of structuralism in relation to food, meanwhile, is the work of the semiologist Roland Barthes (1972) and his followers who have attempted to define a code or grammar underlying food. For Barthes, food items are also items of information, and foods are signs in a system of communication. In Barthes' view, food objects and practices tend to have "apparently natural or commonsense meanings" attached to them and in this way food is seen as central to other forms of social behaviour (Ashley, Hollows, Jones, and Taylor 2004, p.5). Examples from Barthes' work (1972, 1997) provide connotations in relation to a number of foods that are supposed to convey a particularly dense range of meanings about health and sickness, social class and even nationalism. A valuable insight from Barthes is the centrality of food to other forms of social behaviour, closely tying it to modernity and hinting at its connections to spatiality. Barthes describes eating as a behaviour that "develops beyond its own ends" so that it replaces, sums up, and signals other behaviours (Barthes, 1997, p.25). He argues that many situations are expressed through food, including "activity, works, sport, effort, leisure, celebration…We might almost say that this 'polysemia' of food characterises modernity" (ibid).

At the same time, Barthes is very specifically talking about the contemporary food system and expects to be able to derive his food grammar without reference to history. Mennell (1996, p.12) complains that Barthes treats the past simply as a quarry for mining "potent meanings" but not in "any systematic way in order to understand a society's grammar of food". Barthes is compared to Lévi-Strauss in tending to "draw constantly on 'commonsense', taken-for-granted historical knowledge, not always of a very accurate sort" (ibid). This force of this criticism suggests that theoretical insights from Barthes should be approached with some caution in considering food's role in everyday life.

Bourdieu (1984), meanwhile, links taste in food to social stratification and to the notion of the habitus, which he elaborates in a number of contexts. Bourdieu (1993, p.86) explains that the habitus, is more than simply a repetitive habit, rather

"as the word implies, is that which one has acquired, but which has become durably incorporated in the body in the form of permanent dispositions….something like a property, a capital. And indeed, the habitus is a capital, but one which, because it is embodied, appears as innate. [The habitus is] powerfully generative....a product of conditionings which tends to reproduce the objective logic of those conditionings while transforming it. It is a kind of transforming machine that leads us to reproduce the social conditions of our production, but in a relatively unpredictable way" (ibid).

Elsewhere, in a way that seems highly relevant to the food quarter research, Bourdieu draws out the "collective or transindividual" nature of the habitus in order to "construct classes of habitus, which can be statistically characterised" (2000, p.157). So the concept of the habitus, while embodied, describes aspects of taste, behaviour and consumption "which coalesce to create flexible, rather than rigid categories of class, 'taking account of different concentrations of economic and cultural capital'" (Valentine, in Fyfe, 1998, p.196). At the same time, in food terms, Bourdieu has been criticised for the perceived ahistoricity and lack of dynamism in his theoretical approach. First, Bourdieu's snapshot of class stratification in relation to food in France is not thought to justify his argument that only superficial change is possible (Goody, 1982, p.31). Second, the attempt to find a fixed code that underlies people's behaviour would be worthwhile if the code "enabled us to predict a hitherto unknown surface structure" (Mennell, 1992, p.13). However, as Mennell argues,

> "in practice there is no adequate way in which this programme could be carried out. Therefore, because the deep structure is derived from surface elements alone and is unknowable without them, it is meaningless to discuss one as expressing the other, except in a circular, Pickwickian sense" (ibid).

Bourdieu (2000, p.166) answers the first strand of this critique by arguing that the "habitus changes constantly in response to new experiences", undercutting the view that it is entirely an ahistorical, fixed characterisation, and also pointing to its durability. He suggests instead that

> "the adjustments that are constantly required by the necessities of adaption to new and unforeseen situations may bring about durable transformations of the *habitus*, but these will remain within certain limits, not least because the *habitus* defines the perception of the situation that determines it" (1993, p.87).

Reviewing the notion of the habitus, and the various structuralisms discussed above, it seems that they share a valuable sense that meaning is not wholly a private experience. It is only insofar as they focus on an underlying 'grammar' and the prohibition of change (Ashley, Hollows, Jones and Taylor, 2004) that there may be some limits on their usefulness in relation to the research findings analysed in this book, where food sites undergoing rapid transformations socially, economically, environmentally and spatially are being scrutinised. So, for instance, on the one hand the habitus helps to denote the different class positions of place users. It demonstrates the high levels of social capital being formed and expressed through the particular socio-spatial practices of individuals. On the other hand, no claims are being made that the observed practices reflect any kind of deep underlying structure with its own unchanging rules. In other words, the notion of the habitus goes some way to help explain place user behaviour. It may not sufficiently capture issues of change and transformation in socio-spatial relationships related to food as an aspect of everyday life, that are also evident at the food quarters. At the same time, theoretical work linking the habitus and gentrification starts to make more meaningful connections between individual behaviour and spatial change in relation to food that will be discussed later in this chapter.

Another area of sociological enquiry that begins to deal with place-based aspects of designing for food, reflects theorists following the sociologist Norbert Elias (1982; 1994). Elias influentially argues for development of human relationships to food to be understood as connecting in various ways to the civilising of appetites, over time, and across race, class and gender. Elias traces the historical development of the notion of civility and contends that food plays a central role in the process by which behaviour is over time deemed acceptable or unacceptable in public space. Elias suggests that in the Middle Ages the presentation of self was not limited in terms of public eating, belching, spitting, defecation or other activities now frowned on (although it is notable that spitting, urinating and dog fouling seem to again be largely exempt from this social policing in contemporary London). Elias shows how a gradual top-down shift occurred in acceptable public behaviour including in relation to food. Social rules of public self-restraint worked their way down social ranks until they became part of normative everyday behaviour, now widely taken for granted. The transition from traditional to modern food systems, as described later in this chapter, is thought to have had an important impact in the process of civilising appetites (Mennell, Murcott and van Otterloo, 1992) culminating in "the development of notions of self-restraint, embarrassment and shame" (Valentine, 1998, p.193).

Of particular interest in relation to this book's exploration of the relationship between the social and the spatial is how the custom of civilised eating serves to regulate the boundary between public and private space. Eating in public can be considered uncivilised (Valentine, 1998, p.193) as demonstrating a lack of self-control. Rather, it "betokens enslavement to the belly" (Kass, 1994, p.189). Eating in public may even be likened to indecent exposure, whereas, to paraphrase Rudofsky (1980), eating at the table makes the sight of mastication bearable. Moreover, a composed meal at the table requires more sophisticated judgement about the taste of the food and the pace of its consumption than does eating in the street, as well as offering an opportunity for sociability (Visser, 1987; Parham, 1990). Thus, in Elias's terms, table-bound eating is a part of civilising appetites. All of this somewhat problematises the public eating that could be observed at the food quarters. It is also suggestive in relation to their design qualities (of which more later in the chapter). And again the split between the public and the private domain is important because

> "In addition to articulating a nature/culture dichotomy, taboos about eating on the street also articulate a particular understanding of 'public' and 'private'. The street may be a site of consumption but only a particular disembodied form of consumption is civilised – tomato sauce dripping down the chin is not an appropriate public spectacle" (Valentine, 1998, p.195).

These taboos about what is suitable eating behaviour in public space become interiorised. For example, it has been suggested that the tendency towards informalisation in relation to food means that people need to be more self-disciplined. They can no longer rely on formal rules that are shared and act to constrain behaviour. Rather the "predictable orderliness of much interaction among strangers must be governed by a strong sense of individual self-control" (Wouters, 1986, cited in Warde and Martens, 1998, p.152). Foucault (1977, p.155) argues that the "inspecting" gaze as a means of disciplinary power has an important role to play in producing "appropriate public bodily performances" in which each individual becomes his or her own overseer "exercising surveillance over and against himself" (ibid, p.155). Thus, fear of the public gaze – being seen to eat in public – "has served to put a moral brake on the pleasures of street food for many potential consumers" (Valentine, 1998, p.195). The role of the gaze also appears to link the notion of civilising of appetites with that of the habitus, in that the ritual of polite behaviour on the street is part of the appropriate performance of self, and denotes marks of distinction. Taste is embodied and eating on the street is not in good taste; rather it is 'common'.

How then can food quarters be seen as civilised places? As conceptualised in this book, food quarters are primarily public spaces given over to food in all its sensual abundance. They are also sites that operate within social norms that have developed to suggest public food consumption can be a source of shame and disgust to self and others. It may be that the food market and environs are among those culturally sanctioned outdoor spaces that are exempt from the construction of eating as a private activity that is normatively seen as uncivilised in public (Valentine, 1998). This relates to social changes in the image of the street to one that Valentine (ibid, p.198) calls the "self-indulgent street". The argument runs that as the pace of life increases, and work demands grow, people appear to have less time for civilised, slow dining and instead more often eat on the run.

As Warde (1999) has noted, so-called convenience foods help to deal with the perennial difficulties encountered in scheduling everyday lives, and although referring to pre-prepared foods taken home to eat, the timing issue Warde raises remains pertinent for street based consumption too. Snacking in the street, on food bought outside the home, becomes a ubiquitous element in the food environment. A refinement of this argument suggests that as public life becomes attenuated, the private space of the home has been 'transferred' to the street in a domestication of the public sphere (Kumar and Makarova, 2008). With increasing commodification of food and anonymous eating among strangers, comes a decline in "the social stigma of responding to bodily demands for food with instant gratification" (Valentine, 1998, p.200). The codes of fast food have taken over from those of civilised dining. Food courts, as their spatial expression, present the paradoxical development of 'slow' fast food, while movements such as Slow Food and città slow discussed in Chapter 1 in relation to sustainability and conviviality, could be construed as an attempt to combat placeless developments. As will be seen in later chapters those interviewed do not appear to define their own public eating behaviour as in any way uncivilised, speaking to changes in social norms within Elias's terms.

Food system context

The next theoretical areas to be considered are those loosely grouped together under the rubric of the food system (Tansey and Worsley, 1995). Clarity about the nature of the food system is important at two levels. It helps to make clear the economic and political background to specific food production, distribution and consumption patterns evident in the case study areas the book examines. It also sheds light on the way that changes in the broader food system can connect to these specific patterns. In both ways it provides a useful theoretical grounding to the analysis of the food quarters. The food system can be thought of as a kind of shorthand term to represent a

> "complex of interdependent interrelationships associated with the production and distribution of food which have developed to meet the nutritional needs of human populations" (Beardsworth and Keil, 1997, p.33).

The food system can be theorised in terms of its "historical evolution in particular contexts of economy and the exercise of power" (Atkins and Bowler, 2001, p.4). For example, at the more macro level, various theorists have traced particular food commodities to explicate how global economic systems in relation to food operate, to explore their in-built inequalities, and sometimes deleterious environmental effects (Salaman, 1949; Goody, 1982; Mintz, 1985; Atkins and Bowler, 2001, 1997; Schlosser, 2001; Kurlansky, 2002). While such food chain patterns have been conceptualised as a food system, this should not be assumed to exhibit any functionalist-style, well thought-out, formally organised plan or scheme underlying food production, distribution and consumption. At the same time, food system proponents usefully distinguish between traditional and modern forms of the system.

A key aspect of the modern food system is the debate about human relationships to the environment, reflecting sustainability issues discussed in Chapter 1. Perverse effects of the modern food system, in terms of unsustainability and inequality, and their global interrelatedness, have been identified with a range of unfortunate systemic features. These include both widespread and increasing levels of hunger and obesity that are being exacerbated by climate change (Lang, 2004; Patel, 2007). Meanwhile, theoretical work on the *local* nature of the food system also foregrounds sustainability implications, but is a contested area (Hinrichs, 2003). On the one hand, the concept of an alternative, more localised food system has been encapsulated in the concept of the foodshed (Getz, 1991; Hendrickson, 1993; and Kloppenburg et al 1996), which reflects the possibilities for contributing to more sustainable communities through food (Kloppenburg, et al, 2000; Feenstra, 2009). On the other hand, some planning theorists have argued strongly that while this current of food systems research assumes that eating local food is more ecologically sustainable and socially just, this simply constitutes a local trap and local food systems may be no more sustainable or just than those at larger scale (Born, 2006).

Despite such areas of contestation, the critique of the modern food system recognises that there are spatial factors at work in the process by which food is produced, distributed and consumed. This stands in contrast to the sociological problem of aspatiality discussed a little later in this chapter. An aspatial approach leads to some theoretical obscuring of the way that the emergence of the modern food system is in fact closely tied to spatial processes of urbanisation, and the food system's workings over time intertwine with the urbanism that is produced. For example, in the United Kingdom, industrialisation allowed urban development to occur on a previously unparalleled scale and by the 18th century the inability of local food resources to meet burgeoning urban populations' growing food demands precipitated longer distance trade in produce (Oddy, 1990). London was an early example of a metropolitan centre drawing on national and international food sources. In London's case, supply side advances in transport made the movement of food from greater distances possible, including from overseas to 'London's Larder' at Hays Wharf for city wide distribution, while technological changes in food handling and preservation techniques allowed its storage for longer periods. More recently in London, over the latter part of the 20th century, food system shifts have been marked by spatial changes resulting in consumption patterns predicated on car based catchments rather than walkable ones, of which more later in this chapter.

One of the most relevant contrasts for this book in food system terms is between patterns of local, relatively small-scale food production, distribution and consumption which are characterised as traditional within the food system, and large-scale relatively specialised and industrialised forms which are characterised as modern. The detailed study of the food quarters explores aspects of the relationship between traditional and modern spatial scales of production, distribution, and consumption and their implications for sustainable city design. At least five of the characteristics of the modern food system have spatialised effects reflected in city form. These are, broadly, its high degree and large scale of specialisation and industrialisation; that distribution is based on mass markets and buying commodities; consumption emphasises choice and variety; shortages tend to arise from causes other than from absolute food availability; and that the sustainability of the system is debatable (Beardsworth and Keil, 1997).

As the case study results demonstrate in later chapters, the food-centred spaces under consideration challenge central characteristics of the modern food system to varying extents. To give one example, some place users were found to be making choices to avoid or limit supermarket consumption and instead to walk to shop for food at street markets whose economic base was significantly comprised of artisanal foods or foods with low food miles (MacGregor and Vorley, 2006). The main theoretical point is that in food system terms, the socio-spatial practices that were evident at the food quarters, and the urban forms that underpin them, together may support claims for greater urban sustainability and conviviality. The design of these quarters can be contrasted with urban forms and practices that are more passively responding to, or actively engaging with, the modern food system's inequitable and unsustainable structural features.

The cultural and social dimensions of the modern food system can be associated with five main processes, which each represent a distinct phase and focus on specific, characteristic, spatialised loci (Goody, 1982, p.37). As food moves from production through consumption to clean up, the role that the physical qualities of the loci themselves might play receives scant attention in Goody's analysis. However, the conceptualisation of the loci for the food system begins to give some spatial shape to the study of food. It allows theorists to sketch out some of the spatialised processes and material sites that may be involved in food and eating. At the same time, it is limited in dealing with the shift in the locus of cooking, as ready meals that are prepared industrially replace individual cooking, and even private kitchens are omitted from some new apartment developments (Trendhunter, 2008). Aspects of the political economy of such forms of food consumption form a broader context for market-based food buying and are further considered below. Meanwhile, the book focuses on the food system phases of distribution, preparation and consumption, especially as they occur in public spaces in the vicinity of markets in the food quarters.

Food and spatiality

Reviewing relevant work from the sociology of food suggests that until relatively recently, it has been predominantly aspatial in its analysis despite often having "a stake in place" (Gieryn, 2000, p.463). That is, historically the sociology of food has either underplayed spatiality, or simply not conceptualised spatial aspects as part of its theoretical framework, although more recent work suggests this lack of spatial awareness on food topics may be shifting (Lockie, 2001; Morgan, Marsden and Murdoch, 2006; Holloway et al, 2007; Harris, 2010). Sociological and ethnographic work refers to foodscapes (Yasmeen, 1992) of various kinds and scales, in which food has become increasingly commodified as fashion and entertainment, coalescing into the notion of foodatainment (Finkelstein, 1999; 1989) although the spatiality of these spaces may not be foregrounded. The consumption end of the food system has received more theoretical attention than have production or distribution elements (as noted by Beardsworth and Keil, 1997, p.49; Warde, 1997; Murcott, 2011) while the emphasis has fairly uniformly remained on actors and the multiplicity of flows and linkages between them.

There has been less interest discernable in the sociological literature on any role the settings or loci, within which these dynamics have been acted out, may have played in their relationships. Thus, although the "many types of places away from home where currently people may eat a meal in Britain" (Warde and Martens, 2000, p.21) are acknowledged as providing a multiplicity of food consumption contexts, these are seen to bring forward problems of suitable nomenclature rather than of meaning in themselves. Specifically, it appears that food sociology under-theorises the spatial implications and possible influences of food system loci on the shaping of cities, and conversely, the potential of the physical shaping of the city to in turn affect aspects of the modern food system. Equally, within the structuralist tradition the symbolism of food is a well-developed theme around which social differentiation rather than spatiality has been extensively explored (Barthes, 1972; Bourdieu, 1984; Visser, 1987, 1993). While food may be seen more or less convincingly to signify social distinction in terms of nationality, ethnicity, age, class and gender, its capacity to reflect spatial aspects of social distinction appears still to need further work. Bourdieu (1984) does attempt to make distinctions (to Mennell unconvincing ones) between British and French approaches to taste but at the scale of the country as a whole, so the potential effects of supposed national tastes on urban spatiality at a finer grain cannot be readily determined. Given its lack of focus on the spatial implications of food production, distribution and consumption, food sociology may miss or underplay connections to both city form and social relations shaped by and shaping that form. Some of these connections and possibilities are explored later in this chapter, and again through case study results presented and analysed in Chapters 3 to 8.

It is to geographers, urban designers and architects that we should perhaps turn to find more acknowledgement that food relationships may have influences on and be influenced by their urban settings. Geographers have considered the social and cultural meanings of food production and consumption at a number of spatial scales including the body, home, community, city, region, nation and globe (Valentine and Bell, 1995). Urban designers and architects have noted that spatial scales necessarily include, among others, the private spaces of the table, kitchen, dining room, house, and garden; the public spaces of the street, square, neighbourhood, town centre, town, and city; the social spaces of markets, shops and eating places; the productive spaces of the footpath, park, allotment, urban fringe, city region, and countryside; and the global food spaces of the northern and southern hemispheres (Parham, 1991, 1992, 1994). There has also been some work on the spaces of cafes and restaurants (Parham, 2001, 2005; Franck, 2002) and the relationship of various urban scales to their status as public, private or transitional space (Madanipour, 2003).

Thus, although Valentine and Bell's (1995) analysis is suggestive in relation to spatiality, there is still work to be done in determining spatial impacts or effects of food relationships. While Valentine and Bell (ibid) name a series of scales for their exploration of food relationships, there is a need to explore the implications of food places representative of different urban scales in a spatial way. Physical places can then be understood as more than simply being there as locational settings. In current work, there is a risk that place can appear to be a static backdrop rather than theorised as a player in food relationships, with the focus instead on notions of identity and relationships played out as processes between actors within various sites and settings.

For example, in considering the meaning of food in the home, Valentine and Bell define this as about the way individual identities are constructed (op cit). Similarly at the scale of the community (an amorphous term) the discussion centres on interrelationships between various actors. At the larger scale of the city, where they suggest they will deal with the built landscapes of urban food consumption, they do so in terms of defining various sites for consumption and considering the changing social mores governing consumption in those spaces. While architecture is mentioned, the links to spatial design, and between design and the construction of those mores are not explored. Possible scalar and other linkages between food and spatiality have been proposed, but there are limited fieldwork results on which to base conclusions (including Parham, 1998; 1996; 1993; 1992; Franck, 2002; Esperdy, 2002) although more recent work is beginning to address this research gap (Viljoen and Wiskerke, 2012). It appears then that the specific ways in which physical space design may have effects on, or be affected by, food relationships deserve more attention. This book's case study approach to this exploration is explained later in this chapter.

Various strands in the sociological consideration of urban space do have relevant implications for food despite gaps in theoretical work to link the two areas. These include theories of the role of place (Logan and Molotch, 1987), implications of the growth of post urban regions

(Gottdeiner, 1994) and the spatial nature of modernity (Savage, Ward and Warde, 2003), including uneven development (Harvey, 1987, 1989, 2003) and the decline of the public sphere (Habermas, 1989), an area which has become a crowded theoretical field in its own right. Space shaping arguments broadly within sociological traditions (De Certeau, 1984, 1998; Soja, 1989, 1993, 2000; Lefebvre, 1991) also help to explore the notion of the primacy of the spatial in understanding aspects of social relations between people. Some relevant perspectives, such as Warde's (1997) work on consumption, food and taste, are not in themselves spatialised, but help to frame the exploration of the way that food and city form interconnect through the medium of food practices.

Moreover, notwithstanding their relatively small scale, urban areas such as the food quarters are intricately linked in economic, social and environmental terms to a globalised context of urban space that is expanding enormously worldwide. These urbanised spaces can no longer be conceptualised as part of a city-suburb hierarchy or duality as previously configured (Fishman 1987; Rowe 1991; Garreau, 1991; Sudjic, 1991; Frost 1993). As the world becomes mostly urban, "the predominant form of urbanisation is large scale metropolitan areas that link with their surrounding hinterland over vast territory" (Castells, 2000, p.ix) with trends towards the rise of huge "megalopolitan" urban regions covering coastal areas and habitable plains (Sassen, 1991; Gottdeiner, 1994; Konvitz and Parham, 1996; Savage, Ward and Warde, 2003). Therefore, food quarters should not be considered as isolated spatial entities or simply providing venues for discrete units of sociological analysis (Lofland, 1971) but contextualised by these shifts.

Focusing in on the research context of changing spatiality, it is worth noting that like many other cities, London is extremely uneven in its development. Sharpening economic, social and environmental inequalities are played out in its spatial arrangements. In London, as in other large urban conurbations, specific results of growth and restructuring include the deterioration of some traditional centres, the decline of the public realm, and both the clustering and spatial resorting of activities to low density city peripheries (Hall, 1992; Gordon and McCann, 2000; Gordon and Travers, 2010), sometimes operating without traditional centres (Sudjic, 1992).

London's changing spatiality reflects issues including white flight on the one hand and re-colonisation of inner and middle ring suburbs by middle class incomers on the other (Travers, 2004). Many inner areas in London initially declined through the creation of a post metropolitan landscape, but some have now experienced regeneration, waves of gentrification (Smith, 1996; Lees, 2003) and 'supergentrification' (Butler and Lees, 2006). Broadly, post metropolitan regions like London, encompassing both old and newer urban fabric, have undergone a transforming process of urban restructuring, and are now socially fragmented in new ways (Soja; 2000). In this context, the food quarters can also be understood as largely comprising traditionally shaped urban space that sits within an urban world that is changing away from such spatial forms; to develop as part of a spatially complex post metropolitan landscape (Webber, 1964; Self, 1982; Augé, 1995; Soja, 2000).

The book explores the interconnections between the public realm, food and consumption, in the context of well-documented public space decline as a feature of urban development over the last fifty years (Krier, 1979; Kostof, 1992; Jacobs, 1994; Madanipour; 2003). Again, like sustainability problems associated with the advance of modernist thinking in city planning (Holston, 1989; Hall, 1992; Taylor, 1998; Graham and Healey, 1999), public space decline fits well with dominant food patterns in London and elsewhere. These include the expansion of fast food, ready meals, and kitchen-less flats, and dendritic, car dominated and car dependant food space including mall based food consumption, road pantries, and out-of-town hypermarkets (Parham, 1992, 1995, 1996, 2005; Esperdy, 2002). These developments appear to promote homogenous, "nonurban" lifestyles (Lozano, 1996, p.8), and with the same airports, hotels, suburban and post urban areas, allied to increasing segregation by age, class, and race; real experience and social contact with others is replaced by "fantasy of success and power by proxy" (ibid, p.9).

In city centres, public space is both increasingly privatised (Minton, 2009) and substituted for by interaction that occurs in private atriums and malls in corporate headquarters, as well as in hotels and shopping gallerias (Lozano, p.10). The plethora of private eating spaces in office buildings, to which the public normally has no access, is one food-related manifestation. Defying this dominant trend, traditional public spaces are argued to be extremely important in providing the interface between, and maintaining the health of, private and civil society (Rowe, 1997).

One relevant outcome for the public realm in London is that a great deal of food retailing, like other retail sectors, functions as big box or exit ramp architecture (Steuteville, 2000), within a suburban or post metropolitan spatial context. Out of town shopping centres, interior facing 'big box' supermarkets and the development of large-scale malls are symptomatic of this spatial approach to food retailing, in strong contrast to the food-centred spaces under consideration in this book. This trend is also identifiable at a smaller physical scale in reconfigured spaces in established suburbs, where a suburban retailing model of interiorised big box stores, coarse grained frontages and large car parks is imposed on and disrupts traditionally shaped, public realm focused streetscapes. The big box supermarket in these circumstances is often centred on an inward facing, privately owned mall space with parking on the exterior, and pedestrian space within.

In more nuanced versions private space is presented as public space and this, as well as characteristic land use separation and homogeneity are perceived to be threats to the social ecology of urban areas (Lozano, 1996; Minton, 2009), something that dominant design modes in relation to shopping makes clear. "Shopping, for example, is now a strictly functional act of purchasing that involves a simple trip from one's home to a shopping centre (Lozano, 1996, p.7). Paradoxically, more subtly configured big box retailing environments now seek to replicate qualities that once made shopping pleasurable. As Lozano (ibid, p.7) notes

> "urban shopping was once also a social ritual that included window-shopping, promenading, meeting friends informally, and exchanging information. There is still some ritual shopping in a few downtown areas, but the links to community are weakened; many shoppers are suburbanites on an expedition to the city and are thus isolated from the community around them".

In Chapter 3, as part of the process of exploring the food quarters in morphological and design terms; and again in Chapters 4 to 6, in relation to their urban sustainability performance, social use and economic development, there is consideration of some of the food implications of decline and revival of the public realm expressed through food-centred space. As set out above, the context for the food quarters as public food spaces is the spatially much more dominant pattern of post metropolitan development, in which the public realm has been over controlled, diminished, or disappeared altogether (Sorkin, 1991; Davis, 1992; Soja, 1993; Koolhaas and Mau, 1997; Banerjee, 2001; Kolson, 2001; Atkinson, 2003; Minton, 2009). Not only have out-of-town supermarkets and hypermarkets burgeoned, but this has had particular effects on existing retail spaces including the decline of local high streets, with the loss of food markets and local food shops, like grocers, greengrocers, fishmongers, butchers and cafes. In the United Kingdom between 1997 and 2002 such stores closed at a rate of fifty per week, the average person travelled 893 miles a year to shop for food (New Economics Foundation, 2002) and there was further concentration in retailing business ownership (Dobson et al, 2003).

The case study research explored the argument that, by maintaining or reviving food-centred public spaces, the food quarters to varying extents, resisted, modified or reshaped post metropolitan spatiality in ways outlined in the following chapters. For example, the research demonstrated a strong contrast between the well-documented decline of public space in post metropolitan development, and the strength of the public realm in the studied food quarters. Some recent work has reinforced the view that food markets are important *public* sites for social interaction among a diversity of people (Parham, 2001; Esperdy, 2002; Watson and Studdert, 2006) as well as providing high quality, affordable food that reflects a range of food cultures, and is often not available elsewhere (Rubin, Jatana and Potts, 2006). Food markets thus offer

> "possibilities not just for local economic growth but also for people to mingle with each other and become accustomed to each others' differences in a public space – thereby acting as a potential focal point for local communities that could revitalise public space" (Watson and Studdert, 2006, p.vii).

Food quarters and consumption

Looking at food-centred space also means touching on theories of consumption from at least two theoretical perspectives. On the one hand, food markets are public spaces focused on consumption, and thus reflect the nature of the consumption end of the food system and its commodity chains (Mansveldt, 2005). In the modern food system, consumption patterns deriving from the general characteristics described earlier are both spatially and socially located. While Goody (1982) places food markets (in each case at the heart of the food quarter) in the food allocating phase of the food system, this research suggested that as they transformed into 'slow food' courts it was equally valid to consider the studied food markets and their environs as also part of the locus dealing with the consumption phase of the food system.

Meanwhile, food-centred spaces are also sites for everyday consumption, understood in sociological terms. As Warde (1997, p.1) points out, there has been an explosion of interest in consumption within sociology, with some sociologists making "strong claims for the new structural role of consumption practice as a central focus of everyday life", and debating the ways that class, ethnicity and gender impact on consumption practices (Warde, 1991). This in turn reflects the way that consumption of food has become intimately connected to "the consumer attitude" (Bauman (1990, p.204). Because people are increasingly distant from food production, and there are less and less alternatives to buying what we need to eat, the consumer attitude is one of assuming everything can be bought:

> "Hence, the problem of obtaining fresh, tasty, healthy, chemical-free or convenient foodstuffs is perceived and addressed as a shopping problem; where and at what price can the items satisfying my standards be obtained. The spread of the consumer attitude permeates common sense and inserts commercial culture into the core of everyday life" (Warde and Martens, 1998, p.49).

In the context of this high degree of commodification of the food aspects of urban life, consumption at the level of the individual has also increasingly become tied to notions of identity (Knox, 1992), and individualisation (Bauman, 1988; Featherstone, 1987). Through this connection to identity, what is consumed comes to symbolically represent aspects of the self. It also reflects the urban: "consumption is not simply a characteristic of urban life; it is a major factor in determining the nature of that life" (Miles and Miles; 2004, p.3). One sign of this is that consumption's symbolic meaning and significance can itself be spatialised. At the level of the city, for example, consumption has become something that can be invested in or promoted. The city is assumed as not only an arena in which consumption takes place, but a commodity in its own right, pursued through the construction of a cultural economy (Zukin, 1995; Miles and Miles, 2004). The way this played out at the three studied sites is discussed later in the chapter in relation to the nature of the food quarters' development as cultural quarters.

It is possible to read such public spaces of consumption as nostalgic simulacra aimed predominantly at inward urban tourism or harking back to an imaginary past (Watson and Wells, 2005), but neither of these explanations appears entirely convincing in relation to the food quarters as they operated in the period 2005 to 2008. It is certainly the case that the production of urban core space as a "high quality consumption product for foreigners, tourists, people from the outskirts and suburbanites" (Lefebvre, 1991, p.73) is well demonstrated in London and elsewhere. And as its catchment range expanded to encompass visitors from less central urban neighbourhoods, each of the food quarters demonstrated aspects of such a consumption process to varying degrees. However, far from echoing the past, the food-centred spaces focused on Borough Market, Broadway Market, and Exmouth Market appeared to be where new ways of consuming were being modelled and adopted (Thrift and Glennie, 1993), as part of a long-term historical process by which consumption changes in character (McCracken, 1990; Benson, 1994).

The close links between the history of consumption and that of market shopping and related social practices are an important framing element here. The open air market has been conceptualised as the first order of commercial architecture (Betsky, 2000), giving way over time to arcades, then department stores, supermarkets and now the internet (Bowlby, 2000), as shopping has responded to "the demands of a mass production system that required a more rational approach to selling" (Miles and Miles, 2004. p.35), and more recently to sustainability regimes. At the same time, as noted above, the contrast between "faceless and placeless" (ibid) supermarkets and clone town high streets (New Economics Foundation, 2004, 2005) compared with the much more convivial shopping and other socio-spatial practices at and around the food market, is one of the themes explored through the book's case study research.

Food quarters sit alongside, and can be contrasted to, more dominant spatial modes in both urban expansion and renewal contexts. In area redevelopment, as discussed earlier in the chapter, there has been a process of imposition of suburban spatial models for retailing on more urban areas, whereby consumption space created in inner urban areas is predominantly modelled on the sanitised malls of outer suburban areas (New Economics Foundation, 2004, 2005). Examples of this process can be seen all around London and in many other cities and towns in the UK. Moreover, gentrifying areas tend to be marked by street upgrading along these spatially suburbanising lines (Savage, Warde and Ward, 2003). In fact, the research found that none of the three food quarters fitted this suburbanising paradigm in either physical design or socio-spatial practice terms. All three were identified as spatially urban in nature and to provide rich territory for sociability, rather than being bland consumption zones. They were clearly places to go to, as much as through. Thus, a rejection of the suburban mall or clone town model of consumption space was connected to their urban design, both as existing places and as sites for design-based renewal. The case study research showed that this was quite an explicit rejection by designers and some place users, while it constituted a more de facto rejection by others who habituated these food spaces.

A related aspect of the food quarters as rather different kinds of consumption space was the way their temporal qualities were observed to transcend suburban retailing models' highly regulated opening times, behavioural controls and regimented social use. Rather, the quarters showed considerable diversity in use over time, reflecting the "manifold rhythms forged through daily encounters and multiple experiences of time and space" (Thrift and Amin, 2002, p.9). Although less regulated than private space, clear patterns of use over time were documented at each site. The balance of everyday activities shifted with the time of day or night, and the day of the week, as well as varying by week, month and annually, according to the timetable of work, leisure, holidays and festivals. Their physical spaces were shaped and reshaped over time, both to reflect changing practices of everyday life and to influence these (de Certeau, 1988). Each, to a varying extent, comprised at once a site within which individuals played out a well-developed habitus (of which more below), a place for conspicuous consumption *and* a space of social transformation in which less commodified encounters could also be observed.

Food quarters, regeneration and gentrification

An important aspect of the sites' spatiality is the role of food quarters as spaces of regeneration and gentrification. Although a contested term (Furbey, 1999), one workable definition of urban regeneration is:

> "Comprehensive and integrated vision and action which leads to the resolution of urban problems and which seeks to bring about a lasting improvement in the economic, physical, social and environmental condition of an area that has been subject to change" (Thompson et al, 2006, p.17).

Regeneration is therefore posited as being about responding to "the opportunities and challenges which are presented by urban degeneration in a particular place at a specific moment in time" (Roberts and Sykes, 2000, p.3). These responses tend to be area-based (Lloyd et al., 2001) and are aimed at improving urban conditions, including food-related aspects such as health (Curtis and Cave, 2002) with mixed evidence emerging as to their success (Thompson et al., 2006). Much of the focus of regeneration strategies over the last twenty years in the United Kingdom has been on "attracting investors, middle-class shoppers and visitors by transforming places and creating new consumption spaces" (Raco, 2003). By the 1990s, place marketing, focused on retail spaces (Page and Hardyman, 1996), and more recently the development of urban quarters (Bennison et al, 2007), started to be recognised as a mainstream regeneration tool for town centres.

Aspects of the food quarters' functioning could certainly place them in the category of place-marketed regeneration sites. They could equally be seen as demonstrating significant gentrification effects, in which new land users were moving in who were of higher status than the previous occupiers, and were making substantial changes to the built environment in ways that excluded their former inhabitants. Moreover, the food quarters could be seen emerging from this process as the cores of neighbourhoods which were a spatial expression of a particular habitus:

> "qualitatively distinctive in terms of their residents' occupational composition, demographic structure, attitudes, lifestyle preferences, tastes, and consumption profiles" (Butler and Robson, 2003a; Webber, 2007, p.183, based on Butler, 1997).

In order to understand the food quarters' relationship to gentrification, it is perhaps necessary to very briefly review debates in the sociological literature in which competing explanations of gentrification stress either the demand side through the production of space, or the supply side focusing on consumption (Lees, 2000; Lambert and Boddy, 2002, p.2). Two competing views of gentrification emerge. These situate the process as either emancipating the distinctive cultural values of a new middle class or reflecting a class-based conflict in the "revanchist city" (Smith, 1996) whereby the middle classes claims back spatial territory previously lost to them. While in either case poorer residents have lost out, on the revanchist side, the processes of regeneration and urban renewal tend to be treated as normative ways of disguising the exclusion and displacement of poor urban populations (Smith, 1996), with effects on both class and identity. As Tonkiss (2007, p.80) points out in relation to identity formation:

> "Recent shifts at the level of class and capital – the accelerated gentrification of certain parts of the late capitalist city – in this sense produce new patterns of spatial stratification and also alter urban meanings and identities".

Interconnections between gentrification, sustainability and spatiality, in the process of constructing urban identities around food, seem fruitful territory for this book. In such a reading, gentrification is still about class, but identity construction rather than working class displacement takes centre stage. As Butler (2007, p.164) notes, this presents a challenge to a hegemonic critique presented by US theorists on gentrification, in which the concept is simply rolled out without reference to spatial differences. Similarly, Lees (2000, pp.393-405) argues that an "ideology of liveability and sustainability" is now being used to justify gentrification and thus

> "a more detailed examination of the 'geography of gentrification' would constitute a progressive research programme and lead us to rethink the

'true' value of gentrification as a practical solution to urban decline in cities around the world".

Butler (2007, p.162) points to the rise of "greentrification", tying gentrification more explicitly to aspects of sustainability, while Smith and Holt (2007, p.144) allude to the "apprentice gentrifiers", who demonstrate the importance of aspects of place in provincial towns and cities, as well as in more metropolitan contexts. Butler (2007, p.163) also suggests more broadly that residential location has become increasingly important in defining 'who you are', with the spatial context one in which suburbs and other urban locations, as well as city centres, have become places middle class people want to live. Sociological work on middle class households in north, east and south London has in fact shown that "in an urban context such as provided by London, spatial factors are an important mediating variable in terms of identity construction" (Robson and Butler, 2001, p.84).

Another very useful theoretical framing device for understanding the socio-spatial processes that were at work in the food quarters between 2005 and 2008 is the way Bourdieu's work on forms of capital and the habitus has been connected to the spatiality of gentrification. It should be remembered from the earlier discussion of Bourdieu in this chapter that the habitus is essentially an embodied concept, and should not be seen as spatial in itself. Bourdieu (2000, p.130) explicitly ties his conception of the habitus to individual interaction with social rather than physical space. Yet the way that the habitus interconnects with aspects of spatiality and gentrification is particularly interesting. Accounts of gentrification tend overall to emphasise its urbanity. It is situated as occurring in the first instance among people who may have little economic capital but significant amounts of cultural capital

> "deployed in lieu of material capital to achieve distinction. Moreover, the cultural capital used in the case of gentrification is the set of values that privileges pro-urban lifestyles" (Bridge; 2000, p.206).

Paraphrasing Podmore (1998), Bridge suggests that the "gentrified neighbourhood has been seen as the spatial manifestation of the new middle-class habitus" (ibid). Thus the habitus, while remaining tied to the individual, is played out in spatialised ways in and through the gentrified space of the neighbourhood, or in this case the food quarter. A key point is the importance of place. As Butler points out (2002, n.p.r.) in certain areas of London, "the habitus (defined crudely as the attitudes, beliefs, feelings and identities) of our respondents" does connect with place and "this run[s] counter to the accepted sociological wisdom that place is a given". One of Butler's most relevant spatial arguments about the place specificity of the habitus, is that middle class assets

> "will be deployed in different ways which will give particular areas their own distinctive ambiences and that this can be seen as part of the process of class formation in contemporary London. In this sense, the habitus acquires specific spatial characteristics which in turn influence those living in its ambit. In trying to untangle the nature of the urban middle classes in London, the structure of consciousness is likely to prove important and 'place' to be of enduring influence" (ibid).

For the purposes of this research, another very useful extending out of Bourdieu's concept is Butler's (2001) notion of the metropolitan habitus. Gentrification is not just about consumption at the urban centre but explained "by the overall 'pull' of the metropolitan habitus which is strongly associated with being a global city and the associated cultural connotations" (Butler, 2002; n.p.r.). Butler refers here to Bridge (2000) who uses Bourdieu's conceptual framework to develop gentrification as a 'field' within the habitus, in the same way that aspects including housing, employment, and education have traditionally been seen as habitus fields. Such spatialisation is noteworthy in a book looking at food and place because the habitus can then help explain why certain middle class people want to live near each other (Butler, 2007, p.163). Butler draws on Savage's (2005) work in Manchester, which suggests that people operate across a series of fields of work, leisure and home, with the habitus seen to cover each of these fields. "The trick, as it were, is for people to triangulate these fields spatially so that they live with 'people like themselves'" (Butler, 2007, p.175). Savage, says Butler (op cit, p.171)

> "demonstrates that Bourdieu's concept of the habitus is an essentially spatial one that creates a series of 'spatial divisions of consumption' which accommodate to people's economic capabilities and their sense of wanting to `flock' with people like themselves".

Likewise, Bridge's (2006, p.1966) deployment of 'mini habituses' devolved from Butler's metropolitan habitus, seem useful in this research context. Such a mini habitus, representing

> "particular mixes of social, cultural, and economic capital produces a geography of and the development of 'mini' habituses with different neighbourhoods having distinct neighbourhood milieux" (ibid, p.1966).

In the three food quarters, individuals appear to contribute to an overall metropolitan habitus, but their behaviour in each location is subtly different, with users constructing distinct mini habituses in each food quarter. Each individual neighbourhood milieu develops from the metropolitan habitus in a way that seems to support the mini habitus notion and also gives prominence to food as a central unifying factor (Webber, 2007). This has particular resonance in relation to where and how individuals shop for food in the gentrifying spaces of the food quarters, as identity is constructed through the distinctive food practices and liveable spaces of the revived food markets and their surrounding areas. In the context alluded to by Butler (2007, p.167), where the whole of Greater London might be considered "ripe for gentrification", identity construction through food consumption at the micro level of the quarter or neighbourhood, is closely linked to economic and environmental changes in the way food is handled at regional, city wide and broader scales. And, in relation to 'new urban colonist' neighbourhoods, the alternative food geographies referred to earlier in this chapter would seem to be in the ascendant:

> "Taste, it would seem, is a key unifier in these neighbourhoods, in which cooking and the kitchen play a much more central role than in suburban neighbourhoods of similar occupational status. A particularly large proportion of the population are interested in the food that they eat and its provenance, with people being particularly responsive to opportunities to eat foreign foods whether at home or in a restaurant. Ingredients in home-prepared foods are particularly important and consumers go to considerable trouble to shop at upmarket supermarkets offering variety and freshness" (Webber, 2007, p.196).

Meanwhile, although gentrification narratives of displacement may have moved from centre stage, by 1990s London social exclusion was on the rise in regenerating areas (Kleiman, 1998) and working class perspectives on exclusion were themselves being marginalised (Smith, 2005). Relatively recent case study work in London gives empirically-based weight to arguments that connect gentrification and exclusion, demonstrating for example that displacement effects were profound in the 1990s, as working class, elderly and inactive groups were lost from formerly working class areas (Atkinson, 2000). As Chapter 5 demonstrates, the Broadway Market area appeared by the early 2000s to be at the stage of gentrification in which certain middle class fractions were attracted to an urban neighbourhood characterised by diverse populations and relatively affordable housing (Smith and Williams, 1986; Smith, 1996). It then moved on to the verge of the next stage, one that both Borough and Exmouth (in Chapters 4 and 6) seemed to have reached in this gentrifying trajectory. To varying degrees at each food quarter, large-scale capital moved in to scoop up economic value created by earlier urban pioneers, through both food-related and residential developments. As Tonkiss (2007, p.81) describes it:

> "Once the 'gentrification frontier' had been opened up, moreover, the attractions of the inner city came to be less those of social and economic diversity than the effects of gentrification itself: renovated housing, new spaces of consumption and middle class residents".

These processes appear to connect city form and food practices in new ways in which changing relationships between the production and consumption of food and space are both important. On the one side are changes to the production of the economic space of the city; while on the consumption side gentrification stresses culture, lifestyle and patterns of consumption (op cit). Instead of seeing this as two separate processes at work, Tonkiss (2007, p.82) argues that these "gentrifying fractions" are a consumption class because not only do they own housing and have particular consumer patterns but because

> "they are also constituted through changing strategies of accumulation as urban economies are restructured around the production of services, culture and information".

In a now well-documented trajectory, at each food quarter the gentrification processes, at least in the first stage, has gone hand in hand with "an informal urban politics which reject[s] the cultural homogeneity and social conformity of the suburbs" (Tonkiss, 2007, p.85). Yet the narrative is not entirely negative. Also at each food quarter it is clear that incomers have been making an apparently positive input into local political campaigns, for example to protect existing small food businesses from the depredations of property developers. In this way incoming residents have been engaged in struggles to protect local class and ethnic diversity expressed through food. This was an especially clear finding at Broadway Market and is explored in Chapter 5. However, although incomers intended to assist those they might displace, the idealised narratives that Butler (2006) refers to may well have mystified the effects of displacement that were nonetheless occurring. Over the medium term, this process remains one of "social evacuation" in which "displacement removes social problems and rearranges rather than ameliorates the causes of poverty, environmental decay and the loss of neighbourhood vitality. Problems are moved rather than solved" (Atkinson, 2000, p.163).

By the time gentrification enters its mature phase it tends to be accompanied by particular styles of residential architecture (Zukin, 1998) that produce what Tonkiss (2007, p.89) has described as "a mass production gentrification style", currently based on resurgent modernist tropes, judged to produce housing in London of poor quality and inadequate space standards (Greater London Authority, 2006). This has a propensity to homogenise the renewed urban landscapes that are being created, while selling them on the basis of their diversity and chic (Tonkiss, 2007, p.89). The food market as a designed space or spaces plays a major attractor role early in this process, before the arrival of bland food chains signals the beginning of gentrification's more mature phase. Thus, in exploring the rich field of socio-spatial practices embodied in each case study area this gentrifying underside needs to be kept in mind. Likewise, these spatial, economic and social shifts have specific physical design implications and effects that are examined later in this chapter. Chapter 3, meanwhile, provides design and morphologically based examples of the process that was found to be underway in each quarter, while later chapters refer to views from place users and commentators to the same effect.

Food quarters, cultural quarters

The discussion above serves to introduce the development of food spaces in terms of their regeneration into *cultural* quarters (Scott, 1997; Montgomery, 2003; Cameron and Coaffee, 2005) which are sites for various art practices and economic activities related to food. The food quarters provide numerous examples of being attractive to people working in arts and media as places to live, work and visit because of their food qualities. They are also considered particularly suitable sites for undertaking art projects along food-related themes. Some art practice directly focused on the quarters as food spaces was found during case study research and it seems that these spaces increasingly operate as part of London's cultural economy. Not only does more and more arts related economic activity take place in the quarters, they also present a physical and social milieu to which the particular class fraction described above is attracted to live. Their status as more or less recognised food quarters appears very important to their being chosen as sites for art practice and arts-related economic activity, as food is often a central theme. Moreover, as explained below, the physical design of the food spaces appears to be crucial to their development as cultural quarters. Spatial design is part of their development as a favourable milieu for a distinctive, food-related individual habitus. In turn, in each case study area being such a food space appears to contribute strongly to development as a cultural quarter.

A notable aspect of the food space as cultural quarter is the way that such places are subject to wider strategies linking economic and cultural regeneration, becoming urban spaces that are themselves cultural products. This convergence has been theorised as one of the distinguishing features of contemporary cities (Molotch, 1996) within a distinctively post Fordist cultural economy (Lash and Urry, 1994) although some have stressed cultural quarters such as Hoxton in London as more about industry than consumption (Pratt, 2009). In any case, the increasing spatialisation of cultural production has been cited in London with particular reference to these processes at play around Borough Market (Newman and Smith, 2000).

Art processes were also observed and documented during research visits to Broadway Market, while at Exmouth Market "new industry formations" (Hutton, 2004, p.96) include clusters of art, media and architectural practices. This seems to fit within the literature on clustering; the new economy of the inner city and on "the rise and rise of culture led regeneration" (Miles and Paddison, 2005, p.833) in which culture located within 'new economy quarters' becomes a driver for urban economic growth (Hutton, 2004). This, in turn "has become part of the new orthodoxy by which cities seek to enhance their competitive position" (Miles and Paddison, 2005, p.833). The assumption since the 1980s is that cultural quarters will not only support urban regeneration, but also reinforce civic pride and place identity (Hall and Robertson, 2001). Place marketing, described as "the governance expression of this new orthodoxy" (Miles and Paddison, 2005, p.834), is now ubiquitous but the question arises as to how far the food quarters reflect cultural commodification in the following terms:

> "Integral to this—and given clear expression in the city through the spread of processes of gentrification and the development of cultural forms of urban tourism—is the commodification of culture and the spread of cultural capitalism" (ibid).

Such strategies are intended to give rise to a localised sense of place. At the same time, their spatial expression is often of a fast gentrifying urban core ringed by disadvantaged suburbs, and their role in contributing to that gentrification is possibly underestimated (Wilks-Heeg and North, 2004). In London, case studies of such approaches undertaken by other researchers demonstrate how much of the place marketing effort in relation to the commodification of culture has been directed at incomers rather than those already resident in areas earmarked for regeneration, with deleterious effects on indigenous working class populations (Evans and Cattell, 2000). In the food quarters, some observational work and interviews undertaken during research for this book support this notion. It seemed clear that food played a role in a process by which the

> "aesthetic appropriation of place appeals to other professionals, particularly to those who are also higher in cultural capital than in economic capital, and who share something of the artist's antipathy towards commerce and convention" (Ley, 2003, p.2540).

More broadly, while there was evidence from the studied food quarters that they were developing into cultural quarters, attractive to certain fractions of the middle class, they could not be entirely explained in these terms. Rather, in the next sections, other important framing elements for their development are explored.

Food quarters and food governance

Each of the food quarters appeared to demonstrate an alternative economic path to the commonality of much UK urban regeneration which is top down in nature, and allows limited roles for local players in defining desired outcomes and managing the process (Atkinson, 1999; Foley and Martin, 2000; Smith, 2005). Although increasing attention has been paid at policy level to community involvement (Foley and Martin, 2000; Taylor, 2000; Burton, 2003), the renewal process underway at each food quarter foregrounded a lack of practical governance capacity on the part of the relevant local authority to drive forward food-led regeneration. In each case, there appeared to be the perception of an absence from local government of either sufficient strategic planning attention to underpin food quarter development, or day-to-day management expertise.

Although previous good practice was cited in relation to Exmouth Market (Whitelegg, 2007), in each case local government was reported to have placed barriers in the way of food-centred regeneration efforts made by local stakeholders. Despite this, at least two of the quarters developed sets of workable governance arrangements largely through their own efforts, and a third had gone some way towards doing so. At Borough Market (until more recently when some breakdown has emerged) a highly successful form of governance had been implemented through a long established charitable trust that by the time of the fieldwork employed professional market managers. At Broadway Market, a group of entrepreneurial local residents and traders was at the time responsible for an outstanding regeneration process. At Exmouth Market meanwhile, a more informal coalition of 'gastronomic' stakeholders who were running food businesses in the street and area acted as a kind of leadership group, although with more mixed results as far as the briefly revived food market was concerned, as Chapter 6 demonstrates.

Mainstream regeneration processes are generally expected to be partnership-based (Diamond, 2002; Ball and Maginn, 2005); to involve the community in renewal through consultative processes (McArthur, 1993; Lawless et al, 2010); and to stress local capacity building (Diamond, 2004). However, this kind of public-private-third sector partnership, envisaged in public policy as a model for area-based regeneration, has not occurred in a sustained way at any of the food quarters. It is acknowledged in the literature that regeneration partnerships are often the sites for unresolved conflicts between partners (Diamond, 2004) and asymmetrical power relations (Hastings, McArthur and McGregor, 1996; Hastings, 1999). The food quarters certainly demonstrated areas of conflict between local authorities and other stakeholders, with apparently uneasy relationships between local government and others seen at all three places. Governance partnerships tended to develop from the bottom up, or to one side of formal arrangements perceived to be inadequate for reviving and managing the food spaces. These arrangements generally involved community-based or third sector stakeholders alone or in partnership with private sector entrepreneurs from small and medium sized enterprises rather than bigger businesses. At the same time, local authorities appeared to have moved away slowly from a position of managing decline from outside these informal partnerships and coalitions, towards one of more active engagement.

A strong theme emerging from the food quarters was of the critical role played by community leaders and entrepreneurial figures, comprising both social entrepreneurs (Thompson, 2002) and those from more mainstream businesses. There is some discussion in the literature about the possibilities for the emergence of new community leaders as decision makers, in the context of local governance promoted by existing government structures (Hemphill, McGreal, Berry and Watson, 2006). Local entrepreneurship is also a growing trend within regeneration contexts (Porter, 2000). However, in this research, the emergence of community leaders with a vision about the future of their area as a food space appeared to have resulted from their own leadership qualities. It seemingly had not come from a conscious focus by government on local empowerment, but rather a lack of governmental leadership capacity has left space for leadership to develop from the sidelines or below.

At all three food quarters, local community leaders were at the forefront in pursuing a food strategy, although not in all cases with a stated intention to develop a wider renewal programme or lead to significant regeneration effects. At the same time, their leadership qualities were central to the success of both Borough and Broadway Markets and contributed significantly to the food-led redevelopment of Exmouth. The leadership displayed can be read as an example of the way that informal urban actors have taken over leftover spaces in cities and reanimated them through bottom up action (Groth and Corijn, 2005). Also notable has been the mix of social and business entrepreneurialism. Social entrepreneurs are defined as people who have

> "the qualities and behaviours we associate with the business entrepreneur but who operate in the community and are more concerned with caring and helping than with making money" (Thompson, 2002, p.413).

Leaders at Borough, and Broadway appeared to fall within this category, while at Exmouth there was an intriguing straddling of the social and business entrepreneurial divide. Local players at Exmouth Market, in particular, might be defined as gastronomic entrepreneurs, as they had both business and social interests that coalesced around food, and these intertwined interests were played out through food quarter development.

Food quarters and urban design

One context for the food quarters is the way that food is increasingly a conscious focus for spatial design policy at a national and city-wide level (GLA, 2006; DEFRA, 2010; Sustainable Development Commission, 2011) with nationally funded pilot programmes making explicit links between obesity and spatial planning and design (The Guardian, 2008). In London this has included the development of a London Food Strategy that reflects a holistic view of the food system and an explicit focus on its sustainability (Reynolds, 2010). This suggests an emerging narrative in relation to food and area regeneration, focusing on the problematic qualities of this relationship, that is yet to be fully integrated with food discussion situated within a gastronomic tourism mode (Richards, 2002; Quan and Wang, 2004). In both cases, as discussed earlier, there is growing economic, social and environmental unevenness in food aspects of urban development.

The food quarters were therefore striking in the way and degree to which they returned economic value to their local communities (New Economics Foundation, 2005) whereas most urban food space reinforces economic and other inequalities, as the discussion below explores. Linking back to the research concerns set out in Chapter 1, it is important to ask why and how food-centred spaces might manage to support urban sustainability, against the grain of most post metropolitan development which demonstrates a sharpening polarisation between the well-supported and the poorly-served in food terms. Much of the work done in this area is within a paradigm of healthy, sustainable and vital cities (Hancock, 1995; Barton, Grant and Guise, 2003) that situates "food deserts" as places

> "where local food resources are disappearing. This can leave those without cars difficult access routes and little choice for their food supply. As a result, health is further damaged in those already at risk, and local producers lack small-scale local outlets" (Barton, Grant and Guise, 2002, p.137).

Recent research in the United Kingdom exploring food poverty and the associated emergence of food deserts (Webster, 1998; Watson, 2002) seems to reveal increasing inequality of access to inexpensive, high quality food within expanding, spatially transforming urban spaces (Whelan, Wrigley, Warm and Cannings, 2002). Aspects of these conclusions are contested by some studies where food desert effects have not been found to a significant degree, and it has also been suggested that more fine-grained research is required to further test theoretical assumptions about food deserts in real places (Cummins and Macintyre, 2002; White et al, 2004; Short, Guthman and Raskin, 2007). However, it seems fair, on the balance of the considerable research findings available, to argue that food deserts do exist as places in which a significant proportion of people are effectively disenfranchised by lack of access to affordable, healthy local food services (Barton, Grant and Guise, 2003, p.137).

In terms of their spatiality, food deserts may contain substantial numbers of fast food outlets, service station 'road pantries', and food shopping based on high cost but lower quality convenience stores. If the food desert contains supermarkets, the food on offer may be of poorer quality and higher price than that in supermarkets found in more 'gastronomically' entitled areas and will not be within a walkable radius of 400-500 metres for most. Online shopping opportunities may be restricted or non-existent. Take up of food box schemes will be low. All this reflects the spatiality described in an earlier section on trends in post metropolitan development. Thus, while such deserts may be located within well-established areas, they are more likely to be found where traditional urban design principles have not been followed in creating urban form (Parham, 1992, 1995; Lake and Townshend, 2006, 2008).

An associated concern is the relationship between food desert-producing retailing and consumption patterns and the incidence of obesity. Poor food access is correlated with rising levels of obesity in disadvantaged urban dwellers and the evidence about the relationship of obesity and retailing patterns is relatively clear-cut (Cummins and Macintyre, 2006; White, 2007). Researchers now speak of "obesogenic environments" (Lake and Townshend, 2006, p.262), arguing that the

> "obesogenicity of an environment has been defined as 'the sum of influences that the surroundings, opportunities, or conditions of life have on promoting obesity in individuals or populations" (ibid).

The nature of the built form in which obesegenic environments emerge is understood to be a crucial aspect in their creation, with sprawl urbanism posited as central to their development. Supermarkets have been at the forefront of expanding the urban scale of food consumption; avoiding poorer urban areas, a strategy known as 'redlining', and locating on out-of-town sites (Eisenhauer, 2001). They can therefore be seen as instrumental in producing areas where food access is restricted to fast food and convenience stores, which have in turn shown higher obesity levels (Morland, Diez Roux and Wing, 2006; Morland and Evenson, 2009). The concept of "Walmartisation" has entered the language, reflecting the economic planning strategies employed by supermarket giants to increase the spatial scale of food retailing, and pointing to its sustainability consequences (Gardels, 2004). Car dependence has been built into supermarket retailing strategies as part of their efforts to externalise economic, environmental and social costs on to others (Raven, Lang and Dumonteil, 1995; Lang and Caraher, 1998; Lang and Heasman, 2004). There has been in the UK a recent surge in "fake local" stores owned by major food retailers (New Economics Foundation, 2002, p.2), thought to be driving out individually owned convenience food shops from certain inner areas. At the same time, supermarkets' stores still tend not to be located in poorer neighbourhoods and they are predominantly spaced as a smaller number of large stores that are not within walking distance for many. Protests by local food campaigners have accompanied their proposed arrival in recent notable examples. Moreover, as "ever fewer, larger players such as the big four supermarkets capture more of the market, their power means they are able to squeeze ever-better deals for themselves, at the cost of suppliers, farmers and smaller retailers" (ibid).

Supermarkets' retailing arrangements have been judged to support the creation of food deserts (Food Standards Agency, 2006) and some UK guidance on urban design provides explicit design proposals to counter these ill effects (Llewelyn-Davies, 2000; Barton, Grant and Guise, 2002). These guidance documents tend to follow spatial principles associated with design features found in existing food quarters, although such quarters are not explicitly defined as such. The food quarters' spatial design for instance presents a range of food possibilities, including street-based or covered food markets and small, individually owned food shops, cafes and restaurants, all of which are within a walkable catchment area. Such places may also contain a top of the range supermarket and a high level of uptake and availability of organic food box schemes and online shopping delivery services. While location is not prescribed, the data from this book locate a number of food quarters in established urban areas which have been developed along compact city lines, based on walkable food catchments, rather than in newly developed parts of post-urban conurbations shaped by post-war, modernist planning principles. The next section considers these design issues in detail.

Both the food and urban sides of research into food quarters revolve around issues of urban sustainability and conviviality, in part expressed through urban design. In Chapter 1 it was argued that urban sustainability in relation to food is likely to be undermined by dominant spatial design patterns that adversely affect food production, distribution and consumption processes. Conversely, it was suggested that urban sustainability may be supported by food quarter urban design, although food-related design has yet to be fully explored in relation to urban sustainability processes. It is equally important that urban design is approached reflexively, with an acknowledgement that it does not exist as simply a free-floating public good but often as a practice that is poorly grounded in theory (Sternberg, 2000), often undertaken uncritically (Cuthbert, 2002; Hayward and McGlynn, 2002) and may itself be subject to commodification as a part of giving cities competitive edge (Gospodini, 2002, p.59).

Yet, despite these caveats, urban design, if approached with some critical distance, can provide extremely useful insights into place shaping that resonate with the book's concerns. So far this chapter has briefly explored how cities' spatiality is rapidly transforming, in ways that predominantly tend to negatively reconfigure their food relationships (Bell and Valentine, 1997). Such trends are counterpointed by less conventional food geographies emerging in certain places and these developing spatial alternatives offer different "possibilities to those provided by the 'conventional' industrialised agro-food complex" (Maye, Kneafsey and Holloway, 2007, p.1). Like the studied food quarters, they are characterised by short food supply chains, high quality products, and a reconnected, re-localised relationship with consumers (ibid).

Urban spaces that exhibit food quarter characteristics appear likely to demonstrate design that is based on walkable food catchments, within a physical form founded on traditional urbanism (Carmona et al, 2003; Krier, 2006). Food deserts, meanwhile, are significantly less likely to exhibit these features and more likely to exhibit post-war, zoning-based design characteristics (Wrigley, Warm, Margetts and Whelan, 2002; Short, Guthman, and Raskin, 2007). It will be remembered that a key theme within the book is the notion that social, in this context, primarily food relationships, are highly interconnected with spatial processes focusing on walkable, compact urban quarters. Given that human relationships to food are played out spatially day-to-day, it is argued that the critical dimension of space can be explored without physical determinism by examining everyday socio-spatial practices (Lefebvre, 1991; Soja, 2000).

These socio-spatial practices can be better understood if the physical loci for food relationships are investigated with reference to urban design concepts and methods, because these help in revealing the interplay between physical form and socio-spatial practice. Rather than being applied unreflexively, If these design concepts are properly interrogated, they are useful in studying the complex nature and meaning of food quarters; at once commodified, gentrifying spaces *and* sustainably designed, convivial sites for richly lived experience.

The urban food quarter can be understood as both a unit of social science research (Lofland, 1971) and as a physical and social construct spatially based on the European urban quarter (Moughtin, 1996; Montgomery, 1998; Marshall, 2005). Equally, the design of such neighbourhoods can provide insights into the nature of the urban food quarter with relevance to the book topic. This neighbourhood scale of design is a recurring theme in urban design; and is tied to a persistent "search for community" against "threats of ecological degradation, social fragmentation and spatial segregation" (Madanipour, 2003, p.140). Neighbourhood scale design has begun to be explicitly linked to avoiding obesity and promoting health (Parham, 1993, 1992; Jackson, 2003; Sui, 2003; Cummins and McIntyre, 2006).

Therefore, one starting place for exploring food quarters as physical loci for the food system is to consider their scale and the configuration of design elements they display within that scale. Some urban designers have focused specifically on design prescriptions for urban quarters (Gosling and Maitland, 1984; Kostof, 1991, 1992; Moughtin, 1996) and such principles of place making provide a ready basis for exploring the design of urban *food* quarters that are roughly similar both in size and in a range of other more subtle design respects. It is, therefore, worth looking at the sets of design qualities or elements thought necessary to build into urban space to achieve sustainability outcomes at urban quarter scale (as for example, Lynch, 1961, 1985; Alexander, 1977; Bacon, 1982; Bentley et al., 1985; Broadbent, 1990; Jacobs, 1993; Moughtin, 2003; Carmona, 2003; Marshall, 2005; Lessard and Ávila, 2005) given these food-related design implications.

These design elements include experiential qualities of variety, accessibility, vitality, legibility, robustness, identity, cleanliness, biotic support and richness (Bentley, 1990), with vitality judged by Hayward and McGlynn (2002, p.127) as probably "the single most sought after characteristic of good urbanism". Hayward and McGlynn link vitality and civility, in ways that echo the earlier discussion of conviviality in Chapter 1, arguing, "the notion of civility is one of the oldest and most successful in the history of society and urbanism" (ibid, p.127). Quarters require human scale, pedestrian freedom, lasting environments, and the importance of place is stressed (Tibbalds, 1992). Mixed land use and activities are also a preoccupation (Tibbalds, 1992; Roberts and Lloyd-Jones, 1997) as is connectivity for "joined up urbanism" (Marshall, 2005, p.367). Certain designers bring food overtly into the picture, defining design for places that are in Mouzon's (2008) terms, feedable, serviceable, accessible, and frugal, or designed by way of various gastronomic strategies for convivial cities (Parham, 1992, 1993a, 1993b, 1995, 1996). Design codes are posited as a tool to help translate these qualities from theory to design practice (Murrain, 2002; Carmona, 2006).

All these perspectives demonstrate an understanding that public space has primacy over the private domain, and urban design clearly subordinates individual buildings to a collective realm more powerful than them. This in turn relies on "an implicit vocabulary of design and a deference to the larger order of things" (Trancik, 1986, p.11) that until the 20th century was central to town making (Kostof, 1991, 1992; Morris, 1994). Western European cities followed a long-term tradition of an unbuilt space-built space duality in which the built form enclosed urban spaces (Lozano, 1996, p.40), providing a positive context for playing out life in the public realm. A more recent failure to recognise the dialogue between un-built space and built form, treating built form as an independent element in a non-spatial vacuum (ibid), has meant that this collective sense of meaning has been lost, and so too has the understanding that "there are rules for connecting parts through the design of outdoor space (Trancik, 1986, p.11). At the neighbourhood design scale, a number of physical design solutions, largely deriving from traditional design approaches, have been proposed by urban designers to overcome the loss of coherent relationship between built private space and un-built public space. For example, various solid-to-void typologies can recreate conditions where "lost space" (ibid) or cracks in the city fabric (Loukaitou-Sideris, 1996) may be repaired, and outdoor rooms created (Alexander et al, 1977).

It is possible to contrast the neighbourhood form of traditional cities, in which urban spaces demonstrate a strong solid-to-void ratio, with the weak solid-to-void arrangements of modern neighbourhoods. Traditionally shaped neighbourhoods combine formal design strength with well-developed linkages and thus help create a strong "sense of place" (Krier, 1979; Hillier and Hanson, 1984; Trancik, 1986). Such space-shaping principles allow the development of outdoor rooms, displaying an appropriate solid-to-void relationship, and based on a careful interplay between positive and negative space (Sitte, in Stewart, 1965, 1945; Bacon, 1982; Trancik, 1986; Broadbent, 1990; Lozano, 1996; Madanipour, 1996, 2003). These design arrangements are in turn central to food quarter design, in which linked, enclosed outdoor rooms contribute to making a coherent urban fabric focused on food.

Moreover, a sufficient degree of enclosure of space not only makes available outdoor rooms, perceived as physically pleasant to be in, but provides excellent opportunities for serial vision (Cullen, 1994) in which those walking through linked urban spaces have the chance to enjoy a series of impressions, including glimpses of larger spaces beyond. In traditional neighbourhoods, such as those in which the three food quarters are located, achieving acceptable design character is also about designing in, or protecting existing, highly mixed, complex and fine-grained land uses. Again this is inherent to traditional city design, but is counterpointed by functionalist approaches in the latter part of the 20th century city. These created neighbourhoods where the segregation of land uses and the privatisation of public space drained activity and vitality from the public realm.

A number of urban design principles, qualities and elements thus need to be present if urban design is to support food-centred space. The quarter should be centred on exterior street spaces, based on a traditionally balanced mixture of positive and negative space. The heart of each quarter should provide a high degree of enclosure leading to construction of one or more outdoor rooms, while any fragmentation and disruption of this coherent structure needs to be of manageable proportions. The food quarter requires an appropriate physical scale and a fine grain, contributing to an attractive townscape (Cullen, 1971; Ashihara, 1983) marked by qualities of enclosure, permeability, legibility, variety, vitality, and richness (Lynch, 1981; Bentley et al, 1985). It should display a series of positive urban design patterns (Alexander et al, 1977); focus strongly on a convivial public realm; and be based on traditional streets and squares (Zucker, 1959; Barnett, 1982; Bacon, 1982; Greenbie, 1984; Gosling, 1984; Moughtin, 1992; Bentley, 1999; Madanipour, 1996, 2003). The food quarter should demonstrate a subtle handling of space at the small scale, where the possibilities for visual richness, variety and personalisation of space all play a part (Llewelyn-Davies, 2000). The food quarter's capacity to provide positive outdoor space requires perimeter blocks with buildings that edge (or come close to) the street and thus give definition to the shape and function of outdoor space, "to encourage a range of activities to take place...encouraging people to meet, talk and linger" (op cit, p.86).

Moreover, each quarter should exhibit a complex but compatible land use mix within a gradient building up to a node of intensification of activity, to achieve a compact, walkable neighbourhood (Gehl, 1987, 1996; Calthorpe, 1993; Roberts and Lloyd-Jones, 1996; Jenks, Burton and Williams, 1996). The neighbourhood unit of each food quarter should be public transport oriented (Calthorpe, 1993, Llewelyn-Davies, 2000) and form a walkable food catchment radius of 400-500 metres, implying a size overall of approximately 50 hectares (Urban Taskforce, 1999; Llewelyn-Davies, 2007). Crucially, there should be a comfortable walking distance from its central food market space to its periphery (Moughtin, 1996). Leon Krier (in Moughtin, 1996, p.132) suggests an urban quarter configuration housing around 12,000 people at moderate to high densities within urban blocks of four to five stories, where a walk to the market at the centre of the quarter could be accomplished within ten to fifteen minutes. Despite some variation on the question of quarter size and density, the interplay of all these elements and qualities contributes strongly to the urban food quarter achieving a strong sense of place.

A question has been raised as to the applicability of 'European' design ideas in the arguably different urban circumstances of the UK (Nathan and Marshall, 2006, p.1). However, a focus on differences between British and European cities and towns underemphasizes the degree to which European city shaping ideas have influenced city building in the UK over the long term (Girouard, 1985; Kostof, 1991, 1992; Morris, 1994). Moreover, urban design approaches based on traditional European urbanism are now being re-imported from the United States and mainland Europe into the United Kingdom through New Urbanist and European urbanist arguments and projects which are informing influential UK urban design policy and practice (Calthorpe, 1993, 2001; Duany, Plater-Zyberk, and Speck, 2000; Hebbert, 2003; Prince's Foundation, 2007; C.E.U., 2004, 2005, 2006, 2007; among others). Such thinking is also embedded in national and local design guidance currently available in the United Kingdom (Commission for Architecture and the Built Environment, 2000; Department for Environment, Transport and the Regions, 2001; Department for Communities and Local Government, 2007), and is making increasingly specific links between spatial design and avoiding obesegenic environments (The Guardian, November 7, 2007).

Any analysis of the core principles on which such developments are based in the UK, therefore leads directly back to European design perspectives. These in turn appear closely modelled on the European City Model (ECM) defined by Clos (2005) which can be summarized as compact, dense, favouring mobility on foot or by public transport, bringing services closer, used for many purposes in the same area, home to people from diverse backgrounds, and based on public spaces where public transport dominates and the pressure of private cars is limited (Clos, 2005; n.p.r.). Both European traditions, as exemplified by Clos, above, and British traditions in place making, have informed the spatiality of British cities including London (Howard, 1974; Hall, 1988).

As this book focuses on London sites, it is worth noting that the broad expanse of London's metroland (Barnes, 1992; Haywood, 2009) and the villages and towns that have been swallowed up by Greater London, reflect a diversity of design influences over the long term, in complex interplay with landscape and morphological elements. The food quarters themselves thus reflect the principles of the European City Model in their physical shaping, as well as a degree of overlay of other spatial patterns including the imposition of much coarser grained post war zoning regimes. The book research suggests the urban design picture observed at the food quarters was both more similar and more complicated than a simplistic contrasting of British and mainland European urban forms, attitudes, and design practices would allow.

Drawing together the food themes

Chapter 2 has surveyed theoretical areas that frame the research into designing for food, from both sociological and design disciplines, concluding that each has provided important insights into relevant socio-spatial processes. Urban design contributes a useful theoretical backdrop to inform the work, despite its predominantly practice based character. From food sociology, production, distribution and consumption issues, changing food practices and the notion of urban conviviality and civilising appetites are all framing devices. From urban sociological theory the context includes the rise of post metropolitan urban development, the increasing problems of urban sustainability and the decline of the public realm, while the individual habitus and its links to gentrifying space provide valuable insights. The food-related effects of transformations in urban space provided the research context for exploration of particular places that appear to have gone against dominant urban development modes.

Privileging of the spatial has been a way into understanding more about the socio-spatial practices of the food quarters. Three sites on their way to being fully realised food quarters have offered designed settings for exploring relationships between city form and socio-spatial practices, specific to London but with potentially wider food and urban design implications. It has been argued that a number of urban design principles, qualities and elements need to be present if urban design is to support food-centred space. In the next chapter, the focus is on exploring the morphological and urban design aspects of the food quarters using methods described in Chapter 1. This in turn provides a frame for the more sociologically based investigations of Chapters 4 to 6 and the overall analysis and conclusions drawn about food-led renewal in London in Chapters 7 and 8.

PART 2:
EXPLORING THE FOOD QUARTERS

Chapter Three

Food-Centred Space

Why spatiality matters

This chapter looks at the spatiality of the three food quarters; considering the Borough, Broadway and Exmouth Market areas from a design perspective and outlining the results of work informed by morphological and master planning methods. The chapter also acts as a foundation for analysing the relationship between physical design and socio-spatial practices explored in later chapters. There are a number of sources for Chapter 3. Archival material, including maps and historical records, has helped establish how the three studied areas developed as food spaces, and acts as a basis for considering some of the implications of changes in food terms. Site observations, mapping, interviews, and web-based material have provided further data sources that support this morphological research. Urban design analysis in each, meanwhile, has followed some of the conventions of a master planning exercise, beginning with an appreciation of the context, moving on to consideration of urban structure, exploring site connectivity, and finally considering details of the place (Urban Design Compendium, 2000). Again, the focus has been on describing and analysing each quarter to illuminate aspects of the relationship between the areas' design qualities and their roles as food spaces.

This chapter draws on both text and visual methods for the description and analysis of each food quarter, including maps, diagrams, plans, drawings and photographs. The context analysis included preparation of site maps that demarcated the fuzzy-edged extent of each of the case study areas while morphological material was used to trace the physical evolution of food-related land uses, and the mix with other land uses over time. For understanding urban structure, figure-ground analysis provided information about the way the physical fabric has been shaped, helping delineate the interplay between positive and negative space, and thus the degree of enclosure within the street and urban block structure. Urban structure material was also used to reveal key compositional aspects of the urban framework, including landmarks, vistas and focal points; and to give an indication of urban structure in relation to building size, scale, density and active edges.

The connectivity analysis meanwhile included a movement assessment, which demonstrated the level of permeability, legibility and walkability of each case study area. Similarly, the catchment analysis maps made clear the "ped-shed" (Newman and Kenworthy, 2006, p.43) or walkability radius at each quarter, and in this way helped define the spatial range from which visitors would usually be prepared to walk to the market at each quarter's heart. Finally, to establish the details of the place, there was an assessment using text and photographs of the physical qualities that contributed to making the streets and other spaces under consideration into social places within the public realm. The chapter closes with a comparative analysis of the case study areas in morphological and design terms.

Morphology and urban design at Borough Market

Morphological and design research situated Borough Market and its environs as the most mature of the three case study areas in urban settlement terms. Borough was found to be a place that functioned as a food-centred quarter over the very long term, through a complex set of interior, exterior and transitional spaces. In this sense the study area differed from the simpler form of the traditional market street, which typified the core of each of the other two quarters. The map for Borough Market and surroundings (Figure 3.1) identified a complex case study area lying in inner London, just to the south of the Thames and close to London Bridge. In principle, the area could be understood as congruent with the spatiality of an urban quarter, as defined in Chapter 2.

A question arose though as to how far physical case study area boundaries at Borough and the other study areas could be sharply defined. In each case, the areas demonstrated somewhat imprecise edges in spatial and other terms because their food market-related land uses, economic effects, and social and environmental impacts extended outwards in uneven ways and to varying extents. However, there were fairly clear boundaries to how far visitors would walk locally to go to each market (although in each case there were wider catchments using other travel modes discussed below). The ped-shed or walkability area for Borough (shown in Figure 3.1. below) informally defined a certain kind of edge to the urban quarter at a five hundred metre radius. Overall, however, it was not possible to draw a definitive spatial line around each study area and the ped-shed circle in each case should not be read as a definitive limit to the quarter.

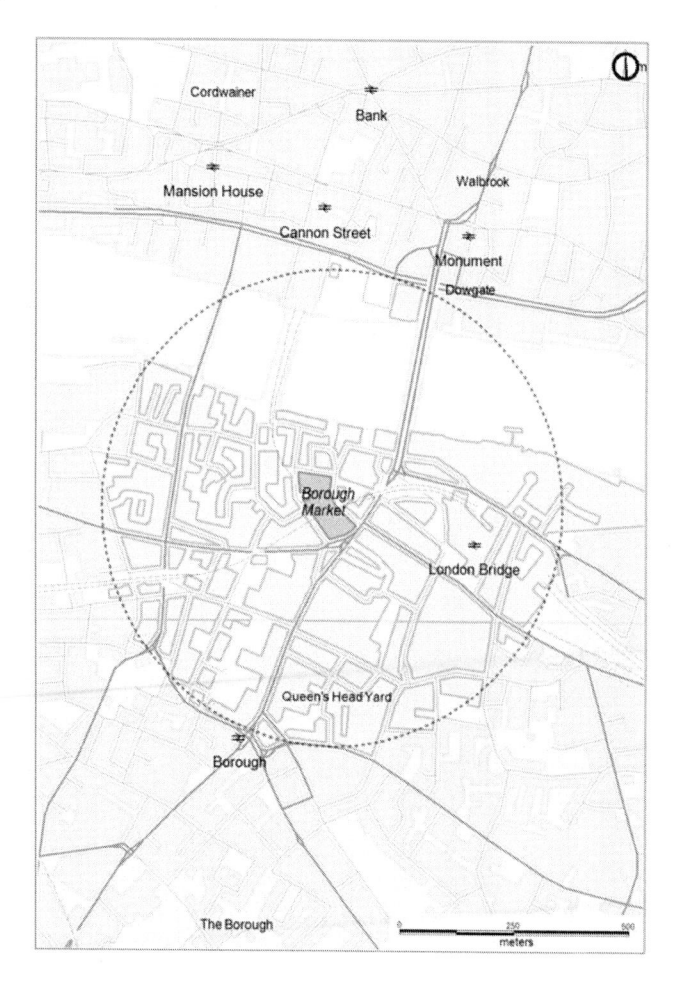

Figure 3.1: *Borough study area walkability radius* Source: Prepared from open source map base by Dominic Honeysett

The urban morphological record showed that food-related land uses have been located in the area of Borough Market's current site over the very long term. The food market was reputed to have pre-Roman antecedents (Passingham, 1935; Forshaw and Bergstrom, 1983) and was at various times positioned on bridges over the Thames and to the south of the river (Inwood, 1998). From the 10th to 18th centuries a series of Royal Charters were granted to Borough Market, and for part of this period it was under the control of the City of London (Forshaw and Bergstrom, 1983; Inwood, 1998). Situated at the meeting point for roads from the south and from the City, the market remained an obvious physical location for trading produce, although its exact site shifted within the Southwark area (Dean, 2005, p.19). Borough Market also acted as a nodal point for the development of new settlement, and by 1600, suburbs were developing around the market in an area which had traditionally mixed rural and urban pursuits, the latter including those less welcome in the City proper: theatres, bear baiting, cock fights and brothels (Forshaw and Bergstrom, 1983, p.16).

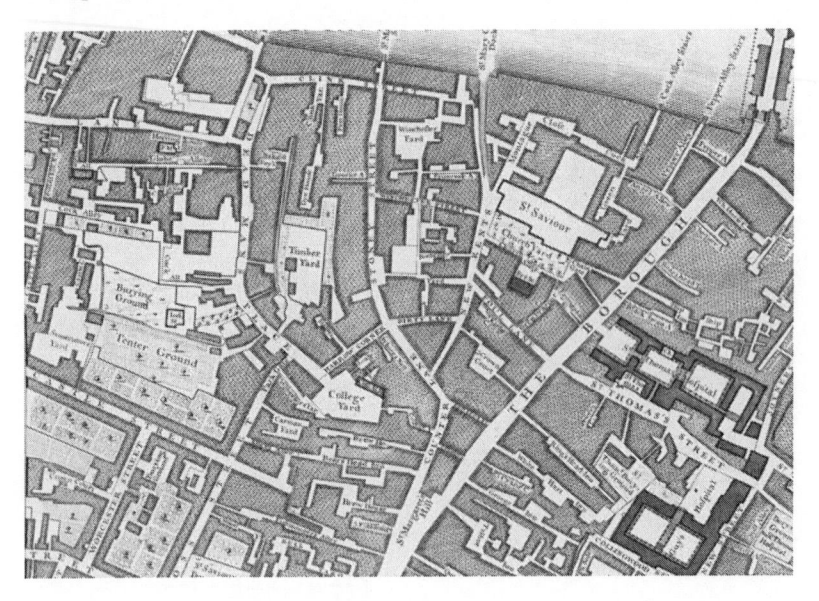

Figure 3.2: *Rocque's map of 1746, detail* Source: City of London, London Metropolitan Archives

John Rocque's beautiful map of 1746 (Figure 3.2) showed a fine-grained urban quarter in the area of Borough High Street, which was then called "The Borough". St. Thomas' and Guy's Hospitals were already in evidence and there was a series of coaching inns and their yards down both the left and right hand sides of the street. On the right, a dense urban fabric was found around St Saviour's Church. This area included brewers, a

"Whore's Nest" (the "stews" of Southwark were famous) and stables, with "Dirty Lane" and "Foul Lane" off Stoney Street suggesting unsavoury activities.

Accounts vary but it appears that by 1754 or 1755, the City of London had tired of running the market with its attendant problems, and control was passed to the churchwardens and parishioners of St Saviour's, Southwark (Borough Market Co, n.d.). A replacement market was created in an area of Southwark known as 'the triangle', "which was far enough away from the main road to avoid congestion" (Dean, 2005, p.19). The maps record supported Dean's contention that the market moved to its current 'triangle' site at around this time.

Horwood's map of 1792-1799 (Figure 3.3) demonstrated that part of Stoney Street was by 1799 called Borough Market, signifying that the market was centred here by that time, away from the main road of The Borough. The loosely triangular shape of the urban blocks in the immediate area offered further support for this view. It was also at this stage that the aims of the market were instituted: "to hold a market, and to contribute profit from the market to the relief of the poor" (ibid). The "trustee option" was introduced in 1756 as a successful form of market management (Smith, 2007, p.40) that remained in force at the time of the fieldwork process.

By 1862, Stanford's map of London and its Suburbs (Figure 3.4) showed that Borough Market still fronted on to Stoney Street, much as in its 1792-99 position. However, Foul Lane and Dirty Lane had disappeared and The Borough had been renamed Wellington Street, no doubt as a result of the Duke's triumphs in the Napoleonic Wars. Many of the inns and taverns also remained along the high street while St Thomas' and Guy's hospitals had taken over more space to the east of the high street, but still contributed strongly defined urban blocks within an enclosed urban structure. Stanford's map illustrated a number of dramatic transport related changes in the morphology of the Borough area since Horwood's map of 1792-99, caused "by a revolution in transportation and movement within the city" (Dean, 2005, p.20). London Bridge had been moved west by some 180 feet, and substantial railway infrastructure developed south of the Bridge. By 1843, railway lines were arriving from both southwest and southeast. The latter required large viaducts to be pushed through the immediate Borough Market and high street area. A further evident transport related change in the 1860s was the clearance of buildings in a sweeping line from the top of Borough High Street round to the west. This was to make way for what was to become Southwark Street, just to the south of the market.

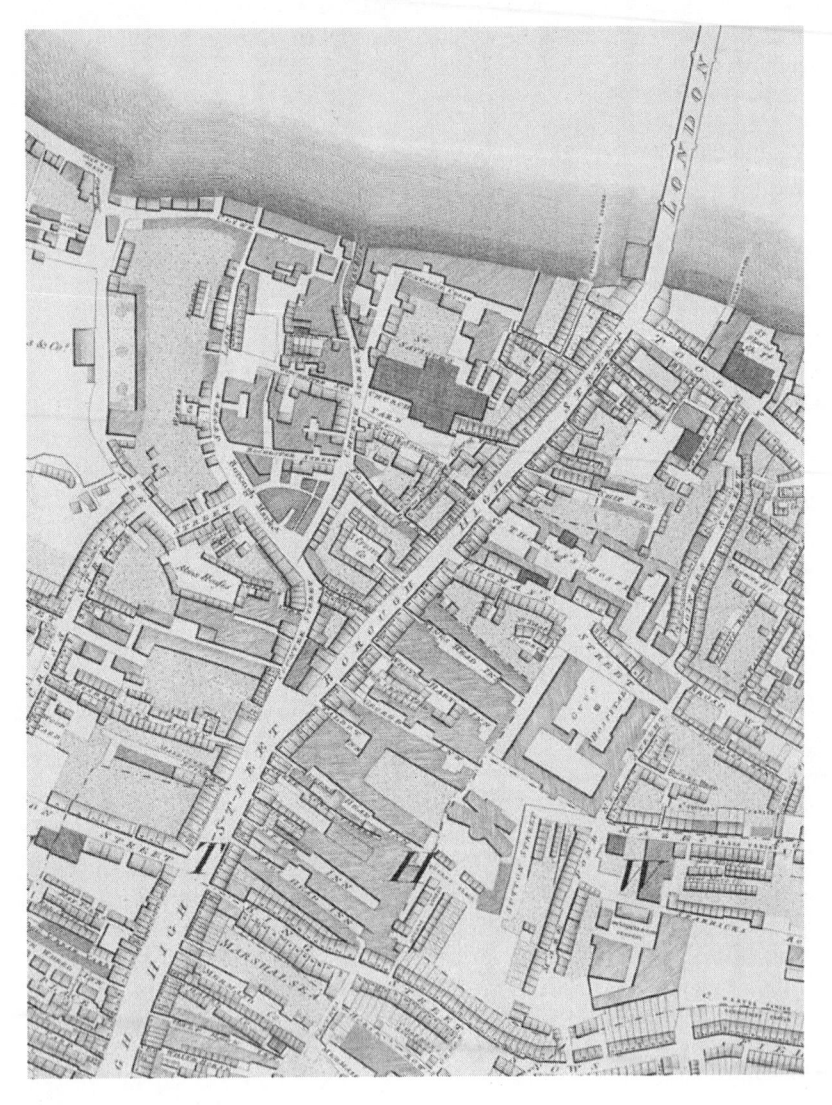

Figure 3.3: *Horwood's map of 1792-1799, detail* Source: City of London, London Metropolitan Archives

Food-Centred Space 81

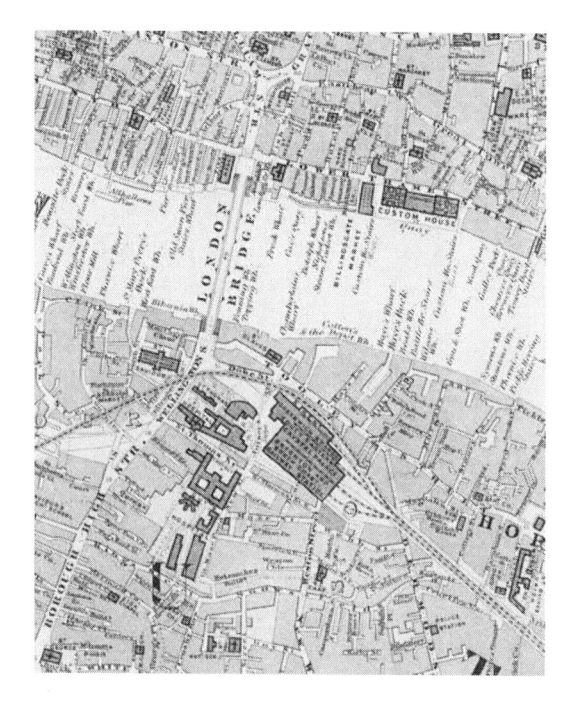

Figure 3.4: *Stanford's map of London and its suburbs, 1862 (detail)* Source: City of London, London Metropolitan Archives

The new railway viaducts "narrowly missed a substantial 88 foot cast iron dome which had been erected over 'the triangle' in 1859 by Edward Habershon" (ibid). In 1880 Henry Jarvis developed ambitious reconstruction plans for the market, but a simpler barrel-vaulted replacement structure was built instead (Dean, 2005, p.22) and a second scheme of barrel vaults by Kinniple and Jaffrey in 1894 did not proceed (French, 2005). Borough Market was designated as a space just to the north of the South Eastern Railway viaduct that looped across it. This space was east of Church Street and north of Bedale Street, rather than the more traditional 'triangle', although the covered halls were still apparent on the map at this location (Figure 3.5).

Figure 3.5: *Ordnance Survey map of Bermondsey and Wapping of 1894 (London Sheet 77)* Source: City of London, London Metropolitan Archives

By the late 19th century Borough Market was one of London's principal fruit and vegetable markets (Porter, 1994) and it continued to flourish as a wholesale market up until the first half of the 20th century. In 1906 new regulations had been brought in for the control of the market, after a series of physical expansions in the late 19th century and by 1914 there had been some further changes to the late 19th century interplay of market and surrounding space. The market was still shown as in the 1894 map, but now the covered structures (market halls) were in a slightly different configuration. A "Borough Market Junction" was shown, where a small entrance to the market met Borough High Street. Just to the south of the railway viaducts was a new space enclosed by built fabric abutting the market halls, now called "Three Crowns Square" (in a position that was to become the 1930s market entrance) and by 1927 the market covered an area of around three acres. Further alterations and additions were made in 1931 "which included the demolition of old Three Crown Square and the building of a new road through the market" (Passingham, 1935, p.110).

The next notable addition was a building comprising an entrance and accommodation for market trustees, designed by Arthur W Cooksey and Partners, in a mix of Art Deco and Neo-Georgian style, which was added on the Borough High Street frontage in 1932. The new entrance was needed to relieve congestion within the market (Maughan, 1931, p.168), which suffered from lack of space and poor road approaches, while "the accommodation there is of a miscellaneous character, and still hopelessly mixed up with other buildings in the vicinity" (Passingham, 1935, p.110). A description of the market's internal arrangement in the early 1930s emphasised its crowded character and gave some insight into the way that wholesale trading was organised in terms of physical form:

> "The market is irregular in shape, hemmed in on all sides as at Leadenhall, and covered by a glazed roof which allows insufficient light to filter through it for the business below. This is in part caused by the two bridges over which the Southern Railway actually crosses the market. ...There are 188 pitching stands let to 81 tenants in the covered portion of the market, while the uncovered part is divided into 203 wagon and pitching stands occupied by growers who bring their produce from the Home Counties south of the Thames. Rents for the outside stands are nominal charges of twenty-one shillings per stand per annum" (ibid).

In the 1930s vegetables and fruit formed "the basis of the business of Borough Market" (Maughan, 1931, p.168). In the (covered) green market, wagons were not unloaded, but fruit and vegetable samples were displayed outside the vans of potential buyers and then packed up by them for distribution onwards (ibid). Produce had to be transferred by hand from street to stalls because of space restrictions so all unloading was done by porters (Passingham, 1935). At that stage the market still largely served south London and the southeastern counties as a wholesale market, as it had done from medieval times (op cit). The market thus retained its nexus position as a physical food trading space at a critical location.

Like much of Borough High Street, Borough Market suffered damage from World War II bombing which destroyed parts of the covered structure on Park Street. Post war the Borough area and the market went into decline, with empty warehouses to the north in the area abutting the Thames, and the market itself, in an increasing state of disrepair:

> "Years of decline in the wholesale trade - a product of changing consumer shopping patterns - had meant that, not only was there a lot of vacant space in the market, but insufficient funds were available to maintain its increasingly decrepit structures and services" (Nicholson, 2005, p.11).

Despite the barriers to the market's continued functioning, from the early 1990s the Market's Trustees launched and managed an ambitious restoration and new development programme for the market and adjoining spaces.

Over the late 1990s and early 2000s, each area of the market was rebuilt, and work to regenerate and improve its physical structures included the re-erection of the south portico of the Floral Hall from Covent Garden. New stall areas were created, with some, but not all, based on the existing pattern of trading 'out' from a space rather from freestanding stalls, while new roofing, walls and flooring were inserted as necessary.

By 2008 plans were afoot for the commercial redevelopment of the area to the northeast of the market, where a new building described as the 'London Bridge Quarter' was proposed to be built next to London Bridge Station. Physical work was underway on this development; by 2010, promoted by its developers as "the capital's most exciting and ambitious new development"…"A truly mixed use vertical city in one building" (The ShardLondonBridge.com, n.d.). Designed by Renzo Piano, the 72 level, three hundred and ten metre tall 'Shard of Glass' was marketed as highly desirable residential, office and hotel accommodation, with linkages to 'attractions' like Borough Market being explicitly made.

Considered in figure-ground terms, the Borough Market area demonstrated a fine-grained urban fabric pattern in keeping with its location near the centre of what the morphological records demonstrated was a very long developed, traditional city quarter. The area exhibited a strong solid-to-void relationship between the built fabric and open space around the market, along the minor Stoney and Park Streets, and a degree of enclosure was also apparent on the more major Borough High Street and Southwark Streets, in which urban blocks were generally built up to street alignments. Within this townscape the railway infrastructure acted as a substantial intrusion, crossing the quarter in a Y shaped form over the market space. The figure-ground analysis also conveyed that the market was predominantly arranged as a set of covered structures tucked under and wrapped around the rail viaducts, within the area bounded by Stoney Street, Winchester Walk, Bedale Street and Borough High Street.

The street and building pattern revealed the imprint of successive layers of settlement from medieval and into early modern times. The elevations from Borough High Street, from Tallis's fascinating 1840 visual survey indicated how coherent this pattern was in the mid 19th century. Tallis's work showed a consistent frontage on both sides of the street, of narrow terraced buildings housing individual shops, surmounted by two to four stories of business and residential accommodation. Gaps in building façades (leading to inns, taverns and their yards) were also narrow and small scale, so that the overall coherence of the façades was not disrupted. Some breakdown of the urban fabric pattern was evident in development dating from this time, due in part to railway line and terminus building described earlier. The impact of this series of transport infrastructures started from this time to contribute to areas of lost space (Trancik, 1996).

Studied together, these visual representations signalled that the area's structure had broken down more seriously by the latter half of the 20th century, when a series of rips and tears disrupted the urban fabric near the food market. These included the development of a number of large-scale buildings comprising housing blocks, hospital-related buildings, and medium and high-rise office blocks, sometimes set back from street frontages. Another evident influence was the relationship to the river to the north. Here lay remnant dock spaces that reflected the area's historically important, but by then superseded, designation as London's larder.

By 1948, as shown in a London County Council visual survey of the time, the building elevation pattern largely remained intact along Borough High Street, although there had clearly been some infill in early modernist architectural style. Some interruption to the fabric could also be seen close to St Thomas' Street, as well as gaps where individual terrace buildings once stood. Somewhat ironically, due to the food market's decline and the lack of redevelopment, by the post war period the area around the market was one of the remnant pockets of fine-grained buildings in the northern part of Southwark, which addressed street frontages in a largely unbroken way.

This morphological view of the Borough case study area provided the groundwork for an urban design analysis to consider how the Borough Market area functioned at the time of the fieldwork process. One obvious conclusion was that the urban blight the morphology revealed had a paradoxical effect on the urban structure at Borough. Many of the market buildings, and buildings surrounding it, were left to fall down rather than being demolished in the 'tabula rasa' fervour that infected nearby boroughs. This meant that when regeneration started in the 1990s it was able to build on a rich stock of local market-related building fabric. The area already had a strong sense of place and environmental harmony even though its commercial viability was deeply compromised and it was extremely physically dilapidated. In the 1990s and early 2000s this intricate building fabric formed the basis for Borough's concentration into an intense activity node, surrounded by a fine-grained mix of land uses including housing, shops, offices, workshops, and studios. In the immediate area of the market an equally rich land use mix could be found, largely focused on food, including food wholesaling premises, stalls, shops, pubs, bars, cafes, and restaurants.

The urban structure analysis identified a range of focal points in the area including the Thames to the north, London Bridge Station to the east

(London's oldest railway station, opened in 1846) and the Underground station entrances on Borough High Street. Within the market, the Floral Hall façade, which was re-erected from Covent Garden, acted as one of the market's focal points, as did the 1930s façade to Borough High Street. Other new focal points included the Monmouth Coffee Store and café on the corner of Stoney and Park Streets, Brindisa's restaurant on the corner of Borough High Street and Stoney Street, and the Neal's Yard Dairy shop and storage premises in Park Street. Meanwhile, landmarks identified in the area included the spire of Southwark Cathedral just to the north of the market, and the George Inn on Borough High Street, which contained parts of London's only surviving galleried coaching inn. The regenerated and newly built market halls, including those at the green market, in the area bounded by Stoney Street, Bedale Street, Rochester Walk, Winchester Walk and Cathedral Street, had themselves become landmarks.

By the time fieldwork was completed the frontage of the Floral Hall on Stoney Street was often being used as a signifier of the market as an iconic space in visual representations of London, in the same way as 'The Gherkin' and more latterly 'The Shard' joined other buildings deployed in images of London's skyline. In a local example of this signification, Neal's Yard Dairy's location map for its shop pointed to some of these landmarks and focal points to help visitors find their way. It also identified other places that might be considered food and drink landmarks at Borough, including Monmouth Coffee Store and three local public houses: the Globe, the Wheatsheaf and the Market Trader. The complex railway infrastructure above the market spaces could be considered another kind of landmark, albeit a less admired one.

The design analysis identified few obvious vistas at Borough, although looking north from Borough High Street; the Borough Market corner above Brindisa's restaurant was one. There were some views in evidence, including west to the entrance to the market from Borough High Street under the railway viaduct. Looking back towards the food market to the south from this position, meanwhile, allowed a rather Gordon Cullen (1971) inspired serial vision view into the market space itself. Another intimate scale view was found by looking north from Park Street back towards the market halls on Stoney Street, while a further view was to be had from the approach from London Bridge Station, looking southwest over the market spaces. The quality many of these views shared was that they allowed glimpses of small parts of a mysterious whole and this added to the case study area's design charm.

The figure-ground findings, historic elevation drawings and photographic record together demonstrated the predominantly fine grain of the urban structure in the immediate area of the food market which by the early 2000s operated as both a wholesale and retail space. The analysis concluded that there was a reasonable degree of coherence in the built fabric in relation to building size, scale, density and active edges in the vicinity of the market. The streetscape analysis showed that the edge of the space, where the pavement met building frontages, was generally active and intricate, supporting vibrant street life, especially, but not only, on market days. Land uses appeared to be compatible, with market-related uses including stalls, food shops, cafes, bars, pubs and restaurants which were developed at a fine grain along each of the streets surrounding the market. Building typologies seemed robust, demonstrating a long life and loose fit quality (Brand, 1994) that contributed to their sustainability. Some buildings could be seen to be undergoing renovation to extend their useful life. The microclimates created by the interplay of buildings and spaces were pleasant, with none of the wind tunnel or sharp updraft effects associated with spaces outside high-rise buildings or in areas that lack enclosure. Taken together, these qualities meant that the area demonstrated a strong visual identity and sense of place based on a complex yet coherent character.

Analysis of the area's design qualities demonstrated that moving further away from the market spaces to the east and northeast in particular (towards the London Bridge transport interchange) there was a sharp deterioration in the quality of the urban fabric. A loss of human scale and active edges was apparent in the net of station approach roads, and exacerbated by the jumble of buildings and spaces of St Thomas' and Guy's Hospitals to the east. Here the coarse grain of high-rise office buildings just to the north and south of London Bridge Station undercut many of the qualities that gave the Borough Market's immediate area such a strong image, sense of place and pleasant microclimate. This wider area was characterised by jarring built form discontinuities and expanses of lost space.

The connectivity assessment built on the analysis of the urban structure and demonstrated that the immediate case study area had a high level of permeability, legibility and walkability. Substantial permeability was demonstrated in a number of ways. First there was the presence of small urban blocks that gave visual cues that help the walker understand how to get from one place to another. There was an avoidance (by and large) of segregation of walking paths from those for vehicles, or the separation of land uses, as is habitual in exclusionary zoning where different land uses are isolated from each other into largely homogeneous districts. There was clearly a road hierarchy in evidence, with Stoney Street, Park Street,

Bedale Street and Winchester Walk the minor roads, and Southwark and Borough High Streets the more major roads, which acted as traffic arteries, but all these roads were also very walkable. The immediate area of the market could also be considered highly permeable because it allowed a considerable number of routes through, avoided confusion about which frontages were the 'public' fronts and which the 'private' backs of buildings, and ensured almost contiguous perimeter block development.

As explained in Chapter 2, legibility is about being able to grasp what is going on in a spatial sense. The design analysis showed that the immediate area of the market allowed a reasonable level of legibility, despite spatial complexities including the overlay of railway infrastructure viaducts (see Figure 3.6) and the substantial level changes to roads as they neared London Bridge. Although configured as a series of complicated spaces, the market area also contributed to legibility by way of its small block structure, strongly thematic quality, high level of path enclosure, nodal nature and the intriguing path sequences it allowed the walker. A little further from the centre of the quarter, legibility declined due to the widely separated land uses of London Bridge Station and the office developments to the north side, with their set back, bland building typologies and overlarge urban blocks.

The catchment analysis suggested that in the period to 2008 Borough Market was highly accessible to a local pedestrian catchment; with the walkability radius encompassing the key transport interchange of London Bridge Station, other public transport nodes such as London Bridge Underground Station, and extending nearly as far as Borough Underground Station to the south. Buss accessibility was also good, covering various bus stops close by the market on Borough High Street, on the southern approach to London Bridge and the bus station adjoining London Bridge railway station. These bus stops served routes from across London as well as the city loop bus route that traversed various transport interchanges and cultural sites on the north and south banks of the Thames.

The public transport accessibility map of Southwark also contributed to the catchment analysis by demonstrating that Borough Market was in the most highly accessible category in the borough (LB Southwark, 2005). The area around the food market was also in this highest accessibility category or one below, which still indicated a very high level of accessibility to public transport, and the likelihood that it would be very accessible on foot. This was not surprising given the area's traditional spatiality, and its proximity to a number and range of transport modes. It reflected that Borough Market had the infrastructural capacity to attract a significantly larger catchment of visitors than those who came from within five hundred metres. The observational findings about Borough presented in Chapter 4 reinforced this 'extended catchment capacity' conclusion.

Figure 3.6: *Market stalls under the railway viaducts across Bedale Street* Source: Photograph by author

Part of the connectivity analysis concerned whether and how street space was shared between different travel and access modes, and the area assessment demonstrated that junctions in the minor streets around Borough Market worked as places, rather than simply as movement corridors for cars and trucks. The narrow streets, and the wealth of activity on streets and street edges, forced drivers to slow down and negotiate their way through. While street space was used by a number of travel modes, car dominance was avoided around the immediate market area, although not on Borough High Street itself. Car parking opportunities were available but very limited. A corner like that of Stoney and Park Streets was a focal point for pedestrian and street activity. These physically tight urban conditions meant that servicing of the food market and attendant shops always had to occur at a reasonably small scale at Borough Market and this remained true during the assessment period. Case study area observations suggested that servicing was handled fairly discreetly, and spatially mirrored the fine-grained economic structure evident in the market. Servicing was typified by numerous small deliveries to the large number of individual businesses, rather than a few very large trucks taking over street spaces.

Turning to the detailed street assessment, this clearly showed that the market hall pathways, and the streets in the immediate area of the market, contributed strongly to its identity and quality. These provided a series of human-scaled spaces that created outdoor rooms, which felt pleasant to be in, rather than simply acting as through ways. The typical height-to-width ratios provided a comfortable level of enclosure. Meanwhile, the public realm was simply detailed, generally with asphalt road surfaces and paving blocks at street edges. Bollards were used to divide off pedestrian from vehicle space in a few places. Until very recently local streets were in poor condition, with ponding and potholes in evidence. While the market's paving surfaces were upgraded as part of the overall regeneration effort, the analysis found that there were still relatively down-at-heel road surfaces and pavements in local streets. Lighting was generally on freestanding poles and there was little in the way of street furniture or public art. There were no street trees but hanging baskets were suspended from poles and building façades here and there. Almost all the public realm drama and visual richness came from the interplay between place users, the market' own stalls displaying produce, the architectural qualities of the buildings and their busy frontages to local streets. Findings reported in Chapter 4 showed that this somewhat rough and ready quality was seen as part of the market area's charm.

In summary, the morphological and urban design analysis suggested that Borough Market was an extremely long-lived food market space. It operated on its current somewhat constrained site for centuries, experiencing substantial changes in its governance, trading arrangements, and physical structures over time. The market's aims and management by trustees were equally long-lived, while the market spaces were of historic, urban design and architectural interest and the area reflected the strongly coherent built form of a traditional urban quarter. This urban fabric suffered transport-related and other incursions in the 19th century, but worse decline came in the post Second World War period, due to structural issues including changes to London's food economy and spatiality. Remarkably, given the scale of post war demolitions elsewhere, the immediate market area remained largely intact as urban fabric, and enjoyed significant regeneration in recent years. At the time the fieldwork was undertaken, the wider area around the market, by contrast, continued to experience a much coarser grained form of development through large-scale, high-rise redevelopment schemes including 'The Shard'.

The different elements of the urban design analysis demonstrated that the case study area had a fine-grained, complex but coherent urban structure. There were both long-existing landmarks in the vicinity, and newer landmarks relating to the food market itself, that helped support its legibility despite a complicated urban pattern. A number of focal points acted as social nodes within the urban fabric. Vistas and views tended to be subtle, giving interesting serial vision opportunities to the walker. The existing, renovated and new built fabric was human-scaled, with active frontages, housing a robust and diverse range of land uses, many related to food. There was a high degree of enclosure in local streets, contributing to the way that public spaces in and around the market worked as outdoor rooms, with simple street detailing that supported the area's distinctive character.

The area allowed a high level of permeability, especially for pedestrians who were unusually privileged in relation to control of street space, as vehicle access was significantly constrained. The transport infrastructure nearby the market also allowed a much broader catchment for visitors from further afield, through a variety of public transport modes. The study area retained a rough and ready character that was part of its identity. All these design elements supported a very particular sense of place by underpinning local intensity in both economic and social activity around food. In Chapter 4 the interplay between these physical elements and the social use of the Borough Market quarter is explored in depth.

Morphology and urban design at Broadway Market

The next section of this chapter turns to the results of morphological and urban design investigations into the physical form of Broadway Market in East London.

The site and walkability radius map for Broadway Market (Figure 3.7) again demonstrates an area with fuzzy edges following the uneven boundaries argued for an urban quarter centred on Broadway Market (the street), running roughly north to south from London Fields to the Regent's Canal.

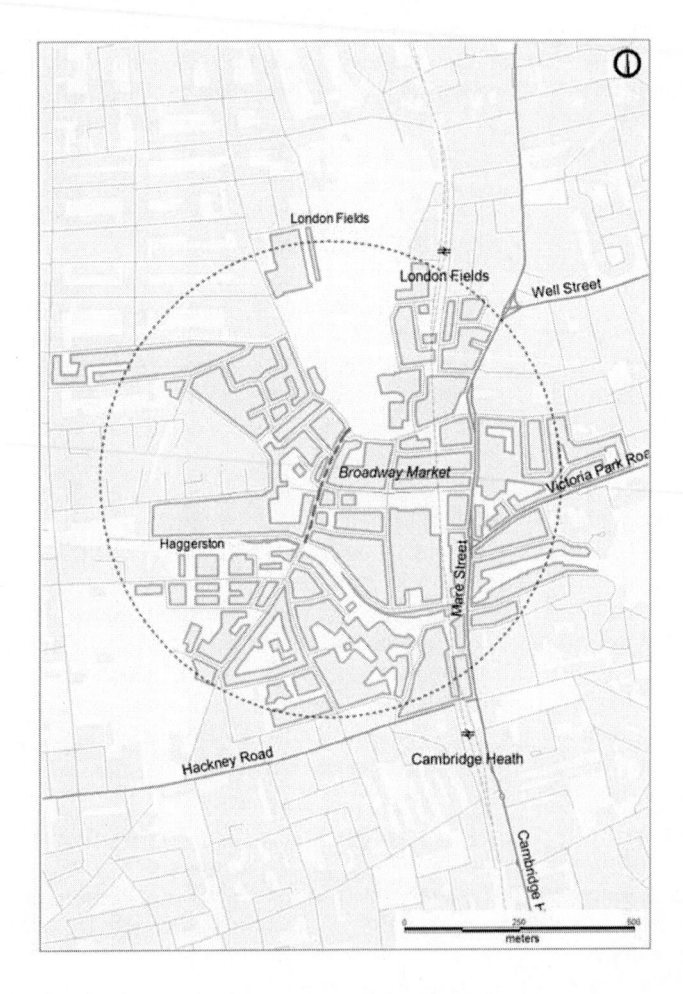

Figure 3.7: *Broadway Market study area walkability radius* Source: Prepared from open source map base by Dominic Honeysett

Most morphological information about the area started from a considerably later period than for Borough, because this neighbourhood was settled as primarily rural rather than urban space until the 19th century. While there were villages in the vicinity, for some centuries Broadway Market was not yet a street or urban area, but simply part of a porters' path along which drovers led cattle into London from Epping Forest and southeastern Essex. Livestock were grazed on London Fields, just to the northeast of

Broadway Market, as it was the last common grazing area before Slaughter Street in Brick Lane or East Smithfield, where London's major meat market was (and still is) located.

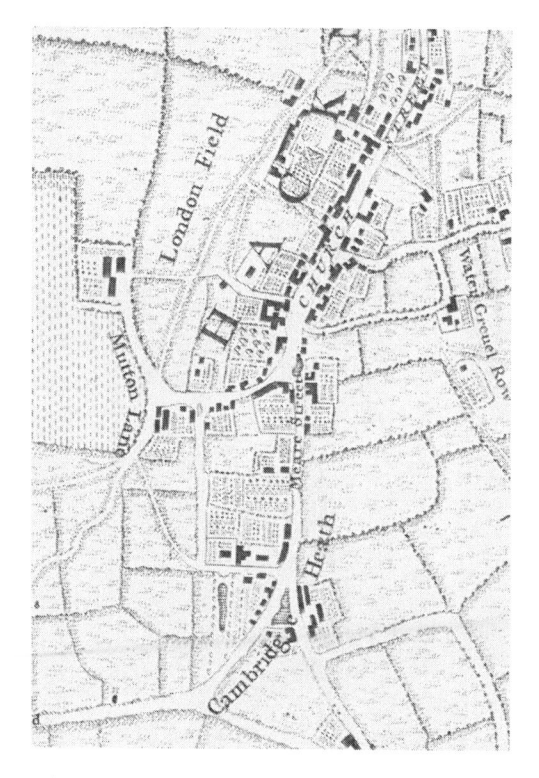

Figure 3.8: *Detail of Rocque's map of London and the Country 10 Miles Round (1746)* Source: City of London, London Metropolitan Archives

At the time of John Rocque's map of *London and the Country 10 Miles Round* of 1746 (Figure 3.8), the drover's path had become a road that traversed rural space, with fields to the west and market gardens to the east. Rocque's map showed the case study area was close to a small settlement just to the northeast in London's rural hinterland, which was centred on Church Street and Mare Street, later to become modern day Hackney's main high street. Mutton Lane, off to the left, could be seen extending south from the bottom corner of the triangular space of London Fields (which were already named on the Rocque map) to eventually join up to Shoreditch High Street and Kingsland Road to the southwest. The urban edge of London could also be seen creeping up from the southwest, with Hoxton at the urban frontier. Peripheral settlements were already in evidence in Bethnal Green and Mile End to the south, where both Old and New Towns were noted, and Hackney and Humerton (sic) to the northeast.

Figure 3.9: *Ordnance Survey map of Dalston of 1870 (London Sheet 40)* Source: City of London, London Metropolitan Archives

Broadway Market was one of the chartered open markets that grew up in London between 1660 and 1840 (Smith, 2006, p.31). Its growth should be situated within London's demographic and physical expansion, which led to rising demand for foodstuffs further out from the centre (ibid). Likewise, its development reflected substantial changes in the "long eighteenth century" in which Londoners underwent a consumer revolution in food marketing toward "decencies and luxuries" (ibid). Some of these changes had spatial expression. For example, suburban expansion in markets mirrored population decline in central areas like the City of London (ibid). "New markets largely depended on the enterprise and wherewithal of private developers at a local level" (op cit, p.32). Such markets were established in areas that were socially mixed and were characterised by diversity and versatility in the foodstuffs they provided. The sharp division between markets for wholesaling and retailing was not yet pronounced.

Maps such as Horwood's (1792-99, 1819) and Stanford's (1862), that gave early morphological information about Borough, did not extend this far out from the geographical centre of London so did not provide primary sources for the Broadway analysis. However, the 1870 Ordnance Survey maps of Dalston, (Figure 3.9), and Shoreditch (London Sheet 51: Scale 1:4340), illustrated that by the mid 19th century there were urbanised areas at and around Broadway Market. The neighbourhood was well established as urban fabric, as was the street of Broadway Market itself. Contiguous development ran along both sides of Broadway Market for its entire length, between London Fields at the northern end and the Regent's Canal (which was completed in 1820) at the southern end. Densely built up urban fabric was evident all around the market street, with small terraced housing generally offering continuous frontages to the street and private gardens behind, on blocks within a traditional grid-based street pattern.

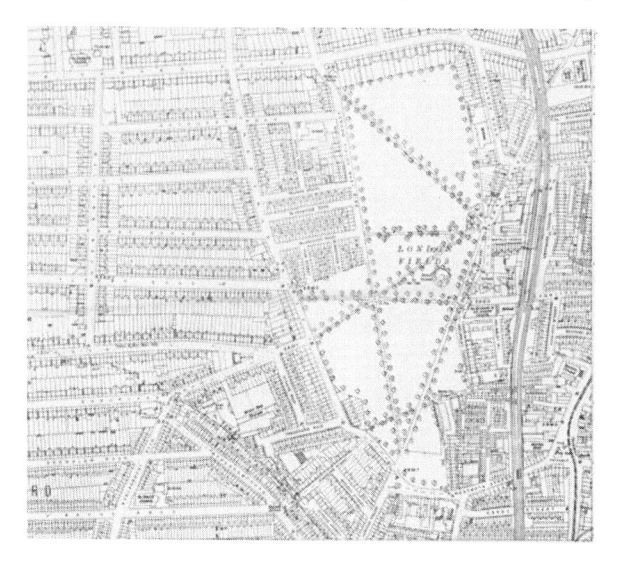

Figure 3.10: *Ordnance Survey map of Dalston of 1913 (London Sheet 40, showing northern end of Broadway Market)* Source: City of London, London Metropolitan Archives

By the time of the Ordnance Survey map of Dalston of 1913 (Figure 3.10), and of Shoreditch of 1914, further changes could be discerned. At the centre of the food quarter, the northern section of the street (called London Fields) extended down from the formally planted urban park of the same name, toward the southern portion of the street known as 'The Broadway'.

Some land uses on the street were named, including the public house on the northern corner where London Fields (the street) met Westgate Street, which ran around the southern edge of London Fields (the park). A small but necessary piece of public infrastructure was the urinal at the centre of the compact, triangular public space in front of the public house at the London Fields end of the street. Two further public houses were shown further south on the street's right hand side; one on the corner of Duncan Road and another on Andrew's Road, the latter facing the canal.

By the early 20th century, various substantial pieces of urban infrastructure could be seen in the vicinity of Broadway Market, demonstrating this was a fully functioning urban quarter with local shops, services, industries, public infrastructure, public transport, parks and housing, as well as the food market at its centre. These land uses included the north to south oriented railway line of the Great Eastern Railway (which had not yet been built at the time of the 1870 map), by then shown as located slightly to the east of the market street; the similarly oriented horse-drawn tramway on Mare Street, again not yet evident in 1870; and the west to east oriented Regent's Canal. The canal dipped slightly southeastwards at this point, to be crossed at the southern end of The Broadway at the Cat and Mutton Bridge. Also just to the southeast was a substantial stone yard, and adjoining that, a gasworks with four large circular gasholders. To the north of the canal and just to the east of The Broadway was a chemical works. The area was thus characterised as a relatively fine-grained mix of dense, working class residential, commercial and industrial land uses, with housing predominating, and providing a substantial local catchment for the food market.

As at Borough, the next era of significant morphological change came about during wartime and after World War Two. While the East End of London suffered substantial bomb damage during the Second World War, it was post war that these boroughs "faced the most relentless enemy of all, the municipal bulldozer" (Inwood, 1998, p.812). Following Abercrombie's Plan of 1948, the intention was to decant population from boroughs perceived as crowded, such as Southwark, Shoreditch and Bethnal Green; the latter two boroughs close to Broadway. Government was committed to the wholesale removal of what were described as "obsolete", "congested" or "muddled" housing, and of "districts of narrow and confined streets lined with outworn and sub-standard building" (op cit, p.821). This resulted in the destruction of substantial amounts of urban fabric that had escaped the bombs, but not the comprehensive development that followed (ibid), and it resulted in urban blight.

From 1954, national government also introduced subsidies for high rise flat development, and

> "the cheaper alternative policy of repairing old houses and providing them with modern heating and plumbing, which was often preferred by tenants themselves, did not attract significant government support, and did not seem to local authorities to offer the mass housing they had in mind" (Inwood, 1998, p.826).

The London Borough of Hackney was among the most enthusiastic tower builders (op cit, p.81) and this left Broadway Market as a traditionally shaped and scaled street marooned in an area seen in the background of Figure 3.11. As Forshaw and Bergstrom (1983, p.46) explain:

> "Broadway Market was a 1960s clearance area; massive modern blocks replaced the little terraced houses and ambitious plans were made for a new shopping precinct. What was once a thriving market serving a strong local community degenerated into a depressing collection of decaying properties".

Figure 3.11: *Housing blocks to the north of Broadway Market* Source: Photograph by author

By 1983, Broadway Market presented a microcosm of the food-related results of local and national governments' post war approach to urban regeneration. In Hackney, for example, a great deal of regeneration funding through the Urban Programme was spent to clean up the area's physical fabric but at Broadway Market, half the shops and pitches were empty (Forshaw and Bergstrom, 1983, p.46). Broadway Market's street was still thought to have character and potential in the early 1980s, despite urban renewal incursions. It retained its cobbles and a large number of its old buildings:

> "some improved, some derelict. The fascia of Geo. Tallet's fish shop can faintly be deciphered above the corrugated iron, seemingly condemned for demolition. Beside London Fields the Cat and Mutton pub has been smartened, and Selby's art gallery is perhaps a portent. The Market House Tavern is painted cheery red, and near the canal estate agents' boards herald bijou residences" (ibid, p.46).

Within a context of decline in the physical form of the place, the beginnings of regeneration of the urban fabric appeared to be stirring. This shift was noted on Broadway Market's website (2007), which mourned that the market had declined almost completely by the 1980s, and pointed to its recent revival:

> "Once a thriving market some thirty years ago, Business then decayed almost into oblivion. Now it is about to become a buzzing centre of the community again" (Broadway Market Co., 2007).

More recently still a trawl of real estate websites showed a number of flats for rent or sale locally described as "located close to the vibrant life of Broadway Market" or "5 minutes walk to Broadway Market and London Fields" (Find a New Home Com, n.d.). As at Borough and Exmouth Markets, the resurgence of the food market heralded substantial new residential development in the Broadway Market area. New mixed-use property developments also began to be built close to Broadway Market. Typical descriptions of new flat buildings include the following:

> "Located on the junction of Westgate Street and Triangle Road overlooking London Fields, this new build mixed-use development is conveniently located in terms of the local amenities in and around Broadway market. A new high quality development, offering a choice of one, two, three and four bedroom apartments".

"NEW DEVELOPMENTS. Enviably located by Broadway Market and overlooking London Fields, is this selection of one, two, three and four bedroom apartments arranged over the upper floors of a stunning new development" (ibid).

The figure-ground analysis of Broadway meanwhile showed that by the early 21st century much of the well-developed fabric in the market street's vicinity had been destroyed. Broadway Market as a street was relatively unscathed in terms of the physical fabric that remained. It still offered an almost continuous built frontage up to the street alignment along its length on both sides. The exception was the area between Benjamin Close (the remnant of Brougham Road) and Duncan Street (on the left hand side of the market street), which lost the triangular building and the rest of the built form that gave this corner its enclosure. The areas behind the street fared far worse, both to the west, and to the east towards Mare Street. In this urban neighbourhood the fabric of terraced houses on Duncan Lane, Duncan Road, Jackman Street, Ada Street, Andrews Street and Urban Place (east-west streets), and Antwerp Street, Sheep Lane (the name possibly retaining the memory of its pre-urban function), and Ash Grove (largely north-south), were hollowed out. Almost all the terraced housing was replaced by large, set back housing blocks, with little ground floor vitality, indeterminate open space and car garaging areas.

On the western side of the road there was less wholesale removal of terrace houses, and rows of these survived in the area between London Fields and Duncan Street. South of here, however, a similar eradication of the fabric created a tabula rasa for the development of more set back housing blocks and a large area for garaging cars owned by these flat dwellers. Also to the west, Benjamin Close was created as a cul-de-sac, with a walkway extending westwards, where once Brougham Road provided terrace lined street access to The Broadway. While the Broadway Market street retained most of its legibility, the permeability and connectivity of the areas immediately around it sharply declined through deliberate decisions to close off streets, as well as through the severance effects of the major infrastructure of the canal to the south and the railway line to the east.

Building on the morphological evidence outlined in the previous section, the urban structure analysis of the Broadway case study area suggested that its traditional pattern of blocks, streets, building, and garden space was severely disrupted in the mid to late 20th century. The demolition of swathes of private houses and gardens and the deterioration of Broadway Market as a high street and market location led to substantial decline in its sense of place and the commercial viability of its centre.

New, large-scale public housing block development undermined the physical character, tenure mix and fine grain of local land uses. Broadway Market, previously a thriving food and social centre for the local community, was reduced to a virtually derelict space. Similarly, the relationship between built form, open space and landscape design was seriously disrupted. The area had in the past been characterised by a strong street grid pattern with buildings close to street alignments on streets lined with trees. This coherent pattern was intentionally destroyed on the basis of assumptions about tabula rasa approaches to renewal. While the area retained a relatively high density of residential development, the result was substantial areas of lost space around isolated residential buildings, and few attractive landscape features or functions left untouched in the remnant, poorly connected public domain.

Following these interventions some amelioration of the effects of decline were instituted to deal with what now seem ill-judged physical renewal approaches. This was most evident in the street assessment of Broadway Market itself, where human scaled buildings along either side of the street largely escaped demolition and were thus available for renovation. Their frontages were renewed in the early 1980s, and this physical regeneration was built on and the street further revived as a physical space in the 1990s and 2000s. As findings presented in Chapter 5 suggest, its restoration relied to a large extent on the high degree of compatibility between its characterful shape and its role as a food space. At the time of the fieldwork, the street functioned on market days as a fine-grained, mixed-use, local activity node, with many of the land uses in evidence having some relationship to food: stalls, shops, indoor and outdoor cafes, pubs, bars and restaurants.

Turning to the urban design analysis, this showed a number of local landmarks in the immediate area: most obviously London Fields to the north and Regent's Canal to the south, while the contentious demolition of Tony's café, a famous local 'caf' on Broadway Market, increased its icon status. Meanwhile local pubs along the street, and certain shops such as Spirit's grocery store (also the subject of redevelopment controversy) and some food stalls similarly acted as focal points, including one that doubled as a coffee bar on market days. The street boasted very attractive views to the north towards the southern tip of London Fields while to the south the canal bridge acted as a vista termination point. Broadway Market was once at the centre of a very connected, permeable and legible street grid that provided a wealth of movement options for pedestrians and other road users, but the comprehensive redevelopment of the 1960s undercut this permeability. Some streets were truncated, while others suffered closures, with deleterious effects on walkability. Broadway Market itself had a road closure installed and by the early 1980s, this closure point provided "a focus for a few hardened traders" (Forshaw and Bergstrom, 1983, p.46).

Catchment analysis of Broadway Market identified a ped-shed or walkability radius of five hundred metres (see Figure 3.7 above) that extended into housing areas to the northwest, northeast and south of the case study area, and into London Fields to the north. It also encompassed the major arterial road and transport hub of Mare Street to the east. While the street provided the nodal point to a relatively walkable area, in reality the catchment was not strictly circular due to the way the street grid was interrupted or severed in certain directions: most seriously to the immediate west and east, limiting pedestrian accessibility in these directions.

By 2008 the area was well served by local and sub-regional public transport, with bus, train, Underground and bicycle options for gaining access to the market street. Transport for London's local Public Transport Accessibility Level map showed Broadway as moderately well connected in public transport terms, with adjoining areas to the east scoring high and very high levels of public transport accessibility. The bus stops and pedestrian paths at the point where Broadway Market met London Fields also contributed to a lively, informal gateway to the street from its northern end. Like Borough Market, the street provided an interesting path sequence for pedestrians, while limiting car access.

The streetscape assessment at Broadway Market (Figure 3.12) demonstrated a high degree of visual richness, due in part to the fine-grained pattern of the frontages. Its human scale led to a significant level of enclosure in which the street acted as a series of outdoor rooms, characterised by active edges on both sides. The height-to-width ratio varied along the street's length but provided a good level of enclosure. Building details were well resolved, with a coherent pattern of façades in relation to the shape of walls, windows and doors, as well as the height, scale and materials in buildings fronting the street. There was simple paving of brick appearance, although a different surface for a bicycle lane was laid down at the London Fields end. A set of gates and bollards half way along added some complexity, and showed the limit of car access during market hours. Lighting and signs were set on poles along the street's length and there was little in the way of street furniture.

102   Chapter Three

Figure 3.12: *Broadway Market streetscape* Source: Photograph by author

Figure 3.13: *Broadway's market in action* Source: Photograph by author

In summary, the morphological and urban design analysis of Broadway Market demonstrated that the food market street sat within what was once a traditional urban quarter of London, located near a number of originally outlying villages, from which urban development expanded. The area had long-term food associations including being on the route of a drover's path into London, and designation as one of London's chartered open markets. The food market and wider local area suffered an almost terminal decline in the post-war period, with much of its housing demolished in the push for renewal based on medium and high rise public housing blocks.

Despite loss of local legibility and permeability through renewal interventions, its physical fabric and social use were significantly regenerated in recent times, especially since the advent of the revived Saturday market (Figure 3.13). The area contained a number of local landmarks, views and focal points, some of which were food-related. Research identified an increasingly rich land use mix, with the range of food-related uses broadening and growing. At the time fieldwork was undertaken Broadway Market operated as an activity node that was both locally walkable and accessible to a broader public transport catchment. As a street, Broadway Market could be seen as an attractive outdoor room with comfortable height-to-width ratios, simple streetscaping details, and highly active frontages; all contributing to a strong sense of place and local identity.

Morphology and urban design at Exmouth Market

The last substantive section of this chapter describes the morphological and urban design conditions that were found at Exmouth Market, in Figure 3.14 below.

The fuzzy-edged case study area was centred on the street of Exmouth Market, running northeast to southwest, parallel with Rosebery Avenue, in the southern part of the London Borough of Islington.

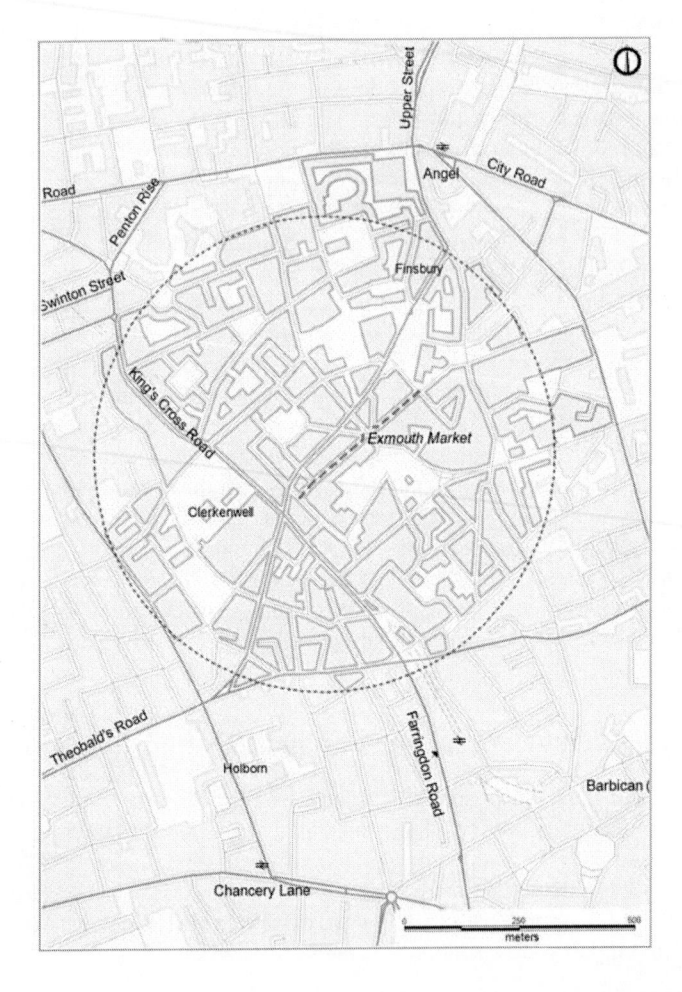

Figure 3.14: *Exmouth Market study area walkability radius* Source: Prepared from open source map base by Dominic Honeysett

Exmouth Market did not exist as a street at the time of Rocque's previously cited London map of 1746. Instead the area was one of market gardens and orchards, just to the south of what became Exmouth Market; and fields and track ways, just to the north. All of these land uses lay at the edge of urban London. The beginnings of what became the urban road structure could already be discerned in the net of pathways, some of which later solidified into streets. However, the quarter was not entirely urban space by the time of Horwood's 1792-1799 map (Figure 3.15).

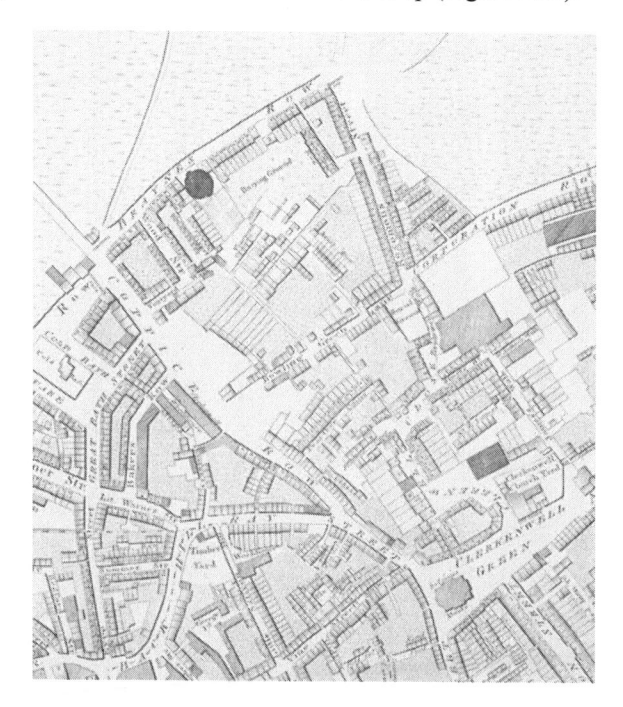

Figure 3.15: *Detail of Horwood's 1792 map* Source: City of London, London Metropolitan Archives

What could be seen in the 1792-99 period when Horwood's map was produced, was that Exmouth Market, named as Baynes Row, was the continuation of a street running north-east up from Mt Pleasant, and crossing the north-south running Coppice Row (later reconfigured as Farringdon Road). The southern side of Baynes Row constituted an urban edge to London at this point, although further north there was already substantial development in Islington village. Terraced housing could be seen all along this southern side of Baynes Row, the line broken only by Spa Fields Chapel and its burial ground (today's remnant Spa Fields). Baynes Row halted at Rosoman Street at its northeastern end to give way to a track across open fields, which stretched towards the New River Head, 'Merlin's Cave' and Sadler's Wells Theatre, and the settled areas north of Winchester Place (later to become Pentonville Road).

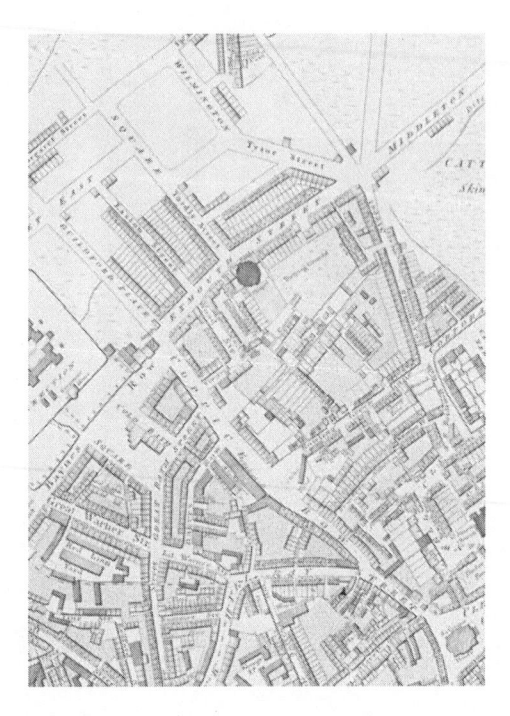

Figure 3.16: *Horwood's 1819 map (detail)* Source: City of London, London Metropolitan Archives

Spa Fields, in the area of what is now the street of Exmouth Market, was in the 18th century "one of London's great rural attractions" where prize fights and fairs were held (White, 2007, p.351). It was also notorious for the footpads who roamed by night, to the extent that theatregoers to Sadler's Wells banded together to cross the Fields supported by linkmen who lit the way for their protection (ibid). By 1816, however, urbanisation was on the way: "the fields around the Spa tea garden were just one more frowsy no man's land at the edge of London, ripe for the house builder's mattock" (ibid). By the mid 1830s Spa Fields was bricked over by the Lloyd Baker Estate and other streets stretched from Kings Cross to Rosebery Avenue (New London Architecture, n.d.).

The Horwood map of 1819 (see Figure 3.16) confirmed that by the early 19th century, Baynes Row had given way to Exmouth Street, and was settled along both sides, with contiguous terraced housing. Side streets on its northern side were Guildford Place, Easton Street, Yardly Street and Tysoe Street, and each had terrace housing developed some way up its length toward the laid out, but not yet developed, Wilmington Square. The urban development on the southern side of Exmouth Street looked very similar to its form in 1792. At the street's northern end, however, a road called Middleton Street had been developed as a continuation of Exmouth Street to the northeast. To the south of Middleton Street, and the east of Exmouth Street, was a designated cattle field of the Skinners Company, furriers who were one of London's 12 great livery companies (trade guilds). In the vicinity was a tiny vineyard, also marked on the 1819 map, just to the south of Exmouth Street. By 1850, Forshaw and Bergstrom (1983, p.118) point out that

> "the spas had disappeared, the wild flowers and fresh air replaced by sweatshops and workhouses, making artificial flowers and clothing, alongside the metal-platers, watchmakers and distillers. Clerkenwell's teeming population was crammed into tight terraces and tenements".

Stanford's map of 1862 (Figure 3.17) meanwhile, showed that all the remaining rural space had indeed been captured for urban development and the street itself, as well as the area to the north and east of Exmouth Street, was now entirely built up. Today's Spa Fields, and a small ring around the New River Head Reservoir, were at this point the only open space left in the vicinity. The street of Exmouth Market could be seen to run directly towards St John Street to the northeast, by way of its continuation (still then Middleton rather than Myddelton Street).

Some of the points about the growth of food markets made in relation to Broadway Market also applied to the evolution of Exmouth, where a street-based food market existed by 1850 and "attracted hordes of street sellers and small shops" (ibid, 1983, p.118). In the 1890s it was still "a relatively new market whose costers were often regarded with disdain by the local authority" (Whitelegg, 2002, p.79). The Exmouth area became known as Little Italy as it attracted generations of Italian migrants who worked as artisans. Their impact on the food trade, such as Gazzano's delicatessen on Farringdon Road, which was still extant as a café and salumeria at the time of the research, and cafes along Exmouth Market itself, was felt from the 19th century until very recent times.

108   Chapter Three

Figure 3.17: *Stanford's map of 1862 (Sheet 7 - detail)* Source: City of London, London Metropolitan Archives

At the time of the Ordnance Survey map of 1894 (Figure 3.18) the entire area around Exmouth Market was fully urbanised and the food market was at the centre of a thriving community. However, by the end of the 19th century, dramatic alterations had occurred in the area's urban form, with Rosebery Avenue carved through in 1891 just to the north of Exmouth Street, running from southwest to northeast. This new major road, and road widening elsewhere in the vicinity, disrupted both existing housing and the urban road and block pattern. For example, a new left over space was created by the way Rosebery Avenue intersected with the southern end of Exmouth Market, as some built fabric was demolished at this point.

Overall, though, the character of the case study area still appeared predominantly of contiguous built development up to or close to the street alignment, in urban blocks demonstrating a high level of enclosure. Particular land uses were altered, such as Exmouth Street's chapel, replaced by a more substantial rectilinear church   (Our Most Holy Redeemer) fronting the street, and the much reduced and relocated Spa Fields was now designated as a playground.

Food-Centred Space

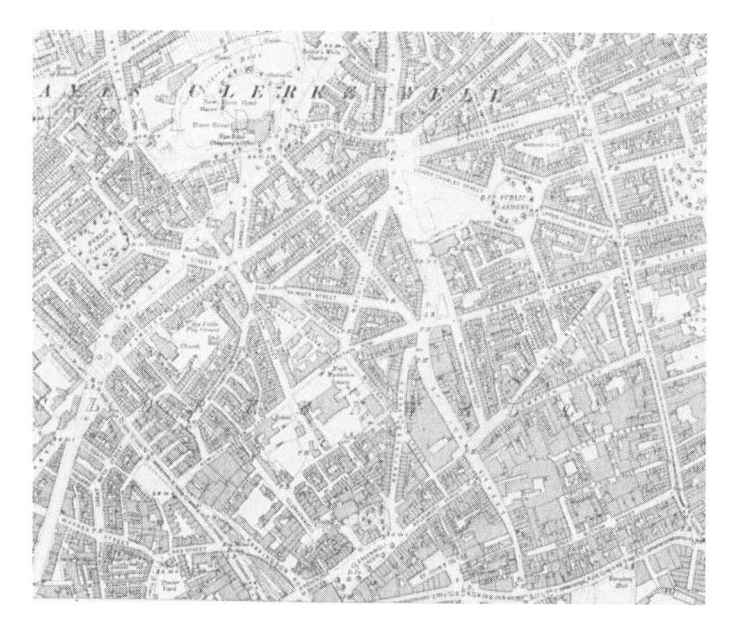

Figure 3.18: *Ordnance Survey 1894 map of Exmouth area (London Sheet 50: detail)* Source: City of London, London Metropolitan Archives

The Ordnance map of 1914 (Figure 3.19) showed little alteration except that Rosebery Avenue now had a tramway, as did Farringdon Road (formerly Coppice Row) and the area was now shown as St James' Ward, Finsbury. The area presented a very coherent morphological picture of terrace housing in traditional London urban streets and squares.

The 20th century morphological record saw the area marked by both decline and regeneration, with the most recent Ordnance Survey map of the area demonstrating substantial changes to the urban form in the vicinity of the street by now designated Exmouth Market. The street itself, like Broadway Market, retained a solid built wall up to the street alignment on both sides, from Farringdon Road at the southwestern end, to the intersection with Tysoe, Rosoman and Myddleton Streets at the northeastern end. However, again like Broadway, but in a more modified form, the most striking alteration was the amount of lost space that had been created, especially to the northeast around post war housing development. There was such leftover space around the estates of high rise and slab block-based public housing, and a rather indeterminate new green area was opened up to the east of Northampton Road, on Exmouth Market's eastern end. Some of this public housing, though, was of significantly higher quality than that found close to Broadway. For example, the Spa Green Estate, designed and built by Lubetkin and Skinner over the period 1936-45, just to the northeast, was Grade II* listed by English Heritage, as an architecturally important example of modern social housing.

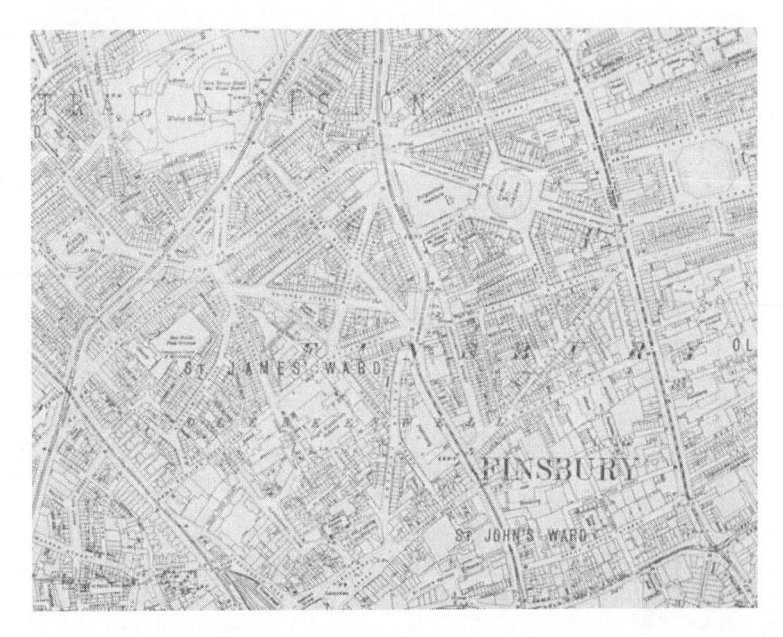

Figure 3.19: *Ordnance Survey 1914 map of Exmouth area (London Sheet 50: detail)* Source: City of London, London Metropolitan Archives

Other spatial changes meanwhile were also physical expressions of economic and social forces affecting the area. For example, Exmouth Market and the wider Farringdon area had long-term connections to cultural institutions and industries, including theatre and printing. This industrial base declined in the 20th century, due to a combination of structural developments (Whitelegg, 2002) that meant

> "Between 1945 and 1980 the accumulation of slum clearance, war damage, closure of factories and the lure of the suburbs had reduced the population to a tiny fraction of what it was sixty years ago; Exmouth Market had become a ghostly and shabby backwater" (Forshaw and Bergstrom, 1983, p.60).

The street was in a very poor state in the 1980s, when a number of physical improvements to its fabric were financed by regeneration funds flowing from national government by way of the London Borough of Islington. At this point, some £146,000 was spent on repaving the street (Whitelegg, 2002). More recent changes to the built form included further streetscape improvements, such as new lighting, paving, the ubiquitous hanging baskets, and street furniture.

It is worth noting that, like Borough and Broadway, the Exmouth Market area became subject to considerable interest from property developers. There were a number of small to medium scale office developments and residential flat building schemes in the vicinity, and at the time of the fieldwork (2005-2008) plans were afoot just to the south of Exmouth Market to redevelop Mount Pleasant, London's biggest postal sorting office. A master plan was drawn up by architect John McAslan & Partners, for a mixed use scheme which comprised a 600,000 square foot (55,741 square metre) sorting office, one thousand-five hundred homes, a public square and a gallery on a twelve acre (4.9 hectare) site. By 2010 however, this scheme appeared to be on hold, and the property press were reporting that the plans were never progressed (Public Property UK, n.d.).

Turning to the urban design analysis, the figure-ground of Exmouth Market showed that most of the built form in the immediate area of the street maintained a strong solid-to-void relationship. The street itself had almost continuous built frontages along both sides, with only small openings to north and south at Spafield Street, and narrow lanes linking the street to Spa Fields Gardens and Rosoman Place. A small public space could be seen at the southwestern end of the street, where it met Rosebery Avenue and Farringdon Road. A much larger open area was apparent at the northeastern end of the street, and another, Spa Fields Gardens, just to the south. The urban structure of the Exmouth Market area predominantly showed a traditional block pattern. This pattern was maintained along the street itself and just to its north, but was disrupted in a number of directions a little further out from this activity node.

The street displayed a finely grained block and plot structure (Figure 3.20), characterised by mixed land uses. There were street level small shops and two-to-three storeys of office and residential above, providing a high residential density and a vibrant activity level. The architecture was not outstanding but provided a solid human-scaled urban fabric framing the public realm and a harmonious environment for the street's increasing commercial viability. The tower of St Saviour's church acted as both a landmark and a vista termination from the north, when viewed down Yardley Street. There was a small urban square formed by the meeting points of Rosebery Avenue, Farringdon Road and Exmouth Market, and Al's Bar on this corner acted as a focal point.

At the early stage of the fieldwork, market stalls were present on market days while later in the research process 'slow' fast food stalls were found here daily during weekdays and constituted a focus for food activity, especially at lunchtime. Another focal point was found about halfway along the street, where there were a high percentage of bars and restaurants. Overall, the coherent built form and public realm underpinned a strong sense of identity and place.

Figure 3.20: *Exmouth Market view looking north-east* Source: Photograph by author

The design analysis identified a number of urban grain and scale issues in the Exmouth area. To the northeast and southeast, the urban clearance process described earlier saw formerly fine-grained, built-up street blocks obliterated and the space redeveloped in a modernist design style. Various set back, separate, large-scale residential, institutional and commercial buildings were awkwardly interspersed with areas of open space. These urban armature elements generally did not present a solid wall to the street, which would help to achieve an appropriate positive-negative space balance. Nor did they possess the fine-grained, human-scaled form that would meld them successfully with the strongly marked local built form context that the morphological research revealed. The contrast was particularly striking at the northeastern end of Exmouth Market, in moving from the enclosed outdoor room of the market street, to an area facing Myddelton Street that lacked coherent urban structure or enclosure.

The connectivity analysis showed that the immediate area was particularly well connected; providing a large number of movement possibilities, through a predominantly permeable urban block structure. It was possible to approach the street from many points on the connected grid that surrounded it in most directions, and the fine grain of these connections reinforced the street's sense of place as a pedestrian friendly, walkable activity node. Traffic management arrangements clearly privileged walking over driving along Exmouth Market. Although the street was still accessible to vehicles, its paving treatments, street furniture, signs, bollards and small number of parking spaces all reinforced the design cues that this was primarily a pedestrian space rather than a through road. Meanwhile, the areas surrounding the street, where the traditional block pattern was erased, conversely exhibited a far lower level of permeability and legibility.

Catchment analysis meanwhile showed that Exmouth Market was highly accessible to pedestrians and had very good transport connections, both for public and private modes. The walkable radius centred on the street took in a number of local residential and mixed land use areas. This showed how easy it was to walk to and through the quarter from most directions, except the public housing areas to the northeast, where the street grid had been broken and legibility significantly reduced. The local Public Transport Accessibility Level Map demonstrated that the case study area was also very accessible in transport terms; reflecting the proximity of various transport modes, including a number of bus stops along Rosebery Avenue, Farringdon Road and St John Street. The advent of the London bicycle hire scheme (with a docking station on Rosebery Avenue) also served to increase Exmouth Market's accessibility even further. Although neither the rail nor Underground stations at Farringdon or at Angel were within five hundred metres, both were less than a kilometre away.

The street assessment demonstrated that Exmouth Market achieved a strong level of enclosure, with a range of detailed street design elements contributing to a perception of the space as a series of outdoor rooms. The height-to-width ratio of the street varied slightly along its length, but averaged at, or a little more than a comfortable 1:1. There was a coherent built frontage on both sides with shop front buildings mostly comprised of robust materials - wood, brick, stone and glass - used in traditional combinations and scales. The footpaths and road surface were paved as a continuous shared space, with a mix of concrete slabs and stone setts. Bollards distinguished the roadway from the pedestrian footpaths to either side, although this separation was somewhat symbolic, as pedestrians habitually used both footpaths and road space. At the Farringdon Road end, seats and tree planting (London Planes) provided a welcome shaded area after the harder edged, largely unshaded street. In principle the sense of enclosure and protection from most car traffic made the space attractive for outdoor seating in front of cafes, restaurants and daily food stalls although benches were often colonised by street drinkers, limiting use by others. The street was lively throughout the week, especially at lunchtimes, and after work.

In summary, the Exmouth Market area emerged as urban space from the middle of the 18th century, as the built edge of London crept northward to encompass the infrastructure of the New River and the attractions of Spa Fields and Sadler's Wells, and their attendant prize-fights and fairs. The area around Exmouth Market was developed as a coherent urban fabric of streets and squares, with terrace housing predominating. The quarter became densely populated, with a strong immigrant presence, and a focus on artisanal and industrial production. There was evidence of the food market existing by the 1850s, with numerous street traders (costers) and small food shops. Italian immigrants were and remained strongly associated with the area and the street as a food space.

The maps and other records showed that major changes included Rosebery Avenue being cut through the existing urban fabric in the late 19th century. There was significant decline in population, industry, and the street and area's physical fabric after World War Two. Large tracts of public housing were built by demolishing traditional terrace housing and streets, under the rubric of slum clearance. The market itself virtually disappeared, leaving a legacy of urban blight. Waves of regeneration efforts to revitalise the physical fabric of Exmouth occurred in the 1980s and 1990s but did not result in the hoped for social and economic improvements. Likewise attempts to revive the food market were largely unsuccessful. However, from the late 1990s the street and area's fortunes rose, with considerable new economic development, in part based on food, and by the time the fieldwork was undertaken in the 2005-2008 period Exmouth was considered a highly attractive residential, business and social location.

At the centre of this fine-grained, mixed-use, dense urban quarter, Exmouth Market showed a strong level of enclosure, with the street working as a series of outdoor rooms. The local area had a predominantly traditional character, based on a grid of streets and contiguous built fabric up to or near street frontages. This provided a strong design context for a focus on a vibrant, human-scaled public realm, with various focal points including food shops and stalls, and landmarks, vistas and views helping establish the legibility of the urban armature. Close by the street there were areas of lost space, as a result of 20th century interventions, especially post war housing and other developments that undermined the street grid and fabric pattern. Exmouth Market itself was at the centre of a highly permeable area, allowing easy access by public transport for a local and wider catchment, and scoring a high walkability rating. Its detailed design helped privilege pedestrian over vehicle movement, making it a pleasant space to be in. This was reinforced by the streetscape qualities, which emphasised both fine grain and visual richness, using simple, traditional materials. These urban design qualities contributed to Exmouth Market's strong identity and sense of place.

Summarising the design basis for food quarter research

Chapter 3 has explored the urban morphology, urban structure, connectivity and details of the place, in each of the three food quarters. Each case study area could be read as fuzzy edged but loosely based in both size and other aspects of spatiality on the European urban quarter. The three areas shared certain important similarities but also showed distinctive features that set them apart from one another. For instance, the urban context of Borough Market was identified as far older than that of either Broadway Market or Exmouth Market. The Borough Market area was settled possibly since pre-Roman times, and was an important, continuous node in London's urban fabric since the 10th century, while the other two areas retained their rural or peri-urban character until the late 18th and early 19th centuries.

Each case study area was characterised by the development of a coherent built fabric and urban structure, which produced "invisible architecture" (Drijver, 2005). This generally did not draw attention to itself but cumulatively provided a strong frame for the intensive nodes of activity created by the food markets and related land uses. Each area historically acted as a focal point for new, mixed-use urban settlement around a food market and attendant food-related activities. Moreover, in each there was a long-term relationship between the market and these other food-related land uses that could be seen to be physical, social and design based. And in each area there was a high density of development from the beginning of urban settlement. Borough Market demonstrated strong urban fabric continuity until the 19th century, when public transport infrastructure was imposed over the existing urban pattern. At around the period when this transformation was underway at Borough, both Broadway Market and Exmouth Market became functioning food markets at the centre of urbanised quarters. Both had previously been outside or on the urban edge of London, which encroached on them in the 18th and 19th centuries. By the end of the 19th century, all three areas were very well connected for walkers and well served by public transport.

However, in all three market areas, the 20th century brought a number of disastrous spatial impacts. Especially in the post WWII period, a series of structural changes including suburbanisation, economic decline, and comprehensive redevelopment affected each of the case study areas in largely deleterious ways. Numbers of residents to support the markets declined in each area in part due to broad structural changes, but also as a result of deliberate post war policies of population decanting and demolition of local housing, that had unexpected consequences. In Borough, the market was left to fall apart, while in Broadway's case, areas perceived as overcrowded were thinned out. Both at Broadway and Exmouth, high-rise buildings and 'slaburbs' (Kegler, 2005) replaced much finer grained housing fabric. All saw their central function as a market dwindle virtually to nothing, and acquired areas of lost space through housing block or other redevelopment which harmed their urban fabric.

Borough became, by the 1960 and 70s, a place to be avoided, while Broadway perhaps suffered the most as more of its fabric was cleared away and the quality of the housing design that replaced the traditional terraced housing was lower than at Exmouth. At Exmouth too, however, serious decline was in evidence in the quality and coherence of the physical space. By the 1980s, regeneration efforts to physically upgrade and regenerate the traditional urban fabric were desperately needed, and were launched at each area. These efforts continued up until the time research for this book was carried out, and for Borough in particular, its strategic central London location close to a major transport hub continued to make it a highly attractive location for major new development, as demonstrated by construction of the misleadingly named London Bridge 'Quarter' (in fact a building). Both the other two case study areas also experienced physical redevelopment trajectories, albeit at a more modest scale.

The detailed physical analysis of the three quarters showed that they each developed a strong identity in the immediate area of the market, but this sense of place fell away sharply further from the food market streets and spaces. Each case study area performed well on movement assessment in terms of permeability, legibility and walkability. Each had a good pedestrian catchment and avoided car dominance, despite some barriers created by poorly designed housing, commercial or transport infrastructure developments in the vicinity. All the quarters were seen to be centred on excellent outdoor rooms with appropriate height-to-width ratios, robust built form and high levels of visual richness, providing an attractive physical setting for a vibrant street life centred on food.

The physical design qualities explored in this chapter provide the groundwork for the socio-spatial analysis of the three case study areas in Chapters 4 to 6. This chapter's consideration of morphological and urban design structure acts as a springboard for exploring in detail the social, economic and environmental life of each of the three food market quarters in turn.

Chapter Four

Designed Renewal at Borough Market

Introducing the Borough Market quarter

This chapter focuses on the case of designed food quarter renewal at Borough Market. It is based on primary research at the market and its surrounding area and refracted through the lens of the sustainable city and the design work of the last chapter. The Borough Market area constitutes the most fully realised urban food quarter of the three case study sites and discussion of its development as a food quarter is structured around the economic, environmental and social dimensions of renewal. These elements provide an overall frame for exploring and analysing the interplay between physical space, economic renewal and everyday socio-spatial practices in and around Borough Market.

Constructing a picture of Borough has relied on semi-structured interviews with visitors, food traders and food and design experts; on numerous informal observational visits to Borough over a three-year period up to June 2008; and on a series of 'head counts' used to distinguish various social practices over a typical Thursday to Saturday trading period, in September 2007. Food mapping of the market and surrounding spaces, undertaken in June 2008, adds a spatial dimension to the research. It is worth noting that the primary research was undertaken before more recent controversy about the future of Borough Market intensified, so that aspects of Borough's current more conflicted situation are mentioned in the analysis rather than central to the narrative accounts here. A map of the area under study, with its five hundred metre 'ped-shed' radius was shown in Chapter 3, but as noted there its edges should be understood as fuzzy rather than tightly defined.

Tracing Borough's triumphant story of economic revival

Borough's economic regeneration has been situated as a story of triumphant revival and the first part of this chapter deals with the economic elements that have underpinned the development of its environmental and social roles and its local governance structure. Borough Market is one of the markets in London run by Trustees, as opposed to local government or a private operator. As previously outlined, its governance arrangements have a very long-term background, stemming from a 1756 Act of Parliament, which brought the market under the control of wardens of the parish of St Saviour. In 1907 it became a Trust nominated through, but not controlled by, the local council. Having operated more or less successfully for centuries, Borough suffered very significant post war decline in both structural and physical terms and by the 1980s was virtually empty. As George Nicholson, former Head of Trustees at Borough Market, explained, customers preferred supermarkets

> "which brought their produce direct from producers, bypassing the wholesale markets. The physical structure was also decrepit and dangerous".

Henrietta Green's Food Lovers' Fair of 1998 is often cited as instrumental in rescuing the market from its moribund state, but other economic and design actions have also been central to its revival. For instance, an unusual route was taken by the market's trustees to kick-start a market regeneration process in the mid 1990s, envisioning an alternative future for the market. Imaginative economic and architectural action to reach their goals marked their approach throughout the decade from 1995. They chose to launch an architectural competition to develop a retail market within the physical structure of the market rather than demolishing it, and awarded the contract to a firm that had recently refurbished Leeds Market. The then Head of Trustees, George Nicholson (2006), explained that the trustees

> "utilised our own unused premises exterior to the core market for new wholesale uses - such as Neal's Yard, something that started in 1996. Previously these had been let to a series of failed wine bars".

The trustees thus helped bring in wholesale food business tenants in the first instance and this led to interest in retail sales as well:

> "Neal's Yard Diary did come in for a cheese storage place. Straight away people starting knocking on their door to buy cheese" (ibid).

The trustees decided to apply for Single Regeneration Budget (SRB) funds to help pay for regenerating the market structures. George Nicholson explained that the application for SRB by the trustees was made in 1996, following a number of unsuccessful previous attempts in conjunction with

Southwark Council. Borough was badged by the trustees as 'London's Larder', the traditional name for nearby Hay's Wharf, which had been historically a centre for London's food imports. £2.5 million was obtained from Single Regeneration Budget funds to refurbish property and pay architectural fees. The trustees had to be creative and take risks in order to pursue their regeneration ambitions for the market, as there were difficult economic issues to wrestle with. One obvious issue was that Borough lay in a cul-de-sac in the river and was not seen as a viable place to set up a retail business. As George Nicholson (2006) commented about the revitalisation strategy:

> *"But if you started a core business (i.e. wholesaling cheese) then you could float the retail off the back of it. The next firm to arrive was Konditor and Cook who just wanted to start a bakery. The Trustees told them they had to also have a patisserie. Next was Fish! who used English Heritage money and their own money to develop their restaurant site...The Trustees discounted the rent".*

As well as the November 1998 food festival involving the food campaigner Henrietta Green (Food Lovers Britain, n.d.), companies like Neal's Yard Dairy started having warehouse sales with invitations sent out through their mail order catalogues. George Nicholson pointed out that the market developed not just as a farmer's market with produce from a narrow geographical catchment; but always had two strands, which supported both food producers in the UK and high quality produce from Europe. Some of the producers invited by Henrietta Green were still trading at Borough at the time that research work was carried out. Meanwhile, over that time the trading interval shortened as the market grew more successful, from quarterly warehouse sales, through monthly to weekly and twice weekly sales. George Nicholson (2006) commented:

> *"Now there are 130 businesses in and around the market. There was also attention to high food quality from the start: "The first thing was to set up a food company to police the quality of what was coming in".*

Alongside these economic regeneration efforts, something had to be done to rebuild the market's physical structures, which were falling apart. As George Nicholson (2006) explained, the trustees *"started thinking about refurbishing, with the architects"*. To do this, substantially more money was needed than trustees had through their Single Regeneration Budget funding and they hoped to obtain a Heritage Lottery grant. Although they were unable to secure enough funds through public sources, the trustees *"were able to sell a couple of warehouses and used the profits to think about more grandly refurbishing the whole of the market"* (ibid). Additionally, in this regeneration effort, the trustees wanted to recycle architectural structures such as the Floral Hall that had been used at the defunct Covent Garden market, which they bought for £1. At the core of the strategy was an intertwining of architectural elements, economic regeneration, and development of a thriving market space and culture. The trustees took note of the experience of developing nearby Coin Street as a mixed-use area, where land uses giving high returns funded social housing. They were able to *"think about constructing a two-level building with market space underneath, and a restaurant on top a la Coin Street. That scheme slowly evolved."* Funding remained a complex area. While the trustees managed to obtain funds from the Single Regeneration Budget, the sale of buildings, and from English Heritage; joint bids with potential funding partners such as the local authority were less successful.

One of the most difficult issues faced in the regeneration effort was in dealing with planned significant changes to the railway infrastructure on site. At the stage when the trustees were planning the regeneration programme, Thameslink informed them that it intended to build a rail line through the market. As a result the trustees decided to split the refurbishment programme into two physical spaces either side of the rail corridor. Thameslink then failed to obtain planning permission for their proposed work, so the trustees were able to fast-forward phase two of their regeneration plans, which was the renewal of the west side of the market. As each section was refurbished, the wholesale market was decanted to other parts of the Halls. The trustees had to tender on the project while the market was growing so *"it was a bit uncertain in design terms"* and George Nicholson commented on the infrastructure related difficulties in the process.

Borough Market experts interviewed made direct links between the economic revitalisation of the market and the details of the design of the market spaces. This relationship had a number of dimensions. For instance, with a market site of about five acres, the process was one in which the trustees both refurbished old structures and created new spaces, with the internal configuration of the market stands as one of the market's design peculiarities. Borough was unusual in that it was able to start from scratch, and, as George Nicholson commented, they could *"kind of make it up as it went along",* devising a spatial model and space structure:

> *"The stand structure of the wholesale market is used for retail. That is quite unlike any normal retail market. You go into each section, not trade out of stands from the centre".*

In spatial terms it was acknowledged that there were possibly economic implications from this design arrangement as it was not very space efficient, but the stand system did allow a unique interplay between interior and urban design, and economic vitality. An architectural expert on the market also reinforced this point:

> *"it allows people to walk in off the street to a store like environment. That's really essential. You don't want to be in the full glare of everybody else".*

The configuration of individual retail elements was deliberate and subtle, with fine-grained attention to the economic and social implications of design. The designers

> *"had a conversation about whether we would have all the butchers together. We sort of did, sort of didn't. None of them front onto each other. If they had all been facing each other the decision comes down to price. There would also be social pressure to buy from the same person all the time. The system of stands offers that choice very well".*

Another facet of the market's relationship between economics and design was the sense expressed by expert interviewees that it was being *"returned to its former glory"* or *"returning to its former grandeur"* as a wholesale and retail space. The architectural expert on the market noted this grand quality in the space, having always been

> *"quite awestruck about market halls, shopping arcades, department stores. They have always been the cathedrals of shopping. The architectural typology of Borough Market is reminiscent of railway station architecture".*

A market trader echoed this view, saying

> *"the ambience of the place is probably one of the key factors...there has probably been a market of some description on this site since the Romans so you are talking nearly 2,000 years of some form of market here".*

The architectural expert similarly made the urban design point that the market's economic sustainability had been in part a function of its urban location in relation to food importing and distribution:

> *"London's Larder – the Pool of London used to be where all food imports came in. It's a most interesting place. Possibly the oldest cross street was London Bridge. A reason why Borough Market is successful/sustainable is where it is. It is one of the best-connected spots in London".*

At the same time, this architectural expert did not think that a strategic interconnection between architectural design and economic issues was at the forefront of all the trustees' thinking when the revival of the market was first being contemplated. This expert described the stance of the trustees as being more about

> *"employment and sustaining the place as a market. Some more enlightened members of the Trust were interested in the heritage of the market. It used to be much grander. [Economic] sustainability was seen as more to do about having always been a market and being on a connectivity hot spot. And a very gritty south London space."*

Individual food businesses grew and thrived economically alongside the market's overall regeneration. This diversification trajectory occurred at an increasing rate, and also took an increasing number of forms, including retailing, wholesaling, restaurant supply, café and restaurant development to showcase products, and food education and training. The Spanish food products firm, Brindisa, for example, began as a wholesaling business that had a retail outlet at the market and eventually opened a very successful tapas bar on a key corner site. The market's redevelopment offered a number of examples of a growth trajectory from wholesale to encompass retail, including most famously Neal's Yard Dairy which had a bustling retail presence at the front of the house it occupied but what was described by George Nicholson as *"a massive business behind this."*

Examples of retail growth were also evident from interviews with traders, and included the example of a trader in Italian products who had started seven years previously at Borough with one stall and by the time of the research had four stalls in the market, covering a range of traditional regional products from Italy. An illustration of a different kind of growth and diversification, into food education and skills development among consumers, was provided by a butcher trading at the market who did

> *"sausage making courses and it's got round to now people will pay as much money to know about a product and see how its made...You can almost make as much money out of your knowledge (laughs) as the product which is quite an interesting fact".*

When talking about the way their businesses had grown, traders mentioned willingness among consumers to learn more about food quality and improve their food buying and cooking skills. Traders also pointed to an increasing consumer focus on understanding more about primary production, sustainable supply chains and product antecedents as part of thinking about what quality meant to them. At the time primary research was undertaken, the growth trajectory was described as not just at the level of individual food traders but a conscious whole market development and management strategy. To build on its economic revitalisation, the trustees developed links with other outstanding markets, twinning with the famous La Boqueria market in Barcelona. The emphasis was always on quality rather than trading down. In fact, interviewees considered one of the keys to the success of the process of economic regeneration so far lay in the structure of the management and governance of the market. Yet this structure appeared to have been largely an unintended consequence of a pre-existing trustee governance model combined with the particular skills of its leadership at a critical juncture.

George Nicholson explained that gaining official charitable status in recent years had a direct link to the market's capacity to economically support small businesses, by, among other actions, keeping rents down so that the local, traditionally working class, population could afford to trade in and buy from the market. The low rents might be expected to be reflected in more affordable prices, but this interviewee challenged the assumption that the market and area were essentially only for middle class consumers because of high food prices. He argued instead that

> "The area's land uses are industrial and commercial with some public housing (Charitable Trusts such as Peabody, Guinness Trust) and traditionally working class. It is not true that working class people don't come to the market".

The rents issue remained an important one though for any researcher. As one trader interviewed argued, rents could go up, with in his view disastrous consequence. He suggested that the market's trustees must continue to support the traders who were the *"people who make the market"*. The architectural expert meanwhile pointed out that the trustees were, uniquely, not driven to make the maximum financial return and so were able to support the sustainable growth of the food market. The architectural expert also argued the connected but more general point that markets were still wrongly seen by local governments as marginal land uses, rather than as a springboard for regeneration. He thought that local governments did not necessarily take a very enlightened view about the best use of their funds in relation to managing markets, tending to favour revenue maximisation over allowing market trustees to build up reserves to run the organisation. This apparent lack of economic foresight linked back to the governance issues raised earlier in the chapter. Borough Market's response was at this stage to try to maintain its independence from local government control by appointing its own trustees. At issue was the trustees' apparently greater capacity than local governments' to maintain a focus on their key objectives for the market. As George Nicholson noted, the trustees

> "have been focused and stuck to it: food - market - quality. Now [trustees] are getting asked to talk to other markets. If you look at what's happened with markets there is only one local authority left that has a markets committee. Markets are a kind of leftover category".

Interviewees argued that the economic benefits of Borough Market's regeneration also extended in the direction of the food producers who provided products for the market. One example was the increasing popularity of the market for producers and traders, with a waiting list for stalls. Attracting a balanced mix of products was a deliberate strategy, as was the specialist food product base. Selling at Borough Market allowed producers to raise their prices to a level that made their production methods sustainable. Referring to the example of a particular meat producer from the north of England, George Nicholson explained, a market butcher

> "managed to persuade six farmers to sell these [lambs with particular geographical provenance]. Their lambs fetched £15 a head. [He] now has 40 to 50 farmers who are making £50 per head. That has a big impact on the Cumbrian economy".

The architectural expert also argued for acknowledgement of a beneficial economic link outward to the community and back to primary producers. This perspective reflected the food chain discussion in Chapter 1 and connected to issues of class, which are relevant to the way resurgent markets like Borough are viewed. A view put by the architectural expert reinforced this point:

> "Historically, good food used to be about all the classes...I resent that whole thing about Borough Market being for rich people. It's not just about people who shop there but people who trade there, who have started business, helped farmers. The town and country always relied on each other. The resurgence of the fresh food market puts wealth back into the rural enterprise, which for a long time drained away through the supermarkets' horrific buying practices. I tend to think we underestimate working class people [about food]".

Issues in relation to class were also apparent in the trustees' conscious focus on the social inclusion of the local population, through rate relief and plans for a food school, among other actions. Interviewee comments suggested that the trustees intended to build on the economic success of the market in future by extending its hours and its range of food services, as well as by reinforcing good management, education and employment related to food. George Nicholson noted that there were around 10-15,000 people visiting Borough Market each Saturday, and an intention to increase the market's reach to Thursdays through special events. From a very tentative start in the mid 1990s the market was now thriving, as a well-managed place celebrated for high quality produce. A market trader summed up that the critical thing for the market in economic terms was the relationship between traders and trustees, which amounted to a kind of informal but mutually rewarding economic partnership:

> "A fairly good relationship with the people that own the market...It's not just a landlord and tenant, whatever. Because everybody fully realises that we are interdependent on each other".

Although views varied between interviewees, a criticism levelled at Borough Market by some was that it was very expensive compared with supermarkets and other more traditional markets. Conversely, one trader suggested that it was high prices allied to high quality that made the market financially viable. Londoners' perceived higher disposable incomes and interest in cooking for dinner parties were thought to be key factors. Another trader argued that higher prices were justified on quality and environmental grounds. This trader thought that artisan products rightly attracted a premium price because of their greater sustainability – a point considered further in the next section:

> "We obviously talk to people, lots of people, one of the biggest complaints you will get about this market is price. Well it's not expensive if you hunt around, but then again, we have been brainwashed into the fact that the cheap supermarket price is the real price of food and it isn't. I'm not saying this is the real price of food but it's far closer".

For some interviewees, the prices issue related to another which was the food market's increasing popularity with tourists who may prefer to simply look than buy. A market butcher pointed out that this had an adverse impact on his stall's trade, although this may be mitigated by mail order sales. Another trader agreed that over a period of time the issue of low-spending tourists had worsened, and tourists were blocking access to stalls for the 'real' buyers:

> "They can't get to the stand because there's too many tourists looking around saying "I'll try this and I'll try that. Oh! Lovely market". They've got short arms and long pockets".

But this was by no means a universal view. A trader in Italian products argued

> "tourists find a lot of things they can't find in their own country. So also tourists are buyers sometimes. They bring back home something particular they found at Borough Market that they couldn't find at home".

One food trader interviewed explained that the market had built up the Borough area

> "without a doubt. All these wine bars and restaurants would never ever, ever be here if it wasn't for the market because they wouldn't put their money where there's no-one here. Now they come here on a Friday and a Saturday and it is heaving and they can see there's potential there".

The architectural expert also noted developers' changing attitudes to markets over the last forty years and the recent recognition of food markets capacity to attract people and regenerate areas through good food:

> "In the 1970s and 1980s developers saw markets as a pain in the arse, a nuisance. They have come gradually to see them as anchors. Now they can see the potential for farmers markets. They don't want markets to be 'down market' but about fresh food. They are a seriously good people drawer".

This view appeared to be borne out by a related consequence of food-based success; that property developers as well as food businesses and their visitors were attracted to the wider area of the food quarter. As noted earlier, the 'London Bridge Quarter' luxury office, hotel and apartment tower development, marketed as "The Shard', was proposed at the time of the research (and was under construction at the time of publication). Its promotional material made reference to Borough Market as a local attraction that added to the area's ambience for the building's potential tenants.

The narrative of fresh food markets, increasingly perceived as local development anchors, connected to the sense that such food places exhibit more authenticity than many high streets, where the conventional assumptions of development economics have led to the creation of a "clone town Britain" range of identical chain shops (Conisbee et al, 2004). As discussed in Chapter 2, authenticity centred on good food can be sold as part of an area's attractiveness for new development and add to development profit. An interviewee (Italian-Australian, in his 30s) commented on this from a place-users' perspective. He cited Brindisa, the Spanish food stall and tapas bar, as an example, saying it might now be considered *"chain-ish"* because it had developed two different outlets (at Borough, and at the time the research was undertaken at Exmouth Market). At the same time, he said,

> "I think there is an appeal because it doesn't feel like another part of London. Coz if you go to any high street you know there's Starbucks, whatever. I think that's a definite appeal about going there".

Exploring Borough's growing role as an alternative food space

Borough's experience reflects the food quarter's occupation of a complex place in the food system. On the one hand the market's regeneration has contributed to sustainability through improved food quality, a focus on provenance, and support for consumer education. At the same time its renewal could be read as giving spatial expression to the contested notion that good food is simply a middle class preoccupation and therefore elitist. Variations on these intertwined themes were found in views expressed by shoppers, traders and experts. An expert in Borough's architecture, for example, argued that places like Borough have emerged in part as more environmentally conscious, educated alternatives to supermarkets. With higher incomes and more consumption choices, supermarket shopping was being challenged and modified by places like Borough. This architect suggested that consumers were *"fed up"* with supermarket food shopping and wanted to

> "find out more about fresh food, enjoy real expertise from sellers. People don't mind spending more time and money. They have a more in-depth understanding of eating...For fresh food we will go to local delis, greengrocers and be quite seasonal. That is how we used to shop".

The architect pointed out that this did not mean people had abandoned supermarkets altogether, but mixed and matched their shopping arrangements, a trend likely to increase in future, in which *"supermarkets are likely to become the centres for distribution of boxed up commodities"*.

This interviewee also felt that food scares had sharpened the interest of Londoners in understanding more about where their food came from and how it was produced. This, in turn, had increased interest in fresh food markets like Borough. Some food traders and shoppers interviewed likewise described Borough Market as a place that focused on getting people back in touch with food. They saw this as at the heart of the market's operations. George Nicholson noted that various stalls had been *"kicked out"* because their produce was not up to standard. A food trader explained:

> *"Well, the whole concept of it is people regain an interest in what they are eating...They can actually talk to people that grow, farm, whatever, instead of being constantly brainwashed by supermarkets into 'you must have this shaped apple'".*

Another trader said in a similar vein that stallholders' product knowledge was critical:

> *"They know where everything comes from and they are quite happy to sit down and talk to people about the food because they passionately love the food and they are proud of what they do".*

A middle-aged, male Viennese tourist seemed to reinforce the point that food freshness, clarity about origins and choice were important to visitors. This interviewee made a link between these food qualities and the social aspects of the market (which are further discussed in the next section):

> *"Well um I think you get a good choice of food. And it's fresh food. You can feel like the origin of where it comes from. And I think that is why I prefer markets to supermarkets. It's not so anonymous. It's got a nice feeling. And seeing all the foods and the fish – it's nice".*

Another market user, a young man in his 20s, who lived locally, also observed the high quality of food available, and argued: *"It's cheaper than the supermarkets. Meat is more expensive but it's justified because of the quality"*. This interviewee made a link to an interest in good food:

> *"I feel very passionate about food. The more people who come here the better. All the people here, farmers, fishermen. I hope they get as many customers as they can get".*

Relationships between different parts of the food chain were considered to be both shorter and more transparent at Borough Market than they were in supermarket-based consumption. A food trader (of meat products), for example, explained his business's direct connections to the farmer who supplied his sausages, to other stalls that sold the raw products, and to the people eating them when cooked. He made the point that these products were unobtainable through the mass food market. At the same time, the distance food travelled to get to the market was of some concern. Another trader (in organics) argued that lower food miles were not by themselves necessarily a mark of better environmental practice. He wanted to support producers of organic food wherever they were, and while he did not use airfreight, he did import *"quite a bit"* that was not produced in the United Kingdom. This interviewee said that refusing to import produce would have a deleterious effect on growers in poor countries:

> *"I don't think we have the moral high ground to say because of food miles we won't take your stuff. Not only that but we've exploited these people for the last 300 years and now we are going to turn round and say 'actually we're not going to have your pineapples'".*

This food trader felt that there was still considerable education needed among consumers about food quality and environmental values. He related this to the dominant food culture, which stressed convenience rather than daily shopping for food in season. Another trader, who sold Italian products, agreed about the importance of clarity about product origin, and explained that his staff tried to educate their customers' food sensibilities. One trader contrasted the UK situation with everyday food practices in Europe, where a more highly developed culture of food was believed to exist; and there were *"people who actually go every day and shop at markets"*. The Italian-Australian shopper quoted earlier reinforced the point that, compared with cities on the Continent, where many people shop at markets daily, a space like Borough was an unusual food environment in the UK. La Boqueria market in Barcelona was invoked as a benchmark of quality (this is the famous market that is 'twinned' with Borough). Class and spatial catchment issues were raised by this shopper; but this time in relation to degrees of familiarity with this kind of consumption:

> *"Whether it's a tapas type restaurant selling great seafood, or whatever it might be, or La Boqueria market, dotted around certain parts of Barcelona. There is a dispersed quality whereas London really doesn't have it, so people will just go to where it is and it tends to be the middle class that have been exposed to it. They've travelled".*

Despite the view outlined above, some traders saw Borough Market food buyers as often more environmentally conscious (or at least interested) than shoppers in the main. A butcher trading at the market noted a symbiotic relationship between sellers of high quality, niche products, and buyers whose knowledge and concern transcended income, or, by implication, their class position or cultural background. The butcher felt that producers came first, providing high quality products, but then

> "You look at some people and they must have spent every penny they have, disposable income, on a lovely joint of pork or wild boar. So I suppose what come first was the producers with their niche products and because of that the 'foodies' if you like to call them that have followed along. I think that's the greatest thing about the market".

This trader suggested that people who came to Borough Market wanted to know about various sustainability aspects of the food they were buying. They showed interest in all facets of the food chain: product provenance, transparency about production methods, food miles, and concern about geographical origin. It was less clear whether this interest arose out of a broad concern with the sustainability implications of food, food ethics, personal health, or a combination of each. The butcher continued:

> "There are a lot of people who are concerned about what they eat and I suppose through ages we've always had that so it's not down to their disposable income".

Again, this concern for food quality was seen as linking to the preparedness of Borough Market customers to pay higher prices. Speaking about the meat he sold, the butcher made connections between greater scrutiny of the production process and preparedness to pay more:

> "Its feeding, its welfare, all the way through the food chain. The slaughtering, the whole process has very much come under scrutiny - which is good...So now it's very much the real artisan producers are at a premium".

The Italian products trader also made the connection back through the food chain to artisans, who produced food in environmentally sustainable ways. He counterpointed the strengths of traditional artisanal forms of production with the lack of quality in industrial production methods, and stressed the importance of seasonality. He explained that the relationships to small, traditional producers were very direct, with sourcing trips undertaken every few weeks:

"Yes, let's say that one of our main concerns is to keep a high quality standard. That's because basically we are passionate about what we are doing. We don't like to sell industrial food. We only like to sell, only sell artisanal food or food made, formed in the traditional way of making cheeses or curing meat".

Knowledgeability among Borough Market habitués was contrasted with a sense that many people had lost connection to food as a central part of everyday life. A food trader in organic products said this might be because people lived *"in such a busy, hectic society we don't actually have time to do anything"*. He suggested that dinner was now something people did *"in between doing something else"*. Another trader argued that people were trapped by overworked lives into a cycle of eating ready meals rather than buying from markets and cooking from scratch:

"There are a lot of people who enjoy good food but maybe because of their lifestyle and the way they work.. a lot of them guys back tonight – nine o'clock, ten o'clock before they get home - and girls - so to go into Marks and Spencer's at Liverpool Street and get one of these ready meals and that's the best they can do".

In this trader's view, places like Borough Market needed to find ways to provide good quality, environmentally sensitive food alternatives, which recognised the lifestyle constraints of long working hours and declining cooking skills among their potential customers. He studied the ready meals that supermarkets were supplying with a view to matching this convenience in his business's own products:

"I said to [assistant butcher] let's go over there and have a look at their chicken Kievs and their porks this...What could we do so people can think 'Ah that would be easy to cook when we get home?' You know, so that's what we've got. So we stuffed some pork chops, we made wild boar sausages, we made some schnitzels and we're trying to create some almost meal-ready things. But how far do we go?"

This trader expanded these points by suggesting the loss of cooking skills reflected changing family patterns, with people *'in transit'* and consequent increases in the need for external education in life skills including cooking. Again comparisons to European experience seemed pertinent to interviewees:

"We have lost that family orientation, where on the Continent you've still got three generations of the family living in the same house type of thing. We don't eat together. We are probably not living with the family, the grandparents. There's probably the old Nanna who had the time to teach

kids to cook etc. I know I learned a lot of cooking from my granddad. And that's been lost. So everything's been in that spiral, you know, the quality of food's gone, schools don't have the cooking we had, the home economics whatever you want to call it, these days".

However this interviewee felt that such skills may be re-emerging as a result of increasing food consciousness and through education, despite 'hectic lifestyles'.

"Hopefully it's all coming back to education. We want to educate people about where the food is from. How you cook it, what do you do with it, you know, it is so easy".

Considering Borough as a uniquely designed social setting for food

The market's physical location and connectivity was seen to be an important backdrop to the social practices and relationships it fostered. The area's very particular sense of place, *"its offbeat flavour"*, was felt by the architectural expert on the market to be an important context for social use of the space:

"In their time, shopping arcades and market halls were the spectacles of their time. They were more architecturally sensational. The more services on top of the fresh food the better".

Various other interviewees reinforced the point about sense of place, character and design quality. The Viennese visitor previously quoted connected this to the market's traditional structures: *"Yes this old structure gives the good touch and a really modern structure wouldn't fit to the spirit of the market I think"*. A food trader meanwhile argued for the interplay of character and design:

"the design is the character. I think English Heritage say stop knocking these buildings down because the character of these buildings is unique".

Just as ambience was previously connected to economic success, the Italian-Australian London resident agreed with others interviewed about the contribution of design and said that:

"there is a series of spaces. There is a sense of enclosure associated with it. I wouldn't say it's entirely the physical environment, but that's a factor".

This interviewee spoke about Borough Market's atmosphere or ambience, and the way this reflected its success as a social space. He also directly linked the atmosphere of the place, in particular the profusion of social interaction, and the quality of the food available there:

> "The space - Borough Market if it's crowded - there is an ambience. It is a place to socialise...Well I think what I like is the quality of what's available in the market and it's relatively central. And it does have a lot of activity in terms of being well used. So there is a certain atmosphere associated with going to the market".

Similarly, the architectural expert on the market made an explicit connection between the design quality of the spaces that emphasised the sensuality of food, and the quality of the social relationship between buyer and seller:

> "It's also about the spaces you are in. You walk into this shop environment, which is quite sensual. You see things in their raw state. There is the relationship at the counter. That is Borough Market".

A food trader interviewed agreed:

> "Although we sell very good food here, very good, top quality food. It's not dressed like Harrods Food Hall. Its quirky, its odd. It has that old London feel about it. It just has a sense of history".

The architectural expert on the market cited expertise and intimacy at the point of sale as being important both socially and environmentally, and qualities that reflected changing consumption arrangements. This kind of retailing space and process could also be read, as the Italian Australian did, as appealing socially to well-travelled, middle class people who liked to socialise in a place that had a particular 'hype' and offered unique products: *"there is a certain crowd that's going"*. Despite the view that Borough attracted 'a certain crowd', the architectural expert strongly argued that Borough's social appeal transcended class. Another food trader also stressed the fact that Borough Market was a social space that was about all sorts of people getting connected:

> "It's become one of the social meeting places as well. You hear people talking to their friends on the phone: 'We'll meet you at so and so'. A lot of people will spend virtually all day here. They'll wander off to Southbank or whatever; people have lunch...I don't think it's just about selling produce.

I think it's also about people being involved in a place they can come to and have a fairly decent, enjoyable experience".

Borough's rich social functioning reflected just how wide the catchment for the market had become, and what kind of people were attracted to visit it for social reasons. One stallholder interviewed did not think the catchment was solely a local one. He said that people came from both London and other parts of the UK but also worldwide. *"If you come to London come to Borough Market – it's an exclusive food market".* Other interviewees made connections between the social use of the space and how much of that involved tourism. A middle aged Viennese tourist explained that

"I just arrived today from Vienna and just taking a look around. Bumped into here. I didn't know anything about the market and so I was interested and it's quite nice".

An American, male, London resident in his late 30s said *"I think this is probably one of the best things about this city - and a lot of tourists don't know to come here".* Meanwhile, from a food trader's perspective, it was thought that people came from

"all over the place. I mean we are now so firmly entrenched on the tourist circuit. People who come to London, um, from all over the country if they are in London for a weekend, if they have an interest in food, they come to Borough Market".

Those interviewed pointed to a large range of socio-spatial practices evident at the food quarter, but gave most prominence to methods of buying produce and various ways of eating in and around the market spaces. For instance, one food trader described a typical buying pattern that covered both local visitors and tourists:

"You know, I will benefit because whoever comes in the market will have a sandwich and a cup of coffee or whatever. They will always have something. It doesn't matter if it's a tourist or not. They won't buy a load of meat and a load of vegetables and take it back to the hotel. You wouldn't do it if you're on holiday".

As the architectural expert pointed out, the market area also provided more formal dining opportunities for Londoners. Business people could come to Borough, as an atmospheric place close to the City of London, and eat in up-market style yet surrounded by gritty market spaces. The counterpointing of luxury and disrepair was one aspect of the market's charm:

> *"When Fish! opened up – you could walk for eight minutes from the Bank of England and have lunch right next to the most decrepit bit of the wholesale market".*

Some interviewees set all these 'extraneous' practices of visitors against the needs of 'real' shoppers, and these patterns clearly had timing implications for the way the market space was being used. The dominant perception of both traders and market users interviewed was that serious shoppers, the "real customers", increasingly came to the market earlier in the day and earlier in the week in order to avoid the tourist crowds. In response to a question about how busy the market appeared to be on Saturdays, one food trader said that: *"it's like everything; the success side to things has brought its own problems"*. Another stallholder concurred about timing for regular customers:

> *"I have to say most of our regular customers, as far as I'm concerned, know when to come. Yeah, like first thing Saturday morning: 'shop there, shop there, shop there'. Certainly before 10."*

A similar comment came from the Italian-Australian shopper, in relation to dealing with large numbers of tourists:

> *"I think it is more of a tourist place. If you want to go there and do shopping it's very difficult because there are long queues. It's very hard to move around. So it's not an efficient place for shopping. I think it's becoming more of a social place. There's nothing wrong with that but I suppose ultimately it may detract from shopping there".*

Food mapping and counting

Food mapping was undertaken as part of research into the Borough Market quarter to help give spatial context to perceptions about social use of the market and surrounding spaces. The mapping recorded the kinds of land uses given over to food in June 2008, and although not claimed to be an exhaustive record, it provided part of the spatial design information about the way that these spaces were being used at that point. The food spaces were named and numbered in a key (Figure 4.1) and shown in a food map (Figure 4.2).

Borough Food Map Key

1. Fish and chip shop
2. Budgen's Express
3. Newsagent/fast food
4. Jade 'caf'
5. The Globe pub
6. Mercats de Barcelona (Boqueria)
7. Gastronomica Piedmont
8. Patisserie Lila
9. "Paella" truck
10. Hobbs roast meat
11. Café (empty)
12. Londis Off License
13. London Bridge Tandoori
14. De Gustibus (bread/café)
15. Silka Restaurant (downstairs)
16. King's Head pub
17. Ristorante Italiano
18. Messr C. Caf
19. Café Rossi
20. Orient Express Café-Rest
21. Lemay Hop Factors Building
22. Entrance to George Inn
23. Slug and Lettuce bar
24. City Tandoori
25. Harper's caf
26. The Hop Cellars
27. The Hop Exchange
28. The Hop Rooms
29. The Southwark Tavern
30. Brindisa Restaurant
31. Elsey and Bent Fruiterers
32. Formaggi Vino
33. Wyndham House butcher
34. Applebee's Fish
35. The Wheatsheaf pub
36. Bangers and Mash café
37. The Market Porter pub
38. German Deli
39. Little Dorrit Tea Rooms
40. Paul Smith
41. Neal's Yard Dairy shop/wholesale
42. Shipp's Tea Room
43. Monmouth coffee shop/café
44. Konditor & Cook Patisserie/café
45. Wright Bros Oyster Bar
46. Vinopolis
47. Black & Blue Restaurant
48. L. Booth Fruiterers
49. Brindisa
50. Charcuterer - The Ginger Pig
51. Borough Cheese Co
52. Olive oil stall
53. Biscuit and cake stall
54. Farmer Sharp Herdwick Butchers'
55. Flour Power Bread
56. Italian cheese stall
57. Wright Bros Oyster Stand
58. Flower Stand
59. Le Marche du Quartier
60. Borough Wines
61. Utobeer
62. Cartright Bros
63. Mrs King's Pies
64. Silifield Farm
65. Roast stall/restaurant above
66. Spanish cooking demonstration
67. Only Organics
68. Mana's Market Café
69. Cranberry (dried fruit/nuts)
70. Ceylon Organic Tea Shop
71. The Fresh Oil Co
72. Ion Patisserie
73. Mozzarella/Prosciutto Stall
74. Gamston Wood Ostriches
75. Monmouth Coffee Stall
76. Chegworth Valley Apples
77. Borough Market Hessian Bags
78. Food plates
79. De Gustibus bread
80. The Flour Station Bread
81. La Tua Pasta
82. Pieminster
83. Argentine Folklore
84. Loch Glen Salmon
85. The Fresh Pasta Co
86. The Veggie Table
87. Pecorino Sardo
88. Sharpham Park (empty)
89. Specialities from Italian Monks
90. Boston Sausage
91. Orkney Rose seafood
92. Mons Fromagier
93. Dark Sugar Chocolate
94. Wyndham House Poultry
95. Burnt Sugar sweets
96. Gastronimica
97. Baxters
98. West Country Venison
99. Furness Fish Markets
100. Turnips
101. Organic Juice Bar
102. Total organics
103. Superfood
104. Shellseekers
105. Northfield Farm
106. Proper Fish and Chips
107. Fishworks restaurant
108. Greens Café
109. Café Brood
110. A. Sugarman Fruit & Veg
111. La Cave
112. Barrow Boy & Banker Pub
113. Malaysian Restaurant
114. All Bar One
115. Polish Deli
116. Burger Van
117. Italian Restaurant
118. Caf

Figure 4.1: *Key to Borough Market Food Uses Map* Source: Prepared by author

138   Chapter Four

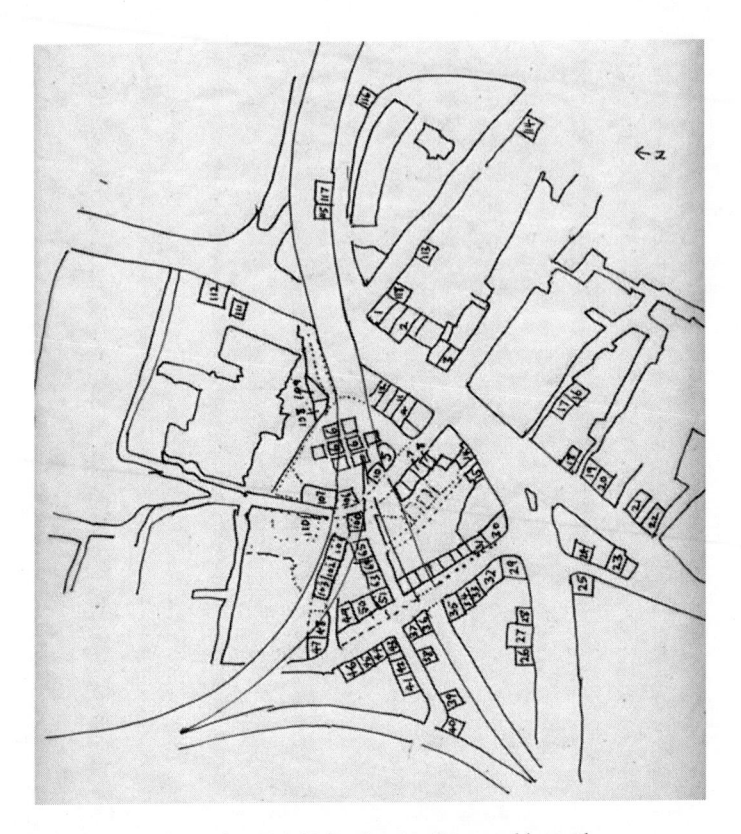

Figure 4.2.: *Borough Market Food Map* Source: Prepared by author

A subsidiary cluster map (Figure 4.3) shows a detail of the market space bounded by Bedale Street, Borough High Street, Stoney Street, and an internal market path, where a particularly large number of food-related uses were found. The map demonstrates some clustering of similar kinds of food and drink uses, such as wine and beer stalls, and an overall cluster of various kinds of fresh foods. On the day that the map was drawn up, the market was hosting a special display of food and drink products from La Boqueria and its produce region around Barcelona. A space normally at that time given over to a mix of fresh fruit and vegetable stalls and charcuterie and cheese (under the railway viaduct) was on this day filled with Spanish food stalls.

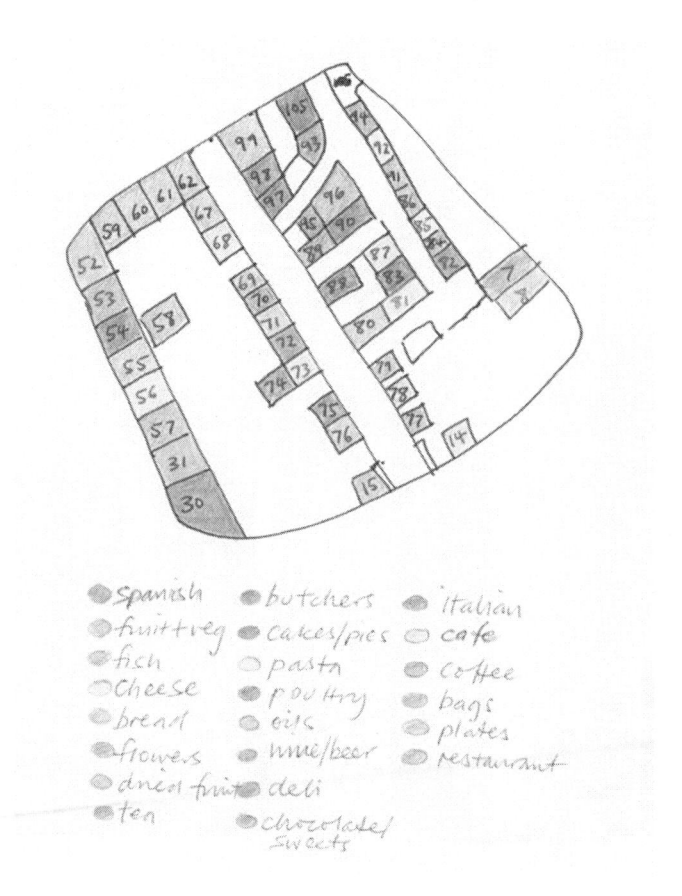

Figure 4.3: *Borough Market Food Cluster Map* Source: Prepared by author

As can be seen from Figure 4.1, 118 food and drink uses were counted in the vicinity of the food market. This compared with the number noted in a contemporaneous publication by the Market, which listed 141 food and drink outlets, caterers and wholesalers of various kinds in a slightly wider area (Market Life, Spring 2008). The key shows their diversity and also that there was a focus on artisanal, organic and specialist food and drink, covering products predominantly from the United Kingdom and mainland Europe. Stalls selling bread, cheese, meat products, fish, vegetables, juices, preserves, confectionary, olive oil and alcohol were particularly well represented, as were food products from the United Kingdom, Italy and Spain. In some cases, similar kinds of uses were grouped nearby, but not right next to each other, as in the case of the three or four fishmongers and oyster bars.

This reflected a retailing design strategy described earlier in the chapter by an architectural expert on the market. There was a loose concentration of butchers in one area, of vintners in another and of greengrocers in a third area, while along Stoney Street there were a considerable number of eating and drinking places, some with open frontages spilling out onto the pavement. Stalls were also sprinkled throughout where it was possible to buy fresh items to eat and drink at the market. A substantial proportion of the food-related uses were for prepared or partially prepared foods. Many had been established since the food market began to revive, but some, especially those along Borough High Street, were longer-term food places that had weathered Borough's decline and enjoyed renewed popularity during its resurgence.

A number of 'head count' observations were made during research into the food quarter, as another way to document the range and type of socio-spatial practices in evidence at and around Borough Market. These were undertaken over the period of 6th to 8th of September 2007 and they generally reinforced and sometimes extended points made by interviewees about the range of practices they could see at Borough. They were also consistent with the configuration of food-related land-uses noted in the food mapping. The head counts illuminated the nature of socio-spatial practices in a variety of ways: in terms of their scale; the balance between them; how that balance shifted over the days and hours of the market's operations; variations observed within similar practices; and any indications that the design of the physical space had impacts on these practices. The head counts were carried out from the same central vantage point at a similar late-morning to lunchtime period, for an hour each, on a Thursday, Friday and Saturday, when the market was operating normally.

The counts tended to confirm interviewees' perceptions that the market became busiest on Saturdays. Overall, over an hour 1019 people were counted on Thursday, 1214 on Friday and 1988 on Saturday. The view that Saturday was so busy that it could be hard for 'real' shoppers to get to stalls, appeared to be supported by the informal observations undertaken alongside the head counts, and was further reinforced by a large number of other informal observational visits. Interviewees also said that 'real' shoppers were coming to the market earlier in the day and earlier in the week to avoid the mass of tourist visitors. The head counts gave some support to this view. For the purposes of the head count, people seen at the market with large food shopping bags or baskets (some also seen browsing at stalls with such bags) were defined as providing a proxy measure for those shopping for food to take home and cook. On Thursday there were 71 such individuals, on Friday there were 57, and on Saturday (the market's busiest day overall) 189 were counted. The number of 'real' shoppers was therefore higher on Thursday rather than the overall busier Friday, but rose again on Saturday, when the market generally was around twice as busy as it was on Thursday.

Interviewees pointed out that, within its three weekly days of operation, the market attracted the most tourists on Saturdays. The head counts strongly confirmed this. As a proxy measure, the count covered those holding or using cameras and/or guidebooks as tourists, rather than individuals from a more local catchment. At the same time, it was not possible to define clearly to what extent the practice of browsing but not buying was in operation among a wider group that might be loosely defined as tourists. On Thursday the count covered eight guidebook or camera holding individuals, on Friday 63, and on Saturday 175. Again the interviewees' view appeared to be borne out by this data. On the Thursday a food book signing could be observed, with a long queue of people waiting to have their Jamie Oliver cookbook signed by the food writer (who was placed in a booth garlanded with flowers and surrounded by burly security guards). There were 100 people waiting for his signature. More generally, on two of the three days of head counts, there was a tiny number of people who could be observed reading: three on Thursday, one on Friday and none on Saturday. It was not possible to see if they were reading Jamie Oliver's book.

The head counts identified some practices not mentioned by interviewees but providing some information about the diversity of socio-spatial use of the food quarter. The most dominant in number terms was the practice of walking around and through the market, but not eating or drinking at the same time. On Thursday 566 people were counted walking alone or in company. On Friday the count included 615 people and on Saturday, 1079. Most people appeared to be walking alone, although there were small numbers of groups, of two and three people walking together, and fewer bigger groups of four people or more. From their demeanour and cameras, the largest groups generally appeared to be tourists, but these were included in the part of the head count documented earlier in this section.

The walkers' pattern shifted somewhat over the three days. On Thursday, in particular, there were more lone walkers, whereas on Friday, and especially Saturday, a substantial proportion of all walkers were observed to be in groups. The other main difference was the increase in scale, with similar numbers on Thursday and Friday and a big jump in numbers for Saturday's market. The inference drawn from this was that Friday and

Saturday constituted the more 'social' days of the market's operation; days on which more people visited and arranged to meet each other at the market. Thursday might be described as more predominantly, although obviously not entirely, the 'real' shoppers day.

Interviewees suggested that many people came to Borough Market for the food-centred ambience, and tended to have something to eat and drink while they were wandering around enjoying the atmosphere. A considerable number on each day were counted holding small food bags, carrying food or drinks, or actually eating or drinking. On Thursday there were 251, on Friday 245, and on Saturday 331. Relatively few people were found sitting or standing still on any of the three days, despite an expectation that there would be considerable numbers of stationery watchers and eaters, but most people seemed to be on the move, even when eating or drinking. This may have been simply to do with the lack of places to sit that could be seen from the observation point, whereas on the other side of the market, just to the north, a lawn connected to Southwark Cathedral was extremely crowded on fine weekday lunchtimes. There were very few benches or other seats in and around the side of the market where observations took place, except for those within or adjoining stands configured as cafes and food stalls. People were found perching where built structures allowed them to do so, at the edge of buildings and on kerbs.

Of individuals observed standing or sitting, a small proportion of whom were also eating, there were 37 on Thursday, 90 on Friday and 78 on Saturday. One conclusion drawn from this pattern was that, very broadly, Thursday was the 'serious' shoppers day. Friday was the day when more local office and other workers visited the market for lunch (many were wearing business clothes), as it was at the end of the working week. Saturday, by contrast was the busiest tourists' day, when most visitors walked around to view different parts of the market without necessarily buying anything.

The head counts documented very few areas of socio-spatial practice where there was any overt sense of conflict between different place users. One such area was the interplay between walkers and those driving through the quarter or making deliveries to the food market or related shops and other food businesses. The pattern was of increasing numbers of cars, vans and trucks observed over the three days, at the intersection of the minor Stoney Street and Park Street. In each case there were somewhat more vans and trucks than cars; the preponderance of such vehicles seemed to fit with the servicing requirements of the market. 58 cars, vans and trucks were counted on Thursday, 104 on Friday and 96 on Saturday.

It may be the somewhat lower number on Saturday reflected the greater volume of pedestrians and thus a decision to avoid delivery and other servicing visits at that time, as well as the need to deliver food for the Friday market trading hours. From the observation vantage point it could be seen that vans and trucks, in particular, often had difficulty navigating the narrow streets and avoiding the large number of pedestrians. There were a number of minor traffic jams, especially at the T-junction. This was less of a problem for scooter and motorcycle riders; four on Thursday, 20 on Friday and 17 on Saturday. It also did not appear to cause problems for the small number of cyclists; with 10 on Thursday, 17 on Friday and 13 on Saturday, when one cyclist was observed with an attached cart for carrying shopping.

Borough Market's transformation into a 'global' food quarter

This chapter has explored the nature of the Borough Market quarter as a food space, through interviews, observations, food mapping and head counts. Together these sources have provided primary research information about the economic context, environmental performance, and socio-spatial practices at the food quarter, and allowed some tentative conclusions to be drawn. Borough's story in the period up until 2008 was one of deep economic decline and equally dramatic regeneration on an area basis. Its outstanding success as a food quarter reflected the operation of more than a standard place-marketing strategy based on investors, shoppers and visitors being attracted to a new flagship tourist space. Borough did not become a bland food consumption space predicated on a suburban mall or clone town model, as the economic, environmental, design and socio-spatial practice findings in this chapter demonstrate.

At the time the research was undertaken, Borough attracted people because it was a complex, interesting and exciting mix of high quality food opportunities within a quirky, characterful setting with a strong sense of place and identity. At the same time the findings suggest that Borough was at a kind of tipping point in which success might generate a new set of problems, and since the book's main research phase was completed these trends have solidified into a substantial area of conflict typified by some as the battle for Borough's soul (This is London Co, n.d.).

At the time of the main research work though, the trustees of the food market at Borough had not only managed a difficult physical regeneration processes in an outstanding way; they had consciously undertaken various actions to avoid or mitigate any negative social and economic effects of success on an existing local population that had once been traditionally working class but was transforming as the area itself changed. The governance and leadership of the market's trustees in the period up to 2008 were an important element in Borough's food quarter development. To situate this more broadly, although many UK regeneration processes have been economically and politically top-down in nature, in this case management was much more bottom-up and locally based. Borough Market had been run along charitable lines for centuries, and over that time its trustees developed a great deal of social capital.

In the story of Borough's renewal, central and local government meanwhile appeared to be largely absent as effective regeneration partners, although they had been involved in earlier stages through, for example, regeneration funding bids. Through the formation of a Development Trust, the locally based trustees positioned themselves to secure regeneration funding at key stages in the 1990s. They employing a risk-taking, imaginative approach to the regeneration process, in which property sales and substantial external funds were secured to finance an architectural competition and design-based refurbishment of the food market, and low rents were used as a strategy to attract food start ups and small scale artisan food producers. Having launched the process with a food festival, a key revitalisation technique was to attract in wholesalers of high-quality food who then chose, or were required by the trustees, to also open retail shops on their street frontages in and around the redeveloping market.

Findings from Borough appear to support a strong link between urban design and food, which in turn underpinned in a number of ways the urban sustainability of both the place itself and its relationship to the food chain. The research findings suggest that in the early 2000s Borough as a revived market functioned well as a sustainable food context. The fine-grained spatiality of Borough was an example of traditional urban space based on the spatial qualities of the European urban quarter. It developed into a very location specific foodscape, which stood in sharp contrast to the placelessness more prevalent in the food environment of the modern food system. This was in turn important to how it operated in economic, environmental and social terms.

Borough offered its users a wide range of food possibilities at a fine grain and human scale within a walkable catchment. In contrast to obesegenic environments (Lake and Townshend, 2006) elsewhere, the quarter underpinned a healthier approach to urbanism by allowing food buyers to walk, cycle or take public transport to the market to buy food. It also supported food distribution processes that were less coarse grained and sprawling. Its revival focused on architectural renovation of buildings and interiors and urban design on the one hand, and on economic revitalisation on the other. On the urban design side the emphasis was on qualities that supported a compact city model. Borough formed a node of intense use within a relatively coherent, dense urban fabric, configured as a series of outdoor rooms in which the public realm contributed to a strong sense of place. This has become an unusual urban food form in a context of the dominance of 'big box' food retailing and wholesaling with its large-scale car parking, and contingent public space decline. Moreover, the sociability traced at Borough suggested that the physical nature of the spaces themselves influenced the way they had been used in the past as well as in more recent times.

Physical refurbishment of the market structures and interiors was an urgent task for Borough's trustees, as by the 1990s the market was falling apart. This refurbishment was undertaken in stages, with the market's operations shifting around the site to avoid building and renovations works. Information from those interviewed fleshed out that provided by the morphological and urban design investigations in the last chapter and confirmed that particular areas of the market were renovated to the design set out in an overall master plan. The market's interviewees referred to *"happening upon"* both a spatial model and a space structure that was unique in design terms for a food market, but reflected well-established urban design qualities such as enclosure, permeability, richness, variety, legibility and vitality. The refurbishment process likewise echoed the market's particular spatial history while directly connecting design to the economic viability of the market's operations.

Market viability was established both at the level of individual traders and businesses and through the market's management and governance overall. Typical growth trajectories for individual food businesses were from wholesale to retail; from running one food stand to a number of stands; and towards diversification in the range of food products, by opening restaurants and cafes, and by expanding into forms of gastronomic education. Traders found that their food knowledge could be as valuable as their food products, a fact that reflected changing social mores in relation to food. Of interest more theoretically, these shifts demonstrated the degree to which cultural capital became a kind of currency in both the formation of Borough as a cultural quarter and formed a part of individual consumption by those who visited.

At the same time, the market's operations reflected a rather complicated relationship with commodification and gentrification. It certainly appeared from the research that some gentrification effects were being experienced at Borough. Economic capital was clearly being extracted in the area around Borough Market from the value created by urban pioneers, market proponents, traders and customers. The findings from interviews and observations suggested though that Borough's trajectory was more than merely an expression of the commodification of urban life, with the space merely to be understood as a high-quality consumption product. Borough equally functioned in the early 2000s as a productive food quarter in which a large number of small businesses were nurtured, where food chain relationships were shortened and made more transparent, and in which opportunities for conviviality were emphasised. While gentrification was clearly underway by this time, Borough could not be understood solely as a gentrifying space, focused entirely on the demands of middle-class incomers. Borough as a developing food quarter also provided production, distribution and consumption opportunities that cut across class, allowed a broad range of positive socio-spatial practices in relation to food to flourish, and brought food and related benefits to some local as well as incoming users.

The chapter has revealed regeneration activity at the level of market management that can be tied into both place-marketing *and* social inclusion readings of the market. The partnerships formed with traders, and cultural and economic links with other European market spaces of high quality (in this case La Boqueria Market in Barcelona), helped publicise Borough internationally, and reinforced the stress on good local food and generation of income for the local community through the Trust. Unlike the mainstream public-private partnership approaches to regeneration, these strategic partnerships emphasised Borough's niche as a high quality food provider, with a stress on artisanal produce rather than as a farmer's market. Borough did not develop strictly as a farmer's market although by the early 2000s it shared some elements with these.

Also different from the usual regeneration approach was the lack of direct public subsidies for ongoing operation and management, although external regeneration funding was used for key aspects of the building programme. Instead, discounting rents was an important tool for attracting, keeping and growing market based food businesses. This socially conscious financial method positively influenced the market's overall economic success as well as supporting what were often fledgling food businesses. One of those interviewed saw the fundamental economic relationship at play as connecting traditional food producers with consumers as directly as could be achieved, with as little mediation as possible. Again, this third sector-private sector partnership seemed to contrast with the way regeneration processes in the UK have tended to operate (and be theorised) whereby top-down subsidies and control from the state are central elements.

A potentially negative aspect of the regeneration programme was the way that property developers commodified design improvements to the area, a tendency that may have increased the level and speed of gentrification. Speculative property development schemes in the area used Borough Market as a local anchor, adding value to property projects. The self-described 'London Bridge Quarter', centred on the high rise Shard building, was noted as the most substantial example of these processes at work locally. Such commodification reflected the way that a proportion of the economic value and social capital created by the market's charitable trustees, individual small businesses, and visitors to the market, was likely to be expropriated rather than being returned to the local community. Set against this, the trustees' charitable objectives also delivered economic benefits to the local area. These occurred directly by operating a market that provided good food, employment and educational services, and generated rate relief for local residents. Benefits were also derived more indirectly, by providing a positive context for broader regeneration efforts in the relatively deprived Southwark area. In so doing, regeneration in practice at Borough's food quarter did not seem to entirely fit with the arguments by Smith (1996) and others, about how gentrification tends to proceed.

After the main research for the book was completed further developments occurred at Borough in relation to its property development context. A major property developer attempted to attract stallholders away from Borough to a new farmer's market style development next to the 2012 Olympic site. In the apparent row at Borough Market over lease terms, the developer was described as hoping "to entice any traders unhappy with the way Borough has gone from wholesale market to tourist trap…(The Guardian, November, 2010). As argued in this account

> "On one side is one of the biggest retail property groups in the world. On the other, a small south London market which, in extolling the virtues of fresh British produce, has helped spur a gastronomic revival in the capital" (ibid).

This situation thus directly relates to arguments about the future of Borough Market that were aired during the research process; reflecting traders' concerns at that time about tourism, and also that the market would lose touch with the wholesaling origins and functions that gave it some of its special qualities. Particularly notable in this regard was the traders' explicit reference to the atmosphere created by the interplay between Borough Market's economic, social and physical structure, which was felt to be unique. This has been reflected more recently in commentary about the attempt to recreate such an atmosphere at Stratford without the same economic and social foundations:

> ""Some are worried that [Borough] will turn into Spitalfields, with chain restaurants and a market in the middle," said one trader. But you can't simply "preserve Borough in aspic…If we did go [to Stratford] it would be in addition [to the stall at Borough]. And it would never have the appeal of Borough, or its lively atmosphere. You can't really bottle it." (The Guardian, November, 2010).

Interestingly, George Nicholson, former Head of Trustees, took a rather different view of this development, arguing that Stratford was

> *"a serious attempt to re-introduce a fresh food element to a shopping centre, reversing a trend that has been pursued in the retail property industry over the last two decades. Secondly, I have always taken the view that London can sustain more than one Borough style market (Barcelona has 40). It is a natural extension of the ethic underpinning Borough to see not just the numbers of businesses grow, but the businesses themselves grow. In that context it is quite natural in my view that some of the businesses could and should trade out of a centre such as Westfield, as well as other markets".*

Since the main body of research was completed for this book, a second substantial area of contention relating to Borough as a regenerating space has been the emergence of gastronomic food spaces nearby, with Maltby Street in Bermonsey, a farmer's market at Bermondsey Square, and weekly food markets on Southbank identified as fledging competitors. A number of Borough based traders who also set up in and around Maltby Street were evicted from Borough Market in 2011, based on the argument that they were damaging Borough by using profits earned from subsidised Borough pitches to *"to put at risk the commercial interests of their fellow traders who trade only from – and remain loyal to – Borough Market and their customers"* (London SE1, n.d). Again, George Nicholson provided an alternative view of this development, seeing this as part of the successful growth of what had been fledgling businesses when they started out at Borough:

> *"It is…part of the reasons underpinning the growth of Maltby Street. As another part of that growth pattern, a new Tapas bar has recently opened in Bermonsey Street - "Jose's" run by the former head chef of Brindisa at*

Borough. Several other traders now have shops in other parts of London too".

At the same time, the emergence of this new element in Borough's food quarter could be seen to reflect the ongoing discussion about the balance between Borough as a food tourism versus a 'real' shopping destination:

> "*The less crowded Maltby Street area has proved popular with shoppers disillusioned with fighting their way through hordes of tourists at Borough*". (London SE1, n.d.).

At the time of writing, this development was unfolding so that conclusions cannot yet be drawn. It would be possible to speculate though that in the longer term these emergent spaces reflect the strength of the Borough food quarter as an alternative food space model in spatial, social and economic terms so should be considered as positive developments in urban sustainability terms.

A significant theme threaded through the discussion of the rise of Borough as a food quarter was about class, with differing opinions expressed by interviewees as to whether the market was of most benefit or interest to middle class consumers for dinner party cooking, or offered more day-to-day food and social opportunities to working-class or lower income food buyers as well. Some of the material collected at Borough supported Bourdieu's (1984) analysis, in which the market space acted as a context for social differentiation, where individuals signified social distinction through the refinement of their taste, and each formed a particular individual although culturally coherent habitus. However, the findings in this chapter also challenged to some extent the notion that only middle class people bought food at Borough Market. A number of those interviewed pointed out that food buyers on very limited incomes also wanted to eat well, and from their experience were willing to buy high-quality, artisanal food that attracted a premium price. Relatively high food prices were in turn argued by both sellers and buyers to be justified on the basis of excellent quality in which real costs were less externalised; were understood to be important to the financial viability of producers and traders; and reflected the requirements of maintaining a sustainable product base and food chain.

The environmental themes that relate to the Borough Market quarter similarly flowed from interviewees' concerns about aspects of both food quality and the nature of consumption. At the time of the research, Borough was clearly a locus for the food system, as discussed in Chapter 2, with both distribution and consumption in evidence. Yet Borough consumers also challenged key aspects of that system, by 'getting back in touch with food' as one interviewee put it, in ways that encompassed food's quality, geographical provenance, production methods and preparation techniques. Market traders and experts suggested this form of consumption as a method by which people could avoid or overcome being 'brainwashed' by supermarkets.

One analysis presented by an expert in market architecture was that such consumption provided an alternative to supermarket shopping, offering far greater expertise, and intimacy 'at the point of sale' as well as healthier food. This was in line with the need to increase the sustainability of consumption practices and support more environmentally friendly production at the same time. Higher prices for some products, especially meat, were justified on environmental grounds. Notions of what constituted sustainable food included a more transparent food chain, in which the origin of food was clearly apparent, and thus the quality of its production methods and food miles could be more easily verified. Food miles remained a complex issue within the research with interviewees pointing to the fact that increased distance from the food market did not constitute a direct linear progression towards unsustainability. They also raised complex geopolitical issues; focusing on the sharp inequalities produced by world food trade, and suggested places like Borough contributed to challenging iniquitous global food trading norms.

In a related way, there were differing views about educating consumers on food sustainability issues, with some of those interviewed believing people had a lot to learn, while others said that Borough Market shoppers tended to be substantially more knowledgeable than most. Some of these views tied in with an identified loss of food skills, which were in turn seen to be related to the decline of the domestic as a locus for cooking, and the advent of ready meals in response to long working hours. Shopping at Borough Market was seen to indicate a higher level of knowledge than apparent among consumers in the main. This knowledge though was not directly correlated to income, and thus by proxy, to class position. A number of market food traders and one of the visitors interviewed suggested that mainland European consumers of all classes had access to high quality food markets as an essential part of urban life, making them better able to understand, appreciate and demand food of high quality, and fitting with de Certeau's (1984) arguments about everyday social practices in relation to food. At the time the research was carried out Borough Market constituted a virtually unique specialist food space in central London for environmentally conscious consumption. In theoretical terms, consumption at Borough could be seen to express a particular individual habitus that also reflected a reshaping of everyday socio-spatial practices for a proportion of Londoners that cut across class and other categories of social differentiation.

A symbiotic relationship was demonstrated at Borough between food producers and traders on one side and food buyers on the other, in which a feedback loop was built-up that supported both sustainable production and consumption. There is a question as to whether these more sustainably grown products could or should directly compete with supermarket-based ready meals. Certain food traders interviewed considered that food market sourced products that mirrored ready meals might be necessary in order to fit in with lives where working hours were long, family patterns had shifted so that food was viewed as less important, and food preparation and cooking skills had declined or were lacking altogether. Warde (1999) has pointed out how hard it is for people to schedule food into the complex demands of everyday life. This is one aspect of the changes in socio-spatial practices in relation to food that were clearly being modelled at Borough and again connected to the notion of the reshaping of everyday practices as argued by de Certeau (1984). A related view from both experts and food traders interviewed was that despite these trends, consciousness about sustainability issues was also rising, leading to a turnaround in this area. This would link sustainability awareness with an increased preparedness by consumers to be more educated about food, as appeared to be the case at Borough. Again this shift was reflected in observed socio-spatial practices, of which more below.

Socio-spatial practices at Borough appeared to be a marker of convivial urbanism. A study of food and space is necessarily also a study of everyday life, in this case one that has explored the links made by food between socio-spatial practice and physical space. On the social side, the Borough Market quarter seemed to be understood by those interviewed as a physical entity that provided both an important backdrop *and* a contributor to everyday socio-spatial practices at the food quarter. Market architecture and design, as well as the local urban fabric, were seen to imbue the area with a strong sense of place. This, in turn, was felt to have positive impacts on the quarter's social use and the convivial practices it generated. Borough Market's architectural framework echoed *"the cathedrals of shopping"* of earlier times and thus, according to one design expert, provided the character and spectacle missing from supermarket-based consumption.

Specific aspects of design thought to contribute to this effect included the series of spaces within and at the edge of the market, the sense of enclosure in the market and surrounding streets, and the strong heritage value of the buildings. The way the stands were configured as *"walk in rather than trade out"* was another specifically design-based intervention argued to be positively affecting social interaction. Borough Market was thought to possess a positive ambience, making it very much a place to socialise. Reflecting its complex morphology, a number of those interviewed were keen to point out that Borough was not mannered or finished, but a raw, sensual and immediate place that was quirky, odd, gritty and grand at the same time.

One visitor to Borough Market said it created a *"hype that attracts 'a certain crowd"*: middle class, well-travelled, food aware, with a European food sensibility, and concerned about style. Again, Bourdieu's notion of the habitus seems congruent with this aspect of the market's social use. A stallholder meanwhile suggested Borough's social space appeal transcended class, and was more about getting connected to others through food, whatever the visitor's cultural or economic background. In this reading, food consciousness was the predominant social link, creating a community of interest, rather than one based on class, ethnicity, age or cultural identity. All sorts of people could become involved in the place and have what was described as *'a fairly decent, enjoyable experience'*. In fact, the quarter's social space catchment was generally agreed to extend well beyond the local area or London more widely, to encompass United Kingdom and overseas visitors. Most were thought to visit intentionally, as Borough received international press coverage, but some simply stumbled across the place.

Eating and drinking informally in Borough's public spaces were among the most dominant socio-spatial practices identified in relation to these visitors through observational visits and interviews. While Borough Market also provided both informal and formal dining opportunities, with the latter being relatively upmarket, many more visitors appeared to visit cafes and stalls in the market than to dine formally there. In this way Borough seemed to challenge Elias's (1982) view that eating in the street is problematic, instead operating as a culturally sanctioned public space in keeping with Valentine's (1998) indulgent street, in which the appropriate performance of self could incorporate public food consumption.

Borough's overwhelming attraction to visitors made it so crowded, on Saturdays especially, that in this way various interviewees believed it risked becoming a victim of its own success. It was uncertain what proportion of those visiting were doing their food shopping at the market, as opposed to, for example, meeting up with friends, as their main socio-spatial practice. The observations, interviews, food mapping and head counts collected at the food quarter did suggest that so-called 'real' shoppers tended to visit earlier in the day and the week. Such shoppers appeared to shop methodically rather than just being at the market to browse more idly or simply enjoy its atmosphere, although this was not demonstrated in a definitive way by the research findings.

Equally, for many visitors observed, the human scale of the market did appear to provide more than simply a locational backdrop for playing out a variety of socio-spatial practices. Individuals seemed to interact convivially at the food quarter, connecting not just with each other but also positively with the spaces of the market itself, as they wandered through, browsed, shopped and socialised. They could, for instance, be seen alone or in company, walking and cycling, taking photographs, leaning on walls, standing around near entrances and gateways, sitting on kerbsides, and perched on benches and seats outside cafes. A substantial proportion of the visitors documented through the observations, head counts and interview narratives appeared to be at Borough Market to not only socialise with each other around food but also to enjoy the ambience of the market spaces themselves.

Foreshadowing the other food quarters

Using a range of methods, the findings from the Borough Market food quarter built up a picture of a physical space with a complex everyday social life centred on food. Borough was seen to play a strong role in sustainability terms within the sustainability framework set out in Chapter 1; reflecting the theoretical context discussed in Chapter 2; and demonstrating various morphological and urban design qualities highlighted in Chapter 3. The chapter's narrative about Borough as an economic, environmental and social space has provided a detailed picture of the way the quarter's functioning in the early 2000s was understood by experts and experienced everyday through the practices of traders and consumers. Borough emerged from this story as both a triumphant success and a place of some – possibly increasing – contestation. In the next two chapters, findings from the case study research at Broadway Market and Exmouth Market demonstrate similar themes in other evolving food quarters, reinforcing the sense that a new and specific form of interplay between socio-spatial and design elements is developing around food in London.

Chapter Five

Renewal 'From Below' at Broadway Market

Broadway Market as a food quarter

This chapter explores the Broadway Market area of East London as an emerging food quarter. It looks at aspects of the relationship between socio-spatial practices focused on food, and the design of physical space that interconnects with these practices. At the time of the research, undertaken over three years to 2008, Broadway Market was not as fully realised a food-centred place as Borough but was changing and developing fast. As at Borough, although on a smaller scale, the findings in this chapter suggest that the revitalised food market rapidly became very successful socially and economically among both a local and wider visitor catchment, while the redevelopment of the market and surrounding quarter likewise demonstrated some areas of contestation.

In a departure from the last chapter, at Broadway a conscious architectural strategy was largely absent from the food market's resurgence, as the market was less dependent on refurbishing built structures than Borough had been. At the same time, as it matured into a food quarter, the local area saw a range of new development. There was certainly recognition from some of those interviewed that architecture and the design of public space were important aspects of place that could affect perceptions and use of the food market and the wider quarter round it. Moreover, it became clear that Broadway Market as a public street had a strong urban design character, which helped to support its social and economic revival.

Constructing Broadway's story of community-based, food-led renewal

The chapter begins by examining the economy of the food quarter, followed by an exploration of its urban design elements, the environmental aspects of its operation as a local quarter focused on a food market, and then discussion and analysis of observed socio-spatial practices. Unlike the last chapter, there is no comparative 'head count' provided from different days, as at the time research was undertaken, Broadway operated as a market only on Saturdays.

Like Borough, the story of the Broadway Market quarter can be situated as one of serious decline and food-led regeneration. Post-war the area was subject to a comprehensive redevelopment process that saw much of the local urban fabric demolished, and the market street dwindle to a remnant space, with few remaining food traders and shops. The role of local leadership has been crucial to Broadway's regeneration, although the local management structure has been 'bottom-up' in a different way to Borough. The push to regenerate the market came from a recently formed group of local residents and traders who organised themselves into the Broadway Market Traders and Residents Association (BMTRA). Under the aegis of a very dynamic local leader in the early 2000s the BMTRA decided to hold a weekly market on Broadway Market. BMTRA's leader became the market's volunteer market manager and was able to flesh out the story of Broadway's revival.

The chapter begins with the market manager's account of the difficult process of restarting the market, which she contextualised by reference to London Farmers' Markets experience generally. The market manager pointed out that the economic regeneration of markets around London fitted within an economic and social movement that people of all classes have taken part in. She made a direct link between the desire for more satisfying consumption and the economic complexities of regeneration as experienced by individuals:

> "About 3-4 years after they [farmers' markets] started the 'white space' brigade, the loft converters, people who had disposable income, started to go to them. Borough was the first. They suddenly realised that it was a very lonely, controlled life".

As at Borough, Broadway's local proponents had a battle on their hands to revive the market, with the local authority, the London Borough of Hackney, perceived as obstructive. The market manager commented

> "We had to fight the council to get it happening. They never said no but they put every obstacle in the way. They couldn't bear the thought of someone else having control and raking in the dough".

In the end, the designation of Broadway Market historically as a chartered market proved critical to its revitalisation, despite apparent council inaction. As the market manager explained, because Broadway had continued to trade through its years of decline, although in a minimal fashion, it was still officially a market:

> "I found a loophole to get the market started. A light bulb went off in my head when I was at yet another meeting with them [the council]. I was looking out of the window at the street sign and I realised Broadway Market is a market. It had two live traders so it was an existing market so Hackney Council can't stop us from trading".

The market manager felt that the council's narrow focus on regulation, without the apparent capacity to properly manage the market, had been a central problem in the regeneration process, and one that left *"a management gap"*. The market manager stressed the bottom-up, community-based nature of the management of the market as a significant aspect in both the process and the structure of its ongoing revival. BMTRA created an unpaid regeneration process that the council would otherwise have had to spend significant funds on.

> "Here we just expanded on what we wanted - a bunch of locals who wanted to shop local. Have camaraderie. Because we're an association - market traders, shops, residents, everyone gets to comment. Look at the whole street, not just the market and shops".

The market manager said that markets like Broadway needed to be understood in much broader economic and social terms than local authorities' traditional approach to market management. She made connections between customers, traders and managers as a kind of partnership-working arrangement:

> "This is the only market I know in the whole country where the market is about the people who live and work directly in that street, everyone's had an involvement and a say".

A stress on creating a *"whole shopping experience"* was contrasted with the traditional trading-down-on-price approach of markets managed by councils. These were typified as a *"dog-eat-dog arrangement where you are forced by market management to compete with your neighbour or they might give someone else the pitch"*. The market manager expanded on her economic and social vision for the market as one that stressed local connections and sense of community:

> "I wanted to work on this market as my family are market traders. I used to work in this market when it was on its last legs. I wanted to create this as a place for the weekly shop, stop and chat, be part of the community. The 70 of us who got together were like that anyway. Old fashioned values, tolerance".

These points were all seen to directly link to the increasing success and growing visitor catchment for the market, from walkable and *"directly local"*, to borough-wide and beyond. The catchment for sellers as well as buyers grew quickly. The market manager commented, *"We started with 23 stalls. We could have filled the whole street in six weeks. I took 500 phone calls in the first weeks"*. Other interviewees also saw the catchment as being primarily local but expanding. One said that over the last 6 years

> "Broadway Market has changed a lot. You can see all the new shops coming in. It's always busy during the week but on Saturdays you get...over time it's just kept developing and developing and its really, really nice. There's more people, more stalls and more stock. We get a lot of regular customers now but then every week you also see new people."

Similarly, another stallholder, argued that this increase in visitors was not caused by mainstream tourism, unlike Borough, but something subtler:

> "it usually seems like that [visitors] are visiting some friend or..because I don't think tourists come here. Loads of tourists come to Borough."

A further stallholder meanwhile similarly said that he thought *"you do get a certain sort of catchment for this area"* while a local resident who visited the market on a weekly basis to do much of his food shopping also suggested the catchment was growing because the market had become cool, and hip journalists had heard about it, or possibly lived near it:

> "It's the kind of thing that will be in the papers, in the Guardian or something; 'a cool place to go at the weekend', so people will come".

One of the contentions by opponents to the changes at Broadway was that long-standing working class residents were unable to afford the food market due to high prices. A related issue that emerged was whether the area's working class population was being excluded from benefits accruing to more affluent incomers, such as increasing property values and an improving quality of life. At the time one critic writing on a weblog argued that Broadway was developing a brand identity, which was based on "an *organic farmer's market catering to inhabitants of the area's mushrooming yuppy apartments, [while] less affluent residents have mainly been victims, not beneficiaries, of this striking transformation*" (Hackney Independent, 2006, n.d.).

By contrast, the market manager argued firmly that the market was affordable:

"Let me take you back to the supermarket - to their finest range. Their finest range is more expensive than what you're getting direct from the producers in my market" (ibid).

Despite these price comparisons, one market-user interviewed put an opposing view, suggesting that the market was *"quite pricy and would demand a certain income"*. This market visitor, who lived locally, commented:

"They are high value added goods here. You have to have a certain income. If you look at prices of cheese, bread, all pricy - you might come here for a treat. It's predominantly people on higher incomes. The exception is the greengrocer who's been here for decades".

Whether Broadway was catering primarily for incomers remained a subject of contention for both those interviewed and commentators (The Guardian, Wednesday 7 December 2005). There was, though, more unanimity about the importance of the market to the area's regeneration and the considerable social mix that the market catered for. One of those interviewed, a food trader, agreed that the food market had led the regeneration of the area and pointed out that residential incomers had been part of what had made Broadway Market sustainable in economic terms. A number of interviewees suggested that the Broadway area was enjoying a mix of incomers and existing residents. A stallholder said that the area could be increasingly recognised as

"middle class from the amount of people with really expensive dogs, people with really expensive buggies and very young children. There are a lot of people in their late 20s, early 30s who have moved into Hackney. There's a lot of media people. It certainly has changed".

At the same time, this interviewee believed that there was

> *"a mixture of people. I do think you get you know you've got the canal and the estates and you know all the other bits of Hackney are right there...Compared with other farmers markets that I do, this market is the...most random mixture of people".*

A number of other traders also stressed the considerable diversity and social mix they noticed among their customers. These views would seem to suggest any stark counter-pointing of working class 'victims' and middle class 'victors', in the market's regeneration would be underplaying the subtleties in the nature of the transformation of the quarter, although changes in class composition locally might reflect the general direction of longer-term trends. Interviewees pointed to the development of an *"arty"* but culturally rather mixed local community coming to the market. A stallholder, for example, said

> *"you know it's quite mixed sort of cultures in this market as well. I think you get in this particular area of Hackney, you get sort of young, up-and-coming, sort of like...There's a kind of arty scene around here. At the same time you've got old geezers as well who've been here... There's a sort of mix in this area. It's quite unique for that".*

The stallholder added that this social and cultural mix contributed to the market's character:

> *"the good thing is the mix of cultures even like the shops that are here on a permanent basis, they work really well, you know, it adds to the feel".*

Another stallholder also noted *"artiness"* in relation to all the people who worked on his stall, most of whom were also *"connected to some kind of visual culture and I think that you would find that here as well" [gestures round]*. A key reason why young and poor artists, students and others with more cultural than economic capital stated that they had moved into the area was because of its relative cheapness. As a local resident and shopper pointed out,

> *"I ended up here because I was a student and it was the cheapest place to live. I'd never been to the market before but now I'm here I don't think I'd leave".*

A stallholder similarly argued that up until recent times the market area had been a cheap place to live because it was poorly connected:

> "It's cheap because its got bad transport links. Depending on where you are. In a way you would think that would effect the market but look at it" [Gestures to busy market].

The area's cheapness, however, appeared to have been a relatively fleeting quality attracting incomers as house price and rent increases were beginning to grip. This aspect of area transformation, associated with growth of the food market, is explored below. Even more apparently than at Borough, the issue of gentrification was an important part of the Broadway Market quarter story. Taken as a whole, the views recorded above suggested that there was a strong community basis for the food-led revival of Broadway Market, but that did not preclude the process from having unintended gentrifying effects, which roused heated local opposition. A market-user argued along these lines:

> "I see the market as gentrifying space. The history of this market: there have been cycles of attempts to have this as a market. First as a traditional market, then there was an attempt to do a flower market, then this high end market".

Both interviewees' views and observations gave weight to the notion that the Broadway Market quarter was in the process of gentrification; a process supported by an influx of professional people, real estate agents and property developers. 'Professional' residents were certainly in evidence during observational visits to the market. Early in the research process a shopper approached to ask:

> "are you doing participant observation? I use mixed methods in my work so recognised what you are doing".

More indirect material suggesting the class position and political orientation of market visitors could be gleaned from the local newsagents' substantial Saturday morning stack of *The Guardian*, (Figure 5.1) whereas conservative broadsheet newspapers were stocked in very small quantities, and there appeared to be few copies of tabloid newspapers for sale (Figure 5.1.). In distinct contrast, graffiti, including anarchist symbols, on a market side street wall (Figure 5.2) showed a less comfortable side of this economic, social and spatial dynamic.

Figure 5.1.: *Broadway Market newsagent selling large number of copies of broadsheet newspaper, The Guardian* Source: Photograph by author

A stallholder argued in relation to this question that *"the gentrification process is so incredible around here"*, and suggested that this was signified directly through food and food spaces. What used to be a working class market the stallholder said now had *"gentrification somehow articulated through food"* and gave the example of the large number of restaurants which had set up in the street, while only one or two traditional food spaces remained (the chip shop and Cook's eel and pie shop). This trader claimed that if such spaces were at Borough they would offer *"sites of authenticity"* but here no one used them. At the same time he went on to say, *"on the other hand I think for the people and for the market it still works as an authentication site somehow."*

Figure 5.2.: *Graffiti on the market street* Source: Photograph by author

A central contention in the claims that this was gentrifying space, was that the council sold off property on and near the market street to developers, instead of to local small businesses, which were sitting tenants and were supposed to have first refusal. The two main examples claimed on web-based accounts were Tony's Café (IWCA, n.d.) and Spirit's grocery store (Hackney Independent, n.d.). A local campaigning group, Hackney Independent, argued that this was a straightforward case of the economic interests of the extant poor on "run down council estates" being marginalised by those of the "self-interested" incoming rich (ibid). The Saturday market was thus viewed as contributing to the gentrification of the area, while its users had no idea of how they were being used by the local council to prop up the local economy (ibid). Another website described the more recent situation with Tony's café and others "forced out" to be replaced by luxury flats (Hackney Independent, n.d.). The notion of an invasion of Broadway Market by property developers was reflected in commentary from Mute magazine, which described the situation as one of "re-colonisation" (IWCA, n.d.).

As these web-based interpretations demonstrate, at the time the fieldwork was undertaken the Broadway Market area was subject to considerable development pressure and some contestation. The previously cited local shopper, who originally came to live in the area because it was comparatively cheap, suggested that a building boom of shoddy new apartments was underway locally:

> *"It is happening though because along the canal there are so many new blocks of flats. And, you know, they're all going to be like the boxy, one bedroom, cardboardy structures but they will sell for loads of money because it's a nice area".*

A stallholder quoted earlier also saw some opposition coalescing around the notion of incomers shaping Broadway Market into a boutique kind of market, inimical to longer standing local people, but in their own view representing a workable social mix:

> *"Yeah, Hackney…there's been quite a lot of opposition to it, let's say, from the working classes I suppose. You know some people, it does upset them, you know, new people coming in. You know, I think the combination works quite well".*

Others also suggested that gentrification was perhaps "a more complex tale" than one of straightforward displacement (Kingsnorth, 2006), arguing that while Broadway Market was further gentrified than five years earlier, it was still a mixed neighbourhood in which older and newer food shops and cafes rubbed along together and incomers supported battles to protect places like Tony's café (The Ecologist, n.d.).

Hari Kunzru, writing in The Guardian (7 December 2005, G2, p.8) also described the regeneration process in a way that accepted it was probably shading into gentrification, but acknowledged the complexities and positive aspects for individuals involved. He noted that there was an economic and social connection between a penchant for living in Hackney because of its individuality and eccentricity; which he described as "a grubby glamour that has not yet been stamped out and flattened into the same cloned corporate hell-hole as the rest of Britain" (ibid) and enjoying what somewhere like Broadway Market's food market brought to the area:

> "But the thing is, I am partial to a nice piece of raclette. I like hanging out at the new street market. And I know the significance of all the high-end prams, the sudden appearance of a yoga parlour, the almost palpable whiff of testosterone emanating from the shiny new estate agencies full of shiny blokes with big, shiny ties and shiny Mini Coopers sprayed in the company colours. The technical term is regeneration. In other words the next phase

of the takeover is underway. People like me - writers and artists - have softened Hackney up. Now comes the real money."

Another description of the area as a residential location, reported in the Evening Standard (Area Watch, Home and Property, Wednesday 7 March 2007, p.7), also demonstrated some of the economic and social complexities embedded in the process for individuals living locally. The Evening Standard (ibid) report provided a kind of incomer's case history:

> "ACTORS Simon Kunz and Caroline Loncq live with their four-year-old son, Jonjo, and their lurcher, Harry, in a large and spacious flat in the London Fields area of Hackney. Simon came to the area from Highgate 12 years ago, not because he loved the area but because he found a flat that he loved at a price (it was less than £100,000) he could afford. Caroline, who came from the Westbourne Grove area, says she and Simon have really come to appreciate Hackney. *"It is very green and friendly, and we like the great ethnic mix. There are lots of Turkish and Vietnamese stores selling lovely fresh produce, and I have never eaten as well as I have here. I know people complain about the public transport, but I have never liked the Tube much, so if I can't go on my bike, I take one of the many frequent buses."* The couple enjoy the nearby Sunday flower market in Columbia Road and the market, shops, pubs and restaurants in Broadway Market. Like a lot of local residents, they have joined the protest in support of Spirit, a long-standing Jamaican shopkeeper in Broadway Market, who is being evicted by his landlord. *"We like the way the local community gets involved in local issues such as this."* A typical Saturday for Simon, Caroline and Jonjo is a stroll down to Broadway Market, a game of ping pong on the outdoor table in London Fields, then home to cook a meal with all the ingredients they have bought in the market".

At one level this could be read as a textbook narrative of first wave gentrifiers or new urban pioneers that fitted very well the community activists' stereotype of the middle class users of Broadway's burgeoning food shops, cafes, and market stalls, and would form the "shock troops" of Hari Kunzru's "softening up" process. However, the account also demonstrated that such incomers could not be solely defined as rich and self-interested. They appeared to be on moderate incomes, with a professional background in the arts. They shopped locally for food, rather than at chain stores, and were involved in local community-based politics to protect working class interests. More broadly, it is worth restating that the market manager did not accept that as the area was being regenerated, this was necessarily to the detriment of longer-term, working class residents. She challenged the use of the word gentrification as a term of opprobrium to describe what was occurring, saying that:

"We got bad press to say we were gentrified. I bawled them out. I don't care how long people have lived here. If regeneration is solely about gentrification, that can't build communities. If it benefits long-suffering residents then you will win. We planned, have created, the first urban village; complimenting the shops that were already here".

In the market manager's analysis the market built on, rather than replaced, local food shops for local people, and a particular spatial model (the urban village) was invoked, of which more below. The market manager argued in a newspaper interview that she believed that market was

"an amazing catalyst for bringing people together. People from all types of background, financially, economically, socially. It's beginning to become a platform for the community. It's real urban space because it's grown up itself. My fear though is that the property market would go nuts and it has. It's gone nuts quicker than we anticipated" (Hackney Independent, n.d.).

When interviewed as part of the research, the market manager pointed out the irony that high housing costs imposed economic constraints on buyers that reinforced the need for them to consume food in a local way:

"Because of the cost of living/housing these people are what I call 'rich poor'. They may have a flat that is worth ¼ million pounds but they have very little disposable income so they are coming to Broadway Market and being very selective about their food and getting the free social aspect".

The market manager saw the possibility of Broadway Market becoming a victim of its own economic success and thus deterring local "core" shoppers. She said that in the previous year she had began to worry that the market was getting too busy:

"We don't want wall-to-wall pressure. We don't want to grow down side streets, as then there is more pressure. Some Borough traders were ringing up more sales but making less money. This would be shoppers buying one or two items. They will deter core shoppers who don't want to stand in a queue. That's what they escaped supermarkets for. On the continent, we go to markets later [in the morning], and let the core shoppers get in earlier".

A stallholder interviewed said that the issue of too many visitors versus 'core' shoppers might not be as significant a problem as it had become at Borough. This, she believed, was due to the market street's location, substantially further from the centre of London, which meant

> "it's always going to have that local aspect. I don't really see it becoming like Borough because it's not quite central enough maybe...I think there is a better mixture here than at Borough. More local and there's less just people who go to look and try but they don't necessarily do their shopping. Here people definitely do and I think with the fact that it's in a place where there are shops, it's not just the market, it means I don't think it will really become that. It's a slightly different thing, a different atmosphere".

A local resident who shopped at the market, interviewed at around 11am on a Saturday morning, did suggest though that *"It will get really busy later on as well to the point when you just get really annoyed walking up and down. It's like at Borough"*. At the time of the research process, the manager had a clear plan for the economic growth of the market over time and believed that local management had been crucial to success so far, by carefully approving potential traders from the *"hundreds of people who want a pitch"*. The intention was to build up numbers of stalls slowly to ensure quality and to manage competition. The market manager argued in the newspaper article quoted above that other local people besides BMTRA could have revitalised the market themselves but did not do so:

> "Where are all the stalls that these people say should be here giving them what they want? Why did they go away in the first place? Because people stopped using this market. They went to supermarkets instead. They let it die. We all let it die. If any one from the local estates wanted to do (something similar) they could have done it too. We're just a bunch of ordinary people. They could've done it themselves. The longstanding businesses (on Broadway Market) would not have been here now if we'd not introduced the market" (Hackney Independent, n.d.).

Exploring the urban design implications of food market led regeneration

Shifting to spatial aspects of the discussion of Broadway's economic revival, an essential aspect of change at Broadway has related to its urban design. Urban design issues and qualities underpinned a considerable number of the points about economic regeneration made by interviewees and observable at the food quarter. A food market stallholder said that the shape of the space was important because the canal at one end formed a *"natural barrier and then you've got the park at the other so it becomes a kind of reach (sic) that people particularly want to [unfinished]."* Another stallholder agreed, mentioning what was, in effect, the street's enclosure as an important factor in building atmosphere:

"*I think it's got that old sort of market feel to it. You've got sort of the shops on one road and the space is quite confined and that sort of builds to an atmosphere to the market. I think that does help this market a lot. Say at other markets I've worked, the space it can affect sort of custom and feel to a market. I wouldn't say its ideal, but it helps*".

A third food stallholder agreed: "*I think it [street shape] helps funnel sort of people in as well. It works well*". One stallholder, meanwhile, contrasted the spaces at Broadway and Borough, seeing the former as an intentionally designed set of spaces that he termed "*a kind of authentic farce*". In regard to Broadway, he wondered if physical design had that much effect, although he did point out some of the less pleasant microclimate effects resulting from where his stall was positioned:

"*Here, in many ways, from a purely practical point of view, it's a pretty bad space because the wind is kind of coming in [gestures to street leading onto Broadway Market behind stall]*".

The spaces at Broadway were also contrasted much more positively with spaces at farmer's markets at Islington and Clapham, with which one interviewee was familiar. This stallholder suggested the high street location at Broadway was very important, whereas

"*places like Islington - and the Clapham one is very similar - it's like a primary school car park. It's not on the high street. There is no flow to it. People have got to know where it is. You've got to come, buy your things and leave. That's it*".

The idea that Broadway was turning into an "urban village", as suggested by the market manager, was one of the connections made between economic and social regeneration and the urban design of the local area. For the market manager, the term urban village denoted an inclusive, community-based place where food needs could be met locally at a reasonable price and with good quality. A market stallholder seemed to support the idea that an urban village was developing at Broadway, as well as giving an indication of typical socio-spatial practices and catchment range, of which more later in this chapter:

"*Yes, in the summer, especially here where our stalls is, people just sit on the pavement, you know, with their coffees if the cafes are really busy, read the papers. A lot of the places are outside things where you can sit. There's music. There's lots of other stalls. There's places with books, you can read. You can have lunch. And it's right next to London Fields so if it's nice.. so *people are definitely using it in that way. I don't know whether it's just people from Hackney, it's really hard to see, but there is a lot of people who live locally it seems".*

The role of connectivity aspects of urban design was also reflected in the way that the area was experiencing an economic upturn at the time of the research. This, in turn, linked to rising property prices. House price increases were related, among other factors, to spatial design changes occurring at a broad level (The Evening Standard's New Homes Guide, Wednesday 20 September 2007, p. 4). The most obvious of these was the development of the new orbital rail network, which at the time of the research was under construction, and once completed would open up new pockets of East London to the Underground. The Evening Standard Guide (ibid, p.4) pointed out that the East London line extension corridor was therefore a property hotspot, and it provided details of residential property for sale close to Broadway Market, while referring in passing to the contested nature of recent changes:

> "Haggerston…is a place to watch. Sandwiched between bar-packed Hoxton to the south and Islington to the north, the pace of gentrification has been slower here, with some determined locals fighting off developers, notably on Broadway Market, where old East End traditions such as a pie-and-mash shop survive alongside a gastro-pub, deli, restaurant and art gallery" (ibid).

At a finer grain, the market manager raised an urban design point about the potential for food market development and new housing to be in conflict with one another, because of amenity issues such as increased noise:

> *"At Columbia Road [flower market close by] developers moved in, values went up, residents started wanting the market to be closed as it was too noisy. That's what's happened at Borough. We've had one or two complaints here about noise. So regeneration has to be community oriented - for both long term and new residents".*

Other physical design issues noted by the manager included safety, which was thought to be likely to increase as an issue if the plans to run evening markets took off. At the time the research was undertaken, the street was closed off at its northern end during market hours. *"I've learnt a lot about street safety etc. going just until 9pm. I can't yet get the council to close the road for this".*

Identifying a 'submerged' account of Broadway Market as sustainable space

This chapter's exploration of Broadway Market's various food roles provides an opportunity to look at its environmental performance, and how at the time of the research this might have contributed to making London a more sustainable city. This part of the chapter draws on semi-structured interviews, online comments and observations made in the case study area in a three-year period to 2008. Those interviewed at Broadway made fewer direct references to issues of environmental sustainability in relation to Broadway as a food space than at Borough, yet a number of comments pointed more obliquely to similar concerns. These views about environmental issues with food were often embedded in interviewees' narratives about Broadway as an economic or social space. For example, the market manager situated the development of Broadway Market within a broader movement of food markets that shared characteristics with formal Farmers' markets, that was strongly environmentally conscious in tone, and which, to some extent, transcended class:

> "London Farmers' Markets has led the way. They arrived at a time when foodies - that's all sorts of people - when I started I was on benefit, but I've always been into cooking food, and was sick of just buying what jumps out at you in the supermarket - for me what happened, that's why they were such a success. People were ready to make a choice".

At the same time, the manager pointed out that Broadway was not a farmers' market and never wanted or claimed to be. Instead, the stress was on good quality food at affordable prices for local people, rather than defining a geographical limit to market suppliers as required by Farmers Market rules. Observations at the market showed that there was emphasis on products from the southeast of the United Kingdom, as well as specialist cheeses, meats, and dried goods from other parts of the country, and from Italy, France, and other European sources.

In relation to stall shopping at Broadway Market, the focus, as at Borough, appeared to be on the knowledgeability of market traders and purchasers about the sources and quality of their products. In interviews, a number of sellers mentioned the geographical background of their products, and from observations, these sources sometimes appeared geographically, ethnically and culturally distinct from those of the purchaser. This suggested reasonable levels of understanding of food products from outside the buyer's immediate background. Thus, for example, one stallholder selling Italian products was observed explaining in considerable detail both the geographical origins of her products, and the right cooking techniques a buyer would need to use to cook them properly. The market manager stressed the point about localism, diversity and quality. *"Broadway Market is about food, diversity, enjoying shopping on a more local, quality basis".* Another stallholder, meanwhile, argued that relatively high prices, previously discussed in relation to economic regeneration, were justified on the basis of outstanding environmental quality, and this was something recognised and accepted by buyers who were concerned with such quality:

> *"I've got to admit some of the stuff we sell, I think, you know, it is slightly on the more expensive side for a couple of things but the quality is there so, you know, it depends how much people are into their food. You know, if you are willing to pay for the good quality stuff people will do that irrespective of how much rent basically".*

There was a suggestion that buyers at Broadway were making conscious choices about their consumption, which were driven by sustainability concerns. At least one blogger about Broadway Market referred to buying patterns based on a desire to consume in more sustainable ways than in the past, with methods used to consume a mix of online and local sourcing (strwberrydelight, 02 Feb 2006). From the limited accounts collected, Broadway appeared to be understood as a place in which individuals modelled aspects of more sustainable consumption, and offered support for more sustainable production and distribution methods. While the accounts in this area were somewhat muted, the stress on food's environmental quality could be discerned from both observations and interviews. There was an emphasis on food localism and small scale, high quality, geographical typification of foods bought, artisanal production and organic produce. It will be remembered from the discussion of the economic resurgence of the market that higher food prices were sometimes considered justified in terms of their relationship to high quality, which was thought in turn to reflect good environmental practice in food production. While food miles were not mentioned, there was an emphasis on sourcing food produce from the southeast of the UK, which suggested a shortening of geographical supply chains. Well-informed buyers and sellers were together allowing sustainable shopping choices to be made by offering attractive alternatives to supermarket-based consumption.

Broadway's socio-spatial food practices: connections to urban design

As at Borough, Broadway could also be understood as a social space, and this section explores a series of socio-spatial practices observed at the case study area and discussed by place users. Like Borough, the study area of the food quarter could be seen to support a substantial range of practices contributing to the construction of everyday life in Lefebvre's (1991) terms, reflecting a distinctive individual habitus as defined by Bourdieu (1984), and contributing to conviviality as explored by Peattie (1998). Observations and interviews suggested that Broadway Market provided numerous spaces for social encounters; many focusing on food buying and consumption, at stalls, shops, cafes and restaurants; and some simply of people meeting on the street in an unplanned way. In each unstructured observation undertaken during market operating hours, a substantial number of casual meetings were noted between individuals in the market area or on the market street. One stallholder said about these spontaneous meetings that

> *"you always see people meeting other people that they know, just bumping into people randomly. There's definitely that thing now where people do know each other and you see the same people here every week".*

In some cases those meeting then went to market-based or nearby cafes for coffee, or walked the length of the market street together. As a stallholder commented, there were

> *"people who come here and literally do their weekly food shopping, and people who come just to buy a couple of things and sit and have a coffee or meet up with other people. If you look around you notice there are a lot of people doing that now".*

Broadway Market's manager saw the local market as the kind of place where a richer social life could be *"nudged along"*. There was an implied commentary about the design of the market spaces in the following comment that expressed conviviality and nodded to Norbert Elias's (1982) arguments on civility:

> *"When the market started, I used to use quotes: "burst your personal bubble, talk to people, smile". People wanted to be a bit more relaxed. The control of etiquette began to relax".*

The physical shape of Broadway Market was viewed by one local place user as particularly well set up to facilitate such encounters: *"We often meet friends here. We don't plan to. It's the physical structure. It's a bit like a promenade in a small town. I end up meeting A, B, C and D".* A stallholder suggested that for some people the market provided a whole day's local entertainment:

> *"Here the farmers market is much longer, from ten to four, and sometimes in terms of people buying things it starts very late. They come in the morning, and get a coffee, have a sit about, have a mooch around, so it's a much longer thing to it. People come and they tend to spend some more time, and they buy their things maybe a bit later on and then they go home and eat or whatever and you can see people are planning on 'I'm going to do this, this evening' or 'we are going to have this late afternoon'. And that's their day really".*

Like Borough, Broadway Market was felt to have a 'hidden gem' quality. A stallholder mentioned that some of her customers stumbled on the market at Broadway by chance, or heard about it through word of mouth, and that it had enriched their social lives:

> *"Sometimes I see people who say 'I live really close by and I've only just discovered the market and isn't it fantastic'. I've had older people come up and say 'oh I used to live close by 20 years ago and it's just incredible how much it's changed and the same time is the same', you know".*

Part of the appeal was that the Broadway Market had become fashionable. Another stallholder argued that Broadway offered the opportunity to see *"a cross section of the trendiest people in London"*. She suggested these were the kind of people who twenty years ago went to Portobello Road or Spitalfields Markets: *"You might see them at Columbia Road on a Sunday possibly...but you see the range, and then, as well as that, there are yummy mummies with kids"*. There was also a feeling that Broadway's catchment was widening: *"I think they're beginning to [come from further afield]. Definitely in the last year or so they're beginning to come as a destination to pose"*. A local resident and shopper agreed that *"lots of people come and they pose"*. One observational visit found talent scouts looking for 'cool' people to feature in a mobile phone advertisement; playing into the notion that Broadway was being recognised as a place to attract and find fashionable people.

As at Borough, walking around the market and to and from it was a socio-spatial practice much in evidence. While most of the observed walking did not appear to be self-consciously reflexive, it often did have performative aspects reminiscent of the Italian passegiatta. While the passegiatta is normally an evening practice, it would be fair to describe some of the combined strolling, socialising and shopping that took place in the Broadway Market space, during the mornings and early afternoons when the market operated, as being in this promenading style. A considerable proportion of walking observed appeared to be slow, thoughtful, observant, and sociable, with aspects of social display relating to fashionable clothes and equipment such as wheeling 'fixie' bicycles. The physical form of the space at Broadway Market also seemed to affect the nature of walking being undertaken. A number of strollers traversed the space end to end, making a slow circuit around the food stalls. A substantial number could be observed arriving from the northeast (London Fields) end, where pedestrian paths, roads and bus links were best developed. The urban design related comments made earlier in the chapter tended to support the view that Broadway Market acted for its users as a kind of linear outdoor room.

As at Borough, shopping at market stalls and in small shops was seen to be a major socio-spatial practice at Broadway Market. Shopping was observed as an enjoyable and even an exciting practice. A number of comments contrasted favourably the experience of food shopping at the street market with supermarket shopping. Interviewees and online accounts were both very positive about Broadway Market as a rejuvenated food market at which to browse and buy at stalls and small food shops. The stalls and food shops that lined the street were important physical elements in the social life of the space, which was described as "an absolute gem" (Anonymous, 04 Apr 2006) and offering "unusual and stunning merchandise at affordable prices" (Huw, 19 Apr 2006). Like these online comments from market users, unstructured observations of behaviour at Broadway appeared to support the contention that considerable enjoyment was derived from browsing the human-scaled stalls, getting close to fresh produce and establishing a direct physical connection to the food and the people selling it. Broadway Market's location made it a good place just to "chill out" (TD, 26 Apr 2006). Few market users interviewed specifically connected their enjoyment of the food market to the nature of the physical spaces within which stall and small shop browsing and buying occurred. However, the observations of their behaviour strongly suggested that visitors liked and felt comfortable in the enclosed space of the street.

Observations undertaken at the food quarter showed a great deal of street-based eating and drinking occurring as a socio-spatial practice at Broadway Market. The stall layout was intentionally organised to include food-eating zones or clusters. Visitors ate food, and drank coffee and juice, from specialist stalls while sitting in, standing around or wandering through the food market. Those eating and drinking could be observed standing, or sitting on the pavement, as well as using folding chairs provided by food vendors at or near their stalls. As at Borough, eating in the street appeared to be exempt from negative connotations about civility in Elias's terms. Instead, eating appeared to be encouraged by both the shape of the space, and the infrastructure provided by market management, stallholders and food business lining the street. A number of visitors were also going to cafes, pubs and restaurants along the market street during market hours. Interviewee comments and online commentary from local people tended to celebrate the eating and drinking diversity available in the area (Anonymous, 05 Aug 2004). Broadway Market's own website noted an eclectic mix of possibilities, and food contrasts in evidence: "a recently refurbished gastro-pub with a sophisticated yet friendly atmosphere sits cheek to jowl with the traditional pie and mash shop." (Broadway Market Co, n.d.)

It was notable that the food market street attracted other kinds of social uses, such as art practice and impromptu music making, to a considerably greater degree than at Borough. During one observation at Broadway Market a number of small computer screens were found in shop windows showing images from the market street. These were part of a performance art process, "Porta Porter", underway over a week at the street, which played on visual and cultural associations with the street as a food market. Observations and interviews also suggested that music was being employed as part of the revival of the food market, as well as occurring in an impromptu way. During observations two kinds of street musicians were seen. The first was a lone acoustic guitarist; the second a group of drummers at the northern park and bus stop end of the street. The market manager commented that the market had *"started having local entertainment etc"*, although such signs of liveliness caused anxieties with the local council. *"The council got rid of the on street entertainment [buskers] as they were worried about risk"*.

One of the most obvious socio-spatial practices seen at the case study area was people doing community based politics. As discussed earlier, in certain respects the future of Broadway Market as a place had for some become a somewhat charged, politicised issue, in which "a greasy spoon café became the front line of a war between locals and developers" (Kunzru, The Guardian, G2, 7 December, 2005, p.8). During one observation at Broadway Market, three groups were handing out leaflets for campaigns on local issues. These included a campaign to halt a luxury residential tower block development in the local area, and support for the previously described "battle" in which local café and shop owners were "forced out by developers". On another observational visit, a group with signs, banners and clipboards was collecting signatures in support of its campaign to reopen the Haggerston pool, recently closed down by LB Hackney.

Broadway Food Map Key Shops etc 1. Fruit and Veg - Off License 2. Nutritious Food Gallery/Fresh Fish 3. Climpson and Son Shopfront - cafe 4. Cat and Mutton Pub 5. Percy Ingle Bakery 6. Organic and Vegetarian Coffee and Tea Room 7. Broadway Café (caf) 8. Broadway Wines 9. H. Tidiman Butcher's and Poulterers 10. La Bouche Delicatessen 11. Costcutter's supermarket 12. Broadway Supersaver - Off License 13. The Dove Freehouse 14. Off License 15. Organic Food Fresh Food and Vegetables	16. F. Cooke - Pie and Eel Shop 17. Solché Grill - Meze Bar 18. La Vie en Rose cafe 19. Broadway Fish Bar Stalls 20. Fresh Pasta 21. Eggs/Poultry/Meat Van 22. Coffee Bar and seating 23. Cake Stall 24. Juice Box 25. Bread Stall 26. Sussex Smokers 27. Roast Meat Stall 28. Olive Oils 29. Fruit and Vegetables 30. German Deli 31. Downland Produce 32. Fruit and Vegetable Stall 33. Olive Stall 34. Bread Stall	35. Meat, eggs etc stall 36. Popina Cakes 37. The Cinnamon Tree Bakery 38. Norbiton Fine Cheese 39. Fishmonger 40. Fruit and Vegetable Stall 41. Flowers 42. Café 43. Cheese and Cured Meat Stall 44. Crepes Stall 45. Damascean Falafel 46. Burgers and other hot food stall 47. The Jewish Deli 48. Flour Power Bread Stall 49. Cookies and Cream 50. Organic Cakes etc 51. Cheese Stall 52. Mushroom Stall 53. Empty Stall 54. Apple Stall 55. Tomato Stall

Figure 5.3: *Broadway Food Map Key* Source: Prepared by author

As at Borough, food mapping was undertaken at Broadway Market in 2008, and generally supported the observations and interviews from the study area. Figure 5.3 provides a key to the various shops, cafes and stalls mapped. At the time the mapping was undertaken, stalls were found along most of the length of the street, halting at the gate near to the canal end, which was closed during market operating hours. The mapping showed loose groupings of both food and non-food stalls, although food stalls predominated. Around half way down the street there was a café 'zone', complete with an appealing clutter of chairs, tables and stools, making use of the broadening out of the space where Broadway met the side roads of Meek Close and Benjamin Close. There was another such zone near the southern end, with stalls selling hot food, coffee, juice and cakes, as well as various places to sit including the road kerbs.

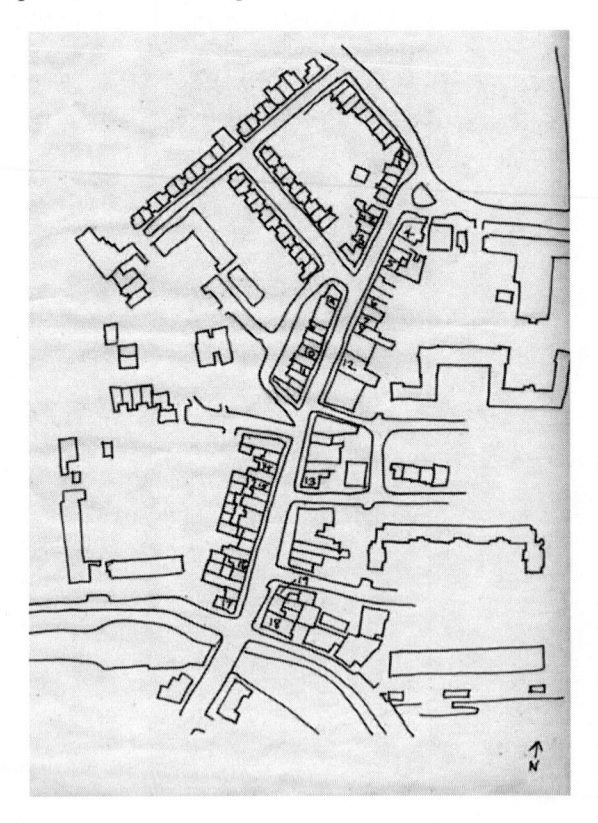

Figure 5.4.: *Broadway Market Food Shops and Land Uses* Source: Prepared by author

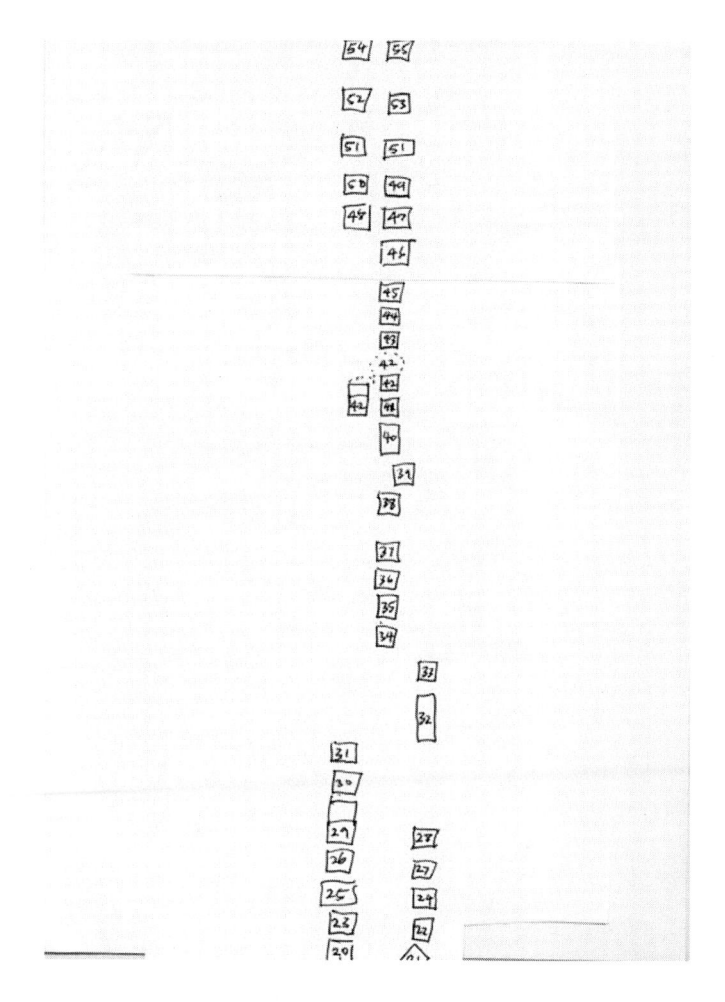

Figure 5.5.: *Broadway Market Food Stalls* Source: Map prepared by author

A wide variety of produce could be found, from fruit and vegetables to cheese, dairy products, pasta, meat, fish and olive oil. There were specialist stalls for particular vegetables such as mushrooms, tomatoes, and apples and pears. The stress was on artisanal, regional and (some) organic produce. Like Borough, the emphasis was on food to take home to cook, but there were also hot foods on offer to eat on the street at the market, including burgers, roast meat in rolls, and cakes. Along either side of the street a number of individual shop fronts were given over to food-related land uses, including off-licenses that sold fruit, vegetables, groceries and wine; and cafes, tea rooms, restaurants, pubs and bars. Many of these had large windows and door openings to the street, and seating against their frontages that was well used during market hours.

Broadway Market's community-led food quarter development

Broadway Market's history to 2008, when the fieldwork was completed, was a story of deep economic decline and rapid food-led regeneration, within a particular urban design frame, that at the time the research was undertaken, gave rise to some intriguing economic, environmental and convivial socio-spatial practices. While not formally a farmers' market, Broadway's revival can be set in the context of a broader movement around alternative food geographies and spaces evident in London through the rise of farmer's style markets. At the same time, apparent local authority governance weaknesses acted as a constraint that had to be overcome in the Broadway Market quarter's rebirth, in a similar way that it did at Borough. In both cases the experience of local food centred renewal contrasted with the predominant mode of top-down regeneration practice in the United Kingdom. The adverse results of apparently poor public sector management of renewal may have been even worse at Broadway than those suffered through ostensible local authority neglect of Borough. After Broadway virtually ceased to function as a market, and the street itself went into seemingly terminal decline, the local authority was claimed to actively obstruct its revival.

Paralleling Borough's experience, the economic development and management gap identified by research respondents was filled by the 'bottom-up' action of the Broadway Market Traders and Residents Association to revive the food market, led by a charismatic and feisty community leader. The volunteer market manager from BMTRA set up a community-based management structure, featuring partnership working between traders, residents and other local stakeholders. Under her leadership, they created a *"whole shopping experience"* centred on conviviality, civility, and a sense of place and community. Again, like Borough, the market avoided *"dog-eat-dog"* competition between pitches, and this was based on the same thinking that too sharp competition too early in the market's revival would be likely to destroy fledging food businesses. Economic success created, and at the same time was created by, an increasing visitor catchment: local, borough wide and eventually extending into other parts of London and beyond. As at Borough in the period to 2008, the market developed a positive economic feedback loop through its subtle handling of growth issues.

The market's economic success had a number of uneven ripple effects in economic areas, which were outside its control. For example, there was thought to be profit taking by property developers and individual house buyers in the area on and around Broadway Market, while some local activist groups argued that catchment growth for the food market signified not just regeneration but gentrification in action. This is very much in keeping with the conventional analysis of gentrification process critiqued in Chapter 2. In this reading of area improvement, regeneration that is based around creation of a new consumption space quickly shades into a gentrification process in the "revanchist" city that benefits incomers and excludes existing populations (Smith, 1996). It was certainly evident by 2008 that incomers, including young media workers, artists, writers, actors, "yummy mummies" and food aware European migrants, found the market appealing as a both a good food place and a fashionable location to hang out. So at one level, Broadway might well be thought to present a gentrifying space, as both a developing food and cultural quarter in which individuals played out a particular 'hip' habitus.

However, there were distinct differences in views held by interviewees as to whether the food market's attraction to those incomers, (who were defined by interviewees as primarily local residents and 'visitors' rather than 'tourists') was predominantly a positive or negative trend. There was disagreement over whether other aspects of the quarter's transformation were simply signs of gentrification or a more positive reflection of renewal attracting a mixed community. Among contested points were whether food prices were higher than supermarkets and whether that signified that the market was only for middle class visitors and buyers. The 'markets are more expensive' argument seemed to be based on assumptions rather than much actual evidence, as when price comparisons were undertaken (as for instance those cited by the market manager) these demonstrated parity or in some cases cheaper food products at markets. However, these views were strongly stated by some interviewed, and perceptions about price differentials may reflect a need to justify a continued preference for supermarket and ready meal consumption that by the early 2000s was normative (an area in which further evidenced-based work would be interesting).

Views differed as to whether the long-term local working class population benefited from economic renewal efforts based on food market-led regeneration. Local critics argued that food led renewal was leading to increasing property prices that working class people could not afford; to their exclusion from the environmental and social benefits of healthy food and from enjoying the market as a social space. Moreover, the view was that gentrification effects were being felt more broadly through new, high-priced residential developments (some of questionable quality), local businesses being driven out, rent hikes occurring, and empty shops and properties potentially undermining the street's vitality. Owners were thought to hold back on developing some of their newly acquired assets to wait for the most financially propitious moment. One argument made locally was that the first tranche of small food businesses in the market would also be likely to suffer in the longer term. Rent rises would force out individual ventures that were catering for the first wave of incomers, and "clone town Britain" chains would then colonise the space.

Points made by those interviewed and observational material, though, both challenged such a straightforward gentrification reading, whereby the food market's revival was simply and clearly instrumental in a classic gentrification process. It has been important to acknowledge the complexities inherent in the regeneration and gentrification processes that were observed at Broadway Market and give space to the range of perspectives relevant to the development of Broadway Market as a highly successful food space. The research suggested that Broadway Market, for many years showing signs of being a food desert, had by the mid 2000s become a vibrant food quarter that served a diverse community of interest in food.

While there was some evidence of place marketing, this was not particularly commodifying in approach. The rise of the food market and the urban area around it could be seen in a nuanced way as typified by a mix of cultures and classes that contributed to its unique character. Food shops and stalls to some extent acted in synergy as part of a deliberate strategy by the BMTRA. At the time the research was undertaken there were no chain stores in the street apart from the local long established Percy Ingle bakery and very few empty shops. Rather, traditional shops maintained some food services for the long-term working class population, while newer stalls, cafes and restaurants extended the range and quality of what was on offer, attracting a wider catchment of visitors.

In relation to the original decline of the street market, the market manager asked if the existing local population was so keen to maintain its traditional street market, why had they allowed it to die away by preferring to shop at supermarkets? One conclusion might well be that this consumption behaviour pointed not to gentrification effects but to powerful, external structural forces in food retailing and marketing, urban political economy and spatiality impinging on and transforming local consumption habits. Equally, the research showed that incomers were supporting campaigns against shop evictions and other local battles against building luxury high-rise flats and the closure of the local swimming pool, and again this did not fit the classic gentrification analysis. In the manager's view the market was about bringing people together and acted as an *"amazing catalyst"*.

Urban design issues and elements clearly interconnected with Broadway's economic revitalisation. Broadway's ambience was as a cool place to hang out, rather than as an architecturally outstanding space developed as the result of an explicit architectural strategy as at Borough. However, case study findings suggested that the quarter's urban design characteristics had both direct and indirect impacts on its economic, social and environmental functioning. Broadway Market displayed compact, walkable urbanism focused on the public realm, and was surrounded in the immediate area by a relatively coherent urban fabric, although this spatiality was fragmented and gave way to various lost spaces a little further afield. Its urban design qualities were embedded in its traditional urban spaces, providing a setting for and underpinning economic revival.

Until recently, Broadway was also a relatively cheap and somewhat inaccessible area of London in which to live that began to attract people who possessed considerable cultural capital but fewer economic resources. Over time, the area changed as some more affluent people moved in, but the market's spatiality continued to reflect a diverse social mix: what local interviewees described as a *"random"* quality. At the same time, some saw revitalisation shading into gentrification as signified through the changing nature of the food on offer, and through the practices of place-users in relation to that food. In this transformation, food was understood to emphasise a certain kind of spatiality by shaping the configuration of food shops, stalls and spaces. In this way, as one interviewee put it, traditional shops on Broadway Market like Cooke's (the eel and pie shop) could be understood as a sign of the area's authenticity for incomers even if those same incomers did not often visit them.

Acknowledgement of the design framework at broad and more immediate spatial scales was often an implicit rather than explicit element in interviewees' accounts, although a number made reference to the qualities of the space that to a designer demonstrate a number of desirable features. The area's spatiality spoke of a traditional urban shaping, which one of those interviewed described as an *"urban village"*, a design concept with significant history (Tibbalds, 1992) that reflects compact urbanism principles including mixed land use, walkability, fine grain and human scale. A connection was made between the urban design of the space and local regeneration objectives. The street's location, between the canal to the south and the park to the north, helped funnel people into and along Broadway Market, and provided an excellent pathway for promenading and serial vision. The street demonstrated a high level of enclosure, generated by fine-grained, active and robust building frontages of shops along each side, and reinforced by stall structures around and past which people flowed. At a smaller scale, it could be seen that the way people used the edge of the space was very intricate and lively, in line with the urban design qualities of vitality and personalisation, and reflected the range of convivial practices noted earlier. The fine grain of activity that the design of physical space allowed at this human scale was another urban design quality richly in evidence. Although there were also negative urban design related effects including noise and wind, and safety effects were also mentioned, in part associated with the market's need to manage the interplay of walking, cycling and driving, these did not undermine the strong sense of place generated by Broadway Market as a burgeoning food quarter.

These urban design qualities underpinned Broadway Market's rapid revival. Unlike Borough, it was generally thought unlikely that the market would develop to the extent to which local shoppers would be deterred by tourist crowds as had been argued at Borough Market. However, the market manager did acknowledge that she feared the property market would *"go nuts and it has"*. This was among the external forces bearing on area regeneration that had a 'macro' urban design component. In this case, the development of sub-regional transport infrastructure (which was in its construction phase at the time the research was undertaken) promised to make the area more accessible in the next few years, and thus a more desirable place to live. This would, in turn, accelerate the pace of regeneration and potentially gentrification. Transport changes, such as the extension of the rail network, were one way that urban design at a broader level was having impacts on the space at the Broadway Market food quarter, and combining with the street and area's inherent design qualities to make the quarter an increasingly attractive place to live.

Moving on to environmental aspects of food-led revitalisation, a number of largely positive sustainability effects were created or accentuated by the Broadway area's development. Like Borough, the market at the core of the food quarter space was a loci for the food system, covering both distribution and consumption phases. The food market was not a formal farmers' market but shared some of these markets' environmental characteristics. Again, like Borough, the market challenged certain aspects of the modern food system by promoting artisanal, small scale, seasonal foods largely bought by a local catchment of people doing their shopping on foot. There was a stress on sustainability embedded in the focus on local, geographically typified foods for sale. Moreover, stallholders played an active role in sharing expertise with consumers, with concern expressed by both sellers and buyers to purchase, cook and eat in an environmentally and gastronomically informed way. High prices (if they are indeed higher than the supermarket, a contested point) were thought to reflect excellent quality and artisanal production methods, and were accepted on that basis by buyers interviewed. Observations and interviews suggested that most buyers were using sustainable means of getting to and from the market by walking there and then home with their purchases. There were also some mixed food consumption methods in evidence that could be judged more sustainable than supermarket based shopping, with buyers reporting a combination of stall and shop buying, with online purchases and home delivered box schemes. All in all these consumption patterns fitted well with the theoretical characterisation of a food quarter's elements, including more sustainable food consumption practices.

Considered as a social space, the food market and its environs at Broadway acted as a rich physical territory for informal and spontaneous social interaction, giving rise to a wide range of opportunities for conviviality. Broadway could be seen as supporting the construction of everyday life in a Lefebvrian sense through unmediated encounters, yet challenging notions of civility in Elias's terms by encouraging street-based eating. Visitors reported Broadway as a perfect space for promenading. For some it provided the context for a whole day's sociability, with various socio-spatial practices enacted over the course of some hours. Many of these practices were focused on food consumption at the market; a typical trajectory was of first browsing, then eating and drinking at cafes and in the street, then again browsing, and finally buying food, followed by making meals at home after market hours.

Like Borough, Broadway Market was described by interviewees as *"a hidden gem"*, discovered by stumbling across it, hearing of it by word of mouth, or reading about it in the print media as a 'cool' place to go. On the one hand, the Broadway Market food quarter possessed a form of stylishness, defined as a place to pose with a *"certain milieu"*. It conformed to arguments about stylish consumption, the development of the space as a cultural quarter, and the construction and playing out of a particular individual habitus. In all these ways Broadway proved similar to Borough, although somewhat less fully realised and more modestly proportioned in spatial and catchment terms. On the other hand, again like

Borough, Broadway as the heart of a burgeoning food quarter also appeared to be expressing a strong sense of community. This was articulated in a variety of ways: through food, fashion, politics, culture, community development, or a mix of some or all of these and others besides. There was a complex array of activities, motives and social positioning at play. The space was not entirely commodified in the way that Lefebvre describes but framed many unmediated encounters reflecting de Certeau's practices of everyday life.

Looking at specific socio-spatial practices identified through the observations and food mapping, walking was singled out as one of the most dominant behaviours. It appeared to be both self-conscious, as in the passegiatta, and less mediated and more instrumental as it related to food browsing and buying. As explained previously, the street's physical shape both acted as a funnel and created an outdoor room that supported pedestrian flow. Food browsing and buying were connected socio-spatial practices, which were seen as very positive and enjoyable. The street was felt to be a good place to visit because of the combination of the attractions of the food market and its proximity to other sites including London Fields, which were among the fundamental elements that constructed the quarter as a spatial entity. Eating and drinking in the street was likewise a very common practice, and there were human scaled food-eating 'zones' created by the relationship of the stall layout and fixed built structures that were intentionally defined in a spatial sense by the market's manager and traders. And, as at Borough, the foodscape appeared exempt from taboos about public eating, as Valentine (1998) has proposed.

While art and music occurred in the street, examples of art practice seen during the research phase seemed to suffer from a lack of substantial local connection to the community, as well as opaque language and objectives. This perhaps reflects art practice norms, in which language and methods speak to the practitioner's peers rather than a wider public, so should not be a surprise. However, it was interesting that the "Porta Porter" proponents, for example, chose Broadway Market as the stage for their art event. It seemed likely that this was because Broadway had become an important local street culturally, and this was in part based on resurgence by way of the food market. It could also be argued that this kind of spatial practice connected to the early 'arty' stage of the gentrification process. Music as a socio-spatial practice, meanwhile, seemed less mediated, and more immediately connected to the place. In part, this was a conscious policy of the market manager; in part, an impromptu practice, but again the council appeared to play a blocking role.

Doing community politics was a common socio-spatial practice, unsurprisingly in a place whose future direction was being to some extent contested. Its prevalence was intriguing in the social and design context of food-led renewal. The substantial number of observations of local political activity tended to suggest that the market street provided a particularly appealing venue for the practice of community politics in everyday life. As the most important node of intensity in a food-based urban quarter, the street market attracted concentrations of people, who could then be approached with campaigning information, or potentially recruited to support local campaigns. It also provided a site for more aggressive graffiti, and while the graffiti writers were clearly taking an oppositional position in relation to incomers, it appeared to be assumed by other less confrontational campaigners that the values of visitors who sought out local, often organic, farmers' market style food, would also be sympathetic to their perspectives on various regeneration issues.

Furthermore, the shape of the space supported this political activity by providing a comfortable outdoor room in which to engage with others. Crucially, this was public space from which campaigners were not going to be moved on or asked to leave, in the way they would in the private space of a shopping centre or mall, as here they were operating in the public realm. And finally in this area, although there were equally vexed issues elsewhere locally, it was the future of this one street that appeared to have particularly fired the local imagination and galvanised political activity in relation to economic and social change. The food street and market might well be conceptualised as both the physical centre of the food quarter and the symbol of local meaning and identity.

The chapter has traced the development of the Broadway Market area as a maturing food quarter in the period up to 2008. In so doing, a number of similarities to Borough's regeneration trajectory emerged but in the context of a more local focus and visitor catchment, based on a highly successful community led approach to food-centred renewal. In both Broadway and Borough Market food quarters, a particular urban design context framed and appeared to actively engage with and influence a range of economic, environmental and socio-spatial practices in relation to food. The next chapter provides the opportunity to compare these two case study areas of food led renewal with the somewhat different experience of a regenerated food space centred on Clerkenwell's Exmouth Market.

CHAPTER SIX

RENEWAL OF A DIFFERENT KIND AT EXMOUTH MARKET

Introducing the Exmouth Market quarter

This chapter explores the way food and place interconnected at Exmouth Market through food led renewal in the three-year period to 2008. The discussion draws predominantly on semi-structured interviews, informal observations and mapping at Exmouth, augmented by press reports and online commentary. As in the other case study chapters, the story of Exmouth Market is refracted through a sustainability prism, and makes reference to findings from the two other study areas and to the theoretical frame for the work.

Much of the discussion focuses on the economic decline and renewal of Exmouth, and the way that the revival of the social life of the street and area in the period up to 2008 was significantly related to its role as a food space. As for the Broadway Market food quarter, while little direct comment was made by those interviewed about Exmouth's environmental performance, at the same time environmental aspects of sustainability permeated much of the discussion.

The narrative of decline and food-led regeneration was a major theme at Exmouth, with the area renewed as a food-centred space even more recently than the other two quarters. Research at Exmouth showed an area with many similarities to the two other sites, including the framework provided by urban design qualities of a particular kind of traditional city form. As at Borough, in the early 2000s Exmouth had became a food space based on high quality, artisanal foods. As at Broadway, the communities of interest within the area's catchment were quite diverse and there appeared to be some disconnection between long term, working class residents and newer, more middle class arrivals within a regeneration context. Food-related land uses, including the revived market, were a focus for community development, and some contention, about the best way forward to revive the area. While eating on the street was a strong feature of both Borough and Broadway's experience, Exmouth's revived market became even more predominantly a 'slow food' market based on hot food stalls, than was the case in the two other spaces. Unlike the other quarters, Exmouth did not successfully redevelop as a fully-fledged street market. Instead, Exmouth's mixture of high quality restaurants and 'slow' fast food gave rise to a somewhat different food focus for convivial socio-spatial practices.

Exploring Exmouth Market's decline and food-led revival

The post Second World War period was bad for Exmouth Market. Like both Borough and Broadway markets, Exmouth Market suffered an almost complete decline as a shopping and market street after the Second World War, despite various regeneration efforts, especially in the period spanning the 1970s to mid 1990s. Unsuccessful attempts were made to revive the market in the 1980s, and again in the early 1990s, including reducing stallholder charges and trying to attract stallholders from waiting lists for other markets (Whitelegg, 2002, p.81). The major landlord in the street, Debenhams, was able to let only four shops between 1988 and 1995, despite substantially lowering rents, and the vacancy rate by 1996 was forty per cent higher than that for the rest of the London Borough of Islington. A number of physical regeneration actions by the local council included major repaving, but by the beginning of the 1990s the street's future remained uncertain. An argument continued over "parking restrictions, poor access, refuse collection, poor lighting and general litter" (*op cit*), and the street was seen to have sunk back to its pre-1986 state of decline. A piece in The Islington Gazette quoted by Whitelegg (*op cit*) noted at the time that, "Exmouth Market, once the thriving heart of village life, is now a squalid and filthy slum - according to the people who live there".

By the late 1990s, though, the street had shifted from a traditional food market in steep decline to a much more upmarket site for restaurants and cafes, serving a predominantly middle class local catchment of businesses and residents (Whitelegg, 2002, pp.83-84). An Islington Council planning decision in November 1996 was seen to be the key to the street's revival (*ibid*). Until 1992 the street had been designated as a protected shopping area and this was reflected in planning policy, which was unrealistically restrictive in terms of possible land uses that could be established in the street. A change to letting policy, to allow up to 50% of vacant property to be let for non-retail uses, was the result of an increasingly partnership-based approach to regeneration between the Debenham Property Trust and the council, who together developed an Exmouth Market Working Party. This was supported by the proactive intervention of council planning officers to drive forward a strategy of regeneration in the street, based on cultural activity and maximising its resources of cultural capital (Whitelegg, 2002, p.82).

Exmouth Market was also able to attract Single Regeneration Budget funds in the mid 1990s, and food was already central to these regeneration plans. Persuading restaurants to locate in Exmouth Market was an explicit aim. The street's revival fitted well with the growth of a new breed of restaurateurs and bar owners in the mid 1990s, with the Chair of Urban Regeneration at Islington talking about "how good restaurants and wine bars would help rejuvenate a dilapidated area, especially when in close proximity to Sadler's Wells" (*ibid*). Debenhams had also proposed a "restaurant solution" in one of its reports. However, in words reminiscent of those used about Broadway Market, a local resident wrote:

> "The more I read...about...the invasion of places like Exmouth Market by trendy restaurants and bars, etc., the more I am convinced that it is a conscious policy of Islington Council to get rid of the working class of this borough to make way for the middle classes" (Letters, Islington Gazette, 28 March, 1998, quoted in Whitelegg, 2002, p.88).

As at Broadway and Borough, it appeared that informal channels of communication, rather than any formal public sector-led regeneration partnership, were the most important in bringing interesting cafes and restaurants to the street. Initially, the café Crowbar, and then a little later, the restaurant Moro, were attracted in, as personal networks came into play to introduce possible restaurateurs to Debenhams. Interviewees shared a similar narrative about the street's revival in this regard. The co-owner of an upmarket restaurant said such networks were crucial:

> *"We have a friend who opened a coffee shop called the Crowbar. Then they came here...then I worked in The Eagle before that as well. So, but in the street there was this place, the Crowbar, and they were friends of ours and they said 'oh the landlords are really nice...and they said there are free spaces. So they were the first people who came down, then Starbucks opened opposite them".*

Debenhams actively pursued restaurateurs who could add to the street's uniqueness, and offered premises on extremely favourable terms. Locating on such an out of the way, down-at-heel street was still a financially precarious business. As the restaurateur explained,

"[Crowbar] were expanded then they went bust. But they were the people that introduced us. [You've been here for the long haul...] "We were quite worried. We were quite worried".

A restaurant manager at another restaurant located on the street traced a similar trajectory of restaurant openings, emphasising quality. *"I think Moro was one of the first, the Eagle was here and then Medcalf...these places provided high quality".* A café owner meanwhile argued that, as the regenerating Upper Street nearby became too expensive to run a restaurant in, Exmouth became more attractive, although rents remained an issue. Despite slightly varying narratives, it is clear that restaurants were essential to the street's revival from the early 1990s to 2008, with Exmouth Market described as "a street of gastronomic renown. Restaurants such as Metcalf, Moro, and the nearby Eagle pub have established the area as being synonymous with good food" (The Evening Standard, 20.09.06, p.36). The restaurant manager referred to the quality of uniqueness apparent among most food businesses at Exmouth Market. *"Everything is individual and unique, apart from Strada really, and a couple of others".* This sense of uniqueness related to individual food shops as well as restaurants on Exmouth Market (Country Life, n.d.). The restaurant manager also made a link to the economic basis for this unique quality. The preponderance of independent businesses was connected by the restaurant manager to achieving a sense of community between traditional and more recent businesses in the street:

"Everything is independent businesses. There's a really nice atmosphere between all the businesses and there's quite a close-knit community in the street. You know all the businesses get on really well. There's a couple of old family businesses...they have been there for a long time, especially the pie and mash shop. And then there's newer people. You know everyone knows everyone's names".

Although restaurants and cafes seem to have emerged independently through informal processes, by the early 1990s, there were also formal regeneration plans developing for the return (in some form) of the street's defunct food market. The local council commented at the time that it was unrealistic to expect there would be any regeneration of Exmouth Market as a street market, with a reduced market the best that could be hoped for (Ham and High, 28 February, 1997, p.7, quoted in Whitelegg, 2002, p.86). An idea for a renewed market was mooted under City Fringe Partnership funding but did not come to fruition. Earlier it had also been suggested that the food market be relocated to the "Farringdon triangle" (that is, the southwestern end of the street where it abuts Farringdon Road and Rosebery Avenue), to increase its visibility, and give an appearance of activity (*ibid*). At the time the research was undertaken this was the portion of the street where the hot food stalls were located, a placement considered later in the chapter in relation to their urban design implications.

A fully-fledged food market?

The unpromising history of regeneration attempts at Exmouth provides a context for the difficulties another attempt to run a fully-fledged food market encountered in the period up to 2008. From around the 21st September 2006 a weekly food market, initially including fruit and vegetables, meat, cheese and hot food stalls, was begun on Fridays and Saturdays at the southwestern end of the street. At that time it was noted that while local restaurants,

> "have enjoyed bustling trade, the numbers of customers at local grocery shops have dwindled. In an effort to draw shoppers back to the area, two of its high profile restaurateurs are launching a farmer's market this Friday" (Evening Standard, 20.09.06, p.36).

A website was set up for the 'farmers' market', and made a direct connection between the nature of the street, as a place that housed small, individual businesses, and the notion of food mix and quality. It pointed to the eclectic nature of the street's available food products and its urban design context:

> "Exmouth Market is a vibrant pedestrianised street in the heart of Clerkenwell flanked on either side by a colourful mixture of small independent design boutiques and long-standing traditional shops, as well as the many bars, cafés and restaurants for which it is well known comprising an eclectic mix to satisfy even the most discerning shopper and gastronome" (Exmouth Market, 2010).

By early in 2008, though, most of the fresh food stalls had disappeared, to be replaced by a Friday-only collection of hot food stalls, rather in the style of a particularly up market 'slow food' outdoor food court. Notwithstanding this change in the nature of the food market, Exmouth clearly enjoyed a very considerable degree of food-related regeneration in the three-year period to 2008. Central to this process were a number of individuals with a strong background in food who established the briefly revived market. Some of those mentioned in accounts at the time were also committee members on the Exmouth Market Traders Association:

> "Sam Clark's Moro triggered a steady regeneration of Exmouth Market upon opening ten years ago, transforming the then run-down, boarded-up street into a focal point for fine food and quirky shops. Now Sam, Monika and Louise have decided that following the success of its annual summer festivals, Exmouth Market is finally ready to have its market reinstated" (My Islington, n.d.).

The market's proponents were reported as saying that the process of the market's re-emergence was inspired by farmers' markets in Marylebone, Stoke Newington and Broadway Market in Hackney, and required "six months of intense negotiation with Islington council" prior to its launch (Evening Standard, 20.09.06, p.36). At the time of the launch, Samantha Clark of Moro restaurant said of the intended nature of the market, that it would be a place for the complete weekly shop and a rich food-centred social experience for the whole community (*ibid*). The intention was that the market would provide a wide range of food rather than simply

> "high end organic produce normally associated with farmers' markets...we thought it would be good for the community to have a market here. It will be a place people can stroll around, have coffee, have lunch, wander into the shops, and look at the stalls. The idea is for people to do their weekly shop here too - buy fish, meat, eggs, everything... we'll have everything from speciality cheese stalls such as Neal's Yard and local bakers from St John Bread and Wine, to traditional greengrocer, Ted's Veg. We want this to appeal to the whole community" (Evening Standard, 20.09.06, p.36).

In a related way, a number of those interviewed for the research suggested that the revitalised food market was a logical outgrowth of the burgeoning restaurant scene in the street. A market proponent explained that one intended role for the food market was to bring more people to the street by acting as a *"magnet"* and emphasised the *"social, positive, life giving aspects of the market really. It means that street's the focal point"*. A restaurant owner interviewed described how it was that the kind of complete food market envisaged failed to work, either in its own terms, or as a catalyst for the street's revitalisation. One issue was that some of the food businesses that were expected to run stalls did not do so. This was described as

> *"slightly chicken and egg. Like places like [name of food business], they said they were going to have.... but they weren't prepared to give it a go.*

> *So some of the big boys didn't come here because they thought it wasn't going to be big enough".*

The new market's apparent decline early in its trading history was contrasted by online commentators with Borough's success (Kristainlondon, 2006) although the market was still attracting around 20 stalls up until mid 2007 whereas "until last year there were just three" (The London Paper, 7th August 2007, n.p.r.).

A number of those interviewed pointed to changes that came about over the course of the market's operation in 2006 to 2007, that were largely viewed as double-edged or negative. By some time into 2007, rather than selling fresh produce, the market had shifted to being largely one comprised of a hot food stalls trade for the lunch crowd on Fridays. One interviewee said *"It's kind of fallen apart a bit, the market, and I think it's closing. It's like on the way out"*. The market, he suggested, had become little more than a fast food space of an unusually high quality kind and should have *"stuck to its original things"*. Now it is *"like decent fast food. Which is OK but it's not what Exmouth Market is about"*. This interviewee made a direct, unprompted comparison with Broadway Market as a food space in relation to the local aspirations for what the food market might have provided:

> *"I thought when they started they wanted it to be more like Broadway, say, with fruit and veg...And I think they did but things have gone a bit.. They haven't really dictated who moves in there and they've found the most popular stalls are the ones who have these food stalls. So we will see what happens".*

A few interviewees appeared to view both the food market's advent and its subsequent changes with some ambivalence. A food business proprietor at Exmouth suggested that the stalls did bring people to the street, but at the same time took business away from existing food traders. An operator of a small food business similarly saw the process as one of unbalanced competition between different kinds of food companies. Food market stallholders were thought to have less stringent hygiene standards and to be paying much lower rates, making them much more competitive and less subject to regulation. Another of those interviewed also believed that fixed food businesses paid higher rates, but viewed the effects of this as much more double-edged. For this person's food business, the atmosphere that the food stalls-style market brought to the street offset any negative effect of these higher charges. For some interviewees the food market was viewed as a failure in terms of its original aims, but not an economic failure. An owner of an upmarket restaurant, for example, pointed out the precariousness for individual stallholders of operating in a new market and the implications this had for the nature of the food market:

> "I mean we all worked quite hard to get it off the ground but some of the stallholders weren't making enough money so...and they can make double the amount of money at the successful places. So it's slightly Catch 22. How long do they stay on until it gets a reputation? But there are fewer [stallholders]. But that's sort of just really...every area is different and you never know until you try what is sustainable".

This restaurant owner felt that the problem of economic sustainability experienced in operating as a 'complete' food market might also have been because there was insufficient passing trade in the street. If the food market had to rely predominantly on local residents doing their shopping there, it was difficult to make some fresh food stalls viable. This interviewee also noted the temporal nature of this issue, with better trade experienced on Fridays than Saturdays because there were more business people passing by. Another potentially contributing factor in the food market's decline as a 'complete' food market was competition between Exmouth Market and other nearby local street markets. Both the long-established Angel, Islington, with its Chapel Market, and the resurgent Whitecross Street market could be alternative destinations for food trips. A café owner argued that the opening of the retail and leisure based N1 Centre at Angel had an effect *"because it has everything under one roof"*.

Meanwhile, Whitecross Street may also have been a source of competition. At the time the research was undertaken, Whitecross Street, another formerly defunct market street to the southeast of Exmouth Market, was receiving substantial regeneration funds from national government through the EC1 New Deal for Communities for a periodic 'fine food festival'. The restaurant owner, though, did not believe that this would be having an effect on Exmouth's viability. Rather he argued that *"the social mix isn't quite right here and also the shopping mix isn't quite right, but it's a very delicate balance"*. The point made by this interviewee brought to the fore comparisons with Broadway Market, where a combination of broad, food-focused shopping and a diverse social mix were referred to as crucial to the street's recovery. Others were more positive about the current social mix at Exmouth. The restaurant manager described a sense of community apparent in Exmouth Market, with a positive if limited interplay between traditional and newer *"yuppie"* incomers attracted to different food spaces in the street and helping to conserve it:

"You know, London's wonderfully mixed and there's two different types of people who are conserving this street: there are the people who've lived here for generations and then there's the yuppies who've moved in. And Ladbrokes, the cleaners, the eel shop, you know, have always been here, and are for the people who have been here always, the families have always been here and then the yuppies are more at the sort of little café style places with.. There is a crossover but not huge".

Problems with establishing the food market's catchment were seen by some interviewees (and others reported in the press) to reflect local authority governance and management issues. Some of these issues were highlighted in a newspaper interview at the time.

"This renaissance [of Exmouth Market] is no mean feat when overstretched councils, which have responsibility for our street markets, have a poor track record for innovation management. And the battle is not over yet" (The London Paper, 07.08.2007, p.10).

Interviewees who were running Exmouth Market-based food businesses at the time the research was undertaken supported this view. For example, a café owner claimed that the problem with the market failing to live up to its initial promise was in part due to poor planning and management by the council. This interviewee argued that the council did not have the capacity to make improvements and had *"ignored"* ideas for streetscape upgrading such as putting in vehicle barriers to pedestrianise it *"like Carnaby Street"*, tree planting, bicycle racks, public toilets and a security presence. Another café owner argued that the council was particularly at fault in the way they managed the market and that this could be seen in a range of examples from the recent past, including the *"inept"* placement of a French Market in the street

"with no consultation whatsoever. They have no idea how to manage any of those things. I couldn't find anyone to talk to there called a market manager.. There is in theory but they certainly don't encourage it".

Perceived ineptitude was especially noticeable in the way that the council was felt to have failed to consult with local traders and other food businesses at Exmouth Market, on managing competition. This resulted in a perception there were unresolved spatial issues, for example, about the placement and nature of food stalls in front of fixed food businesses that were thought to have undermined competition. A café owner explained that they did not think that the food market would change for the better in the foreseeable future, not only because of the perceived inadequacy of council management, but also because of other food traders unrealistic expectations. This food business owner argued that the problems encountered were inherent to the proposal to revive the food market and that subsequent decline was inevitable given it was a flawed concept in the first place. *"I said to them if you do this, the market will be a failure. And it has been a failure. They will never learn because they don't want to listen"*. An additional factor for this interviewee was the role played by upmarket food shops in the street:

> *"And that market was originally a forum for the sale of food from [food business names]. They were pushing all the time but then they pulled out also. Their expectations didn't come true".*

A number of those interviewed were aware of Broadway Market's revival, and made unprompted comparisons between the two places. A café owner critically compared Exmouth with the management of Broadway Market's revival:

> *"I live in London Fields so I saw how Broadway was and I then saw what Broadway became. It was sort of moribund. Which was why I was so keen for something similar to happen here and it just never did".*

This interviewee suggested that while the renewal order in each place was somewhat different, with restaurants followed by a food market at Exmouth rather than a food market then food shops, cafes, pubs and restaurants as a basis for regeneration at Broadway, both ways of managing regeneration might have been workable:

> *"What was great about Broadway Market was it grew organically. It was about the community. There's things wrong with it but I still think it's a very good market".*

The interviewee argued that the economic strategy pursued at Broadway also worked better because a conscious element of careful placement of market stalls to maximise synergies between businesses:

> *"I mean I know that [name] who organises it very consciously puts certain kinds of stalls together....kind of zones...there's the fresh food, then there's the bakery bit. I think it's really smartly done and I think that's how I always hoped it would be here. Sadly it hasn't".*

A somewhat different analysis of the way the street had been redeveloped was presented by one interviewee, who felt that there was a much more 'us and them' situation between existing long-term working class residents on council estates and newer middle class residential and business incomers:

> *"I also think that the big problem is local people feel let down. That's right. They feel left out. This has been their street for donkey's years. Yuppies come in, you know. Sandwiches are expensive. There are probably a few places they'll use down here but not many".*

A restaurant owner agreed that there was something of a two-speed economy in the street in relation to food, with incomers not likely to visit traditional food and other shops very often. *"You know the yuppies will go and have a pie and eel, a pie and mash now and then, and probably have a bet now and then but not very often"*. Another interviewee conjectured that other, more economically inclusive, ways to regenerate the street could have been chosen, over what was perceived to be a food market for yuppies. A distinction was made between the food market as launched, stressing very high quality, artisanal foods, with ideas for what was described as a more *"normal"* market. An interviewee saw the need to develop a more broadly based retail strategy for the street; covering both market stalls and fixed shops, and based on analysis of the street as it was then operating. *"Then once you have analysed you only allow specific stalls that will attract more people here".*

Online commentary provided an additional insight into some of the food-related changes to the street and the sense among those who could be defined as 'urban pioneers' or first wave gentrifiers that the street had lost some of its traditional food appeal in the process of regenerating:

> "In 1978 I took on a studio in Clerkenwell, Easton St, just off Rosebery Avenue. In the 8 years that I was there Clerkenwell was discovered and in the last decade Exmouth Market has become a retail and culinary destination. But in the transition most of the shops and cafe's (sic) that gave it its colour have gone. Now, I absolutely don't miss the Wimpy Bar but I do miss Dino's Diner and the Quality Chop House. Yes, the Chop House is still there but only in a rather 'New Labour/Islington' sort of guise. You don't go in at 06.30am and get liver-egg-bubble-fried slice, two crusty slices with butter and a mug of tea as a hang-over cure" (London SE1 Forum).

The process of regeneration in Exmouth Market was situated by some as a straightforward case of gentrification in action, in which political machinations were at the heart of the regeneration process (Independent Working Class Association, 1999). Interviewees' comments generally suggested a more nuanced analysis of Exmouth' transformation than this 'us and them' reading of the street and area. They saw that aspects of gentrification were occurring in relation to food, yet at the same time acknowledged that high quality restaurants were a crucial basis for the social and economic revival of the street and wider quarter. The majority of interviewees who commented on this theme, said that the resurgence of the street and the Exmouth area, led by food businesses, was broadly a good thing, and one to be celebrated. Moreover, for some of those interviewed, food led renewal was not problematised at all. The restaurant manager interviewed, for example, argued instead that new restaurants in the area did not just serve an entirely new population coming into Exmouth but attracted longer-term local residents as well. There was a very high density of *"fantastically high quality places"* within a confined local radius such as

> *"Moro, Medcalf, Brindisa, and its fantastic. The Eagle at the end of the road, the Quality Chop House, and even in the surrounding area, The Easton. And then St John Street has St John, you know, so within a mile, 2 mile radius it's got some of the best restaurants in London".*

Asked who comprised the visitor catchment for such restaurants and for the market, the restaurant manager suggested that this varied over time, between lunch and dinner and between weekdays and weekends. Lunch was for local working people, while for dinner *"it's definitely residential... in the evening people who live in this area or towards Lamb's Conduit Street, that way"*. In terms of the catchment's class origins it was apparent that the perceived variation for this interviewee was within a relatively narrow band of middle class business and residential visitors. There were also views expressed by the restaurant manager about the kinds of industries attracted to the area since its revitalisation, and those likely to eat there, which again gave clues to class change over time:

> *"For us it changes. At lunch its people who work in the area because there's a high density of architects, a high density of media type people. EMAP have just moved but, they've just all gone up to Mornington Crescent. The Guardian are obviously just over there. There is a mixture of architects. There is the highest density of architects in Europe I think in this area".*

There was some speculation about why this restaurant-led regeneration process worked in Exmouth Market despite the problems with the development of the food market. One interviewee pointed to the catchments generated by the theatre, large-scale businesses, and public institutions like the Family Records Centre and courts, combined with cheap rents. *"And that's why Exmouth Market became a food market. The rents were cheap, but now they're not."* The impact of large rent increases was noted in exploration of the regeneration process in the street in the 1990s (Whitelegg, 2002, p.87) and remained a live issue at the time of the research. It was reported in the 1990s that large rent increases would be likely to drive out small businesses, to have them replaced by large scale multiples, such as chain food businesses (*ibid*). In this way it was feared that the uniqueness that drew individual food businesses to the street would be destroyed. In fact, by 2008 this had not happened to a substantial degree although there were now three food business chains present so the risk remained.

Another financial issue raised by some of those running food businesses at Exmouth was that changes in the nature of the catchment population, from primarily business to more predominantly residential, might seriously affect the viability of their food trade in the future. Asked if that would that help generate a bigger food catchment for the street, one argued that it was all a question of maintaining the right balance between different population segments. Press reports (Evening Standard, Homes and Property, Wednesday 21 February, 2007, p.5) meanwhile suggested that the balance was tipping towards residential land uses. The Guardian newspaper's site on Farringdon Road close to Exmouth Market had planning approval for 118 flats, while the Mount Pleasant Royal Mail Sorting Office site, just to the southwest, was described as the key to the regeneration of "a neglected triangle of land that links Kings Cross, Clerkenwell and Bloomsbury...with potential for a 1.75 million sq ft redevelopment" (*ibid*). Under a master plan developed by architects John McAslan and Partners, the 11 acre site at Mt Pleasant was proposed to be redeveloped as 1,500 homes, a public square, gallery and new sorting office. Proximity to Exmouth Market was one of the strongest aspects of its likely appeal to investors and new residents (*ibid*).

This situation was reminiscent of the real estate 'boosterism' occurring at both Borough and Broadway Market quarters at around the same time, in which the appeal of the nearby food spaces was an explicit element in property marketing efforts. It also supports the view that the area had shifted upmarket to become more middle class by the early 2000s. Exmouth's burgeoning role as a food quarter and the related gentrifying effects, were noted in press reports:

> "Historically, Mount Pleasant has been a village in its own right, employing about 3,000 postal workers. In recent years, surrounding neighbourhoods have become gentrified. Exmouth Market, opposite Mount Pleasant, used to be all betting shops and cafes. Now it's trendy bars and

restaurants. The balance has shifted away from a working-class community to a more affluent one" (*ibid*).

While Exmouth Market became something of a food destination in inner London, views varied between those interviewed as to the role played in this by restaurants and the shifting forms of the food market. A restaurant owner said that certain restaurants were a destination for dinners, but neither the street nor the food market were yet a destination for most:

> *"Well there's a minute amount of walk-in trade but a lot of it is business or residential so we are not a destination yet. Moro is [a destination]. But you know the market itself isn't a destination".*

Again, comparisons were drawn with Broadway Market, and the point made that a visit to Broadway Market could be part of an East End day out that could take in other local attractions for visitors. *"You know they do a little East End thing, but they don't really do that here. But if there was another thing here which drew them then they might".* Asked whether people might come to Exmouth Market then go south to St John Street, and perhaps Smithfield or the Barbican, the response was that this would be fairly unusual tourist behaviour. Rather, Exmouth Market might be a food stop for people going to Sadler's Wells theatre. *"So sometimes they'll come here to have a pre-theatre supper. At that time the [food] stalls will still be out, so that's quite positive".* Another of those interviewed echoed the view that Moro restaurant clearly attracted people as a destination, but that other food shops in the street too might be a destination for some:

> *"There's really nowhere to touch Moro in terms of providing really high quality food but also food that you can't really eat anywhere else. You can get variations on it, but it's quite specific. And, to a certain extent, Brindisa."*

The view was that the qualities of friendliness and community were also an important part of Exmouth Market's attractiveness to people as a food place:

> *"I've worked in the street for 8 years, so much of it is tied in with the friendliness and community. I know and like people in all the shops that I go to, so for me it's almost as much a kind of social thing".*

Exmouth Market was understood as a social connector and this was an important part of its appeal. A café owner argued that the place acted to support developing social networks and that his shop provided a social space for people to network with each other to mutual advantage, but also for less instrumental reasons. Asked whether the advent of the food market had made any difference to the number of people coming to the street, or the mix of people, the café owner suggested that there may have been a *"marginal increase"* on Fridays but was not sure how well the food market worked in terms of its original aims. *"I still think it's a really positive thing, but in terms of business or changing the face of the market, not really"*.

Most of those interviewed thought that Exmouth Market had gone significantly *"upmarket"* over the years that the restaurants, and more latterly the food market, had been in operation. The street had become less *"rough"* than in the past. The restaurant manager, for example, saw this as most likely the result of a conscious strategy by the local Exmouth Market Traders Association to benefit the community. This interviewee also noted the more visible presence of community policing officers in the street, concluding, *"I think it's probably tried to go upmarket…a lot more care is taken of the community"*. Another of those interviewed made reference to a history of anti-social behaviour in the street. For example, in its early days as a food space in the late 1990s, Moro was *"witnessing several alarming scenes with local youths"*, thought to be related to anger at older businesses it was claimed by some were being 'forced out' of the street by rent increases (Whitelegg, 2002, p.87). It is possible to speculate that if this behaviour reflected local resentment, it could also be fuelled by witnessing scenes of conspicuous consumption in a once predominantly working class area. The restaurant manager explained that when there was anti-social behaviour it was responded to. *"Yeah last summer there was a spate of like bikes being stolen and so they just, you know, stamped on that. It's gone now. It doesn't happen"*.

Connecting regeneration and urban design

A central aspect of Exmouth Market's redevelopment in the late 1980s and early 1990s was the physical renovation programme to improve its streetscape, especially through paving and lighting treatments. The street's vehicle space was narrowed, and more room was given to shared pedestrian space which could also be used for outdoor tables for restaurants and cafes. These design changes

> "became an object of hostility from the Neighbourhood Forum, as older residents in particular found it difficult to negotiate their way around the tables and found themselves increasingly forced into the road, which was still not completely closed to traffic" (Whitelegg, 2002, p.86).

Pedestrianisation remained an issue for a number of those interviewed, but there was little support, and sometimes active disapproval, for the idea of Exmouth Market as a fully pedestrianised space. A café owner, for instance, was vehemently opposed to pedestrianisation, and provided the example of Covent Garden in support of the view that it creates *"soulless places"*, although recognising not all agreed. At the same time, a number of those interviewed appeared to approve of a design arrangement that supported walkers more than vehicles and gave pedestrians a safe and pleasant walking route along Exmouth Market.

Various comments from those interviewed touched on a range of other aspects of the design of Exmouth Market's physical space, and the ways that this interconnected with various social uses of the space. One respondent described Exmouth Market as a *"secret space"*, in a markedly similar way to views expressed about Borough and Broadway Markets in previous chapters. Like those spaces, the street demonstrated a high level of containment and enclosure, which kept it hidden from view until in its immediate vicinity. For one interviewee this physical design quality built on and reflected the street's obscurity:

> *"The most interesting thing I find is that I grew up in London and I'd never heard of Exmouth Market. It's a well-kept secret. The number of people that I tell that I work in Exmouth Market and they say 'where's that?' Yeah and it's actually five minutes, ten minutes from right in the centre of London, from Oxford Street...I can never decide if that's a good thing or a bad thing because I think it's nice that it's a secret but kept away but then you want more people to come".*

Views about Exmouth Market as a secret, interesting space also built on a perception that Clerkenwell had become a less rough area, and this in turn was seen to have spatial aspects. One interviewee said that the street's location was an important element in its transformation:

> *"I think this street is in a really nice position. Its location is so good that you can't really take that away from it. You know, ten years ago this used to be quite a rough area. Now it's a pleasant area. It's only really going to go in a good direction".*

The food market (in its changing forms) was viewed by some of those interviewed as demonstrating commitment to the public realm, and supporting a kind of democratic process in terms of relation to setting up a business at Exmouth Market. One view was that

> "restaurants are behind closed doors and [gestures to exterior space], that's what this street is designed for. Well, you know, at the end [gestures westward to food court style market] it works very well. It was designed for that...Also, anyone can just put up a stall there, so it's bringing people in from outside the area as well, which is good".

At the same time, in good weather there were large numbers of restaurant tables to be seen in front of restaurants in the street, and street design similarly was thought by a number interviewed to have a direct effect on how people used Exmouth Market in food terms. An interviewee compared Exmouth Market favourably with Bloomsbury to the west, commenting in particular on Exmouth Market's prettiness, human scale and small business frontages, whereas the latter was deemed

> "not a place where you can come and walk up the street and see the selection that you can see here. Exmouth Market is very nice because you've got everyone in a such small area and it's a really pretty street....the frontages are unique and there's some of the old...you know, the family businesses".

The street was described by some of those interviewed as comfortable and being like a pedestrianised street in that its layout privileged walking over motorised traffic, despite some difficulties with enforcement of traffic restrictions. One commented that it was a really comfortable street to walk down. *"It's got a nice set up to it. It's almost like a pedestrianised street although its not pedestrianised but it feels pedestrianised".* The interviewee noted that regulations were in place to control the hours within which vehicles could use the street. Another described a typical visitor (pedestrian) journey along the street from its southwestern to northeastern end, and believed that by far the largest proportion of visitors to the street arrived from the southwestern end, where the street joined Rosebery Avenue and Farringdon Road:

> "You can see it starts at the top [the western end?] Yeah and it's going down the street. It started with Al's Bar on the corner and you know that's where everyone comes into the street. If someone did a survey on how many people come into the street in an hour there it would be like 85% [starting from there]".

Another interviewee also described a spatial 'triangle' about half way along the street, made up of three food business, and a further couple of food business attractors nearer the northeastern end of the street:

> *"There's Moro and then Medcalf and [Café] Kick making a kind of triangle there... and there is [restaurant name] and Sweet [patisserie] down there, and then there is Santori, so its filtering down this way, and I think eventually the whole street will be as busy as one another".*

The design configuration of the street, with its main road access from the southwestern end, meant that end of the street would always remain busier:

> *"Just for the fact that that's on Farringdon Road, so I think that is always going to be the busier end of the street...a lot of those businesses pick up a lot more people just by being in that location. We are in our own little sub location".*

This interviewee also commented on the way the urban design of the street interacted with temporal aspects such as the rhythm of an evening out. The street's shape was thought to increase the capacity to socialise outside in the public realm, giving it a

> *"European feel. Here you can get all parts of your evening. You can go outside for a coffee, then you can go outside for a drink, have a meal then go somewhere else for a drink. Do you know what I mean? It's got a really European feel, everyone outside".*

A number of those interviewed referred to the design relationship between the two ends of the street in terms of the catchment for food business. It was often mentioned in relation to the subtleties of food space catchment changes over the length of the street. One view was that there were substantial walkable catchment differences that affected the use of the street:

> *"It sort of attracts everyone up that [southwestern] end. Now people - what they can buy there - they don't need to walk down here to see what they wanna buy. So we tend to suffer."*

This interviewee felt that their business was declining as a direct result of the interplay between the physical layout of the street, and the location of the food stall market located at its busier southwestern end. *"You usually see your regular customers actually walking past you to go up there".* However, given that both ends of the street are within a 500-metre walkability radius, the explanation for this business being ignored in favour of arguably more fashionable food stalls could instead relate to the way each individual habitus is played out, rather than being explained by design changes along the length of the street.

As well as the temporal changes noted on a day-to-day basis in relation to the catchment for the food market, one interviewee referred to seasonal changes connecting the street's design to its various food spaces. They pointed out that summer weather allowed people to make more use of exterior space and this was when the street's enclosed, human-scaled public realm really came into its own. This interviewee explained that until recently people would go no further northeast along the street's length than to Medcalf, a restaurant and bar located around half way along Exmouth Market:

> "It's almost like when [restaurant name] first opened it was like a force field at the end of Medcalf. People would be like a scrum. I don't know if you have seen it in the summer, and it's really, really dense. Everyone goes to a few bars and drinks".

From these accounts, it appears that the social need to be seen near a stylish place was having a spatial expression. Place users did not want to stray too far from the hip centre of gravity. The interviewee pointed out that by the time they were being interviewed, visitors to food businesses were making use of the street's whole length, suggesting this may be because restaurants, cafes and bars near the northeastern end had by this stage become *"cool"*:

> "Now it's OK because people know us but when we opened we didn't really do PR. We would have like loads of empty tables and people would be there at Medcalf, but people would not push themselves down the street. It has got quite an interesting geography although it's quite a small street. It can only really improve".

The comment about the street's *"interesting geography"* seemed to reinforce the notion that Exmouth Market benefited from being a fine-grained space with a number of narrow frontages of individual, often food-related, businesses. By contrast, two interviewees saw the physical shape of the street and its frontages as placing constraints on business development. One suggested that continuity in relation to colour treatments of frontages and improvements in lighting could help improve the quality of the public realm. However, they did not approve of the lights strung on lines across the street and fixed to building frontages. Instead they believed a bespoke system should be developed to give particular character, *"something that will be completely unique to the street".*

Another interviewed also argued that the spatial qualities of the street had paradoxical effects:

> "Number one is that the council use the shape of the street and the fact that it was organised as a market 20 years ago as a justification for saying 'and therefore we can put a stall in front of your shop and that's fine'. Because historically it had been done. It's not a good policy".

This interviewee also believed that the process of redeveloping the street and running the market could have allowed for more creativity in design terms. This would include making positive connections between market stalls and other streetscape arrangements in the space, especially at the southwestern end where Exmouth Market met Rosebery Avenue and Farringdon Road:

> "The council have been asked so many times to do something more creative with the space at the end, but they failed radically every time".

Some of those interviewed linked Exmouth Market's urban design with crime. An Islington Crime and Disorder Audit of 1998 - 2001 identified Exmouth Market area as a moped theft hotspot. One interviewee suggested that the street's shape made it easier to commit crimes such as bicycle theft:

> "Ironically it's a perfect street for stealing things from. It's a very short street, there's an alleyway. You can be into the block of flats…it's great for people stealing bikes. Absolutely fantastic".

This interviewee also believed it would be possible for the council to deal better with other design related antisocial behaviour and streetscape issues that had emerged. These included dumping rubbish, redundant telephone boxes, and street drinkers colonising the seating space at the southwestern end of Exmouth Market, at the Farringdon 'triangle':

> "And it could be - it seems like a classic urban design conundrum - you've got this place. If you put benches people drink, sit there, and create havoc, and people dump stuff under the trees, so how do you make it better?"

This interviewee explained that the traders asked the council to remove the telephone boxes *"because people use them as toilets and the answer was they couldn't do that'… For whatever bureaucratic reason they couldn't move them"*.

Exmouth as a street for eating: passegiatta and proximity

Exmouth emerged from these accounts as a place that in the main 'worked' for eating. Many of the points made in relation to its regeneration and urban design had socio-spatial practice implications or were reinforced by findings about these practices. Food mapping and interviews with place users visiting the 'slow' fast food market in 2008 generated a number of points about social use that tended to confirm the views of fixed business food traders and stallholders. Findings were in part gleaned from interviews with those visiting the food market, and these tended to be young adults, both male and female, and from a variety of ethnicities, with most working or studying in the area. They were interviewed after the food market had transformed from a *"whole market"* into a kind of outdoor slow food court. Much in evidence were the linked socio-spatial practices of browsing and buying prepared foods at food stalls, then sometimes eating in the street. Various food market visitors interviewed mentioned that they discovered Exmouth Market by chance. The sense of pedestrian priority offered by the street appealed to a number of them:

> *"I think it helps that it's a pedestrian street basically. The fact that it's pedestrianised is great. If it wasn't it would be almost impossible. The traffic noise that's going along there [indicates Rosebery Avenue behind] that's ridiculous".*

Despite changes to the nature of the food market dealt with earlier, there remained a form of passegiatta at Exmouth, although with differences to promenading practices found at Borough and Broadway. Observations showed that some food market visitors made their way along the whole length of the street, but most arrived from the southwestern end so only walked a short way along, browsing the food stalls. A kind of spatially short and temporally brief promenading was apparent. Various interviewees also mentioned the ambience of the street as a contributing factor in their decision to come to the food market, which was largely driven by the high quality lunch choices on offer. One said, *"I quite like the atmosphere, but it's mostly the choice"* while another commented that *"I suppose it creates a sort of ambiance"*.

Some visitors ate while at the street while others took their food back to the office, in some cases reluctantly. A comment about this was that, *"It would be nicer if there was somewhere to sit. I don't particularly want to take it back to the office"* while another explained that, *"If the weather's nice we sit in the green spaces around here"*. In terms of visitor catchment size, it appeared that the majority of visitors were coming from close by, with one saying

> *"it's just round the corner from where I work"* and *"we've been here for a week. There's a course down the road. So we just walk up here and see what's available".*

Some visitors to Exmouth Market's food stalls came from further afield:

> *"I've been about three of four times before and I work down on Holborn Viaduct. Usually it's like my Friday treat".*

A number cited the quality and variety of the food on offer as the main attraction. One said that

> *"I usually just come here because I can get a decent vegetarian meal"* while another noted that *"personally I would much prefer to come here than go to a sandwich shop".*

A typical response was

> *"there's lots of good stalls. And it's the nearest place to where I work that's got that kind of choice".*

Unlike Borough and Broadway, lunchtime food market visitors did not spend a significant amount of time at Exmouth. Rather, most observed appeared to visit to browse stalls, buy food, and take it away to eat elsewhere (the point about the lack of seats may have something to do with this behaviour). Despite this rather instrumental quality, they also seemed to be individually playing out a kind of habitus. Buying lunch from stalls at Exmouth Market was a hip thing to do.

Like Borough and Broadway, Exmouth was food mapped using techniques discussed in Chapter 3, to understand more about the range and configuration of food available there. The mapping results lent support to interview findings, visitor comments and case study observations. The food-related uses identified are listed in Figure 6.1.

Exmouth Food Map Key	19. Lemon and Thyme Café	39. Little Bay Café/Restaurant
1. Al's Bar and Café	20. Santoré restaurant	40. Gazzano's Salumeria
2. Gulshan Tandoori	21. Mark's caf	41. Giveaway Food Vouchers
3. Sofra restaurant	22. Starbuck's	42. Brindisa Chorizo
4. Strada restaurant	23. Sweet Patisserie/Café	43. Freebird Steak
5. Café Nero	24. Jessop's Bakery	44. Hot Satay Beef
6. China Silk restaurant	25. Rhum Jungle	45. Moro Paella
7. Exmouth Arms Pub	26. Cotton's Caribbean restaurant	46. Gujarati Rasoi
8. Harput Charcoal Grill takeaway	27. Wilmington Pub	47. The Veg Table
9. Colossi Greek restaurant	28. Rosebery Kebab	48. Fruit and vegetable Stall
10. Brill - Music, Coffee, Bagels	29. Perfect Chicken	49. Cake Stall
11. Brindisa Shop	30. Mix Grill	50. Turkish Food Stall
12. Moro	31. Di Popolo Deli	51. Koenwah Salads
13. Medcalf	32. Royal Caf	52. Jollof Pot
14. Café Kick	33. Tito's Sandwich Bar	53. Thai Stall
15. Ayla's Snacks and Café	34. Dollar Grill Bar/restaurant	54. Italian Sausage Stall
16. Clark's Pie and Mash Shop	35. Golden Fish restaurant	55. Crepes and Galettes Stall
17. Pride of Siam	36. Golden Fish Bar	56. La Porchetta Pizzaria
18. The Ambassador restaurant	37. Farringdon Grill	57. The Old China Hand bar
	38. Quality Chop House	

Figure 6.1.: *Key to Exmouth Market Food Map* Source: Prepared by author

As interviewees noted, the weekly food stalls formed a cluster at the southwestern end of the street, while there was an informal triangle of cafes, bars and restaurants mid-way along the street, and a further clustering of cafes and restaurants at the northeastern end (see Figure 6.2.). Two of the three chain food businesses established at Exmouth were found at the busier end of the street, facing onto the Farringdon 'triangle'. The different kinds of food-related land uses mapped included two pubs, two bars, two bar/cafes, four bar/restaurants, thirteen restaurants and seven cafes. There were five food shops, fourteen food stalls, and six fast food/takeaway places. Cafes and restaurants mapped meanwhile ranged from the upmarket Moro, Ambassador, and Medcalf restaurants and bars, to the more informal Little Bay and Gulshan, and the highly traditional Clark's Pie and Mash Shop. Food shops equally varied widely, but there was a preponderance of high-end food outlets such as Brindisa (closed since the research was completed, to be replaced by the fashionable Morito - offshoot of Moro) and the very long established Gazzano's Salumeria. As at Borough and Broadway, there was a very clear focus on independently owned and operated artisanal, organic and specialist food and drink businesses.

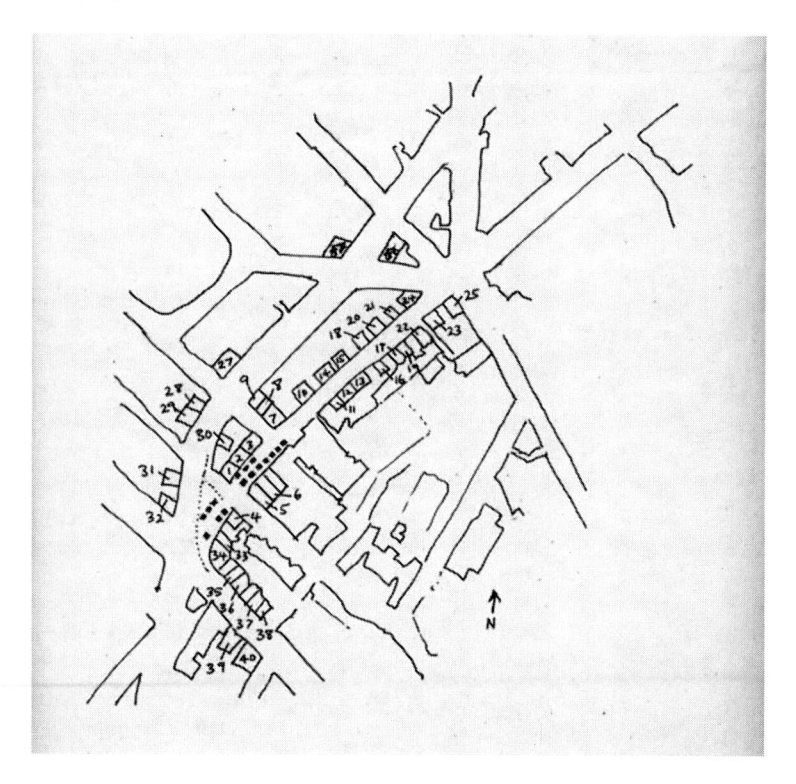

Figure 6.2.: *Food Map of Exmouth Market (black squares on the map are stalls)*
Source: Prepared by author

Drawing conclusions from Exmouth Market's food-led renewal

This chapter's findings broadly support the view that at the time of the research the Exmouth Market quarter was evolving as a convivial food-centred space. Its food-related regeneration trajectory encompassed socio-spatial practices with strong similarities to those found at Borough and Broadway, as well as providing some distinct contrasts. Governance issues were important in the revival of Exmouth Market, and, as at Broadway, food entrepreneurs and community-based players were central in the quarter's revitalisation. Within a broad narrative of urban improvement, there was considerable agreement, as well as some difference of opinion between those interviewed, about the nature of the quarter's food-led renaissance. Exmouth Market, as the street on which the quarter focused, emerged as a destination for certain kinds of stylish food consumption. This consumption in turn could be considered to constitute an individual habitus for some visitors and residents that was both food-led and focused. At the same time, the street could still be understood as a food desert for other long-term, working class inhabitants who were unable for economic and social reasons to take an active part in this food-centred experience.

Exmouth Market's recent history can be read as a narrative of food-centred regeneration, focused on restaurants and bars, as well as several incarnations of a revived food market, in a process that shaded into gentrification. Prior to regeneration efforts that began in the 1980s, Exmouth Market was in a similar position to the areas around both Broadway and Borough Markets, with a moribund food market, empty shops and a declining population base in the surrounding neighbourhood. In this way, its story resonated with the long-term economic and spatial processes set out in Chapter 2, which connected structural transformations in relation to food and urbanisation in London. However, the outcomes from food-centred regeneration efforts in the Exmouth Market quarter played out somewhat differently from those in the other two case study areas.

At Exmouth Market the loss of the fresh food market in the 1960s and 1970s came to symbolise the way the street and the surrounding urban space were shifting from a solid working class area based on traditional trades to a remnant space and then to a more affluent, hip location for arts, architecture and media companies. A scheme of physical regeneration gave way in the early to mid 1990s to a more nuanced cultural regeneration strategy emphasising partnership between the local authority and other stakeholders, but perhaps failing to engage as successfully with the area's remaining working class residents. Changes to local planning policy helped support a regeneration focus on "the restaurant solution". Its implementation was based on both formal and informal networks encompassing council proponents and influential property owners actively pursuing potential restaurateurs to tenant empty shops and help attract cultural industries to the quarter. The local working class community, apparently left out of this regeneration loop, in some cases resorted to oppositional politics.

By the early 2000s the vision of reviving the food market in a more modern form had started to solidify, but by this time, as at Borough and Broadway, local government appeared to be judged an ineffective partner or stakeholder in these processes. What was proposed in food terms at Exmouth was similar to a farmer's market but not bound by the environmental criteria these impose, such as food mile restrictions. The idea of restarting a food market came to be seen, by now well-established restaurateurs and other influential local food business people, as a logical extension of the very successful 'destination dining' occurring in the street. However, certain other food traders in Exmouth Market saw the concept as flawed from the start, based on insufficient research and analysis to determine its likely feasibility. Notwithstanding these dissenting views, a revived food market was launched in 2006, using a combination of expertise from Broadway Market, and high-powered proponents with food credentials stretching well beyond the confines of the local area, to mentor and manage the process.

Action taken to revive Exmouth's market was somewhat different from the bottom-up activity of traders and residents at Broadway Market. Nor did it or arise from the leadership of a long established community based charitable trust as at Borough. Instead, the regeneration process might be described as more of a 'sideways' move rather than a typical public sector led, top-down approach. Despite the market's gastronomic proponents possessing very significant social capital in London food terms, difficulties still arose in implementing the food market as originally envisioned. A range of other factors may have played a part. The length of time it took to build up food business at a virtually new market clearly had a deterrent effect on stallholders. This was exacerbated by other issues. There was apparently an insufficient local residential population catchment to support this kind of revived market. Additionally, there was competition from nearby food markets at The Angel, Islington (in the form of a long established traditional street market at Chapel Street) and slightly further afield from Whitecross Street (a newly resurgent, directly competitive street food market supported by substantial regeneration funding).

Among the revived market's proponents at Exmouth, the thinking appeared to be that the street's substantial cultural capital based on uniqueness, social mix and high food quality could be built on to run a successful market in the Broadway Market mould. Features including fine-grained design, a preponderance of independent food shops, and the presence of 'destination' restaurants such as Moro were all key elements in this mix. The role of the street's physical shape was identified as important in providing a desirable backdrop to the food market and broader regeneration efforts, although no conscious architectural or urban design strategy could be discerned, in contrast to the case at Borough. At the same time, the public realm as a social and physical space was identified as an important focus at Exmouth, as were third places in various food businesses and cafes. A renewed food market was seen as a good thing in itself, as well as a tool for bringing more people to the street to reinforce regeneration efforts focused on food.

Fairly sophisticated place marketing was undertaken, but even so the food market started to decline as a source of fresh produce soon after its launch in 2006. A number of the food business *"big boys"* either did not set up stalls as promised, or stopped running stalls quite quickly, apparently preferring to concentrate their efforts on other more successful farmer's style markets. Relatively soon the complexion of the food market started to change from one focused on fresh produce into a kind of 'slow' fast food court in the street. This second wave food market was typified by food stalls selling items like burritos, chorizo sausages in rolls, and Thai and Ghanaian foods, to workers and students walking there at lunchtime from local businesses and educational institutions.

There was a feeling expressed by some of those interviewed, that while this alteration in the nature of the food market might represent a successful financial strategy for the stallholders, for some it was *"not what Exmouth Market is about"*. These interviewees were perhaps referring to the sense of community they identified at Exmouth Market: and signifying that the food market in its latter incarnation did not contribute particularly strongly to this aspect of local place shaping. On these grounds Exmouth Market was adversely compared with Broadway Market. Some interviewees saw the revived market as a failure in terms of the original vision of a community centrepiece based on food, although not a wholesale commercial failure. There was also an alternative view, from one interviewee that the evolving food court style market was an economic threat to existing fixed food businesses in the street, with stallholders benefiting from advantageous competition through much lower rates and less strict hygiene standards. For other food businesses interviewed at Exmouth Market, the busy atmosphere the food court style market brought to the street was thought to offset any possibly harmful effects on their own trade. For visitors to the food stalls, meanwhile, the market was simply judged a success in its own terms.

One of the food market's proponents described its decline as a fresh produce market as reflecting the difficult economics of getting a food market off the ground. They noted a Catch 22 situation in which stallholders needed to keep trading despite very poor returns, but being unable to do so because they were generating such low incomes. Temporal aspects were also thought to have played a part, with the stronger Friday catchment for the food market unable to make up sufficiently for the low turnover on the much quieter Saturdays. Catchment size was clearly an issue. The decline of the market as a fresh produce space suggested a number of factors may have contributed. Explanations offered included that there was too small a residential community in the quarter, there was too little passing trade, and that (some) local residents were unwilling to buy food from the market. Both the prices and style of the market were identified as aspects that did not appeal to local working class residents. This was the view held by at least one interviewee who described the new market (in its early phase) as not aimed at this population, and in fact likely to exclude them. As at Borough and Broadway, interviewees' narratives indicated that Exmouth might continue to operate as a food desert for some while developing into a convivial food quarter for others, albeit with a somewhat different kind of food focus than a complete food market would offer.

While interviewees did not believe that competition from other food markets like Whitecross Street or Chapel Market, or shopping centres with large supermarkets like Angel, was taking trade away from Exmouth Market, this remained a possible if partial explanation. It should be remembered too, that very substantial regeneration funding was going into Whitecross Street to support a food market modelled on Borough Market at the same time that Exmouth was trying to establish itself as a revived market without this support. This sustained level of support could well help draw potential visitors there, instead of to Exmouth Market, which had no such public funding base available at the time of the research. There may also have been a question about getting the shopping balance right. One interviewee pointed out that Exmouth Market may have had insufficient 'cool' shops to attract enough visitors to in turn make the market viable. Again, there were some comparisons made with Broadway Market's well-honed shopping and social mix, which was understood as critical to successful food-led regeneration efforts in that food quarter.

As with the other two food quarters, it was impossible to avoid discussing issues of gentrification in relation to Exmouth Market given its connections to food-led revitalisation. Two contrasting narratives emerged in this area. The first suggested that Exmouth Market displayed a *"wonderful mix"* of traditional working class and newer, more affluent incomers who together acted to conserve what was best about the street, while developing it economically for the future. This kind of view challenged conventional gentrification arguments by largely denying Exmouth was a contested space. The second narrative, by contrast, saw the street as subject to aggressive competition for social and economic resources where the traditional community felt excluded from regeneration activity, and was unlikely to benefit from it or may even be driven out by gentrification. The stress on the notion of urban mix in Exmouth Market, in which the old rubbed shoulders with the new, was contrasted with a reading of Exmouth as

> "more about underpinning property prices and fusing 'culture' with 'consumption'. As this consumption becomes increasingly conspicuous, as the 'swells' occupy the outside tables, the extent to which culture becomes implicitly exclusive is obvious" (Whitelegg, 2002, p.90).

For some of those interviewed, food-centred gentrification was not being problematised in this way. One interviewee saw Exmouth Market as simply a great place for social mixing and networking. Others situated Exmouth Market as a stylish and even unique food destination that was part of what would make the development of high quality residential units in the quarter increasingly socially and economically attractive to investors and incoming middle class residents. Interviewees may not have been aware of the ways that Exmouth Market's transformation reflected a classic gentrification trajectory, and their stories could thus be understood as "idealised narratives" (Butler, 2006), in which conflict was smoothed over. Moreover, Exmouth Market's growth did appear to fit well with certain features of arguments that position the development of cultural quarters as expressions of gentrifying forces. In particular, Exmouth could be seen as a quarter in which space itself was increasingly becoming commodified through cultural production and as a site for its consumption.

Interviewees' stated fear, however, in this case, was more often not whether gentrification would drive out traditional communities but whether the shift to residential over business land uses in the vicinity might adversely affect the numbers visiting the street for food. At the time of the research these visitors were predominantly composed of business users. Already catchment variation from day to evening, from weekday to weekend and across the seasons was evident, and food businesses were not sure more residents replacing office workers would mean more business for them. In effect Exmouth was carving out a niche as a food destination for high quality restaurant food, and for pubs, bars and cafes, but not as a fresh food market, and these catchment issues may have been critical to the development of that situation. Within the scope of the research it was less clear to what extent the increasing level of residential development may have contributed to working class displacement effects and there was still substantial public housing in the vicinity at the time of the fieldwork. However, given high rents and sharply rising house prices in the area, the food-led transformation of Exmouth Market seemed likely to be at least contributing to some working class flight.

Again, as for the other two food quarters, local government did not fare well in any of the interviewees' accounts of how the street and wider quarter developed as a food space. Local government was acknowledged to have played a useful regeneration role in the 1990s but a perceived lack of management expertise and governance capacity more latterly, allied to what was described as occasional, inept interventions and defensive attitudes, seemed to sum up the view of most. Some food traders felt that their ideas about developing Exmouth Market as a food street were ignored and most expected little improvement to emerge in either management practices or consultation on the street's future. An unspoken but possibly relevant issue was that regeneration funds and attention were going to Whitecross Street rather than Exmouth Market (although this was not a council led initiative). The food market's gastronomic stakeholders also came in for some criticism from one interviewee for *"not listening"* and going ahead with a food market thought to be under-researched and likely to fail. Overall, these issues provoked unenthusiastic comparisons with excellent community-based market management at Broadway Market at the time. There was disappointment expressed that Exmouth Market was not able to regenerate in the way that Broadway Market had, as an apparently organically growing food space *"all about community"*.

Turning to the interplay between physical design and food-related socio-spatial processes at Exmouth Market, a number of relevant urban design points emerged. Findings at Exmouth in the main supported those from Borough and Broadway. Exmouth's experience demonstrated that physical design was significant to how the street was used as a food space in the past, and had been experienced in relation to food in recent times. The street benefited from being the traditional centrepiece of the local quarter, with a human scale public realm well designed to house a food market. Despite the depredations of post-war redevelopment, Exmouth remained highly suitable in physical design terms for this kind of public space use. The area and the street itself was repeatedly referred to by those interviewed as both well-located and a *"secret space"*, a description that reflected its high level of enclosure which was similar to the height-to-width ratios of primary food streets at both Broadway and Borough Markets. The design of the space underpinned the potential for people to set up stalls in the public realm and thus, in turn, attract more people to the street. It was variously described as pretty, small-scale, pedestrian-friendly and having unique frontages. Exmouth's physical design elements reinforced its attractiveness to people as a setting for conviviality and they supported its particular sense of place. Again, physical comparisons with Broadway and Borough's fine-grained, compact, walkable spatiality seemed very clear.

Looking at the street as a sustainable space, the environmental aspects of its resurgence produced little in the way of direct research findings, yet many environmental points seemed implicit in interviewees' comments and were further supported by observations and food mapping. Market proponents spoke of providing local people with the opportunity to buy good quality fresh fruit and vegetables locally. Although the positive sustainability implications of doing so were not explicitly drawn out, the stress on making good quality fruit and vegetables available in the area reflected an informed perspective about sustainable food. Likewise, the intention to increase the surrounding community's capacity to buy food locally within a walkable catchment had other implicit social and economic sustainability benefits. For example it would have positive effects for individuals in avoiding obesegenic environments (Lake and Townshend, 2006). Increased local food buying would also contribute to making the city more sustainable through careful use of food resources and production of less waste and pollution. In the latter stages of the research, a number of the comments made by place-users buying food from stalls at the 'food court' iteration of the market, suggested they were attracted by the bespoke, (sometimes) organic nature of what was on offer, so were choosing to avoid food chains and supermarket sandwiches, at least for lunch. Again, these choices had positive sustainability implications, spelt out in Chapters 1 and 2.

Turning to the social life of the street, the overarching point emerging was that the food quarter's economic, environmental and design complexities influenced socio-spatial practices that were observed, mapped, photographed and discussed with interviewees. Overall, interviewees emphasised what a convivial place Exmouth Market was for them, while referring to the differences between the street's southwestern and northeastern ends. The southwestern end of the street was identified as busier, with visitors to the market, cafes and restaurants often arriving by way of the two major intersecting streets of Farringdon Road and Rosebery Avenue. Various food-related sub-locations were identified, and one intriguing finding was the perceived need by visitors to maintain a close physical proximity to stylish food places along the street's length.

The fairly subtle physical configuration of the space seemed to have shaped its social use in relation to food to a significant extent, including determining the location of the revived market. While the northeastern end of the street was initially less frequented, this changed as larger numbers of hip food business established there. Meanwhile, the Farringdon 'triangle' at the southwestern end of the street presented some design challenges despite its attractive paved and tree shaded character; most notably to deal with anti-social behaviour, and to develop an acceptable configuration of food stalls from a fixed business point of view.

The research also found an interplay between design quality and the temporal aspects of the street's food-related use, with the shape of the street lending itself to what was seen by some interviewees as a rather 'European' style day and night time use. Place users would move from one food-related outdoor space to another, and the public realm would be fully exploited for socialising. The perceived 'European' nature of the social and spatial practices encouraged by the design of the street was reminiscent of visitors' comments about Borough and Broadway, and again reflected the sense that living convivially in the public domain was understood as a European lifestyle. Analysis of food mapping also demonstrated that the space was one where eating in the street was not only a popular social practice but appeared to others to be an acceptable form of civilised behaviour. All of this seemed to reflect the development of a distinct individual habitus being played out in Exmouth Market of stylish consumption, located in the indulgent street (Valentine, 1998).

In the three-year period to 2008, Exmouth stood in marked contrast to the two other food quarters in some respects but also shared significant common ground with them. One of the clearest differences was that unlike the other food quarters, the revived food market did not succeed as a produce market, although the Exmouth quarter overall developed into a successful food-centred space of a somewhat different complexion. Like the other two case study areas it shared strong thematic terrain in terms of food-led regeneration shading into gentrification. Like them it developed as a cultural quarter, in which certain individuals played out a habitus of a similar kind. All demonstrated the development for some users of a food quarter from a food desert, while others were left behind. In Exmouth's case, urban design features and elements, both traditional and new, supported the quarter in playing a role both as gentrifying space and as an increasingly convivial and sustainable place within a more alienating and unsustainable city.

The last three chapters have explored areas defined as food quarters emerging across London - with varying design, conviviality and sustainability results. The final part of this book considers how far the research findings support the book's fundamental questions about the relationship between physical form and socio-spatial practices relating to food. Chapters 7 and 8 provide the opportunity to draw together the elements of the analysis in more detail within the frame provided by relevant sociological and design theory, and based on the range of sociological, design, and morphological work this book documents. The final chapter then offers a chance to outline some overall conclusions from the food quarter research about changing relationships between food and urban form.

PART 3:

SUMMING UP THE FOOD QUARTERS

CHAPTER SEVEN

FOOD-LED RENEWAL IN REVIEW

Drawing comparative conclusions

The focus of this book's research has been on places argued to be emerging food quarters in formerly rundown areas of London. The research grew out of a long term exploration of food and city shaping, with the studied spaces understood as an element in that wider field of enquiry. The central claim is that food quarters may represent a new, connected phenomenon of alternative food spaces in which food-centred place design and food-led regeneration have been based on the revival of remnant food markets and areas around them. This chapter starts to draw together findings about three closely studied food-centred areas – at and around Borough, Broadway and Exmouth Markets - and reaches the conclusion that these developing food quarters are at once fast gentrifying spaces and ordinary places (Knox, 2005, p.1) for playing out authentic everyday food relationships. It concludes that the development of these nuanced quarters may have contributed to making more convivial, sustainable cities through the interplay of their physical design and the socio-spatial practices of everyday life. At the time of the research, these quarters also represented a break from the past, by fostering interactions between distinctively new combinations of social practices, existing spatiality and physical design features.

A significant area for investigation is the double-sided nature of the food quarters and the questions this raises for research in delving into their real character. How is it that they have operated simultaneously as zones of gentrification that may have excluded some, yet equally appeared to defy dominant spatial trends evident in London and elsewhere that are producing food related sprawl and 'obesegenic' environments (Lake and Townshend, 2006)? Are these places informed by the same kind of food economies and cultures as the 'fat cities' cited in Chapter 1 where the combination of a well-developed gastronomic townscape and convivial practices helps keep people thin? How is it that they have developed in a more convivial, gastronomically rich and sustainable way than some other areas of London? Can the benefits they offer involve people of all classes or are they only for gentrification's winners? Are the conditions and processes found in these quarters possible in other places in London and beyond? This chapter reflects on the food quarters' complex nature in the light of the book's research findings and analysis and offers some tentative conclusions in each area.

The book has sought to apply spatialised thinking (Soja, 1980, 2000) about aspects of food and urban space to a number of case study areas in London. It has done so in part by analysing their urban design elements and in part through exploring the ways these design elements appeared to influence the socio-spatial practices found there. The studied spaces were found to be based in spatial terms upon a size and physical design configuration analogous to a typical urban quarter within traditional European urban space (Moughtin, 1992). The research findings showed strong links in design terms between the emerging food quarters and such traditional urban spaces. In exploring these quarters, the book has also reflected and drawn theoretically upon an increasing interest in food, the body and everyday life within sociology (Zukin, 1995; Lupton, 1996; Beardsworth and Keil, 1997; Amin and Thrift, 2002, 2004). A number of different sociological strands have proved relevant, including structuralist perspectives from Bourdieu (1984), while from historical sociology there has been work on food within an urban setting from Elias (1982) and Mennell (1992) among others. Urban sociology has acted as a way into spatialising the analysis.

The book has crossed a number of boundaries between theoretical areas within sociology, and also between sociology and related disciplines; seeking insights from urban geography, morphology and urban design when sociological thinking proved insufficient. This has been necessary in order to make relevant connections between spatiality understood in sociological, geographic and design terms, on the one hand, and individual socio-spatial practices on the other. The work has sought to overcome the identified research problem of aspatiality in regard to sociological theorising on food. So key theoretical insights in relation to socio-spatial practices were derived from the work of Bourdieu (1984), whose notion of the 'habitus' was important for framing the discussion around structural issues evident in the case study areas, as these were represented in individual behaviours. Work by Bridge (2000), Butler with Robson (2001), Butler (2006, 2007) and Webber (2007) has all been very useful in connecting the habitus to spatialised aspects of gentrification. The work of de Certeau (1984) and Lefebvre (1991) meanwhile has helped in constructing an analysis of the making of everyday life through the socio-spatial practices found at the case study areas. Norbert Elias's (1982) theorising of the civilising process has offered insights into how public behaviour in these places was developed and modulated in a dynamic way.

Meanwhile, the case study areas have been defined as food loci within the food system (Goody, Beardsworth and Keil, 1997), and seen to play both allocation and consumption roles, while challenging some of the inequitable and unsustainable aspects of that system. The contribution of spatiality has been further explored by analysis of the changing political economy of these quarters over time, through their contested regeneration and gentrification. This aspect of the analysis has made use of the work of, among others, Zukin (1995), Smith (1996), Whitelegg (2002), Miles and Miles (2004), Mansvelt (2005), and Butler (2007) to trace the quarters' decline and resurgence, and explore how their regeneration and gentrification, as particular material places, has been critical to their social and design development.

Spatiality has also been approached through insights from urban morphology from Whitehand and Larkham (1992) among others. From urban design, the work of design theorists including Alexander et al (1977), White (1980), Bacon (1982), Greenbie (1984), Hayward and McGlynn (1993, 2002), Gehl (1996), Madanipour (1996, 2001, 2003), Bentley (1999) and Cuthbert (2006) has helped focus on the shaping of the quarters' physical character over time. Work that interconnects food, urban design and health (Parham, 1992, 1993; Lake and Townshend, 2006) suggested that a particular urban form character has played a distinct role in the quarters' development as social spaces, in sharp contrast to obesegenic environments and food poverty related deserts found elsewhere. The study revealed that the physical settings of the food quarters played active roles in the social, economic and environmental processes of food allocation and consumption. It also helped to make clearer the social distinctions evident in the habitus played out by individuals engaging with these settings.

The whole research focus has been undertaken within the paradigm of urban sustainability, helped by the work among others of Hough (1984, 1994), Stren, White and Whitney (1992) and Haughton and Hunter (2003) which has been employed to frame and bring together key aspects of food and spatiality in the analysis. Equally relevant has been the analysis of the quarters in terms of their contribution to a more convivial ecology in urban space. In this regard their physical features have provided the frame for emergent forms of socio-spatial practice that, as was argued in Chapter 1, reflect increased conviviality in everyday urban life (Maitland, 2007).

This brief introduction to the perspectives that have framed the work sets the scene for exploring conclusions from the morphological and urban design investigations in a comparative way from across the three food quarters. Tracing how their physical and gastronomic character has altered over time, helps contextualise broader conclusions about food quarters that follow in Chapter 8. The socio-spatial practice conclusions in this chapter meanwhile start to focus in on the way physical space and social practices have interconnected at the quarters through regeneration processes and urban design.

The legacy of urban continuity and coherence

After setting out the stall in a theoretical sense, the book's research enquiry began in Chapter 3 with a morphological and urban design investigation of the physical features identified through primary research into the three food quarters. This enquiry used visual methods to both contextualise the food quarters and explore their gastronomic character, by tracing their changing physical form over time. The morphological research material, based on maps, photographs, plans and written records, was used to follow the physical evolution of food-related uses, and the mix with other land uses at the food quarters, drawing out food and design implications from this longitudinal analysis. Each of the quarters was defined in fuzzy-edged terms by their pedestrian catchment, which approximated the physical extent of each of the areas as a walkable space. The maps record for each quarter helped identify some of their salient land use features in food and design terms.

So, for Borough for instance, it was possible to discern a complex series of built, transitional and public spaces connected to food; with a triangular shaped overlay of major rail infrastructure dominating the urban structure of the market area. For Broadway, by contrast, the main market street could be traced as a clear public space pathway from north to south, running between London Fields and the Regent's Canal. Exmouth similarly showed a quarter centred on a primary food market street, extending southwest to northeast within a complex urban street pattern; itself the product of successive layers of urban development. For all three areas, various disruptions to streets and urban blocks could be seen in fairly close vicinity to the main market street or market structures. The various site maps demonstrated that the traditional urban structure was both complex and fine-grained in each food quarter, but the urban fabric suffered some serious interruptions to its pattern, mostly in the 20th century, that undercut its overall physical coherence.

Despite many waves of urban development and redevelopment, especially in Borough's case given its very long urban history, all three quarters could be judged as legible places in built form terms over a substantial time period, up until the late 19th century in Borough's case, and the mid 20th century for Broadway and Exmouth. Each quarter was closely associated with food markets, from the beginnings of their emergence as urban space. For Borough, the antecedents of this urban form were extremely long term, possibly pre-Roman. For the other two case study areas, materialisation as urban space went hand in hand with development as public food markets in the 18th and 19th centuries, when both were for a short time at the urban edge of a rapidly expanding London.

All three case study areas also began with close links to food production or distribution. Borough was home to market gardens and other agricultural land uses until quite recently in its history whereas Broadway's emergence as a street began as a drover's route into London. Exmouth, meanwhile, was part of a field track close to a cattle field for the Skinners Company, a London trade guild. While none of the case study areas' relationship with food was immutable in land use configuration terms, they all continued to operate as food-centred spaces in an unbroken line until the mid 20th century. Borough was always a food market, although the market's location locally shifted a number of times over the centuries before finding a permanent home (with associated built structures) on its current site. At both Broadway and Exmouth, the street's built frontages meanwhile provided a backdrop to food markets which changed in character over time, but continued to operate as fresh produce markets without interruption until the 1960s.

In each case, the food market acted as a nodal point and focus for urban settlement and intensification based on food-related and other land uses, that mixed residential, work, leisure and cultural activities. Each area developed into a dense, fine-grained urban quarter, with a thriving local economy in which the food market played an important role physically, socially and economically. The maps record and other visual material demonstrated very strongly how coherent the street pattern, block structure, and built form remained through successive layers of urban development until the latter part of the 19th century when the first major infrastructure intrusions began to occur.

Within the framework provided by the overarching similarities between the three quarters there were also significant differences identified. Borough was unlike the other two areas, not only because it was settled for a far longer period, but because it was for many centuries one of

London's principal wholesale food markets, whereas both Broadway and Exmouth were primarily retail markets (although the distinction between retail and wholesale was blurred) serving much more local catchments. Borough and Exmouth, as sites closer to the centre and thriving heart of London, were both spaces where, for a time, marginal and radical social and political activities found a home. This was far less the case for Broadway given its further removed location, and it remained as a village settlement outside built up London for longer than the other quarters.

Then, from a period that started in the mid to late 19th century for Borough, and the mid 20th century for Broadway and Exmouth, substantial physical changes began to significantly weaken the consistency of each of the food quarters' urban form. While the food market at the centre of each case study area was not completely destroyed, each area suffered serious urban decline that was both a result of planned physical changes and external structural forces impinging on its character. At Borough, railway infrastructure was a prominent feature, while at Broadway and Exmouth this was the consequence of approaches to regeneration that stressed wholesale demolition of traditional housing and streets by way of comprehensive housing 'renewal'.

At Borough, the decline of the wholesale market from the middle part of the 20th century was due, to a substantial extent, to external structural forces described in Chapters 3 and 4. Most notable were changing distribution and shopping patterns that saw food wholesaling methods and infrastructure alter in ways that Borough could not accommodate within its limited physical space. Lack of space, and poor road approaches, reinforced the operational problems created by miscellaneous market accommodation, and the railway viaducts cutting off light and access to and through the market. At Borough, by the post Second World War period, the market itself was very badly rundown and the surrounding urban fabric had been partially demolished. At Broadway and Exmouth, meanwhile, the retail markets similarly declined in response to the same broad structural forces. These were related to alterations in food distribution and consumption on the one hand and post industrial decline in each area's local economy on the other. The effects were exacerbated by the comprehensive renewal post war, "the municipal bulldozer" (Inwood, 1998, p.812) which led to demolition of substantial areas around the markets, and loss of community focus and catchments for them. All three areas suffered much more physical harm from post-war interventions than from bomb damage during WWII.

None of the areas' urban decline was entirely due to the destruction of large parts of their physical fabric, but these actions contributed materially to their decay from thriving food-centred spaces to remnant urban pockets, in Exmouth's case, described by their own residents as "slums". In each case, a series of lost spaces in Trancik's (1986) terms was created: in part by the unwontedly perverse outcomes of public policy for urban renewal and in part by structural changes to urban form brought about by the wider political economy of London. One result was a breakdown in each of the quarters' urban structure. The areas surrounding the market streets declined from human-scaled, fine-grained urban fabric, with solid-to-void relationships and levels of enclosure that made for excellent outdoor rooms focused on food retailing, to a series of depressed and depressing places, that had lost their identity, largely lacked sense of place and demonstrated minimal urban functionality in food terms.

The morphological findings showed that in more recent days, predominantly since the 1980s at all three quarters, there was substantial physical redevelopment and revitalisation of the built fabric of the market buildings, market streets and market areas. At Borough, decrepit market structures were redeveloped through an ambitious staged programme of restoration and rebuilding. New frontages and buildings were inserted into the ensemble of existing, very dilapidated market halls. Beyond the market, existing buildings were renovated and new apartment buildings built, or planned by developers, including the "shard of glass" tower block still at the time of publication under construction next to London Bridge Station. At Broadway, physical improvements to market spaces were modest but included gates at either end of the street, for closing the road to vehicles during hours of market operation, and some refurbishment of shops and other building frontages by private owners. Again, substantial new building, mostly residential, was underway in the area by 2008 as developers took advantage of economic value created by an up and coming area. At Exmouth, meanwhile, two programmes of streetscape improvements were undertaken, and the street's carriageway reconfigured to partially pedestrianise the space. In the wider area, a number of new residential and mixed-use buildings were built or were planned by developers, including the redevelopment of the substantial Mt Pleasant Sorting Office site.

The quarters as food-centred public realm

The book's morphological investigations acted as a basis for considering each quarter's urban structure in a design sense, with this analysis using a palette of master planning methods explained in Chapter 3. This analysis helped to reveal compositional aspects of the urban armature at the three sites that supported their emergence as food quarters. Through this analysis, the urban structure was defined in terms of urban block layout; and building size, scale, density and active edges; while landmarks, vistas and focal points were identified. Figure-ground diagrams prepared as part of the fieldwork showed that the physical fabric at each quarter displayed an excellent balance between positive and negative space, and thus a good degree of enclosure within the street and urban block structure. In each case, the food market's outdoor rooms and covered spaces acted as focal points in the public realm within the surrounding urban fabric.

At Borough, the food market's landmarks were at once strongly evident yet shared this role with other important foci in the area. Broadway and Exmouth, meanwhile, featured more modest landmark elements. In each case, landmarks in the immediate area of the market worked as both vista terminations and social meeting points for market visitors. Among other examples, the Monmouth Coffee corner played this role at Borough; while the junction of Broadway Market and Dericote Street at Broadway; and the Farringdon triangle at Exmouth acted in a similar way. Sometimes food businesses became social and physical landmarks themselves – Monmouth Coffee and Brindisa tapas bar at Borough, and Moro and Medcalf restaurants at Exmouth, seemed to fall into this category. Each market space also provided interesting serial vision possibilities for the walker. This was especially marked at Borough, where numerous possible path sequences encompassed a great deal of visual richness and variety focused on food. Intriguing path sequences with a food focus could also been seen more modestly at both Broadway and Exmouth.

The urban structure analysis starkly demonstrated the destruction of physical fabric in the 20th century, although the immediate area of the food market in each case escaped more unscathed than did the wider area around it. Each of the markets' immediate physical settings retained a strong solid-to-void relationship, and high levels of enclosure, but Broadway's traditional fabric in particular became marooned in a tabula rasa of poorly enclosed redevelopment space after WWII. The retention of remnants of traditionally shaped fabric in the markets' immediate area was not sufficient in the subsequent period to protect the food market as a fully functioning land use in any of the three case study areas. As its surrounding fabric was erased, including even portions of the street grid itself, each market declined and virtually disappeared. The market buildings at Borough, and the streetscape in all three sites, became dilapidated, empty and even dangerous places to be. By the 1960s and 1970s, each was at risk of further destruction through proposed additional demolition, driven by notions of modernity and progress in housing, road design and retailing.

Despite these depredations, each space continued to possess rich urban structure qualities. Each had a fine grain of buildings up to street alignments, with active frontages, or frontages that could be reactivated, on ground floors. These buildings were rich in detail and proved robust over time; reflecting their long-life, loose-fit qualities (Brand, 1994). The streets themselves retained human scale, with excellent height-to-width ratios and degrees of enclosure, good microclimates and high levels of connectivity, helping each quarter keep a strong sense of place at its centre. Further out this had declined, as the urban fabric was coarsened in both grain and scale by what in review appeared to be predominantly unfortunate interventions. In each case, these wounds in the urban fabric seemed to be mirrored locally by a post war history of dysfunction and incoherence in social, environmental and economic terms.

Following on from the urban structure analysis, the book's connectivity research into the food quarters included a movement assessment, which helped demonstrate the level of permeability, legibility and walkability (as defined in Chapter 3) of each study area. Catchment maps were created to show the 'ped-shed' or walkability range, which helped in defining the spatial area from which visitors would generally be prepared to walk to the food markets at the heart of each quarter. The assessment at each quarter showed that its food market had once been at the centre of a very permeable, legible and walkable street grid, but each suffered considerable damage to this connective tissue through active design interventions of various kinds. These included major transport infrastructure overlaying or bisecting the area; 'slaburb' (Kegler, 2005) housing developments breaking up the surrounding street grid and block structure; and segregation of pedestrian paths from the street network undercutting path permeability. In each case, the immediate food market area remained very permeable and walkable, but legibility was significantly compromised by intrusions including those described here.

The catchment analysis suggested that each food quarter had a strongly developed 'ped-shed' and retained a high degree of connectivity. In part, this reflected the well-connected pattern of the immediate street network. Despite some interruptions, this offered walkers many ways to get to the food markets in all three quarters. It also reflected the way that pedestrian use of the streets had been subtly privileged over cars and servicing vehicles. The walkability radius was reinforced in each case by excellent wider public transport links. In Borough's case, the ped-shed encompassed London Bridge Station, a major transport hub for Underground and surface rail lines. For the other two areas, major railway stations lay slightly beyond 500 metres, the established ped-shed radius, but were within walking distance, and they also enjoyed multiple bus links. At the time of the research Broadway was due to benefit from major rail improvements in this sub-region of London, once the East London Line was completed, and the area would be even better connected in the future. Each food market could be judged as highly accessible not only to a local catchment arriving on foot, but to visitors from further afield, using a range of public transport modes. Overall, the conclusion was that the areas' excellent connectivity, allowing easy access by a local and broader visitor catchment, was one of the factors that underpinned their success as revived food-centred spaces.

The detailed street assessment for each quarter built on these urban design investigations. It demonstrated that at the centre of each area, in the immediate vicinity of the food market, the buildings and spaces contributed strongly to sense of place and local identity. Among the positive design elements in play were the series of active frontages built up to street alignments at a fine grain and human scale; street and open space height-to-width ratios that supported the creation of a series of outdoor rooms; the dominance of robust building typologies; the well-composed streetscaping and lighting arrangements; and the visual richness provided by the details of the place. This was not to say any of the three food quarters was found to be a mannered or finished space in design terms. Their design elements predominantly arose from the existing built form and its careful redevelopment, rather than being built in as new in a more artful way.

In fact, each food quarter's rough and ready quality was understood by place users to reinforce its unique character and identity, and support its authenticity. This raw quality was most pronounced at Borough, and while the market spaces there received the largest amount of overt design attention, and benefited from an ambitious building programme, this quality was carefully protected. Where, as at Borough, there was substantial physical renewal, it occurred in a highly contextual manner, through careful, staged infilling and renewing rather that demolishing and transforming the basic urban structure. At Exmouth, meanwhile, the physical design improvements carried out in the 1980s and 1990s were much more modest in scope, and did not include any built structures apart from streetscape elements such as paving and bollards. The street's inherent qualities were allowed to remain largely untouched. At Broadway there was even less overt design intervention but the street, like Exmouth, had 'good bones' to start with. The overall conclusion from the street assessment aspect of the urban design analysis was that the existing traditional design elements, already found at each site prior to regeneration as a food space, formed a very important and positive streetscape context for that redevelopment to occur. Newer design interventions were generally intended to reinforce existing qualities of place through a contextual design approach.

Urban regeneration and food space: melding economics and design

This is not just a book about physical design; important player though that is in the story of the rise of these food quarters. The research findings also suggested some conclusions about the interplay between design on the one hand and the social, environmental and economic aspects of the renewal of these food-centred spaces on the other. The story of the emerging food quarters, as one of urban decline and regeneration, was a central, shared narrative among those interviewed that was reinforced by site observations and food mapping. As was clear from the physical design exploration, in each food quarter a long-term process of decay left the food market as remnant space, within a deteriorating broader physical environment. When regeneration occurred, the two examples that were most successful as fresh produce markets benefitted markedly from the leadership and skills shown by community-based individuals and organisations.

At Borough Market this was in the form of a well-led, very long established charitable trust, and at Broadway Market, an innovative leader of a more recently emerging, active local traders and residents association. At Exmouth, by contrast, the food market's proponents were predominantly made up of gastronomic stakeholders who ran restaurants and food businesses in the street. In all three cases, the market advocates demonstrated a strongly altruistic sense of purpose about reviving their food market. They also all spoke of their desire to have a positive impact on local sociability and community in the surrounding area. A conclusion from the research, especially from the experience at Exmouth of the food market failing to thrive, was that the altruism and goodwill of key local players was vital, but not sufficient alone to ensure food market success. Both Borough and Broadway market proponents had exceptionally good links into the local community, or were more clearly seen as part of it. This may have been one determinant for their food market success that was not sufficiently in evidence at Exmouth, although it did not constrain the quarter's broader revival as a food-centred space of a different kind.

All three places demonstrated that architecture and design played a very important part in food-based urban renewal as an economic activity. This was notwithstanding that there was substantial variation between the food quarters in terms of design as part of a conscious strategy for this renewal. Architecture and design were most clearly articulated as tools for renewal at Borough, where design was used as a conscious regeneration instrument, by employing professional, architects and designers highly experienced in food led renewal to master plan the proposed built form changes. As was described in Chapter 4, a substantial design programme was a central aspect of the regeneration effort over the medium term at Borough. This occurred at a number of scales. Redundant warehouses were sold to help fund the regeneration programme; new infill buildings, frontages and covered spaces were designed and built; and existing structures were sympathetically renovated. The logistics of undertaking these major works and continuing to run a successful market were cleverly handled. For the design of market stalls, a new spatial model for retailing was developed, based on the design of Borough's unusual traditional food stand system. In all these ways design was central to an economic revitalisation strategy based on the food market.

At the other two quarters, meanwhile, design also played an important part, but in a somewhat different way. Broadway and Exmouth both demonstrated the shape and quality of the street space was important to attracting visitors. At Broadway, it seemed that while urban design was not employed in a self-conscious way, the market's proponents did speak about the street as being designated a market and how important this was to them in reviving it. There was a real sense that reviving Broadway as a traditional market space was an important part of their thinking at the outset in making the market a financial and social success. Additionally at Broadway, the street's structure provided an attractive, traditionally shaped urban space, which possessed the necessary design qualities to make a comfortable outdoor room. In other words, at Broadway Market, even without a self-conscious design strategy, not only was there some spatial awareness but the existing spatial structure made the space human scaled, fine grained, mixed use and highly walkable. For these reasons the space was – and was understood to be – very suitable to support food-centred revitalisation. As one stallholder commented

> "I think it's got that old sort of market feel to it. You've got sort of the shops on one road and the space is quite confined and that sort of builds to an atmosphere to the market. I think that does help this market a lot".

At Exmouth Market, again, the existing spatial design structure of the market street suited the redevelopment of individual food shops and a food market, reflecting the strengths of traditional, vernacular urban space design. There appeared to have been somewhat more consciousness expressed at Exmouth than at Broadway that the shape and design of the street played an important part in making it the centrepiece of an attractive food space, but one that needed to be looked after. At the time of its 1980s physical upgrade, Exmouth was perceived as a place that had "once been the heart of village life" but was now described by local people as a "squalid and filthy slum" (Whitelegg, 2002, p.81). The research findings suggested that there was understanding of the need for both physical and economic renewal in the planning of the physical renovation of the street in the 1980s and 1990s. More recently, accounts of developing the revitalised market at Exmouth in 2007 highlighted the explicit focus on the street itself as public social space, rather than remaining associated only with restaurants *"behind closed doors"*. The focus on the public realm of the street was described as enabling businesses to *"give something back to the street"*.

Community-based stakeholders at all three food quarters seemed to have shared a strategic vision in which food was central to the revitalisation strategy. Although there were certainly differences evident within the strategic approach, including the varying levels of conscious focus on design aspects, the overarching similarities were striking. As was explained in Chapter 4, Borough Market experts believed that the wholesalers who located at the food market in its early days of renewal were critically important in getting the regeneration process underway. Food businesses like Neal's Yard Dairy, Brindisa and Monmouth Coffee originally intended just to run wholesaling from their premises, but Neal's Yard, for example, were asked to sell cheese to people who turned up there *"from day one"*. In other cases, the trustees required wholesalers to also establish a retail presence. Such businesses were very important to the initiation and expansion of the Borough food market, as their individual growth trajectory first prefigured, then later mirrored, and created synergies which benefitted the growth of Borough Market overall.

The strategy was described by one interviewee as running the retail trade *"off the back of the wholesale"*. A small retail space might thus have a substantial wholesale operation behind it that cross-subsidised its retail component, even if this was not apparent to retail buyers. A related strategy of discounting rents, to attract fledging businesses, was also important to bringing excellent, individual food retailers and wholesalers to Borough in its early days. The stress from the outset was on high food quality and the sociability of the shopping experience. In its more mature phase Borough saw a number of food businesses add retailing to their wholesaling base, then set up restaurants, and finally offer other food-related products and services.

At a more modest scale, as was described in Chapter 5, there was a similar emphasis at Broadway Market. The food market regeneration strategy was conceived of as a *"whole shopping experience"*, counterpointed against the 'trading-down-on-price' approach attributed to the local authority. There was a great stress on the importance of both food quality and making Broadway Market into a highly sociable place, that local people of all backgrounds would be glad to shop at. Like Borough, the focus from the outset was on supporting small-scale individual businesses and traders, and creating synergies between market stalls and food shops, cafes, pubs and restaurants. Actions included charging low rents for stalls (and local shops where the markets had control over these spaces) to support renewal. It was clear from Chapter 5 that despite an enlightened approach from community-based management of these markets, that some traditional food shops and cafes lost out through what has since been described as the local council's "haphazard and uncoordinated approach" (Hackney Citizen, August 2010, n.p.r.) and allegedly through the actions of property developers. At the time the research was undertaken, despite an apparent public sector governance absence, clever market management from community based managers at both Borough and Broadway contributed strongly to highly successful overall renewal strategies.

At Exmouth Market, the food strategy was considerably more restaurant and bar focused from its inception than at either Borough or Broadway. In the mid 1990s this was partly because local government appeared to not believe that it would be realistic to successfully revitalise the food market, after failed attempts to do so from the late 1980s (Whitelegg, 2002). Changes to planning regulations helped open up permitted land uses and allowed a new breed of restaurateurs and bar owners to establish there in the latter 1990s (*ibid*). This so-called "restaurant solution" was a conscious strategy by local government and its regeneration partners at the time, making use of both the street's walkable catchment and its perceived "destination dining" capacity. By the early 2000s, Exmouth Market was being described as a street of gastronomic renown, whose uniqueness was based on high quality, individual food businesses.

As at Borough and Broadway, low rents were initially one of the main strategies for attracting restaurateurs and bar operators to Exmouth Market in the mid to late 1990s. Just as low rents helped food wholesalers to set up and remain viable, despite thin early trading times at Borough, they seemed to have provided an important element in the burgeoning restaurant scene at Exmouth. More recently, rent increases at Exmouth had some impact on fledgling food businesses' viability. It was evident that some cafes that were early players (Crossbar was one example) did stop trading. As the street became more established as a food destination, there was a greater likelihood the food chains would move in and emphasise these economic disparities, and by the early 2000s, Starbucks, Cafe Nero and Strada had a presence in the street. Given that chain food businesses are usually better capitalised than small food businesses tend to be, they are generally more able to wait to become viable while sitting out the competition. They sometimes employ 'hub and spoke' saturation tactics as Starbucks is known to do (Bridge and Dowling, 2001) to further improve their market position in favoured locations, and in this case these outlets may have been 'spokes' within such a strategy for each firm.

External regeneration programme funding played an important but somewhat mixed role in supporting food-centred space renewal in two of the food quarters, but appeared to have played almost no role in the third. For instance, the role of external funding could be judged as important at key points in the regeneration of Borough Market. National sources of funding, most notably Single Regeneration Budget (SRB) funds, were employed by the food market's trustees to part finance their ambitious redevelopment plans. At the same time, this was by no means a simple or straightforward process. Changing funding criteria and funding levels, uncertainty about availability, and the failure of strategic economic partners to go through with planned bids (the local authority was cited by one interviewee in this regard) meant that the trustees' ability to obtain such funds at critical points was limited. It said much for the trustees' canniness that they were able to deal successfully with these complexities, and match external regeneration funding with income derived from strategic property sales of surplus market building stock, to find their way through a complex external funding thicket. In the event, they proved extremely adept at leveraging in the regeneration funds they needed from public, and more importantly their own sources from property sales in the 1990s and early 2000s, to redevelop the food market's decrepit physical structures and underpin its economic revitalisation.

At Exmouth Market, meanwhile, external regeneration funds were also involved in the redevelopment process, through renewal money allocated to the street and surrounding area for physical upgrading in the 1980s and 1990s. The main sources were again from national government, channelled through City Fringe Partnership and Single Regeneration

Budget (SRB) funding, and managed through local government led partnerships. Some of these external regeneration funds were used to finance physical refurbishment of streetscape elements at Exmouth. More recently, the focus of attention in food-related regeneration at local authority level appeared to have shifted, with substantial regeneration funds through the EC1 programme going to Whitecross Street Market to the south, rather than to Exmouth Market. In any case, it should be remembered that the externally funded physical interventions were perceived in the 1990s as insufficient alone to turn the street around from its decayed and very economically depressed state. It was notable that it was only more latterly, once the emphasis moved to private sector efforts in relation to food business development, and other structural changes occurred in both food consumption patterns and the wider political economy of London, that the regeneration of the street as the centrepiece of a food quarter really accelerated.

Although both Borough and Exmouth in particular made use of external funding, this appeared to play a subsidiary role in all three food quarters, compared with the economic action generated by pivotal local stakeholders and 'gastronomic entrepreneurs' themselves. In Borough, external regeneration funding was useful, but the trustees seemed to have generated more significant, reliable and timely income through strategic property sales. At Exmouth, externally funded streetscape improvements were felt to have had little effect on deep-seated decline. And at Broadway, external regeneration funding appeared to have played almost no direct role in the regeneration process. One of the most remarkable aspects at all three areas, but especially at Broadway in its rise as a widely recognised food quarter, was that the process was almost entirely generated, governed and financed by local leaders, the community of market users and food traders.

At all three emerging food quarters, the research findings seemed to suggest real public sector frailties in funding and partnership terms. In the period 2005-2008, it appeared that the relevant local authority in each case either did not assist financially (through specific renewal funding targeted at market improvements) or had done so in ways that were perceived as partial, poorly timed or minimal. At both Broadway and Exmouth, some interviewees saw the relevant local authority as having placed economic, management and regulatory barriers in the way of the regenerating food market space, while proving a poor financial manager of markets themselves. In Broadway's case, these judgements were supported by a very critical report into market management in the borough reported in the local press (Hackney Citizen, August 2010, p.1).

Overall, then, it seemed that external regeneration funds could have a very useful role, especially where substantial refurbishment and infilling of built structures was needed. However, Broadway, in particular, demonstrated that - among other factors, most notably exceptional local leadership - external regeneration funds were not absolutely necessary for viability. In this case, the traditional market street provided a highly suitable design frame for the food quarter without substantial regeneration funding intervention. In fact, external public funds alone were not a sole requirement for food led regeneration in any of the three quarters. One highly successful example managed to develop without such support (Broadway), and two others (Borough and Exmouth) with limited regeneration funding help. While external funding could be very useful, what appeared to be critical to success at the time the research was carried out was an appropriate physical design frame, allied to inspired leadership, an ability to generate funds from non-governmental sources, good ongoing governance, and sensitive community-based management.

A strong theme running through the regeneration narrative at each food quarter was the role of partnership working between individuals and organisations involved in the area's development. Partnership-based action was critical to the revival of each space to transform it into a food quarter. However, within that overall judgement, considerable differences in approach were evident, and significantly influenced the nature of the food-centred space that resulted. At the time the research was undertaken, Borough was characterised by a very interesting mix of partners, encompassing local trustees with substantial regeneration skills; gastronomic leaders and entrepreneurs; and architects and designers with a strong food consciousness. This alliance worked together closely, within a regeneration plan based on strategic, governance and master planning elements. Equally, at Broadway, regeneration action was pursued through a resourceful partnership of local traders and residents; formalised through an association, and more latterly a community interest company. The rise of the food market at Broadway, to develop the Broadway Market quarter, represented highly successful community-based action in partnership.

Both Borough and Broadway's success appeared in part to have transcended gentrification processes and class differences, to appeal to a very diverse catchment that also constituted a community of interest in food. The food market was the catalyst and material site for bringing different people together socially, economically and environmentally. At both Borough and Broadway, partnership working formed the basis of the food market's governance relationship to its financial strategy. Community-based structures of governance, through trustees at Borough, and local traders and residents at Broadway, worked very successfully to regenerate the food markets and – to varying extents - the wider physical space in which they operated. By contrast, although Exmouth did have a traders association that overlapped with a more 'gastronomic' partnership, it was not able to sustain a *"weekly shop"* food market.

While partnership working was important at various stages at Exmouth too, the development of the area into a food quarter took a somewhat different path and produced a space of a somewhat different kind. In the late 1980s, local government regeneration officers were instrumental in creating a formal regeneration strategy based on bars and restaurants, in conjunction with the street's main landlord, among others. However, it seemed that it was not so much this formal structure but more informal food links and networks between the main landlord and food entrepreneurs that were most important in attracting restaurateurs and bar operators who had a vision for the street as a food space. Accounts from this time suggest that the landlords pursued those they hoped would start food businesses there. Fledgling food businesses, which were driven by a passion for good food, had the courage and commitment to set up in what must have appeared to others as a very unpromising location. Partnership working was again crucial in this context, but it took a somewhat different form.

Across the three quarters there was an apparent inability of local government to provide consistent leadership and vision for area-based renewal at either a strategic level or in day-to-day management. Interviewees in each case considered that the incipient food market experienced either poor or no support from the relevant local authority, and this left a yawning management gap. At Broadway the situation appeared to be particularly serious and since the book's research was completed, as noted earlier in this chapter, a very critical report on the management of this borough's markets reinforced the points made by those interviewed at Broadway Market. As reported in the local press, the report referred to the markets as experiencing a *"haphazard and uncoordinated approach to all aspects of their management"*, and a council *"either unable to or ineffective at managing its markets at a strategic or tactical level"* (Hackney Citizen, August 2010, p.1).

This situation was perhaps unsurprising. The three study areas were beginning their regeneration efforts in the late1980s when local government had fewer than ever governance tools to assist them. In London, as elsewhere, there was a deliberate political process underway at national government level to undercut the possibility of instituting any strategic planning for London as an entity. Despite the existence of some national regeneration funds, there was arguably a loss of management skills and focus locally, so the capacity to recognise and build on the food potential of these areas was very limited. The market pioneers' nuanced thinking about food was by no means widely shared in national or local government although the local authority in Exmouth's case did appear to have a good sense of what might work in terms of food in the early days. Councils were not helped either by powerful external changes in food retailing and consumption practices impinging more broadly on food market viability. By the 1990s, the residualisation of food markets and their management reflected a retreat from traditional service provision to markets, in a wider climate of managerialism in the public sector (Clarke and Newman, 1997). Insofar as local government focused on these spaces, they generally did so from within a regeneration context. There was little sense that market spaces were viewed as places requiring new kinds of food market management based on a positive vision about what such markets could offer in food terms.

In each developing food quarter, an inescapable conclusion was that local government performed poorly at both a political and managerial level in relation to food markets. Until very recently local authorities seemed to have largely seen food markets as sites in which they would need to manage decline, if they were to manage them at all. At the time of doing the primary research, local authorities looked to be somewhat overwhelmed by the rapidity of the social and economic transformations underway in these spaces. For the most part, the appearance was of councils unable to adequately provide economic and sustainability strategies, governance capacity, management and administration support, and partnership working processes with their local food market proponents. All in all, despite positive elements in individual performance that should not be overlooked - the leadership role of the local authority's regeneration officers in the 1990s in relation to Exmouth Market is one example cited by Whitelegg (2002) - local government did not emerge with a great deal of credit from the narratives of food-led renewal in the three studied spaces in the early 2000s.

However, during and since the research for this book was completed, it is worth noting that some signs of improvement have been perceptible at a London wide and local authority level. A London Food Board was established in 2004 to advise the Mayor of London, and the Mayor's food strategy and programme cover five key strategic objectives, of which a number have an explicit sustainability remit (LDA and Mayor of London, 2006). In 2009 in his initial proposals for the review of the London Plan, which is the capital's overarching planning framework, the Mayor of London announced his intention to support street and farmers' markets and their development and expansion. Third sector groups including Sustain have been advocating for a consciously sustainable relationship between food and cities to be fostered through more enlightened planning regimes. Various local authorities in London have similarly stated their intention to be better market managers in future. LB Hackney for example, the local authority area in which Broadway Market is located, announced a three-year programme of investment in improvements to its markets, as well as recognising

> *"the need to provide more effective management....We are committed to ensuring that problems we have experienced in the past are not replicated. We will work to ensure that Hackney's much loved markets are successful in the long term"* (Hackney Citizen, August 2010, p.1).

As described in Chapter 4, at Borough the local authority was seen as unable to work as a reliable financial, strategic planning or design partner with the nascent food market and redevelopment of the wider quarter in food terms. Implicit in the narrative of renewal was a sense that those involved in redeveloping the market quarter had to work round rather than with the council to regenerate Borough Market. Taking up the slack, it was fortunate that at the time (over the 1990s and into the early 2000s) the trustees in Borough's case had the skills, knowledge and leadership qualities to work through complex regeneration issues and barriers to develop and implement an innovative food-led vision for the future. However, as reported in Chapter 4, the more recent changes proposed by market management for the future direction of the market seemed to represent a significant move away from this approach, potentially undermining previously positive sustainability and conviviality results.

At Broadway, meanwhile, local government was described as not simply a neutral bystander but actively putting impediments in the way of reviving the food market. The borough was judged by some interviewees to have shown a lack of management skills and effective interest in Broadway as a developing food-centred space. Various more serious allegations about local government activities in relation to the market were also raised in local media and online accounts at the time of the research (see for example the views of Hackney Independent cited in Chapter 5). In this case, the most favourable judgement could be that the focus of regeneration was perhaps too narrowly conceived by the local authority, which did not appear able to deal sufficiently well with the social and economic aspects of 'bottom-up', community-based management founded on partnership working. More recent reporting about apparent ineptitude in local authority market management terms has reinforced this view

(Hackney Citizen, August 2010, p.1). In the event, the community-led network established through the traders and residents association was critical to the food market's renaissance, as was the leadership of the volunteer market manager, who played a central role in the food quarter's successful regeneration process.

The situation at Exmouth was slightly different again. A number of those interviewed compared Exmouth Market's partnership working capacity with Broadway Market where regeneration management was handled notably well by local community players. At Exmouth, partnership did start with the local authority, and it appeared that individual regeneration officers in the 1990s had a strong vision for the street as a food space. However, the formal regeneration partnership at that time was judged by interviewees to have been less effective than later informal networks of gastronomic entrepreneurs, including restaurateurs and other local business people with food interests. These informal connections seemed to be most successful in attracting food businesses to the street. During the time research was being undertaken for this book, the focus of regeneration partnership managed through the local council was on other food-centred places in the borough, notably Whitecross Street. Interviewees described recent governance interventions by the local council at Exmouth meanwhile as both inconsistent and inept. The council in this case was claimed to have shown a poor grasp of the governance, planning and management tasks needed; to have failed to listen to local views; and to lack a sufficiently nuanced analysis of food market development and management practice over the medium term, to successfully manage a food market centred space.

Gentrification: competing narratives and paradoxical processes

An inescapable conclusion is that at the time of the research all three food quarters were gentrifying areas. And while gentrification was a significant issue in all three places, the way its causes and effects were playing out varied considerably across the quarters. One point that emerged strongly was that gentrification could not be simply defined as wholly and inevitably negative in its effects on each place. Instead, there were competing narratives about the trajectory of redevelopment at the three food quarters, and the results were often complex and even paradoxical. Despite the argument discussed in Chapter 2 that an ideology of liveability and sustainability could be used to justify gentrification (Lees, 2000), the food quarters tended to exhibit other, more nuanced characteristics in practice. What did seem clear was that in all three emerging food quarters, the arguments about gentrification revolved around whether the food spaces created or promoted the local social exclusion and displacement effects that a typical gentrification trajectory demonstrates. The question was whether food quarters were only likely to attract middle class visitors and fuel trends toward the dominance of incoming house buyers, thus dislodging existing working class communities.

At Borough, for example, most interviewees lived experience of the place was telling. Market experts, traders and visitors largely rejected the view that the food market was socially and economically exclusionary in nature. Instead they said that the revived Borough Market and its surrounding area drew a very broad range of visitors at all income levels and represented a wide diversity of ages, cultures, nationalities and ethnicities. One interviewee spoke of people spending all their money to buy a good quality piece of meat. Another suggested that the assumption that only people on higher incomes cared about good quality food was mistaken in his experience of working with customers at this and other food markets. Although Chapter 4's case study suggested gentrification was occurring in aspects of the development of Borough Market as a food quarter, this did not seem to be a central theme in the narratives, design analysis, observations and mapping from the quarter. Rather, gentrification was contained as a spatial regeneration subtext within an overall view of the food quarter as a wild success. That success was seen as particularly inclusionary in nature – socially, environmentally and to an extent – economically.

At the same time classic gentrification signs were plain to see. The Borough Market quarter was experiencing both substantial office building activity and rising housing prices in its limited residential stock. Property developers mentioned in Chapter 4 described the food market as a key local attraction, of which incoming property purchasers would wish to take advantage. At the time the research was undertaken, the charitable objectives of the Borough Market Trust, and the charitable commitment of the trustees, ensured that the food market and attendant services were run to benefit the local community, not only through rate relief and good quality food, but as the market matured, through more diverse benefits such as food skills training, jobs and food education. Economic benefits also rippled back along the food chain as Chapter 4 demonstrated. All these positive activities and results acted as some counterbalance to the undoubted property market led gentrification underway in the wider quarter.

As touched on earlier, since the time the main research was undertaken a substantial dispute emerged about the direction of the market, with traders reported to be launching a court battle to *"save the soul"* of Borough Market (Evening Standard, Tuesday 31 August 2010, p.21). The argument revolved around the future of long established fruit and vegetable wholesalers who were reported as being forced out of the market to make way for *"fancy retailers"* who would *"kill the diversity of the market"* (ibid). This dispute might be considered an argument about the best way to capture the value created by increasing success for socially constructive purposes rather than simply arising as a result of gentrification effects.

The research findings showed that gentrification effects played out differently in relation to Broadway Market, and was a theme in relation to the market's revival for which there were competing narratives. For some, the renewed food market and its wider quarter unwittingly contributed to significant gentrification that benefitted richer incomers over a poorer indigenous population. In this view, as documented in design and morphological terms in Chapter 3 and in observational ways in Chapter 5, the area was in the first stage of a classic gentrification arc, with working class local people potentially excluded from the food market's social, economic and environmental benefits. It was suggested that they might then be squeezed out of the area altogether by rising house prices which were indirectly a result of the market's success. Within this analysis, not only was food seen as the currency of urban change but the food market was defined as the lynchpin of the gentrification process, even though this might be largely unintended and a view explicitly rejected by market proponents.

It was certainly the case that retail and residential redevelopment on and around the Market street, and apartment building in the Broadway area were underway at the time of the case study research. Over the course of the research Broadway became a more expensive place to rent or buy housing. Chapter 5's case study showed that the success of the food market contributed to a sense that the area's building stock was rising in economic value and thus becoming more attractive to developers. However, development activity and rising house prices in London were not confined to the Broadway Market area but a trend across many parts of the capital at the time, so such changes could not be causally linked only to the market's success in any very clear way.

Equally, 'us and them' arguments, that situated local working class residents solely as victims and incoming *"yuppies"* as victors, did not deal sufficiently with the subtleties of the process as experienced by both indigenous and incoming individuals. Gentrification arguments about Broadway Market seemed to underplay the degree to which local people of all backgrounds used and enjoyed the benefits of the food market; positive effects that were shown in both research interviews and observations. Additionally, more recent incomers could be seen to often support local campaigns to protect traditional residents and food traders: it was not a coincidence that the food quarter was the site for significant political, social and cultural action aimed at supporting diversity and the socially excluded. Incomers often had a considerable amount of cultural capital but were cash poor. As one interviewee put it, newer local residents were often *"rich poor"*; just able to fund a substantial mortgage but therefore on a tight budget so more likely to shop and socialise near home, providing a ready catchment for the market.

Therefore, it should be acknowledged that while some gentrification effects were in evidence, the catchment for the food market at Broadway was typified by a mix of cultures and classes taking up opportunities for more convivial and sustainable ways of interacting in relation to food, and doing so in ways that supported a lively public realm. Their focus on liveability and sustainability could not simply be ascribed to gentrification nor act as a justification for it. Instead, a focus on developing Broadway as a kind of "urban village" based on food occurred in part as a result of deliberate synergy effects aimed at by the market's clever proponents. As at Borough the community basis for the market at Broadway, originally through a very active traders association and then formalised in a community interest company, was a crucially important aspect in mitigating less appealing gentrification effects.

Gentrification was also problematised at Exmouth Market, where there were diverse communities of class and interest, and some reports of what seemed to be class-based conflict in the course of the regeneration process. As was shown in Chapter 6, for one of those interviewed, the story was of 'us and them' between local working class social housing tenants, and those described as *"yuppie"* incomers, taking local jobs and creating a demand for expensive housing for sale. The Exmouth area became an economic cluster for architecture, design, media and arts jobs; and as in the other two food quarters, some significant building projects were planned in the vicinity for mixed-use, predominantly high-cost, residential development. Property developers began to incorporate Exmouth Market's food status into marketing and publicity material. In a 'gentrifying space' argument, the street and the market as food spaces were not viewed as socially inclusive enough to appeal to the longer-term working class population at Exmouth. One point made by an interviewee was that the proposed market was not *"normal"* but *"too farmers' market"* or artisanal in nature to suit working class members of this community. This was interesting in habitus terms, of which more below.

Based on these perspectives it would be possible to argue that for some local people food-related changes were the source of discontent. The new restaurants that arrived in the 1990s, more latterly the food market in its different forms, and the second wave of restaurants and cafes since the early 2000s, might all have been a focus for contestation because working class residents felt excluded and marginalised by economic and social changes to Exmouth Market associated with food. This might, in turn, connect to why this significant part of the local population did not seem to support the new fresh produce market in numbers sufficient to help make it viable. Contrasting narratives reported on in Chapter 6 conversely suggested that for some restaurateurs and food business owners, the interplay between the existing working class population and incoming middle class residents and businesses created *"a wonderful mix and sense of community"* encompassing old and new. The re-launched food market was expected to be an economic and social attractor, but the outstanding success of Exmouth Market as a street in attracting visitors from outside the area to eat and drink, was not matched by drawing sufficient local people to buy at a fresh produce market. One tentative view about Exmouth was that both narratives might be right in part. For some, the space was felt to be marginalising while for others it really was experienced as wonderfully mixed.

Overall, drawing on evidence at the three quarters, gentrification seems to have been a very relevant aspect of the development of food-centred space of the kind studied in this book, but this needs to be understood in a nuanced way. The quarters' upward social and economic trajectory was being enjoyed by more affluent incoming residents and visitors and exploited by property developers. Some negative effects on existing populations were being reported as a result of these shifts. Food was one of the ways in which this gentrification was expressed. The food quarters provided findings that are particularly interesting in demonstrating the way gentrification interconnected with the development of an individual habitus in which food, as Bridge (2000) and Savage (2005) suggest, was a 'field' like housing, employment and education. As Butler (2007) points out, gentrifying neighbourhoods could be understood as spatial manifestation of a new middle-class habitus in which food was crucial to the construction of stylish individual personae.

At the same time, positive sustainability and conviviality effects did arise from urban change focused on food in the three quarters. Many of the alterations that produced food quarters failed to easily fit a gentrification template. Gentrification in the context of the food quarters was a more subtle and complicated process than displacement related explanations alone adequately describe. Not all working class people in all circumstances in the three quarters were excluded from the benefits of developing food-centred space. Not all middle class residents and visitors were unaware of, or insensitive to, the displacement and other effects of their arrival. Instead, at each food quarter the effects of gentrification were varied, complex and sometimes paradoxical. For instance, while food quarter development may have increased competition for resources such as housing, and effects on food prices were uneven, there were also significant food-related opportunities. These included food-related jobs, and better quality food that was not necessarily more expensive than supermarket comparators and had a much better environmental performance.

Burgeoning food quarters also offered space for political and cultural activity in the public realm. Importantly, the development of the quarters has supported sustainable urban place shaping and benefitted local communities in ways summed up in this chapter, as well as possibly challenging, and indirectly contributing to wider processes of exclusion and displacement. In the next and final chapter these elements of food quarters are explored and some discussion of the potential for development in future considered.

Chapter Eight

Food Quarters for the Future?

Understanding the quarters as a new kind of food space

The previous chapter concluded that in the three year period to 2008 the studied food-centred spaces each traced a unique but similarly highly successful economic path towards physical and social renewal based on their food status; but that in each case issues of gentrification arose in part as a consequence of this food-led renewal. This final chapter draws together conclusions about the aspects of the quarters' development that underpin their development as arguably a new element in the spatiality of London; reflecting an increasing level of sustainability and conviviality in relation to food.

The findings from the field suggest that each revived food market was consciously developed into the centrepiece of a new kind of food space, defined in this book as a food quarter. Each of the three sets of market proponents – at Borough, Broadway and Exmouth Market - planned to make a food market that was the centrepiece of a vital local area in which food was at the heart of neighbourhood life. It was clear from their accounts that each of these proponents envisioned a new and distinct food market form that stressed good quality fresh produce, with a clear provenance, available to the whole community within their local area, and in Borough's case, also with a wider spatial catchment in mind.

This economic, social and environmental model – articulated in different ways - was interconnected with the market as a set of food spaces from the start. Being clear about the nature of the food market, as one based on high quality food and also with good levels of local accessibility, but not strictly a farmer's market, mattered to market proponents in each food quarter. This was because they were trying to create something they perceived as new and better than what had gone before in relation to the social, environmental and economic aspects of sustainability in a local area. They were effectively challenging the status quo of what was available within existing local food supply and retailing arrangements.

This intertwining of a particular food market model with a distinctly food-centred spatiality was fundamental in each case.

In each place the revived food market was consciously built on but was also unlike previous food market forms. In each, the aspiration was loosely to create a farmers' style market, incorporating typical elements such as the stress on high quality produce, short supply chains, and artisanal agriculture, without having the restrictions that would be imposed by seeking official farmer's market designation. At Borough, for instance, the food market was developed to be like a farmer's market in ethos and overall approach but without a farmers' market's strict provenance rules. At Borough there was a direct link made between the market's physical refurbishment, and its financing strategy based on a farmers' 'style' market.

Equally, the principles of Slow Food and Slow Cities (città slow), discussed in Chapters 1 and 2, appeared highly relevant to the Borough approach, both in terms of the community centred, sustainable food process and its human scaled and convivial spatiality. At Broadway meanwhile the food market was described by an interviewee as *"not a farmers' market"* but it shared a number of such markets' values, including commitment to food quality and clear product sourcing. Likewise at Exmouth, the food market was originally intended to be like a farmers' market in relation to food quality but broader than such a market as a place where everybody in the community could do their weekly food shop. In a spatial sense 'community' was convenient shorthand for describing the local area and again, there was an emphasis on produce of high quality in sustainability terms.

Once set in train, food market and wider food-related development took on a life of its own. In each quarter, new or revived food spaces started to emerge that were not simply modelled on what had been there prior to decline. A distinctive and complex pattern of food-related economic, environmental, and social activities began to take shape. These, in turn, developed a complicated interplay with both the existing spatiality of the place, and new urban design and architectural interventions. First of all the economic and social forces of revitalisation began to ripple out in ways that could not be entirely forecast, directed or controlled. In each case, the food market changed over time, but in somewhat different ways. At the time of writing, both Borough and Broadway retained significant links to the original aspirations set out for them but were again altering in economic, social and governance terms in ways that were bringing fresh issues to the fore. Equally, their proponents may have been surprised at just how successfully and quickly these food spaces evolved and grew, with success bringing a new set of issues into play relating to commodification and gentrification.

At Exmouth, by contrast, as was described in Chapter 6, the alteration in the nature of the food market was not through any identified strategy. Instead, the revived food market declined as a *"whole market"* first because the range of stalls expected to set up did not materialise. Then some of the stalls that did establish on the street fairly rapidly stopped trading, as they were not generating sufficient business to stay viable. The original aspirations for Exmouth's revived market were not met, but success as a food quarter was achieved through a somewhat different route, based on restaurants, bars and a 'slow food' food court of street-based stalls.

In counterpointing Borough and Broadway's market based revival with Exmouth's somewhat different food-centred experience, the reasons seem to be at least partly to do with distinctions in catchment viability. Borough and Broadway succeeded as fresh food markets while Exmouth did not, but it did succeed as a food space in other ways. The varying economic experiences of the three quarters may have reflected marked differences in the formation of social capital in Bourdieu's terms, as discussed in Chapter 2. At Broadway, in particular, the impetus for the food market arose from players within, or with close links to, the local community, so local social capital was strong. Borough, meanwhile, combined both local social capital and broader gastronomic capital, so that its broader catchment did not undercut its local viability. At Exmouth, the community was more clearly a community of interest in gastronomy with its 'local' social capital supplied by the workers buying from the hot food stalls. It is reasonable to conclude though that at all three quarters visitors – local or not - represented a community of interest in relation to good quality food and a particular way of consuming.

Unpicking this a little further, the most recent attempt to revitalise Exmouth Market as a fresh food market came from a grouping of individuals with substantial gastronomic credentials in broader London terms. For these players it was a logical outgrowth of their restaurant and retailing trade and their altruistic food vision for the street. However, the re-launched market's rapid decline showed there was not at the time a sufficient local catchment for its produce. One interviewee suggested there was insufficient research into the likely local visitor catchment to see whether a food market would be feasible. Other factors may also have come into play, including the land use mix providing too few local residents to visit the market. There were also pull factors to other food locations. Competition from nearby supermarkets, supermarket-owned convenience stores, and the traditional street market at Angel, Islington may have drawn trade away. A new 'gastronomic' food market at Whitecross Street to the southeast may also have played a part by attracting different segments of the available visitor catchment. In contrast to Exmouth Market, Whitecross Street received substantial regeneration funding and attention focused on growing its local economic and social presence as a food space. A local interviewee said that despite Exmouth Market being *"wonderfully mixed"* the balance wasn't yet quite right between kinds of food shops, and there were not yet enough hip shops to attract people as a destination that would support a food market in the way they visited Borough or Broadway.

At Borough and Broadway both infrastructure constraints and opportunities shaped the development of their food quarters. The physical constraints were most clearly apparent at Borough, where the redesign of the food market and surrounding food retailing spaces had to take into account both the existing tangle of railway lines and bridges, and the proposed development of a new rail line over the market space. This considerably increased the complexity of the regeneration staging and physical upgrading programme. Paradoxically, the overlay of rail lines from the 19th century was also seen to positively shape the spaces at Borough in a design sense. Interviewees described the spaces' unique character as a central element in their appeal and a support to economic success. Meanwhile, at Broadway, wider connectivity improvements to the local area, through the development of new rail infrastructure at sub-regional level (the East London line extension opened shortly before publication of this book), are likely to give a strong boost to the area's economy and attractiveness to incomers. The Exmouth Market quarter alone appeared to have no obvious infrastructure related constraints affecting its development as a food-centred space. Instead Exmouth benefitted economically from its excellent level of connectivity while retaining a secret space quality. Since the main research was completed both Borough and Exmouth became part of the area in which the London bicycle hire scheme was established and early reports of the scheme's success suggested this should increase the food quarters' connectivity even further.

The research demonstrated unequivocally that people liked going to these markets, and the extent and nature of the visitor catchment drawn to each food-centred space was a focus for the research. Catchment findings broadly supported the notion that a new kind of food-centred spatiality was acting as a basis for successful redevelopment. These food spaces became highly attractive to local users and visitors from further afield.

Borough was notable in drawing an extremely wide range of people: locally, from central and greater London, from other parts of the United Kingdom and from overseas. By the time of writing its visitor catchment was thought to be global. It will be remembered from Chapter 4 that Borough Market was argued by some to be at risk of becoming a victim of its own success. Those wishing to buy food there were described as having difficulty making their way through the crowds who visited as tourists of the food-centred spectacle rather than being regular food buyers. Observations suggested this was particularly apparent on Saturdays, signifying that Borough exhibited a strong leisure time focus for visitors. In fact, observations also showed that many of these visitors did buy food at Borough; but often they purchased hot food to eat there rather than raw ingredients to take away.

At Broadway, meanwhile, as noted in Chapter 5, the catchment was mostly local, although attracting visitors as tourists from other parts of Hackney and London as a 'hip' weekend destination. Here, again, the visitor catchment shifted over the day and week. At the time of the research most appeared to be visiting during market opening hours on Saturdays. However, the rise of the market also generated considerable economic activity besides the food stalls, including cafes and restaurants, and this contributed to making the street livelier at other times too. The issue of *"core shoppers"* versus tourists was found in modified form at Broadway because the catchment balance was more weighted towards weekly shoppers than other visitors. At Exmouth, by contrast, the visitor catchment issues played out differently given the demise of the short-lived fresh produce market. When Saturday was still operating as a fresh produce market, there was an evident split in the visitor catchment between Fridays and Saturdays. Friday's visitors to the market were predominantly drawn by the hot food stalls, rather than those selling fresh produce. In any case, some local interviewees said they believed the food market in its later 'slow' fast food stall form only made a difference to the liveliness of the street overall during the weekday lunchtime period.

In fact, the role of high quality restaurants was arguably more important as a consistent social attractor at Exmouth, in the period before (as well as during and since) the fresh produce market started and stopped again. The most long-term 'anchors' for food visitors to the street included well-regarded restaurants such as Moro and Medcalf (and more recently the very fashionable Moro offshoot, Morito, and the highly rated Caravan), based on good quality, regionally specific food. In one case the food business was further supported by cookbooks showcasing the recipes and food culture presented in the relevant restaurant. Restaurants and bars, rather than a full food produce market, were instrumental in widening out the spatial range and the scale of the visitor catchment. Visitors were not only drawn from local business people, middle class residents and those visiting other local cultural attractions such as Sadler's Wells Theatre, but included diners coming from other parts of London, for whom these places were a destination in themselves. Connected to these trends, the local area was seen as gentrifying, through the effects of food-led regeneration, a point reviewed at some length in the last chapter.

Some concern was expressed during the research process, that, as the nature of the area's demography shifted due to an increased residential population (which would result from housing led redevelopment schemes such as the Mount Pleasant Mail Sorting Office site for example), this might adversely affect the nature of the visitor catchment for the street. However, this anxiety seemed unwarranted, as these residential incomers were likely to provide an additional catchment for the street's restaurants if less for its 'slow' stall based food. Moreover, with a residential tipping point reached a whole market might again be a possibility. As it stood, Exmouth Market, as the centrepiece of a food quarter, was clearly acting as an important social and economic condenser for a diverse food-centred land use mix and an increasingly broad catchment of people involved in business, retail, and cultural activities.

Whether food market, 'slow' fast food stall, or restaurant led, or a combination of all of these, food-centred regeneration was critical to greatly increasing visitor catchments for each of the three food quarters. In each case, the catchment was mixed in terms of size, spatial reach and demographic composition, encompassing both local people and incoming visitors and tourists, although the balance between these shifted according to area specific and temporal conditions. It was clear that in each quarter, food spaces and businesses worked as critical local anchors and attractors for visitors who were in the post tourist (Lash and Urry, 1994; Judd, 2008) mode as discussed in Chapter 1. In theoretical terms this could be seen as leading to increasing commodification of space based on food and design improvements, and to some extent food was part of a place marketing strategy in each quarter.

At the same time, none of these spaces could be considered *"just for tourists"* and having no internal, uncommodified life. Each demonstrated an appeal to a broad range of visitors buying and eating food as an integral part of their everyday lives. This authentic lived experience seemed to undercut the argument that such spaces could be dismissed as no more than packaged nostalgia zones, and were only developed as tourism simulacra, a point discussed in Chapter 2. It may be that at this point in their evolution, all three food quarters reflected Bell's (2007, p.19) notion of the development of a kind of hybrid hospitality that was in part commercially driven, but was also more authentically convivial than a place predicated solely on commercial transactions.

Situating food quarters as expressions of urban sustainability

Research into the food quarters suggests that they have helped in supporting London as a more sustainable city by both reflecting the existence and reinforcing the development of a sustainable urban form and processes. In these three cases the quarters were shown to be both distribution and consumption loci of the food system with strong links to food production loci elsewhere. In fulfilling these roles, they achieved some of their potential to strongly influence important aspects of urban food sustainability explored in Chapter 1. As emerging food quarters, the case study areas seemed to work in broadly positive ways in sustainability terms, and the resulting sustainability effects were mostly desirable ones. The thinking behind the development of these food-centred spaces seems a good place to start to unpick how this sustainability focus worked.

While no one interviewed mentioned Slow Food and Slow Cities (città slow); as discussed in Chapter 1, these linked movements appeared to have strong similarities in sustainability terms to the thinking behind the food spaces' development. Although individuals buying and selling at the food quarters were not necessarily part of any organised sustainability group, the capacity to support more environmentally-conscious, discerning shopping choices was identified as a factor pulling them towards using the markets, especially at Borough and Broadway. This was occurring in the context of concerns for food quality, purity, authenticity, healthfulness, production ethics, waste, food miles, and increasingly, food security and urban resilience. Shopping locally for products in season and region was motivating some interviewees to change their food buying behaviour. Some or all of these concerns also acted as factors pushing food buyers away from supermarkets and industrialised food products. Implicitly reflecting the discussion in Chapter 2 about the (contested) role of supermarkets in obesegenic environment creation, interview and online comments made about the food markets referred to opposition to industrialised farming, supermarket dominance, poor food quality, unhealthy products, wasteful packaging, and long, opaque food chains.

The development of such food markets could reasonably be situated within a wider movement towards urban food sustainability, with a strong localism slant, that includes farmers' markets and markets with some farmers' market-like attributes. Shopping at such markets was perceived as a way to avoid both supermarket shopping, and being *"brainwashed by supermarkets"*. Some interviewees said they were trying out new combinations of shopping methods and types of shopping, including online shopping and vegetable box schemes. For some these were quite deliberate choices in order to make their food consumption more sustainable. Certain market traders and stallholders also saw visitors as being increasingly informed buyers, and stressed the sustainability aspects of the buyers' interest in food quality. This was repeatedly described as *"people wanting to eat real food and know where it has come from"*.

The situation was somewhat different at Exmouth, given that the food market did not develop as expected, but the street gained a reputation based on high quality, individual restaurants and food stalls and this had sustainability implications. As documented in Chapter 6, there was a degree of discernment in relation to sustainability issues among a number of those interviewed about the market in its different forms. Findings from Exmouth about these concerns, while more muted, tended to reflect the same perspectives on urban sustainability issues as for Borough and Broadway.

Part of this was about achieving a symbiotic relationship with food producers: stressing environmental standards, quality and food skills. Shortening food supply chains, to make them more direct and transparent, also had positive economic implications for regeneration. The effects were not just local in the emerging food quarters, but in rural places supplying the food markets at each quarter's heart. At both Borough and Broadway, a symbiotic relationship with producers developed through the resurgent food market. A *"foodie"* community of interest at the consumption end of the food chain was thought by some to largely transcend class differences. It might also be thought of as an aspect of a particular individual habitus' through a display of knowledge and discernment.

At the other end of the food chain, demand for high quality, more sustainably produced foods encouraged artisanal producers. It allowed them the economic space to develop the food supply in more environmentally and spatially sustainable ways, which in turn positively affected both rural and urban ends of the food system. At Broadway, the sale of artisanal produce from Italy benefitted both producer and consumer, in relation to quality and environmental standards. At Exmouth, food shops like Brindisa and restaurants like Moro supported artisanal food producers in Spain. Reinforcing the sense that Exmouth experienced a restaurant led revival, after primary research work was completed the food shop Brindisa closed and was replaced by a fashionable restaurant (Morito tapas bar, an offshoot of Moro restaurant). At Borough, meanwhile, connections with farmers in Cumbria had a positive effect on their viability as small scale, rural producers. Insofar as the food quarters helped sustain, and sometimes revitalise, otherwise economically marginalised producers within the United Kingdom, they also made a contribution to national food security and community resilience.

At the same time, findings about the related issue of food miles raised sustainability questions that the research did not resolve. For instance, interviewees tended to see increasing the number of food miles as presenting complex issues rather than simply being a straightforward problem solved by always buying food from within a limited geographical area. At both Borough and Broadway, the markets were not strict about the food catchment for produce, and it was argued by traders that the emphasis was on quality, rather than *"artificially"* limiting the geographical area for suppliers. The food miles implications of this approach deserve further attention, as does the contribution food quarters could make to achieving food resilience if they became a more prevalent urban form.

Connected to developing relationships between producers and consumers was the demand shown by both for high environmental standards in food produced and sold at the markets. At Borough, these higher than mainstream standards reflected the sustainability concerns of both buyers and sellers. There also seemed to be a predominantly (but not totally) shared agreement at Borough that higher prices for some foods captured their better quality and more scrupulous environmental standards, and this helped to produce a sustainable production base and food chain. At Broadway, similarly, the food sold was of high quality, and connected to an increasing environment consciousness, although not necessarily based on food being organic.

As at Borough, claims of higher prices were both contested and justified in terms of high quality and better environmental standards. This was not simply defined by interviewees as about food's organic status, but about knowing its origin and the methods by which it had been produced. In both cases, there was clearly increasing interest in food provenance, its geographical origin, artisanal production and ethical considerations in production. Concern about provenance was most evident at Borough but was also seen at Broadway, with observations showing buyers very interested in their food's origins. While no visitors interviewed mentioned food security or resilience directly, a number stressed local food as important to them and an interest in food miles and food security could be inferred from their responses.

Food browsing and buying behaviour observed at Borough and Broadway could often be seen to demonstrate a concern for food quality. From comments made by buyers, it was evident that such concern was sometimes matched by sophisticated food skills and cooking knowledge, but this was not always the case. The research observations and interviews also showed a distinct lack of food knowledge (and an implied lack of skills) among a proportion of buyers about what to buy, when to buy in season, or how to prepare the food they had bought. Loss of food skills was explored particularly in Chapter 4's study of the Borough quarter, and it will be remembered that traders perceived this as being about a disconnection to food production that was linked to and exacerbated by fast-paced urban lifestyles. These traders' attempts to match the supermarkets ready meal offerings were one strategy to respond to the perceived need for quick-to-prepare food while maintaining slow food quality. Overall, buying at the food markets clearly provided a way to educate consumers who were already sympathetic to a sustainable food agenda but were not necessarily very clear about how to express that in a practical way through their own food consumption practices.

Proposing food quarters as sites for increased conviviality

Through the research the studied food quarters were seen to be 'ordinary' places (Knox, 2005; Maitland, 2008) that also provided rich sites for increased conviviality in everyday life. These emerging quarters offered their users ample opportunities for expressing richness in human interaction, based in various ways on food. The market areas at the core of each of the food quarters appeared to fit with Valentine's (1998) view of public food space exempt from, or reshaping notions of, what constitutes civilised behaviour. As explored in Chapter 2, eating in the street clearly signifies a lack of restraint in Norbert Elias' (1982) terms. Yet at the same time, at each of the quarters this kind of eating in the public domain offered place users opportunities for conviviality which were in contrast to the meagre prospects for social contact in relation to food found in less developed food spaces; spaces that have been entirely commodified by food chains; or those spaces that operate predominantly as food deserts.

The three food quarters provided a considerable number of examples of users constructing new socio-spatial patterns through their everyday activities in relation to food. There seemed to be examples of Bell's (2007, p.19) hybrid hospitality occurring in each of the quarters' third places, where the transactions made about food appeared more authentic than purely commercial interactions would do. For instance, restaurateurs were selling commercial services yet at the same time there was a sense that they also shared a knowledgeable and enthusiastic interest in gastronomy and conviviality that was not about profit making. These examples of hybrid hospitality, as well as more unmediated encounters in Lefebvre's (1991) terms, such as those in which visitors made connections simply by meeting up in the street, appeared to be influenced by the design of the spaces themselves, and the opportunities this presented for food-based social life.

The narratives of interviewees suggested that the food quarters were understood as unique spaces for those who lived and worked nearby, and those who visited them from further afield. All three food-centred spaces at the centre of the quarters were described as having a *"hidden gem"* quality; so part of the atmosphere derived from the sense that these were spaces that visitors had the opportunity to discover and explore for themselves. The distinctive spatial design quality of the food quarters equally promoted a large number of socio-spatial practices in relation to food: strolling, browsing, buying, conversing, eating, and drinking, among others. Together, these aspects supported the development of a convivial ecology as defined by Bell and Binnie (2005) through which each food quarter demonstrated a strong sense of place.

At Borough, the morphological and socio-spatial practice results showed a traditional urban structure connecting to a strong sense of place, and there was a complex interplay between urban character, design and food quality. At Broadway Market, too, the streets around the market and the pathways through its various sections were a rich set of spaces for spontaneous social encounters. These could be unmediated in Lefebvre's terms, as well as for planned social meetings and even a day's food-based entertainment. The place, as a physical entity, contributed to the development of a community of interest centred on the food market. Broadway Market, meanwhile, was physically organised to allow for social encounters and this was expressed through the fine grain of its design at a suitably human scale. At the broader level, the shape of the street funnelled people along; and at a smaller scale, subtle, fine-grained urban design changes along the street's length including its highly active frontages, helped create a series of social spaces as outdoor rooms.

Like Borough and Broadway, Exmouth's high degree of enclosure as a street allowed it to be seen as something of a secret space. Its fine grain, and the variety and richness of its detailing in urban design terms, reinforced the sense that it was both unique and well adapted for socio-spatial practices associated with food. The street was originally designed to house a food market, and at the time the research was undertaken provided a renewed focus on a public realm that was human scaled and enclosed. Like Broadway, the space was divided in design terms into a number of smaller outdoor rooms, including the Farringdon 'triangle' at its southeastern end. There was also a less formal, food-defined spatial triangle between Morito, Moro and Medcalf restaurants and the Kick bar. The shifting temporal aspects of the relationship between design and social use were also palpable at each food quarter, with public realm-focused food journeys encompassing daytime food browsing and buying, and evening and night-time drinking, socialising, and dining out. Overall, in all three quarters, the physical backdrop provided an apt setting for a rich sociability based on food, and thus what appeared to be an increased degree of conviviality over that found in surrounding areas.

A question that arose from this conclusion, though, was whether this was conviviality for all and how this connected to habitus construction. It was striking how disparate a range of people in terms of class, occupation, ethnicity, gender and age were drawn together in a community of interest at each food quarter through their awareness of food. At the same time, not everyone was using the food spaces in the same way. Each space could be understood as presenting a kind of continuum from a well-realised food quarter for some, but closer to a food desert for others. The food quarters did not present a sharp choice to their users between complete exclusion and complete incorporation in food terms. The research demonstrated rather that individuals were differently situated in relation to each quarter even in regard to their own socio-spatial practices over time. At each space, they might be on the inside in some respects, such as buying market food, but on the outside in not being able to afford to eat at restaurants associated with the food market.

This notion of the food continuum could be connected to the idea of the individual's habitus in all three places, with each market offering a food space described as one that attracted a *"certain crowd"*. In this way each food quarter provided the context for a developed habitus for individuals, contributing to a "mini habitus" in Bridge's (2006) terms, in which visitors played out their own social distinctiveness through proximity to the good taste that the market represented in cultural terms. By visiting the food street or market they were expressing marks of distinction as defined by Bourdieu (1984). Each food quarter in this way represented a space for the construction of social capital. At Borough, for instance, visitors were typified by some interviewees as middle class and food aware, although this ascription was contested by others, and the case study research showed a very diverse buyer profile and catchment at the market. Similarly, at Broadway and Exmouth, there was a sense that the place both attracted and created what one interviewee called *"a certain milieu"* and expressed a form of stylishness.

Creating a new phenomenon in urban development?

Among the most fundamental conclusions in this book is that the studied food quarters constitute a new kind of place in London. This is a place in which a novel socio-spatial phenomenon appears to have emerged as a result of the interplay between particular physical form and food-centred socio-spatial practices. Given the centrality of food to the development, shaping and functioning of these areas, it seems reasonable to suggest that at the time of the research these spaces could be described as urban food quarters. Through the construction of everyday life played out in the form of daily practices focused on food, occurring within spaces where design has been amenable to these practices, place-users helped a particular kind of urban spatiality to emerge. Through food, they could be argued to contribute to the emergence and construction of a more economically, environmentally and socially sustainable urban form.

A major factor in this phenomenon was the very close relationship between socio-spatial practice and physical design, identified and confirmed through design research and observational and interview results. Visitors were attracted to spend time at the quarters by the interplay between distinctive, human-scaled physical space and opportunities for food-based conviviality. These quarters were not simply instrumental places, or contexts for conspicuous consumption, although those aspects played a part, as discussed earlier. These were also places actively being shaped to allow for unmediated encounters in which food had a key role. The very well developed passegiatta that could be seen in each quarter demonstrated a wealth of these kinds of meetings, as people strolled along, as well as browsing and buying food. Food was the medium for unmediated social interaction, through eating, drinking and talking in the street and at stalls and stands. The strength of the urban design qualities of the food quarter spaces meant that minimal specific physical infrastructure in the way of seats and other street furniture was needed to support this social richness.

At the same time, there were clearly tensions between instrumental and social use. In both Borough and Broadway, the head counts reflected the perceived gap between *"food tourists"* and *"real shoppers"* referred to by interviewees. It was clear from observations, especially at Borough, that large numbers of visitors could make it difficult for shoppers to get to food stalls through the crush of people. In all the food quarters, the sheer range of socio-spatial practices in relation to food reinforced the sense that these quarters were becoming the new centrepieces of social life for expanding visitor catchments. Yet, at the same time, their futures as food-centred urban spaces were hotly contested because they came to matter to many people, and what food meant was at the core of this contestation.

It was notable, for example that at Broadway, community politics became an aspect of the quarter's development. Broadway was a site for engaging people with local political issues and campaigns, but it was the street's role as a food space that was most disputed. After the fieldwork was completed this debate became much sharper at Borough Market, and conflict about the place's food future grew more heated (The Independent, 14th May, 2011, n.p.r.). The tension between space for 'real shoppers' and tourists, and over the future direction of the market between management and some traders, was touched on in Chapter 4. Borough became connected to a major shopping centre developer's 'raid' on market stallholders, and on the development of a 'competing' food space locally at Maltby Street in Bermondsey, which was described as "London's latest food destination" (Time Out, n.d.):

> "Maltby Street is emphatically not a street market - it's merely a collection of rented railway arches, experimenting with opening to the public on Saturday mornings. Cheap rent and a proximity to Borough Market led several traders to set up wholesale or storage operations in the arches." (ibid).

The point is that food-centred spatial design – combining existing, reshaped and newly created elements – has been a central factor in shaping the development of this new phenomenon in urban development. As was discussed in Chapter 2 this kind of food-centred urban shaping has largely gone against the grain of dominant spatial, food retailing and urban design trends. Prevailing spatial expressions in contemporary urban form have tended to produce coarse-grained, mono-functional urban space at low densities, with 'clone town', mall based and big box food shopping spaces. Large scale, widely spaced food retailing and wholesaling spaces requiring large, car-based catchments have reflected these dominant patterns.

By contrast, the food quarters emerged as spaces that resisted the imposition of these influential but damaging developments. The quarters' shaping was important to this resistance. Borough was seen to have an extremely fine urban grain, made even finer by the numerous small-scale food businesses supported by the market's stand system. There was a conscious strategy to keep chain stores out of the food market. Similarly, Broadway Market, and the broader area of Hackney within which it sits, attracted incoming residents because they were not clone town places, even though the very qualities that attracted incomers were thought, as Hari Kunzru argued, to have "softened Hackney up" for gentrification. Exmouth Market, too, avoided developing as a clone town food street, as its food-related land uses were predominantly made up of numerous, individually owned small businesses, housed in a fine grain of frontages to a street that acted as an enclosed outdoor room.

Ironically, the avoidance of clone town qualities made the emerging food quarters particularly attractive to property developers who wished to commodify these areas or 'borrow' their social capital for other developments. At Borough Market, one significant local example was the 'London Bridge Quarter' tower building. Another was the action of a very large property development company that sought to attract stallholders away from Borough Market to their own retail space next to the Olympic site at Stratford. It was interesting that the qualities that appealed at Borough were thought to be applicable as a kind of gloss in a 'farmer's market style' development in a privately owned mall elsewhere. At Broadway, meanwhile, commodification was also occurring through development of residential and other land uses, although place branding had a less formal cast in relation to the market's publicity material than it did at Borough. Similarly though, this process was brought about in part by the resurgent food market making the local area more attractive as a place to live, buy food and socialise. At Exmouth, meanwhile, the food quarter appeared to be at the planning stages of a substantial commodification process, with large mixed-use schemes proposed, such as the redevelopment of the Mt Pleasant Mail Sorting Office site. In each case, the place branding efforts of the food markets themselves may have keyed into these property development processes even where food proponents were actively opposed to these wider changes.

In all three emerging quarters, trends towards commodification could be set against the way the food market's governance worked to deliver local and wider benefits. At the time the research was undertaken, the charitable trust in Borough's case, the traders and residents association at Broadway (later a community interest company) and the gastronomic stakeholders at Exmouth (in a somewhat different way) delivered economic and social benefits to the local community. This was variously through design and architecturally based improvements, rent relief, food of high quality, food-related educational services, food skills training, and food jobs. More broadly, each market also helped support the growth and sustainability of shorter and more environmentally sound food chains.

Turning to spatial aspects, it seemed clear that architecture and design contributed to a rich sociability at each food quarter. At Borough the area's design was broadly agreed by those researched to be unique and characterful, and design contributed largely to the atmospheric quality of the market at Borough's centre. A strong sense of place underpinned social life at the market, in which character and spectacle were important elements. Specific urban design qualities identified as valuable at Borough include spatial enclosure; subtle transitional spaces; the richness of the built edges of the space; the possibilities for serial vision and complex path sequences; the unusual design of the stall system as mini shops; and the heritage value of the buildings. It was important to both market designers and users that the space was not too mannered but retained a raw and rough edged quality, even if this was somewhat artfully presented in places.

At all three food quarters, a relevant related design aspect was the high degree of temporal change in social life over the day, week, season and year. Such change was connected to design, in the sense that human scaled and focused public spaces allowed a subtle shifting in social and economic practices at a variety of spatial and time scales. While food markets are traditionally morning places, changes in food-centred practices (as well as the desire to increase economic value) broadened out their use over time in nuanced ways. In Exmouth's case, and increasingly at both Borough and Broadway, with the focus on dining and bars, this temporal shift to the evening was especially strong.

At Broadway, the street was not judged architecturally outstanding, but was an example of solid, traditional urban fabric where design qualities had a positive impact on the social use of the space. Broadway Market was described by one of those interviewed as *"an urban village based on food"*. As explored in Chapters 3 and 5, in this way the design of the space directly linked to the traditional urbanism of the city quarter with a food market at the core. Meanwhile, comments about design qualities tended to be inferred rather than direct at Broadway, but included that the shape of the space was important. The canal at one end and the park at the other made the street a channel that reinforced Broadway Market as a promenading space, and contributed to a market feel in a confined area. Equally, at Exmouth, a solid street design supported a walkable catchment and promoted public space use; and its *"hidden gem"* quality caused those using the space to feel they had made a special discovery. Overall, views both directly given and implied reinforced the sense that the nature of design and architecture expressed in the food quarters was central to developing the sociability of the food-centred space.

An important question from the design and architecture of the emerging food quarters was whether they were designed predominantly for middle class users, as a stylish backdrop for their conspicuous consumption, to the detriment and exclusion of others locally. Exploring this question in the field also reflected the habitus discussion earlier in this chapter and elsewhere in the book. For example, there were reports of contestation over space at Exmouth Market, read by some as working class resentment at conspicuous middle class consumption of space and place. Taken alongside other research findings in the previous chapters, and touched on above, food-centred design at each quarter could be problematised as simply a technique for advancing gentrification. However, that seemed to present some evidential difficulties as set out in earlier chapters. A considerable proportion of the research supported the view that at least some of the design appeal of each food quarter transcended the class position of the users, or the playing out of a personal habitus where conspicuous consumption of high quality food was a mark of distinction. Additionally, some of those interviewed raised the 'gentrified design' point simply in order to argue against the proposition, so it remains a mixed and nuanced picture.

At the same time, if each food quarter represented the development of spatialised social capital, it is worth considering whether that process did by its nature exclude those who were not part of developing that capital. In each case there were varying views among those interviewed as to whether or not local working class people were the victims of food-led change connected to the market or wider food space. Indicators included growth in the local housing market and the arrival of more affluent incomers. At Broadway, it was suggested that this social mix was what gave the food market and surrounding area its unique cultural diversity and "arty" sense of place; and this might suggest the whole community, existing and new, benefitted in certain respects in social capital terms. As explained in Chapter 2, at least two of the food quarters - at Broadway Market and Exmouth Market - could also be understood as developing cultural quarters. In design terms, the notion of social mix was both focused on the food spaces and contested in relation to those spaces. Examples at both Broadway and Exmouth were the pie and eel shops whose frontages symbolised and gave design expression to the traditional food businesses in the street. One interviewee claimed the pie and eel shop in Broadway Market was rarely visited by most newer residents and visitors, but observations at Exmouth conversely suggested a mixed clientele enjoyed the experience, and some online accounts seemed to bear this out.

Each of the food quarters demonstrated clear links between spatial design and visitor catchment, which in turn reflected the particularity of their regeneration and gentrification process. At Borough Market, design was thought to influence the balance between local people and those from further afield, with larger numbers coming from a distance, to visit a space voted in 2007 as London's best shopping experience (Borough Market SE1, n.d.). It was evident through the research that a very broad visitor catchment enjoyed Borough as a set of designed social spaces, (despite the emergence of dissenting perspectives especially since the fieldwork was completed). At Broadway, meanwhile, the catchment reflected the changing nature of the local community. As part of a general spatial resorting in which the locus of hip London was moving further east, young couples and families were moving in, with many involved in work areas such as new media, fashion and the arts, yet drawn by the street's traditional spatial design appeal. These "shock troops" of regeneration were also beginning to be priced out of the area. A somewhat different process of food catchment growth was underway at Exmouth, reviving as a mixed-use cultural quarter, already close to a mixed but gentrifying residential area and likely to shift further in this direction in future.

The conclusion from these identified shifts is that the positive interplay between food-centred social practice and particular forms of spatial design created a specific phenomenon in urban development, at least in these three quarters, and arguably something similar is occurring in other places in London and beyond. The quarters' spatial model relied on a context of traditional urban fabric (which clung on at the centre of each space despite 20th century interventions), and that fabric acted as more than just a sympathetic backdrop. There was an active interplay identified between the physical spaces and the socio-spatial practices provoked by revived food markets focused on sustainable food and farming. In this way the fabric of each place helped support a form of food-led renewal that could not be written off as simply a mix of commodified property relations, urban gentrification and conspicuous consumption. In the last section of this chapter some implications for London – and possibly elsewhere – are drawn from these findings and conclusions, about the role food-centred renewal could play in making more sustainable cities focused on food.

Potentials for food-led renewal in London – and elsewhere

In the last part of this chapter it seems useful to explore the potential that the emergence of food quarters may have for London and elsewhere for increasing both urban sustainability and conviviality. First, it is clear that area based regeneration and retrofitting of built form in London could be more food-led than is currently the case in most renewal processes. Food-led renewal may have more chance of success in enhancing sustainability, and adapting to and mitigating climate change shocks, if it can be focused on formerly leftover or ordinary spaces. These may be places that have previously housed food markets that became moribund, or retain markets that are in serious decline, rather than flagship development sites that have already been thoroughly commodified.

The research documented in this book gives some pointers about how this process of food-led renewal has been handled successfully in a food market or 'slow food' stall-based form in such places. It suggests that space for the bottom-up, place making actions of local leaders and communities within food-led regeneration can strongly contribute to the development of a food quarter. Conversely, top-down, externally driven activity on food-led revival has not always been helpful, timely or sufficiently adept, but stakeholders including local governments could play a more productive policy, governance and economically supportive management role in future.

Second, the physical shaping of place plays an important part. Food quarters have emerged in run down places that have traditional urban design qualities, and where economic, environmental and social life focused on food can reflect and build on these intrinsic qualities of place. Borough, for example, may now look like a flagship development site but, as detailed in Chapter 4, at the start of its renewal process this was not at all evident. What it did have was 'good bones' in an urban design sense. The case of the Broadway Market study area, likewise shows that food-led revival can happen in ordinary places in London, even when only remnants of solid urban fabric remain, and can help these places to avoid becoming clone towns as they are revitalised.

London has a wealth of places physically and socially configured to provide the basis for food-led regeneration, and in a number of locations not researched for this book it is clear that this is starting to happen. In others, though, where the food conditions would seem promising, positive change is not occurring. Instead, as discussed in Chapter 2, there are numerous examples of the parachuting in of an over-scaled, large floor plate suburban retailing model into existing more urban retail centres. This spatiality matters because of the environmental sustainability implications discussed earlier, because it reflects problematic aspects of the food system, and it actively discourages conviviality. Instead of shorter food chains and a diverse range of food businesses, these food-retailing models are based on and extend the economic dominance of a few large players.

The findings also show that food-led regeneration has the potential to help combat or minimise the growth of obesegenic environments by, among other elements, supporting walkable spaces, localising consumption, and emphasising food quality. In all these ways, such food-led regeneration process can contribute materially to producing the urban sustainability and conviviality effects that were discussed in Chapters 1 and 2.

This book's food quarter elements and development trajectories offer useful examples to urban design and regeneration practitioners, as they demonstrate how the positive interplay of urban design and social and economic processes can occur in relation to food. These examples also illustrate that such interconnections cannot be oversimplified or reduced to a solely commercial approach. From an urban design point of view the physical shaping of renewal of Borough Market looks relatively similar to that of, say, Spitalfields Market next to London's financial district. However, despite some design similarities in streetscape terms of infill redevelopment around and within a traditional market space, Borough has become the centre of a robust, fine grained, economically diverse food quarter while Spitalfields has been turned into a soulless, commodified retail zone that lacks charm, character or significant economic diversity. Here the remnant market provides a sense of synthetic spectacle for drinkers and diners in chain restaurants and bars. With minor exceptions, such as the independent Verde, this simulacrum of vitality lacks the short food chain based economic structures or spatial design qualities that underpin authenticity.

Such examples are instructive, as when it comes to food, urban design needs to be approached in a nuanced way and its roots in the political economy of the city properly understood. In practice, reshaping space for food should be approached at a fine grain, with recognition of the unique qualities of particular places and an acceptance that the public realm comes first. Single developer approaches are unlikely to produce anything other than *"false variety"* (Hardy, personal communication) in which different facade treatments attempt to give the appearance of multiple ownerships at a fine grain. In the same way, food spaces in which supermarkets and food chains are allowed to preponderate cannot truly animate the public domain in the way that more diverse food spaces can do.

Urban design practice could become more developed in its approach to food: events, processes and spaces, and in turn be reflected in urban design policy and guidance for London and elsewhere that is more sensitive to food. Equally, urban design and master planning guidance for food could be improved, for example, in relation to the specific areas of movement and connectivity, urban structure analysis, and establishing design details of the place.

A central linked theme running through this book is that design for food-led regeneration has the potential to contribute very significantly to urban sustainability. The book's analysis brings the sustainability implications of food in London into the picture in a spatialised way and makes a series of connections to urban design and changing socio-spatial practices. In the context of the identified need for greater localism of consumption in the light of climate change and food resilience concerns, it appears that the food quarter should be taken seriously as a way of helping regenerate London's urban space to more sustainable, food secure ends.

A fourth, linked, area of potential is in relation to food-led regeneration in terms of urban policy development for London. By better understanding the relatively new urban phenomenon of the food quarter it should be possible to include food-related insights (about both the positive potential and apparent risks of developing such places) in policy setting for local government in London. This should be useful in planning and regeneration contexts in inner London but may also suggest transferable lessons in outer London, for new area development on London's fringes, and in the wider conurbation of Greater London. As the book notes, London as a megalopolis has significant issues in its food spatiality. Food is also increasingly a focus for planning and regeneration policy. The previously mentioned governance, leadership and sustainability issues that need to be taken into account in food-led regeneration could be pursued at a London conurbation wide level.

There are clear lessons for London's regional and (especially) local governments, that they should avoid treating food markets and the quarters around them as leftover or residual spaces in which they need merely to manage decline. Instead they have opportunities to connect up their strategic planning and day-to-day management of food spaces to a broader interest in, and understanding of, the planning, retrofitting and regeneration implications of urban food production, distribution and consumption. In this way food-led planning and regeneration could benefit from a more informed approach that would link a number of these aspects. These encompass design for walkable food consumption spaces; attention to food and health concerns including the problem of obesegenic environments; issues of food space management, funding, and retailing strategies; and the need to involve local leaders, listen to stakeholders, and accept the long term nature of social capital building that food market centred quarters require. The food-led design, planning and regeneration potentials of the food quarter are as yet insufficiently explored but offer substantial opportunities for remaking London's urban spaces – and possibly those of other cities – in more sustainable and convivial ways.

Last thoughts about the food quarters

It seems evident that food quarters are emerging and developing in London. The book's research largely supports the view that there are a range of socio-spatial practices that together underpin the emergence and development of a number of food quarters located in traditionally designed urban space, yet remaking and interconnecting with that space in new ways. Each of these developing food quarters is found a substantial way along a regeneration trajectory that shades into gentrification in some respects, and each may also be experienced as excluding from some, or all, of its positive food aspects. The research suggests that despite these experiential differences, each food-centred space allows enriching food-related opportunities for conviviality for a considerable number of people, and that this interplay between space and practice often transcends class and other aspects of distinction; helping to develop a recognisable community of interest in food at each site.

In each case, the social, environmental and economic features that attract a growing number, spread and diversity of visitors to the emerging food quarters are strongly related to traditional design of the urban fabric, and have been augmented by contextual infill architecture and design approaches. So, although design and architectural qualities have not created food quarters in themselves, the strength of the relationship between a particular set of urban design features and a new combination of socio-spatial practices is very strong indeed. Moreover, contextual urban design has been critical to the creation of successful food-centred space in each of the three food quarters. All three food quarters can be understood through a narrative of urban regeneration – and to a degree gentrification – that is food-led, and in which the themes of food quality and contextual design have been woven together in ways that are highly appealing to an increasing number of people.

The gentrification aspects of food quarter development are the most problematised and the most problematic of the themes studied. However, it appears that the forces leading to gentrification in food quarters stem more from external causes residing in urban political economy, than the results of food-led revitalisation strategies or the individual actions of food space managers themselves. Gentrification may be the unavoidable accompaniment to any successful regeneration programme, not just those focused on food. Given the food quarters' identified benefits to local communities the existence of gentrification should not be used as a basis for ignoring or discounting the urban potential of food-centred design in social, environmental and economic terms.

Each emerging food quarter studied here presents a strongly marked example of urban redevelopment that has gone against dominant spatial trends. The research findings suggest that they have been broadly an economic, social and environmental success, in part for that reason. Food quarters centred on farmers' style 'hybrid' markets, located in outdoor rooms within finely-grained, richly-detailed, legible and walkable urban space, have worked as convivial urban places on a number of levels. They have increased the opportunities for economic regeneration and diversification of deprived areas even where external funds and planning and governance support has been limited or absent. They have offered opportunities for playing out more sustainable production, distribution and consumption patterns that challenge unsustainable aspects of the modern food system and its sometimes harmful health and sociability effects on individuals. They have helped revive areas of cities at risk of becoming or remaining food deserts because traditional food patterns have been undermined. They have helped combat the unsustainable physical design approaches that produce "clone towns". Finally, and perhaps most importantly for individuals, food quarters have offered opportunities for unmediated social encounters that enrich the making of everyday life in ordinary places, not just a few flagship development areas.

The hope is that these conclusions about the nature of emerging food quarters in London provide a useful addition to sociological enquiry into urban spatiality and useful insights for urban design theory and practice. The growth of food quarters appears to be an urban phenomenon offering significant opportunities to increase the conviviality and sustainability of London. Further work on food-centred space should help to determine whether this combination of urban design and socio-spatial practice within cities' traditional fabric creates possibilities elsewhere for remaking urban space in similarly enriching ways.

APPENDIX 1

INTERVIEWS MATRIX

Expert Interviews	Place User Interviews		
	Borough Market	Broadway Market	Exmouth Market
1. Architect and master planner for Borough Market	1. Viennese tourist, middle aged, white male	2. Husband and wife, market users, white American, doctors, in their forties who live with their small child at London Fields	1. Operator of small traditional café, male, thirty something, white, Londoner
2. Architect and Urban Designer - Space Syntax Expert	2. Café stall owner, white, British, middle aged	2. Olive seller, twenty something, male, European	2. Manager upmarket café restaurant, white male, twenty-something, Londoner
3. Urban Designer - Expert on inclusive design	3. Butcher's stall holder, a professional butcher, British, middle-aged white male	3. Local market user, twenty something, white male, Londoner	3. Owner/operator organic café, white male, fifty-something, Turkish background
4. Former Head of Trustees, Borough Market	4. Organic vegetable stall holder, middle-aged, white male, British	4. Female trader, white, middle class London accent, in her forties	4. Chef, food writer and part owner 'landmark' restaurant, white male, thirty something, British
5. Voluntary Market Manager and head of BMTRA - Broadway Market	5. Italian-Australian, white male, architect and urban designer	5. Fish pie stall seller, twenty-something, white, female, Londoner	5. CD and coffee shop owner, white male, forty-something, Londoner

Interview Matrix

	6. Food shop and stall manager who specialises in Italian products, Italian, white male, forty-something	6. Tomato stall seller, twenty-something, white, male, Londoner	6. Group of three women queuing at food stalls, twenty-something, British, mix of ethnicities
	7. Australian tourist, just arrived but previously resident in London, middle-aged, white male		7. Local worker in media, twenty-something, white male, Londoner
	8. Couple who live locally 'round the corner' for the last year, twenty-something, white		8. Mixed group of students, four twenty-something, white Europeans
	9. Tourist, American, white, male, in late 30s		9. Local worker in design industry, thirty-something, white male, Londoner
			10. Local office workers, group of three twenty-something women, mix of white, black and Asian

BIBLIOGRAPHY

ACKERMAN, Diane 1990 *A Natural History of the Senses* London: Phoenix
ADAMS, Tim 2006 *The Observer Food Monthly,* April, page 34
ADLER, Patricia A & ADLER, Peter 1994 "Observational Techniques", in N.K. Denzin & Y.S. Lincoln (Eds) *Handbook of Qualitative Research* Thousand Oaks, CA: Sage, pages 377-92
AGRIFOOD STANDARDS (n.d.) *News* [online] Available at: <http://www.agrifoodstandards.net/en/news/global/report_says_too_m any_supermarket_practices_are_unhealthy_unjust_and_unsustainable. html>
ALASUUTARI, Pertti 1995 *Researching Culture. Qualitative Method and Cultural Studies* London, Thousand Oaks: Sage
ALDOUS, Tony 1988 "Inner City Urban Regeneration and Good Design" London: HMSO
—. 1992 *Urban Villages. A Concept for Creating Mixed-Use Urban Developments on a Sustainable Scale* Urban Villages Group
ALEXANDER, Christopher, ISHIKAWA, Sara & SILVERSTEIN, Murray 1977 *A Pattern Language: Towns, Buildings, Construction* New York: Oxford University Press
ALEXANDER, Christopher; NEIS, Hajo; ANNINOU, Artemis & KING, Ingrid
—. 1987 A *New Theory of Urban Design* New York, Oxford: Oxford University Press
ALEXANDER, David 2008 "Food Matters" Town and Country Planning, Vol. 77, No. 10 October, pages 420-424
ALL-PARTY PARLIAMENTARY SMALL SHOPS GROUP 2006 "High Street Britain: 2015" London
AMIN, Ash & GRAHAM, Stephen 1997 "The Ordinary City" Transactions of the Institute of British Geographers, Vol. 22, No. 4, December, pages 411-429
AMIN, Ash & THRIFT, Nigel 2002 *Cities: Reimagining the Urban* Cambridge: Polity 2004 (Eds) *The Blackwell Cultural Economy Reader* Malden, Mass, Oxford: Blackwell

ANDERSEN, Hans Thor & VAN KEMPEN, Ronald (Eds) 2000 *Governing European Cities: Social Fragmentation, Social Exclusion and Urban Governance* Aldershot: Ashgate
ANONYMOUS, 5th August 2004 *Broadway Market* [online] Available at: <http://www.urbanpath.com/london/food-markets/broadway-market.htm>
ANONYMOUS 4th April 2006 *Broadway Market* [online] Available at: <http://www.urbanpath.com/london/food-markets/broadway-market.htm>
ASHIHARA, Yoshinobu 1983 *The Aesthetic Townscape* London, Cambridge: MIT Press
ASHLEY, Bob; HOLLOWS, Joanne; JONES, Steve; & TAYLOR, Ben 2004 *Food and Cultural Studies: Studies in Consumption and Markets* London and New York: Routledge
ATKINS, Peter AND BOWLER, Ian 2001 *Food in Society* London: Arnold
ATKINSON, Paul & HAMMERSLEY, Martyn 1994 "Ethnography and Participant Observation" in N. K. Denzin and Y. S. Lincoln (Eds) *Handbook of Qualitative Research* Thousand Oaks, Calif.; London: Sage
ATKINSON, Rowland 2000 "Measuring Gentrification and Displacement in Greater London" Urban Studies, Vol. 37, No. 1, pages 149-165
—. 2003 "Revenge on Urban Space? Control and Empowerment in the Management of Public Spaces" Urban Studies, August 2003 Vol. 40, No. 9, pages 1829-1843
—. 2004 "The Evidence on the Impact of Gentrification: New Lessons for the Urban Renaissance?" European Journal of Housing Policy, Vol. 4, No. 1, April, pages 107–131
ATKINSON, Rowland & BRIDGE, Gary (Eds) 2005 *Gentrification in a Global Perspective: the New Urban Colonialism* London: Routledge
AUGÉ, Marc 1995 *Non-Places: Introduction to an Anthropology of Supermodernity* London: Verso
BADLAND, Hannah & SCHOFIELD, Grant 2005 "Transport, Urban Design, and Physical Activity: An Evidence-Based Update", Transportation Research, Part D, 10, pages 177–196
BACON, Edmund 1982 *Design of Cities* London: Thames and Hudson
BALL, Michael 2004 "Co-operation with the Community in Property-Led Urban Regeneration", Journal of Property Research, Vol. 21, No.2, pages 119–142
BALL, Michael & MAGINN, Paul J 2004 "The Contradictions of Urban Policy: the Case of the Single Regeneration Budget in London",

Environment and Planning: Government and Policy, Vol. 22, pages 739-765

—. 2005 "Urban Change and Conflict: Evaluating the Role of Partnerships in Urban Regeneration in the UK", *Housing Studies*, Vol. 20, No. 1, pages 9-28

BALL, Michael; LAURENT Le Ny & MAGINN, Paul J 2003 "Synergy in Urban Regeneration Partnerships: Property Agents' Perspectives" Urban Studies, Vol. 40, No. 11, pages 2239-2253

BANERJEE, Tridib 2001 "The Future of Public Space. Beyond Invented Streets and Reinvented Places" Journal of the American Planning Association, Vol. 67, No. 1, Winter, pages 9-24

BANKS, Marcus 2001 *Visual Methods in Social Research* London: Sage

BANKS, Marcus & MORPHY, Howard 1997 *Rethinking Visual Anthropology* London. New Haven: Yale University Press

BARNES, Julian 1992 *Metroland* Vintage Books: New York

BARNETT, Jonathan 1982 *An Introduction to Urban Design* New York. London: Harper and Rowe

BARNETT, Jonathan 1986 *The Elusive City: Five Centuries of Design, Ambition and Miscalculation* London: The Herbert Press

BARTHES, Roland 1964 *Elements of Semiology* London: Noonday Press

—. 1972 *Mythologies* London: Paladin

—. 1997 "Towards a Psychosociology of Contemporary Food Consumption" in C. Counihan and P. van Esterik (Eds) *Food and Culture: A Reader*, London: Routledge

BARTON, Hugh (Ed) 2000 *Sustainable Communities. The Potential for Eco-Neighbourhoods* London: Earthscan

BARTON, Hugh; GRANT, Marcus & GUISE, Richard 2002 *Shaping Neighbourhoods: Health, Sustainability, Vitality* London: Routledge

BATCHELOR, Anna & PATTERSON, Alan 2007 *"Political Modernization and the Weakening of Sustainable Development in Britain"* in Rob Krueger and David Gibbs (Eds) "The Sustainable Development Paradox: Urban Political Economy in the United States and Europe" New York. London: Guilford

BEARDSWORTH, Alan & KEIL, Teresa 1997 *Sociology on the Menu: An Invitation to the Study of Food and Society* London. New York: Routledge

BEATLEY, Timothy 2004 *Native to Nowhere: Sustaining Home and Community in a Global Age* Washington, DC: Island Press

BENNISON, David; WARNABY, Gary & MEDWAY, Dominic 2007 "The Role of Quarters in Large City Centres: A Mancunian Case

Study" *International Journal of Retail and Distribution Management*, Vol. 35, Issue 8, pages 626-638
BENTLEY, Ian 1999 *Urban Transformations. Power, People & Urban Design* London: Routledge
BENTLEY, Ian et al 1985 *Responsive Environments: A Manual for Designers* Oxford: Butterworth Architecture
BELL, David 2007 "The Hospitable City: Social Relations in Commercial Spaces" *Progress in Human Geography*, Vol. 31, No.1, pages 7–22
BELL, David & BINNIE, John 2005 "What's Eating Manchester? Gastro-Culture and Urban Regeneration" in Franks, K (Ed) *Food and the City* Architectural Design, Vol. 75, No. 3, pages 78-85
BELL, David & JAYNE, Mark 2004 *City of Quarters: Urban Villages in the Contemporary City* Aldershot: Ashgate
BELL, David & VALENTINE, Gill 1997 *Consuming Geographies. We Are Where We Eat* London: Routledge
BENEVOLO, Leonardo 1980 *The History of the City* London: Scolar Press
BENSON, John 1994 *The Rise of Consumer Society in Britain 1880-1980* London: Longman
BETSKY, Aaron 2000 "All the World's a Store: The Spaces of Shopping" in J. Pavitt (Ed) *Brand.new*, London: V & A, pages 108-144
BIDDULPH, Mike 2001 *Home Zones: A Planning and Design Handbook* Joseph Rowntree Foundation: Policy Press
—. 2003 "The Limitations of the Urban Village Concept in Neighbourhood Renewal: A Merseyside Case Study" Urban Design International Vol. 8, No. 1-2, June, pages 5-19
BLOWERS, Andy (Ed) 1982 *Urban Change and Conflict: An Interdisciplinary Reader* London: Harper & Row in association with the Open University Press
BONIFACE, Priscilla 2003 *Tasting Tourism: Travelling for Food And Drink* Aldershot: Ashgate
BORN, Branden 2006 "Avoiding the Local Trap, Scale and Food Systems in Planning Research", *Journal of Planning Education and Research*, Vol. 26, No. 2, pages 195-207
BOURDIEU, Pierre 1984 *Distinction: A Social Critique of the Judgement of Taste* Trans. Richard Nice London: Routledge and Kegan Paul
—. 1993 *Sociology in Question* Sage: London, Thousand Oaks
BOROUGH MARKET (n.d.) *About* [online] Available at: <http://www.boroughmarket.org.uk/index.php?module=about:19>
BOROUGH MARKET (n.d.) *News* [online] Available at: <http://www.boroughmarket.org.uk/index.php?module=news>

BOWLBY, Rachel 1985 *Just Looking: Consumer Culture in Dreiser, Gissing, and Zola* New York: Methuen
—. 2000 "Supermarket Futures" in J. Pavitt (ed.) *Brand.new* London: V & A. page 152
BOYER, Christine 1994 *The City of Collective Memory. It's Historical Imagery and Architectural Entertainments* Cambridge. Mass; London: MIT Press
BRAND, Stewart 1994 *How Buildings Learn: What Happens After They're Built* New York, NY; London: Viking
BRIDGE, Gary 2002 "Bourdieu, Rational Action and the Time-space Strategy of Gentrification", Transactions of the Institute of British Geographers, Vol. 26 Issue 2, 17 December pages 205-216
—. 2003 "Time–Space Trajectories in Provincial Gentrification" Urban Studies, Vol. 40, No. 12, pages 2545–2556
—. 2006 "It's Not Just a Question of Taste: Gentrification, the Neighbourhood, and Cultural Capital" Environment and Planning, Vol. 38, pages 1965-1978
—. 2007 "A Global Gentrifier Class" Environment and Planning, Vol. 39, pages 32-46
BRIDGE Gary & DOWLING, Robyn 2001 "Microgeographies of Retailing and Gentrification" The Australian Geographer Vol. 32, Part 1, pages 93-108
BROADBENT, Geoffrey 1990 *Emerging Concepts in Urban Space Design* London, New York: Van Nostrand Reinhold
BROADWAY MARKET (n.d.) [online] Available at: <http://www.broadwaymarket.co.uk/>
BROADWAY MARKET (n.d.) *Information* [online] Available at: <http://www.broadwaymarket.co.uk/info.html>
BROADWAY MARKET 2007 *History* [online] Available at: <http://www.broadwaymarket.co.uk/history.html, 2007>
BROADWAY MARKET (n.d.) [online] Available at: <http://34broadwaymarket.omweb.org/modules/wakka/HomePage>
BROMLEY, Rosemary D. F; TALLON, Andrew, R & THOMAS, Colin J 2005 "City Centre Regeneration through Residential Development: Contributing to Sustainability" Urban Studies, Vol. 42, No. 13, pages 2407–2429
BROTCHIE, John F; BATTY, Mike; BLAKELY, Ed; HALL, Peter & NEWTON, Peter W. 1995 *Cities in Competition: Sustainable and Productive Cities for the 21st Century* Australia: Longman
BRUEGMANN, Robert 2005 *Sprawl: A Compact History* Chicago, Ill.; London: University of Chicago Press

BRYMAN, Alan 2001 *Social Research Methods* Oxford: Oxford University Press
BURNETT, John 1979 *Plenty and Want: A Social History of Diet in England from 1815 to the Present Day* Revised Edition. London: Scholar Press
BUTLER, Tim 2002 [Online] "Thinking Global but Acting Local: the Middle Classes in the City" Sociological Research Online, Vol. 7 Available at: <http://www.socresonline.org.uk/7/3/timbutler.html>
—. 2003 "Living in the Bubble: Gentrification and its 'Others' in North London" Urban Studies, Vol. 40, No. 12, pages 2469–2486, November
—. 2007 "For gentrification?" Environment and Planning, Vol. 39, pages 162-181
—. 2008 [Online] "In the City but not of the City? Telegraph Hillers and the Making of a Middle Class Community" London: King's College London
BUTLER, Tim & LEES, Loretta 2006 "Super-gentrification in Barnsbury, London: Globalization and Gentrifying Global Elites at the Neighbourhood Level" Transactions of the Institute of British Geographers, NS 31, pages 467–487
BUTLER, Tim & ROBSON, Garry 2001 "Social Capital, Gentrification and Neighbourhood Change in London: A Comparison of Three South London Neighbourhoods" Urban Studies, Vol. 38, No. 12, pages 2145–2162
BUTLER, Tim with ROBSON, Garry 2003 *London Calling: The Middle Classes and the Re-Making of Inner London* Oxford. New York: Berg
COMMISSION FOR ARCHITECTURE AND THE BUILT ENVIRONMENT 2000 "By Design. Urban Design in the Planning System: Towards Better Practice" London: DETR
CABINET OFFICE (n.d.) *Food Policy* [online] Available at: <http://www.cabinetoffice.gov.uk/strategy/work_areas/food_policy.aspx>
CALTHORPE, Peter 1993 *The Next American Metropolis* New York: Princeton Architecture Press
CALTHORPE, Peter & FULTON, William 2001 *The Regional City: Planning for the End of Sprawl* with a Foreword by Robert Fishman, Washington, DC: Island Press
CAMERON, Rondo & SCHNORE, Leo (Eds) 1997 *Cities and Markets: Studies in the Organization of Human Space* Lanham, Md.: University Press of America

CAMERON, Stuart & COAFFEE, Jon 2005 "Art, Gentrification and Regeneration - From Artist as Pioneer to Public Arts", European Journal of Housing Policy, Vol. 5, No. 1, April, pages 39–58
CARLEY, Michael; KIRK, Karryn & MCINTOSH, Sarah 2001 "Retailing, Sustainability and Neighbourhood Regeneration", Joseph Rowntree Foundation
CARMONA, Matthew 2003 *Public Places - Urban Spaces: The Dimensions of Urban Design* Oxford: Architectural Press
—. 2006 *Design Codes: Their Use and Potential* Amsterdam; Oxford: Elsevier
CARMONA, Matthew; PUNTER, John & CHAPMAN, David 1996 "Controlling Urban Design - Part 1: A Possible Renaissance?" Journal of Urban Design, Vol. 1, No. 1, pages 47-73
—. 1996 "Controlling Urban Design - Part 2: Realizing the Potential" Journal of Urban Design, Vol. 1, No. 2, pages 179-200
—. 2002 *From Design Policy to Design Quality: The Treatment of Design in Community Strategies, Local Development Frameworks and Action Plans* London: Thomas Telford
CARMONA, Matthew; DE MAGALHÃES, Claudio; & HAMMOND, Leo 2008 *Public Space: The Management Dimension* London: Routledge
CARMONA, Matthew & TIESDELL, Steve (Eds) 2007 *Urban Design Reader* Oxford: Architectural
CASTELLS, Manuel 2000 Preface, in Peter Evans (Ed) *"Liveable Cities? Struggles for Livelihood and Sustainability"* Berkeley: University of California Press
CHAPLIN, Elizabeth 1994 *Sociology and Visual Representation* London: Routledge
CHASE, John; CRAWFORD, Margaret; & KALISKI, John 1999 *Everyday Urbanism* New York, N.Y.: Monacelli Press
CITTASLOW (n.d.) [online] Available at: <http://www.cittaslow.org.uk/>
CITY FRINGE ORGANISATION [online] Available at: <http://www.cityfringe.org.uk/>
CLARKE, John; GEWIRTZ, Sharon & MCLAUGHLIN, Eugene (Eds) 2000 *New Managerialism, New Welfare?* London: Sage
CLARKE, John & NEWMAN, Janet 1994 "The Managerialisation of Public Services" in: J. Clarke, A. Cochrane & E. McLaughlin (Eds) *Managing Social Policy* London: Sage, pages 13–31
CLARKE, John & NEWMAN, Janet 1997 *The Managerial State: Power, Politics and Ideology in The Remaking of Social Welfare* London: Sage

CLARKE, Graham; EYRE, Heather; & GUY, Cliff 2002 "Deriving Indicators of Access to Food Retail Provision in British Cities: Studies of Cardiff, Leeds and Bradford", Urban Studies, Vol. 39, No. 11, pages 2041–2060

CLOS, Juan 2005 "Towards a European City Model" in *London: Europe's Global City?* Urban Age Conference Newspaper, London: LSE and Alfred Herrhausen Society

CLOUT, Hugh (Ed) 1991 *The Times London History Atlas* London: The Times

COATES, Sam 2006 "The End of the Corner Shop is Nigh as 10,000 Go Under in Five Years" London: The Times, Monday 2nd January

COFFEY, Amanda & ATKINSON, Paul 1996 *Making Sense of Qualitative Data: Complementary Research Strategies* Thousand Oaks, CA: Sage

COHEN, Philip & RUSTIN, Michael J. (Eds) 2008 *London's Turning: Thames Gateway - Prospects and Legacy* Aldershot: Ashgate

CONISBEE, Molly; KJELL, Petra; ORAM, Julian; BRIDGES-PALMER, Jessica; SIMMS, Andrew & TAYLOR, John 2004 "Clone Town Britain. The Loss of Local Identity on the Nation's High Streets" September, London: New Economics Foundation

COOK, Ian 2000 (Ed) *Cultural Turns/Geographical Turns: Perspectives on Cultural Geography* New York: Prentice Hall

CORBIN, Juliet & HOLT, Nicholas 2005 "Grounded Theory" in Bridget Somekh & Cathy Lewin (Eds) *Research Methods in the Social Sciences* London Thousand Oaks, New Delhi: Sage

COUNTRY LIFE (n.d.) *Foodies London* [online] Available at: <http://www.countrylife.co.uk/culture/article/78975/Foodies_London.html>

COUPLAND, Andy 1997 *Reclaiming the City: Mixed Use Development* London: E & FN Spon

COWAN, Robert 2002 *Urban Design Guidance: Urban Design Frameworks, Development Briefs and Master Plans* London: Thomas Telford Publishing

—. 2003 *The Dictionary of Urbanism* Tisbury: Streetwise Press

CRESWELL, John 1994 *Research Design. Qualitative and Quantitative Approaches* Thousand Oaks, London: Sage

CROWHURST LENNARD, Suzanne & LENNARD, Henry 1987 "Livable Cities: People and Places: Social and Design Principles for the Future of the City" 1st International Conference on Making Cities

Livable: Selected Papers, Southampton New York: Center for Urban Well-Being

CULLEN, Gordon 1971 *The Concise Townscape* London: The Architectural Press

CURTIS, Sarah & CAVE, Ben 2002 "Is Urban Regeneration Good for Health? Perceptions and Theories of the Health Impacts of Urban Change", Environment and Planning C: Government and Policy, Vol. 20, pages 517-534

CUMMINS, Steven & MACINTYRE, Sally 2002 ""Food Deserts" - Evidence and Assumption in Health Policy Making" British Medical Journal Vol. 325, No. 24, pages 436-438

—. 2006 "Food Environments and Obesity - Neighbourhood Or Nation?" International Journal of Epidemiology No. 35, pages 100–104

CUTHBERT, Alexander 2006 *The Form of Cities. Political Economy and Urban Design* Malden Mass., Oxford: Blackwell

DANTZIG, George & SAATY, Thomas 1973 *Compact City. A Plan for a Liveable Urban Environment* San Francisco: WH Freeman and Company

DAVIS, Mike 1992 *City of Quartz. Excavating the Future in Los Angeles* London: Vintage

DE CERTEAU, Michel 1984 *The Practice of Everyday Life*, trans. S. Rendall, Berkeley, CA: University of California Press

—. 1986 *Heterologies: Discourse on the Other* translated by Brian Massumi; foreword by Wlad Godzich, Manchester: Manchester University Press

—. 2000 *The Certeau Reader* edited by Graham Ward, Oxford: Blackwell

DE CERTEAU, Michel; GIARD, Luce & MAYOL, Pierre 1998 *The Practice of Everyday Life, Vol. 2: Living and Cooking* University of Minnesota Press

DE ROO, Gert & MILLER, Donald (Eds) 2000 *Compact Cities and Sustainable Urban Development: A Critical Assessment of Policies and Plans from an International Perspective* Aldershot: Ashgate

DEPARTMENT FOR COMMUNITIES AND LOCAL GOVERNMENT 2006 "Preparing Design Codes - A Practice Manual" 30 November, London: HMSO

DEPARTMENT FOR COMMUNITIES AND LOCAL GOVERNMENT (n.d.) *Sustainable Urban Design* [online] Available at: <http://www.communities.gov.uk/archived/generalcontent/citiesandregions/sustainableurbandesign/publicationsaboutsustainable/>

DEPARTMENT FOR ENVIRONMENT, FOOD AND RURAL AFFAIRS 2010 *Food 2030* HM Government

DEPARTMENT OF THE ENVIRONMENT, TRANSPORT & THE REGIONS 2000 "By Design, Urban Design in the Planning System: Towards Better Practice" HMSO: London
DEPARTMENT OF THE ENVIRONMENT, TRANSPORT & THE REGIONS & THE PRINCE'S FOUNDATION FOR THE BUILT ENVIRONMENT 2001 *Sustainable Urban Extensions* London
DIAMOND, John 2002 "Strategies to Resolve Conflict in Partnerships: Reflections on UK Urban Regeneration", The International Journal of Public Sector Management, Vol. 15, No 4, 2002, pages 296-306
—. 2004 "Local Regeneration Initiatives and Capacity Building: Whose 'Capacity' and 'Building' For What?" Community Development Journal, Vol. 39, No. 2, pages 177–189
DINES, Nicholas & CATTELL, Vicky with GESLER, Wil & CURTIS, Sarah
—. 2006 "Public Spaces, Social Relations and Well-Being in East London" Queen Mary, University of London; Joseph Rowntree Foundation: Policy Press
DOBSON, Paul. W.; WATERSON, Michael & DAVIES, Stephen. W 2003 "The Patterns and Implications of Increasing Concentration in European Food Retailing" Journal of Agricultural Economics, Vol. 54, pages 111–125
DOEL, Christine. M. 1996 'Market Development and Organisational Change: The Case of the Food Industry', in N. Wrigley and M. Lowe (Eds) *Retailing, Consumption and Capital: Towards the New Retail Geography* London: Longman
DOLPHIJN, Rick 2004 *Foodscapes: Towards a Deleuzian Ethics of Consumption* Delft: Eburon
DOUGLAS, Mary 1978 *Purity and Danger. An Analysis of Concepts of Purity and Taboo* London: Routledge and Kegan Paul
DREIER, Peter; MOLLENKOPF, John & SWANSTROM, Todd 2004 *Place Matters: Metropolitics for the Twenty-first Century* 2nd Edition revised. Lawrence, Kan.: University Press of Kansas
DRIJVER, Peter 2004 "Invisible Architecture" New Civic Architecture, Triennale IV of Architecture and Urbanism, October, Bologna
DUANY, Andres 2011 *Garden Cities: Theory and Practice of Agrarian Urbanism.* London: The Prince's Foundation for the Built Environment
DUANY, Andres & PLATER-ZYBERK, Elizabeth 1991 *Towns and Town Making Principles* New York: Rizzoli International Publications
DUANY, ANDRES; PLATER-ZYBERK, Elizabeth & SPECK, Jeff 2000 *Suburban Nation: The Rise of Sprawl and the Decline of the American Dream* New York: North Point Press

DUNHAM-JONES, Ellen 2011 *Retrofitting Suburbia: Urban Design Solutions for Redesigning Suburbs* Hoboken, N.J.: Wiley; Chichester: John Wiley

DURUZ, Jean 2003 "Eating at the Borders: Culinary Journeys" *Environment and Planning D: Society and Space*, Vol. 23, No. 1, pages 51-69

EBBELING, Cara B; PAWLAK, Dorota B & LUDWIG, David S 2002 "Childhood Obesity: Public-Health Crisis, Common Sense Cure", The Lancet, Vol. 360, Issue 9331, pages 473 – 482

THE ECOLOGIST (n.d.) [online] Available at: <http://www.theecologist.org/archive_detail.asp?content_id=593>

EDWARDS, Ferne & MERCER, Dave 2010 "Meals in Metropolis: Mapping the Urban Foodscape in Melbourne, Australia" Local Environment Volume15, Issue 2, pages 153-168

EDWARDS-JONES, Gareth et al 2008 "Testing the Assertion That 'Local Food is Best': The Challenges of an Evidence-Based Approach" in *Towards Sustainable Food Chains: Harnessing the Social and Natural Sciences*, Trends in Food Science & Technology, Vol. 19, Issue 5, pages 265–274

EID, Jean; OVERMAN, Henry G.; PUGA, Diego & TURNER, Matthew A. 2008 "Fat city: Questioning the Relationship Between Urban Sprawl and Obesity" Journal of Urban Economics, Vol. 63, Issue 2, pages 385–404

EISENHAUER, Elizabeth 2001 "In Poor Health: Supermarket Redlining and Urban Nutrition" GeoJournal, Vol. 53, pages 125–133

ELIAS, Norbert 1982 *The Civilising Process* Translated by E. Jephcott, Oxford: Blackwell

ELKIN, Tim with MCLAREN, Duncan & HILLMAN, Mayer 1991 *Reviving the Cities. Towards Sustainable Urban Development* Friends of the Earth

ELLIN, Nan 1996 *Postmodern Urbanism* Cambridge, Mass., Oxford: Blackwell

ENTEC 2006 "Greater London Authority Sustainability Appraisal of the London Plan (First Review)" Scoping Report, Greater London Authority

ESPERDY, Gabrielle 2002 "Edible urbanism" *Architectural Design,* 72, pages 44–50

EUROPEAN COMMISSION EXPERT GROUP ON THE URBAN ENVIRONMENT 1995 "European Sustainable Cities" Final Report, European Commission

EUROPEAN COMMISSION, DIRECTORATE-GENERAL, JOINT RESEARCH CENTRE, EUROPEAN ENVIRONMENT AGENCY 2006 "Urban Sprawl in Europe: The Ignored Challenge" Copenhagen: European Environment Agency
EXMOUTH MARKET (n.d.) [online] Available at: <http://www.exmouthmarket.co.uk/>
EVANS, Bob; JOAS, Marko; SUNDBACK, Susan & THEOBALD, Kate 2005 *Governing Sustainable Cities* London, Sterling, VA.: Earthscan
EVANS, Graeme & SHAW, Phyllida 2004 "The Contribution of Culture to Regeneration in the UK: A Review of Evidence" A report to the UK Department for Culture, Media and Sport
EVANS, Mel & CATTELL, Vicky 2000 "Communities or Neighbourhoods? Place Images, Social Cohesion and Area Regeneration in East London" Rising East, Vol. 4, No. 1
FAINSTEIN, Susan 1996 "Justice, Politics, and the Creation of Urban Spaces" in Malcolm Miles, Tim Hall with Iain Borden (Eds) *The City Cultures Reader* 2000 London: Routledge, pages141-155
FEATHERSTONE, Mike; HEPWORTH, Mike; & TURNER, Bryan (Eds) 1990 *The Body: Social Process and Cultural Theory* London: Sage
FINDAHOME (n.d.) *New Homes For Sale* [online] Available at: <http://www.findanewhome.com/s/ai/5661/rs/1/pt/2/new-homes-for-sale.fap>
FISCHLER, Claude 1988 "Food, Self and Identity" Social Science Information Vol. 27, No. 2, pages 275-92
FINKELSTEIN, Joanne 1989 *Dining Out. A Sociology of Modern Manners* Oxford: The Polity Press
—. 1999 "Foodatainment" Performance Research 4, pages 130–36
FISHMAN, Robert 1987 *Bourgeois Utopias. The Rise and Fall of Suburbia* New York: Basic Books
FLYNN, Thomas 1994 "Foucault's Mapping of History" in G. Gutting (Ed) *The Cambridge Companion to Foucault*, Cambridge: Cambridge University Press
FOOD LOVERS BRITAIN (n.d.) *Borough Market London* [online] Available at: <http://www.foodloversbritain.com/FoodMatters/This-Month/Borough-Market-London/>
FOOD STANDARDS AGENCY, 2004 "Do Food Deserts Exist? A Multi-Level, Geographical Analysis of the Relationship Between Retail Food Access, Socio-Economic Position and Dietary Intake (N09010)" Project Report, Monday 17 May, London: Food Standards Agency

FOLEY, Paul & MARTIN, Steve 2000 "Perceptions of Community Led Regeneration: Community and Central Government Viewpoints", Regional Studies, Vol. 34. No. 8, pages 783 - 787

FOUCAULT, Michel 1993 "Space, Power and Knowledge" in During, S. (Ed) *The Cultural Studies Reader* London: Routledge

FRECKLETON, Ann M et al 1989 "Public Perception and Understanding" in C.R.W. Spedding (Ed) *The Human Food Chain* London: Elsevier Applied Science

FRENCH, Stuart J 1983 *Urban Space A Brief History of the City Square* Dubuque, Iowa: Kendall/Hunt

FREY, Hildebrand 1999 *Designing the City: Towards a More Sustainable Urban Form* London: E and F N Spon

FURBEY, Robert 1999 "Urban 'Regeneration': Reflections on a Metaphor"1999 Critical Social Policy, Vol. 19, No. 4, pages 419-445

FYFE, Nicholas. R. 1998 *Images of the Street. Planning, Identity and Control in Public Space* New York, London: Routledge

GABRIEL, Yiannis & LANG, Tim 1995 *The Unmanageable Consumer. Contemporary Consumption and its Fragmentation* London: Sage

GARCÍA, Beatriz 2004 "Cultural Policy and Urban Regeneration in Western European Cities: Lessons from Experience, Prospects for the Future" Local Economy, Vol. 19, No. 4, pages 312–326

GARDELS, Nathan 2004 "Globalization Bites Back" New Perspectives Quarterly, Vol. 21, Issue 2, Spring, pages 66-71

GARNETT, Tara 1996 "Growing Food in Cities. A Report to Highlight and Promote the Benefits of Urban Agriculture in the UK" SAFE Alliance

GARREAU, Joel 1991 *Edge City: Life on the New Urban Frontier* New York: Doubleday

GEERTZ, Clifford 1973 *The Interpretation of Culture* New York: Basic Books

GEHL, Jan 1996 *Life Between Buildings: Using Public Space* Copenhagen: Arkitektens Forlag

GEHL, Jan & GEMZØE, Lars 1996 *Public Spaces, Public Life* Copenhagen: The Architectural Press

GEIST, Johann Friedrich 1983 *Arcades. The History of a Building Type* MIT Press

GERMOV, John & WILLIAMS, Lauren (Eds) 1999 *A Sociology of Food and Nutrition. The Social Appetite* Oxford, New York: Oxford University Press

GIDDENS, Anthony 1990 *The Consequences of Modernity* Cambridge: The Polity Press

GIERYN, Thomas F 2000 "A Space for Place in Sociology" Annual Review of Sociology, Vol. 26, pages 463-496

GILLHAM, Oliver 2002 *The Limitless City: A Primer on the Urban Sprawl Debate* with aerial photographs by Alex S. MacLean, Washington, DC: Island Press

GIROUARD, Mark 1985 *Cities and People. A Social and Architectural History* New Haven and New York: Yale University Press

GLASER, Barney 1992 *Basics of Grounded Theory Analysis* Mill Valley CA: Sociology Press

GOLLEDGE, Reginald G 1978 "Learning About Urban Environments" in T. Carlstein, D. Parkes, and N. Thrift (Eds) *Timing Space and Spacing Time: Making Sense of Time*, London: Arnold, pages 76-98

GOMEZ, Marie-Léandre 2011 "The Emergence of an Influential Practice: Food for Thought" *Organization Studies,* July, Vol. 32, No. 7, 921-940

GOODY, Jack 1982 *Cooking, Class and Cuisine. A Study in Comparative Sociology* Cambridge, London, New York: Cambridge University Press

GORDON, Ian & TRAVERS, Tony 2010 "London: Planning the Ungovernable City" City, Culture and Society, Vol. 1, No. 2, pages 49-55

GORDON, Ian & McCANN, Philip 2000 "Industrial Clusters: Complexes, Agglomeration and/or Social Networks?" Urban Studies, March, Vol. 37, No. 3, pages 513-532

GOSLING, David 1996 *Gordon Cullen. Visions of Urban Design* London: Academy Editions

GOSLING, David & MAITLAND, Barry1984 *Concepts of Urban Design* London: Academy

GOSPODINI, Aspa 2002 "European Cities in Competition and the New 'Uses' of Urban Design" Journal of Urban Design, Vol. 7, No. 1, pages 59–73

GOTTMAN, Jean & HARPER, Robert 1990 *Since Megalopolis, The Urban Writings of Jean Gottman* Baltimore and London: The Johns Hopkins University Press

GOTTMAN, Jean 1978 *Forces Shaping Cities* Newcastle upon Tyne: University of Newcastle, Department of Geography

GOTTDEINER, Mark 1994 *The New Urban Sociology* New York: McGraw Hill

—. 1995 *Postmodern Semiotics* Cambridge, Mass, Oxford: Blackwell

GOULDSBLOM, Johan & MENNELL, Stephen (Eds) 1998 *A Norbert Elias Reader* Oxford: Blackwell

GRAHAM, Stephen & HEALEY, Patsy 1999 "Relational Concepts of Space and Place: Issues for Planning Theory and Practice" European Planning Studies, Vol. 7, No. 5, pages 623-646
GREATER LONDON AUTHORITY 2006 "Mayor's London Food Strategy" London: GLA
—. 2006 "Sustainable Design and Construction" Supplementary Planning Guidance, May, London: GLA
—. (n.d.) [online] Available at: <http://www.london.gov.uk/gla/publications/housing.jsp>
—. (n.d.) *Growing Food* [online] Available at: <http://www.london.gov.uk/priorities/environment/urban-space/growing-food>
GREED, Clara & ROBERTS, Marion (Eds) with contributions by Hugh BARTON et al 1998 *Introducing Urban Design Interventions and Responses* Harlow: Longman
GREENBIE, Barrie 1984 *Spaces: Dimensions of the Human Landscape* New Haven. London: Yale University Press
GROTH, Jacqueline & CORIJN, Eric 2005 "Reclaiming Urbanity: Indeterminate Spaces, Informal Actors and Urban Agenda Setting" *Urban Studies*, Vol. 42, No. 3, pages 503–526
GRONOW, Jukka & WARDE, Alan (Eds) 2001 *Ordinary Consumption* London: Routledge
THE GUARDIAN 7th December 2005 *Market Forces* [online] Available at: <http://shopping.guardian.co.uk/food/story/0,,1660557,00.html>
—. 1st November 2007 *Healthy Communities* [online] Available at: <http://www.guardian.co.uk/society/2007/nov/01/health.communities>
—. 10th November 2008 *Healthy Towns To Fight Obesity* [online] Available at: <http://www.guardian.co.uk/society/2008/nov/10/obesity-healthy-towns1>
—. Monday 1st November 2010 *Borough v Westfield: Food Fight As Stratford Takes On South Bank* [online] Available at: <http://www.guardian.co.uk/uk/2010/nov/01/borough-westfield-market-london-olympics>
HABERMAS, Jurgen 1989 "Modern and Postmodern Architecture" in *The New Conservatism: Cultural Criticism and the Historians' Debate*, translated by Shierry Webe Nicholsen, Cambridge, MA.: MIT
HACKNEY INDEPENDENT (n.d.) [online] Available at: <http://www.hackneyindependent.org/content/view/170/2/>
—. (n.d.) *Saturday Market Debate* [online] Available at:

<http://www.hackneyindependent.org/news_archive_2006/the_saturday_market_debate.html>
HALL, Peter & WARD, Colin 1998 *Sociable Cities The Legacy of Ebenezer Howard* Chichester: John Wiley
HALL, Peter 1992 *Cities of Tomorrow: An Intellectual History of Urban Planning and Design in the Twentieth Century* Oxford: Blackwell
HALL, Peter & CASTELLS, Manual 1993 *Technopoles of the World: The Making of 21st-Century Industrial Complexes* London New York: Routledge
HALL, Stuart (Ed) 1997 *Representation: Cultural Representations and Signifying Practices* London: Sage
HALL, Tim & ROBERTSON, Iain 2001 "Public Art and Urban Regeneration: Advocacy, Claims and Critical Debates" Landscape Research, Vol. 26, No. 1, pages 5–26
HANCOCK, Trevor 1995 "Urban Planning, Sustainability and Health" OECD/WHO International Healthy and Ecological Cities Congress, March, Madrid: OECD
HANSON, Julienne 1989 *Order and Structure in Urban Space. A Morphological History of the City of London* University of London
HARRIS, Edmund M 2010 "Eat Local? Constructions of Place in Alternative Food Politics" Geography Compass, 4, pages 355–369
HARRIS, Marvin 1986 *Good to Eat: Riddles of Food and Culture* London: Allen and Unwin
HARDY, Matthew (Ed) 2008 *The Venice Charter Revisited: Modernism, Conservation and Tradition in the 21st Century World*, Newcastle-upon-Tyne: Cambridge Scholars Publishing
HARDY, Matthew, 2005 Discussion of the Principle of Variety in Urban Design [Conversation] (Personal communication)
HARVEY, David 1985 *The Urbanisation of Capital* Oxford: Blackwell
—. 1987 "Flexible Accumulation Through Urbanisation: Reflections on 'Post Modernism' in the American City" Antipode, 19, pages 260-286
—. 1989 *The Condition of Post Modernity* Oxford: Blackwell
—. 2002 "From Managerialism to Entrepreneurialism: The Transformation in Urban Governance in Late Capitalism" in G. Bridge and S. Watson (Eds) *The Blackwell City Reader* Oxford: Blackwell, pages 456-463
—. 2003 "The City as Body Politic" in J. Schneider & I. Susser (Eds) *Wounded Cities: Destruction and Reconstruction in a Globalized World* Oxford: Berg, pages 25-46
HARVEY, Mark; MCMEEKIN, Andrew & WARDE, Alan (Eds) 2004 *Qualities of Food* Manchester: Manchester University Press

HASTINGS, Annette 1999 "Analysing Power Relations in Partnerships: Is There a Role for Discourse Analysis?" Urban Studies, Vol. 36, No. 1, pages 91–106

HASTINGS, Annette; MCARTHUR, Andrew & MCGREGOR, Alan 1996 *Less Than Equal? Community Organisations and Estate Regeneration Partnerships* Bristol: The Policy Press

HAUGHTON, Graham & HUNTER, Colin 2003 *Sustainable Cities* London and New York: Routledge

HAYDEN, Dolores 1995 *The Power of Place Urban Landscapes as Public History* Cambridge, Mass., London: MIT Press

—. 2004 *A Field Guide to Sprawl* with aerial photographs by Jim Wark, New York, London W.W. Norton

HAYWARD, Richard & MCGLYNN, Sue (Eds) 1993 *Making Better Places. Urban Design Now* Oxford: Butterworth Architecture

—. 2000 "Editorial" Urban Design International, Vol. 5, pages 61-62

—. 2002 "Editorial" Urban Design International, Vol. 7, pages 127-129

HAYWOOD, Russell 2009 *Railways, Urban Development and Town Planning in Britain: 1948-2008*, Farnham: Ashgate

HEATH, Gregory W; BROWNSON, Ross C; KRUGER, Judy; MILES, Rebecca; POWELL, Kenneth E & RAMSEY, Leigh T 2006 "The Effectiveness of Urban Design and Land Use and Transport Policies and Practices to Increase Physical Activity: A Systematic Review" Journal of Physical Activity and Health, No. 3, Supplement 1, pages S55-S76

HEBBERT, Michael 2003 "New Urbanism — the Movement in Context" Built Environment, Vol. 29, Issue 3 New Urbanism, pages 193-209

—. 2005 "Engineering, Urbanism and the Struggle for Street Design" Journal of Urban Design, Vol. 10, No. 1, February, pages 39-59

HEDMAN, Richard & JASZEWSKI, Andrew 1985 *Fundamentals of Urban Design* Planners Press

HEMPHILL, Lesley; MCGREAL, Stanley; BERRY, Jim & WATSON, Siobhan 2006 "Leadership, Power and Multisector Urban Regeneration Partnerships" Urban Studies, Vol. 43, No. 1, pages 59-80

HILLIER, Bill 1996 *Space is the Machine. A Configurational Theory of Architecture* Cambridge: Cambridge University Press

HILLIER, Bill & HANSON, Julieanne 1984 *The Social Logic of Space* Cambridge: Cambridge University Press

HINCHLIFFE, Steve & WHATMORE, Sarah 2006 "Living Cities: Towards a Politics of Conviviality" Science as Culture, Special Issue: Technonatural Time-Spaces, Vol. 15, Issue 2, pages 123-138

HINRICHS, Clare C 2003 "The Practice and Politics of Food System Localization", Journal of Rural Studies, Vol. 19, Issue 1, pages 33–45
HOCKINGS, Paul (Ed) 1995 *Principles of Visual Anthropology* 2nd Edition. Berlin: de Gruyter
HOLLOWAY, Lewis; KNEAFSEY, Moya; VENN, Laura; COX, Rosie, DOWLER, Elizabeth & TUOMAINEN, Helena 2007 "Possible Food Economies: a Methodological Framework for Exploring Food Production–Consumption Relationships", Sociologia Ruralis, Vol. 47, pages 1–19
HOLLAND, Caroline; CLARK, Andrew; KATZ, Jean & PEACE, Sheila 2007 "Social interactions in urban public places" The Open University, Joseph Rowntree Foundation: Policy Press
HOLSTON, James, 1989 *The Modernist City: An Anthropological Critique of Brasilia*, Chicago: University of Chicago Press
HOUGH, Michael 1984 *City Form and Natural Process. Towards a New Urban Vernacular* Croom Helm: London
—. 1990 *Out of Place Restoring Identity to the Regional Landscape* New Haven, London: Yale University Press
HOWARD, Ebenezer 1974 *Garden Cities of Tomorrow* London: Faber
HUW 19th April 2006 *Broadway Market* [online] Available at: <http://www.urbanpath.com/london/food-markets/broadway-market.htm>
ILLICH, Ivan 1973 *Tools for Conviviality* London: Calder and Boyars
IMRIE, Rob; LEES, Loretta & RACO, Mike (Eds) 2008 *Regenerating London: Governance, Sustainability and Community* London: Routledge
IMRIE, Rob & RACO, Mike (Eds) 2003 *Urban Renaissance? New Labour, Community and Urban Policy* Bristol: The Policy Press
THE INDEPENDENT (n.d.) *Bermondsey Seven Evicted as Food Market Tensions Grow* [online] Available at: <http://www.independent.co.uk/news/uk/home-news/bermondsey-seven-evicted-as-food-market--tensions-grow-2283885.html>
INDEPENDENT WORKING CLASS ASSOCIATION (n.d.) *Information* [online] Available at: <http://www.iwca.info/>
—. (n.d.) [online] Available at: <http://www.iwca.info/cor/cor0034.htm>
JACK, Ian (Ed) 1995 *Food. The Vital Stuff* Granta, No. 52, Winter
JACKSON, Laura 2004 "The Relationship of Urban Design to Human Health and Condition", Landscape and Urban Planning, Vol. 64, Issue 4, pages 191-200
JACOBS, Allan B 1993 *Great Streets* Cambridge, Mass., London: MIT Press

JACOBS, Jane 1994 *The Death and Life of Great American Cities* Harmondsworth: Penguin in Association with Jonathan Cape
JACOBSON, Howard 1999 *The Mighty Waltzer* London: Jonathan Cape
JANES, Hilly 2002 "Local Heroes?" Saturday, March 2, The Guardian
JABAREEN, Yosef R 2006 "Sustainable Urban Forms: Their Typologies, Models, and Concepts" Journal of Planning Education and Research, Vol. 26, No. 1, pages 38-52
JARVIS, Helen; PRATT, Andy & CHENG-CHONG WU, Peter 2001 *The Secret Life of Cities: The Social Reproduction of Everyday Life* London: Prentice Hall
JAYNE, Mark; HOLLOWAY, Sarah L. & VALENTINE, Gill 2006 "Drunk and disorderly: alcohol, urban life and public space" Progress in Human Geography, Vol. 30, No, 4, pages 451–468
JENKS, Mike 2000 *Compact Cities: Sustainable Urban Forms for Developing Countries* E. & F.N. Spon
JENKS, Mike; BURTON, Elizabeth; & WILLIAMS, Katie (Eds) 1996 *The Compact City A Sustainable Urban Form?* London: Spon
JOHNSTON, Josée & BAUMANN, Shyon 2010 *Foodies: Democracy and Distinction in the Gourmet Foodscape* London: Routledge
JUDD, Dennis. R. 2008 "Visitors and the Spatial Ecology of the City" in L. M. Hoffman, S. S. Fainstein and D. R. Judd (Eds) *Cities and Visitors: Regulating People, Markets, and City Space* Oxford: Blackwell
KASS, Leon 1994 *The Hungry Soul: Eating and the Perfecting of Our Nature* New York: Free Press
KEGLER, Harald 2005 in S. Parham (Ed) "The European City, 30 Years: Review & Prospects" Report of C.E.U.'s First International Congress 9 - 10 September, Berlin, Germany
KHARE, Ravindra. S & RAO, Madhugiri S.A (Eds) 1986 *Food, Society and Culture Aspects in South Asian Food Systems* Durham. NC: Carolina Academic Press
KIRWAN, James 2004, "Alternative Strategies in the UK Agro-Food System: Interrogating the Alterity of Farmers' Markets", Sociologia Ruralis, 44, pages 395–415
KLEINMAN, Mark 1998 "Include Me Out? The New Politics of Place and Poverty" CASE Paper, Centre for Analysis of Social Exclusion CASE/11, London School of Economics,
KLEMEK, Christopher 2011 *The Transatlantic Collapse of Urban Renewal: Postwar Urbanism From New York to Berlin* Chicago, Ill.: University of Chicago Press

KLOPPENBURG, Jack JR; LEZBERG, Sharon; DE MASTER, Kathryn; STEVENSON, George W & HENDRICKSON, John 2000 "Tasting Food, Tasting Sustainability: Defining the Attributes of an Alternative Food System with Competent, Ordinary People, Human Organization" Vol. 59, No. 2, pages 177-186

KNOWLES, Caroline & SWEETMAN, Paul (Eds) 2004 *Picturing the Social Landscape: Visual Methods and the Sociological Imagination*, London : Routledge

KNOX, Paul L 2005 "Creating Ordinary Places: Slow Cities in a Fast World" Journal of Urban Design, Vol. 10, No.1, pages 1-11

KNOX, Peter 1992 "The Packaged Landscapes of Post-Suburban America", in J. Whitehand and P. Larkham, (Eds) *Urban Landscapes: International Perspectives* London: Routledge

KOETTER, Fred & ROWE, Colin 1978 *Collage City* Cambridge, Mass.: MIT Press

KOLSON, Kenneth 2001 *Big Plans: The Allure and Folly of Urban Design* Baltimore and London: Johns Hopkins Press

KOSTOF, Spiro 1991 *The City Shaped Urban Patterns and Meanings Through History* London: Thames and Hudson

—. 1992 *The City Assembled The Elements of Urban Form Through History* London: Thames and Hudson

KRESS, Gunther & VAN LEEUWEN, Theo 1996 *Reading Images: The Grammar of Visual Design* London: Routledge

KRIER, Rob 1979 *Urban Space* New York: Rizzoli

KRISTAIN LONDON (n.d.) *Exmouth Market* [online] Available at: <http://kristainlondon.typepad.com/dining/2006/10/exmouth_market_.html>

KUMAR, Krishan & MAKAROVA, Ekaterina 2008 "The Portable Home: The Domestication of Public Space", Sociological Theory, Vol. 26, Issue 4, pages 324–343

KUNSTLER, James 1996 *The Geography of Nowhere The Rise and Decline of America's Man Made Landscapes* New York. London: Simon & Schuster

KURLANSKY, Mark 2002 *Salt: A World History* London: Jonathan Cape 1997 *Cod: The Biography of a Fish that Changed the World* Toronto: Alfred A Knopf

LAKE, Amelia A & TOWNSHEND, Tim G 2006 "Obesogenic Environments: Exploring the Built and Food Environments" The Journal of the Royal Society for the Promotion of Health, Issue 126, pages 262-267

LAKE, Amelia A; TOWNSHEND, Tim G & ALVANIDES, Seraphim (Eds) 2010 *Obesogenic Environments: Complexities, Perceptions and Objective Measures* Chichester, West Sussex: Wiley-Blackwell

LAMBERT, Christine & BODDY, Martin 2002 "Transforming the City: Post-Recession Gentrification and Re-urbanisation" CNR Paper 6, Centre for Neighbourhood Research

LANG, Jeremy F 2000 *Pierre Bourdieu: A Critical Introduction* London: Pluto Press

LANG, Tim 1997 *Food Policy for the 21st Century. Can it be Both Radical and Reasonable?* Thames Valley University Centre for Food Policy Discussion Paper No 4

LANG, Tim; BARLING, David & CARAHER, Martin 2009 *Food Policy: Integrating Health, Environment and Society* Oxford: Oxford University Press

LANG, Tim & HEASMAN, Michael 2004 *Food Wars: The Global Battle for Minds, Mouths, and Markets* London; Sterling, VA: Earthscan Publications

LANE, Andrea J 1993 *Urban Morphology and Urban Design A Review* University of Manchester, EIA Centre

LASH, Scott & URRY, John 1994 *Economies of Signs and Space* London: Sage

LAURIER, Eric & PHILO, Chris 2004 "The Cappuccino Community: Cafés and Civic Life in the Contemporary City" ESRC Project July 2002-December 2004, Reference No.: R000239797, Department of Geography & Topographic Science, University of Glasgow

LAWLESS, Paul, FODEN, Michael; WILSON, Ian & BEATTY, Christina 2010 "Understanding Area-based Regeneration: The New Deal for Communities Programme in England" Urban Studies, February, Vol. 47, No. 2, pages 257-275

LEES, Loretta 2000 'A Reappraisal of Gentrification: Towards a "Geography Of Gentrification"', Progress in Human Geography, Vol. 24, No. 3, pages 389-408

—. 2003 "Policy (Re)Turns: Gentrification Research and Urban Policy - Urban Policy and Gentrification Research" Environment and Planning, Vol. 35, pages 571-574

LEGATES, Richard & STOUT, Frederic (Eds) 1996 *The City Reader* London and New York: Routledge

LEFEBRVE, Henri 1991 *The Production of Space* Oxford: Blackwell

LESSARD, Marie & AVILA, Milian 2005 *"A Contribution to Urban Sustainability: Analaco, a Historic Neighbourhood in Puebla, Mexico"* Urban Design International 10, pages 39-50

LEVI-STRAUSS, Claude 1994 *The Raw and the Cooked: Introduction to a Science of Mythology* London: Pimlico

LEY, David 2003 "Artists, Aestheticisation and the Field of Gentrification" Urban Studies, Vol. 40, No. 12, pages 2527–2544

LIBCOM 27th March 2006 *The Battle of Broadway Market* [online] Available at: http://libcom.org/news/article.php/broadway-market-hackney-270306

LINDELOF, Anders; NIELSEN, Claus V & PEDERSEN, Birthe D 2010 "Obesity Treatment - More Than Food and Exercise: A Qualitative Study Exploring Obese Adolescents' and Their Parents' Views on the Former's Obesity" *International Journal of Qualitative Studies on Health and Well-being* Vol. 5, No. 2

LLOYD, Greg; MCCARTHY, John; BERRY, Jim & MCGREAL, W. S 2001 "Fiscal Incentives for Urban Regeneration" ESRC Report, Award No. R000223122

LLOYD, Kathleen & AULD, Christopher 2003 "Leisure, Public Space and Quality of Life in the Urban Environment" Urban Policy and Research, Vol. 21, No. 4, pages 339–356

LOBSTEIN, Tim; BAUR, Louise & UAUY, Ricardo 2004 "Obesity in Children and Young People: A Crisis in Public Health" Obesity Reviews, Vol. 5, pages 4–8

LOCKIE, Stewart 2001 "Food, Place and Identity: Consuming Australia's Beef Capital" Journal of Sociology, Vol. 37, No. 3, pages 239-255

LOFLAND, John 1971 *Analyzing Social Settings: a Guide to Qualitative Observation and Analysis* Belmont, Calif.: Wadsworth Publishing Company

LOGAN, John & MOLOTCH, Harvey 1987 *Urban Fortunes. The Political Economy of Place* Berkeley, London: University of California Press

LOMBARDI, Patrizia Lucia 1999 "Understanding Sustainability in the Built Environment. A Framework for Evaluation in Urban Planning and Design" PhD Thesis, University of Salford

LONDON DEVELOPMENT AGENCY & MAYOR OF LONDON 2006 *Healthy and Sustainable Food for London*, The Mayor's Food Strategy

LONDON BOROUGH OF SOUTHWARK 2005 Transport Topic Paper

LONDON EVENING STANDARD 2007 Homes and Property, Wednesday 21 February, page 5

—. 31st August 2010 *Traders Battle to 'Save the Soul' of Borough Market* [online] Available at:
<http://www.thisislondon.co.uk/standard/article-23872328-traders-launch-court-battle-to-save-the-soul-of-borough-market.do>

LONDON SE1 (n.d.) *Forum* [online] Available at: <http://www.london-se1.co.uk/forum/read/1/34280>
—. (n.d.) *News* [online] Available at: <http://www.london-se1.co.uk/news/view/5278>
LOPEZ, Russ 2004 "Urban Sprawl and Risk for Being Overweight or Obese" American Journal of Public Health, Vol. 94, No. 9, September, pages 1574-1579
LOUKAITOU-SIDERIS, Anastasia 1996 "Cracks in the City: Addressing the Constraints and Potentials of Urban Design" Journal of Urban Design, Vol. 1, No. 1, pages 91-103
LUPTON, Deborah 1996 *Food, the Body and the Self* London, Thousand Oaks, New Delhi: Sage
LYNCH, Kevin 1961 *The Image of the City* Cambridge, Mass: MIT Press & Harvard University Press
—. 1985 *A Theory of Good City Form* Cambridge, Mass. London: MIT Press
MCARTHUR, Andrew A 1993 "Community Partnership - A Formula for Neighbourhood Regeneration in the 1990s?" Community Development Journal, 28, pages 305-315
McCRACKEN, Grant 1990 *Culture and Consumption: New Approaches to the Symbolic Character of Consumer Goods and Activities* Bloomington and Indianapolis: Indiana University Press
MACGREGOR, James & VORLEY, Bill 2006 "Fair miles"? The Concept of "Food Miles" Through a Sustainable Development Lens" International Institute for Environment and Development, Sustainable Development Opinion Papers, October
MADANIPOUR, Ali; CARS, Göran; & ALLEN; Judith (Eds) 1998 "Social Exclusion in European Cities: Processes, Experiences, and Responses" London, Philadelphia: Jessica Kingsley
MADANIPOUR, Ali 1996 *Design of Public Space. An Enquiry into a Socio-Spatial Process* New York: John Wiley
—. 2003 *Private and Public Spaces of the City* London: Routledge
MADANIPOUR, Ali; HULL, Angela & HEALEY, Patsy (Eds) 2001 *The Governance of Place: Space and Planning Processes* Aldershot: Ashgate
MAITLAND, Robert 2007 Conviviality and Everyday Life: the Appeal of New Areas of London for Visitors" International Journal of Tourism Research, Vol. 10, pages 15–25
MANSVELT, Juliana 2005 *Geographies of Consumption* London, Thousand Oaks, New Delhi: Sage
MARSHALL, Stephen 2005 *Streets and Patterns* Spon Press: London

—. 2005 "Joined-Up Urbanism" Town & Country Planning, December, pages 367-371
MARTE, Lidia 2007 "Foodmaps: Tracing Boundaries of 'Home' Through Food Relations" Food and Foodways, Vol. 15, Issue 3 and 4, pages 261-289
MARVIN, Simon & MEDD, Will 2006 "Metabolisms of Obecity: Flows of Fat Through Bodies, Cities, and Sewers" Environment and Planning, Vol. 38, pages 313-324
MASSEY, Doreen, ALLEN, John & PILE, Steve (Eds) 1999 *City Worlds* London: Routledge in association with the Open University
MAYE, Damian; HOLLOWAY, Lewis & KNEAFSEY, Moya (Eds) 2007 *Alternative Food Geographies: Representation and Practice* Amsterdam, Oxford: Elsevier
MAYER, Heike & KNOX, Paul L. 2006 "Slow Cities: Sustainable Places in a Fast World" Journal of Urban Affairs, Vol. 28, pages 321–334
MAYOR OF LONDON 2003 "Sustainable Development Framework" London: GLA
MENNELL, Stephen; MURCOTT Anne & VAN OTTERLOO Anneke 1992 *The Sociology of Food: Eating, Diet and Culture* London: Sage
MENNELL, Stephen 1996 *All Manners of Food* Urbana and Chicago: University of Illinois Press
MILES, Malcolm; HALL, Tim & BORDEN Iain 2000 *The City Cultures Reader* London. New York: Routledge
MILES, Malcolm 1997 *Art, Space and the City* London and New York: Routledge
—. 1998 "Strategies for the Convivial City: A New Agenda for Education for the Built Environment" The National Society for Education in Art and Design
—. 2000 "Café-Extra: Culture, Representation and the Everyday" in Nick Stanley and Ian Cole (Eds) *Beyond the Museum: Art, Institutions, People* Oxford: Museum of Modern Art, pages 30-37
MILES, Steven & MILES, Malcolm 2004 *Consuming Cities* New York: Palgrave Macmillan
MILES, Steven & PADDISON, Ronan 2005 "Introduction: The Rise and Rise of Culture-led Urban Regeneration" Urban Studies, Vol. 42, No. 5/6, pages 833–839
MILLSTONE, Erik & LANG, Tim 2003 *The Atlas of Food: Who Eats What, Where and Why* London: Earthscan
MINTON, Anna 2009 *Ground Control: Fear and Happiness in the Twenty-First-Century City* London: Penguin

MINTZ, Sydney 1985 *Sweetness and Power: The Place of Sugar in Modern History*, New York: Viking
MONTGOMERY, John 1995 "Urban Vitality and the Culture of Cities" Planning Practice and Research, Vol. 10, No. 2, pages 101-109
—. 1998 Making a City: Urbanity, Vitality and Urban Design" Journal of Urban Design, Vol. 3, No. 1, pages 93-116
—. 2003 "Cultural Quarters as Mechanisms for Urban Regeneration. Part 1: Conceptualising Cultural Quarters", Planning Practice and Research, Vol. 18, No. 4, pages 293-306
MORGAN, Kevin; MARSDEN, Terry & MURDOCH, Jonathan 2006 *Worlds of Food: Place, Power, and Provenance in the Food* Chain Oxford University Press
MORLAND, Kimberly B. & EVENSON, Kelly R 2009 "Obesity Prevalence and the Local Food Environment", Health & Place, Vol. 15, Issue 2, June, pages 491–495
MORLAND, Kimberly; DIEZ ROUX, Ana V & WING, Steve 2006 "Supermarkets, Other Food Stores, and Obesity: The Atherosclerosis Risk in Communities Study" American Journal of Preventive Medicine, Vol. 30, Issue 4, pages 333–339
MORRILL, Calvin; SNOW, David A & WHITE, Cindy H (Eds) 2005 *Together Alone: Personal Relationships in Public Spaces* Berkeley, CA: University of California Press
MORRIS, A. E. J 1994 *A History of Urban Form Before the Industrial Revolutions* Harlow. New York: Wiley, Longman
MOUGHTIN, Cliff 1992 *Urban Design. Street and Square* Oxford: Butterworth Architecture
—. 1996 *Urban Design. Green Dimensions* Oxford: Butterworth Architecture
MOUZON, Steven 2006 "Feedable Places" Southlands Charrette, The New Urban Guild, Miami Beach
MURCOTT, Anne 2011 [Online] "The BSA and the Emergence of a 'Sociology of Food': A Personal View" Sociological Research Online, Vol. 16, No. 3, page 14. Available at: http://www.socresonline.org.uk/16/3/14.html 10.5153/sro.2344
MURRAIN, Paul 2002 "Understand Urbanism and Get Off Its Back" Urban Design International, Vol. 7, Numbers 3-4, pages 131-142
MUSTERD, Sako; MURIE, Alan & KESTELOOT, Christian (Eds) 2006 "Neighbourhoods of Poverty: Urban Social Exclusion and Integration in Europe" Basingstoke: Palgrave Macmillan
MY ISLINGTON (n.d.) *New Exmouth Food Market* [online] Available at:

<http://www.myislington.co.uk/islington/fe-community_new-exmouth-food-market.htm>
NACHMIAS, Chava & NACHMIAS, David 1992 *Research Methods in the Social Sciences* Sevenoaks: Hodder
NATHAN, Max & MARSHALL, Adam 2006 "Them And Us, Britain and the European City" Centre for Cities Discussion Paper No. 7, London: Institute of Public Policy Research
NEAL, Peter (Ed) 2003 *Urban Villages and the Making of Communities* London: Spon Press
NEAL, Zachary 2006 "Culinary Deserts, Gastronomic Oases: a Classification of US Cities" *Urban Studies* 43, pages 1–21
NEAL'S YARD DAIRY (n.d.) *Our Shops* [online] Available at: <http://www.nealsyarddairy.co.uk/ourshops.html>
NEW LONDON ARCHITECTURE (n.d.) *The Great Estates* [online] Available at: <http://www.newlondonarchitecture.org/media/exhibitions/catalogues/TheGreatEstates.pdf>
NEWMAN, Peter & KENWORTHY, Jeffrey 2006 "Urban Design to Reduce Automobile Dependence", Opolis: An International Journal of Suburban and Metropolitan Studies, Vol. 2: No. 1, pages 35-52
NEWMAN, Peter & SMITH, Ian 2000 "Cultural Production, Place and Politics on the South Bank of the Thames" International Journal of Urban and Regional Research, Vol. 24, No. 1, pages 9-24
NICHOLSON, George *Presentation to Academy of Urbanism Delegation*, London, August 12, 2006.
NORTH, Pete 2000 "Community Capacity Building: Maintaining the Momentum" Local Economy, Vol. 15, No. 3, pages 251–267
ODDY, Derek J 1990 "Food, Drink and Nutrition" in F.M.L. Thompson (Ed) *The Cambridge History of Britain 1750-1950* Vol.2 *People and Their Environment*, Cambridge: Cambridge University Press
OLDENBURG, Ray 1989 T*he Great Good Place: Cafés, Coffee Shops, Community Centers, Beauty Parlors, General Stores, Bars, Hangouts, and How They Get You Through the Day* New York: Paragon House
ORAM, Julian; CONISBEE, Molly & SIMMS, Andrew 2003 "Ghost Town Britain II" London: New Economics Foundation
PAGE, Steven J & HARDYMAN, Rachel 1996 "Place Marketing and Town Centre Management A New Tool For Urban Revitalization", *Cities* Vol. 13, No. 3, pages 153-164
PARHAM, Susan 1990 "The Table In Space: A Planning Perspective" Meanjin, Vol. 49, No. 2

—. 1992 "Gastronomic Strategies for Australian Cities" Urban Futures, Vol. 2, No 2
—. 1993a "Gastronomy and Urban Form" South Australian Winter Planning Seminar, Adelaide: Planning Education Foundation Papers
—. 1993b "Convivial Green Space" Proceedings, Seventh Australian Symposium of Gastronomy, Canberra
—. 1995 "Megalopolis" Arena, No.16, April/May
—. 1995 "Strategic Issues for the Ecological City", OECD/World Health Organisation Symposium, Conference Paper, Madrid
—. 1996 "Gastronomic Architecture: The Cafe and Beyond" Architecture Bulletin, October Sydney: RAIA
—. 1996 "Food and Megalopolis" Proceedings, 9th Symposium of Australian Gastronomy, March, Sydney
—. 1998 "Fat City. Why Bologna Works" Australian Financial Times, Saturday Review Section, February
—. 2005 "Designing the Gastronomic Quarter" in K. Franks (Ed) *Food and the City* Architectural Design, Vol. 75, No. 3
—. 2006 "The European City Model and Its Critics", Discussion Paper, Urban Age Programme, LSE, January
—. 2008 *"The Relationship Between Approaches to Conservation and the Idea of Nostalgia: Looking at Food-Centred Spaces Within Cities"* Chapter, in M. Hardy (Ed) *The Venice Charter Revisited: Modernism, Conservation and Tradition in the 21st Century World,* Newcastle: Cambridge Scholars Publishing
PARHAM, Susan & KONVITZ, Josef 1996 *Innovative Policies for Sustainable Urban Development* Paris: OECD
PARRY, Jayne & JUDGE, Ken 2005 "Tackling the Wider Determinants of Health Disparities in England: A Model for Evaluating the New Deal for Communities Regeneration Initiative" American Journal of Public Health, Vol. 95, No. 4, pages 626-628
PASSINGHAM, W J 1935 *London's Markets: Their Origin and History* Sampson Low
PATEL, Raj 2007 *Stuffed and Starved. Markets, Powers, and the Hidden Battle for the World Food System* London: Portobello Books
PEATTIE, Lisa 1998 "Convivial Cities" in M. Douglass, & J. Friedmann *Cities for Citizens, Planning and the Rise of Civil Society in a Global Age* Chichester. New York: John Wiley and Sons, pages 247-253
PETERS, Toby 2000 *The Crisis in UK Local Food Retailing* Thames Valley University, Centre for Food Policy
PINK, Sarah 2008 "Sense and Sustainability: The Case of the Slow City Movement" Local Environment, Vol. 13, Issue 2, pages 95-106

PINK, Sarah; KURTI, Laszlo; & ALFONSO, Ana Isabel (Eds) 2004 *Working Images: Visual Research and Representation in Ethnography* London: Routledge

POLLAN, Michael 2008 *In Defence of Food. A Food Eater's Manifesto* New York: Penguin Press

PORTNEY, Kent E 2003 *Taking Sustainable Cities Seriously. Economic Development, the Environment, and Quality of Life in American Cities* Cambridge Mass, London: MIT Press

POTHUKUCHI, Kameshwari & KAUFMAN, Jerome L 1999 "Placing the Food System on the Urban Agenda: The Role of Municipal Institutions in Food Systems Planning" Agriculture and Human Values, 16, pages 213–224

PRATT, Andy C 2009 "Urban Regeneration: From the Arts 'Feel Good' Factor to the Cultural Economy: A Case Study of Hoxton, London" Urban Studies, Vol. 46, No. 5-6, pages 1041-1061

PRÉTECEILLE, Edmond 2007 "Is Gentrification a Useful Paradigm to Analyse Social Changes in the Paris Metropolis?" Environment and Planning, Vol. 39, pages 10-31

PRETTY, Jules N; BALL, A.S; LANG, Tim & MORISON, James I.L 2005 "Farm Costs and Food Miles: An Assessment of the Full Cost of the UK Weekly Food Basket" Food Policy, Vol. 30, Issue 1, pages 1-19

PROJECT FOR PUBLIC SPACES (n.d.) *Placemaking in a Down Economy* [online] Available at: <http://www.pps.org/info/newsletter/Placemaking_in_a_Down_Econo my/think_global_buy_local>

PROSSER, Jon (Ed) 1998 *Image-Based Research: A Sourcebook for Qualitative Researchers* London: Falmer

PUNCH, Keith 1998 *Introduction to Social Research. Quantitative and Qualitative Approaches* London, Thousand Oaks: Sage

RACO, Mike 2003 "Remaking Place and Securitising Space: Urban Regeneration and the Strategies, Tactics and Practices of Policing in the UK" Urban Studies, Vol. 40, No. 9, pages 1869-1888

RAGIN, Charles & BECKER, Howard (Eds) 1992 *What is a Case?* Cambridge: Cambridge University Press

RAVEN, Hugh & LANG, Tim 1995 *Off Our trolleys? Food Retailing and the Hypermarket Economy*, Institute for Public Policy Research

RAVETZ, Alison 1986 *The Government of Space* London: Faber

RAVETZ, Joe, with the Sustainable City-Region Working Group 2000 *City Region 2020. Integrated Planning for a Sustainable Environment* London: TCPA and Earthscan

REDFERN, Paul 2003 "What Makes Gentrification 'Gentrification'?" Urban Studies, Vol. 40, No. 12, pages 2351–2366

RELPH, Edward 1987 *The Modern Urban Landscape* Baltimore: Johns Hopkins University Press

REVEL, Jean-Francois 1982 *Culture and Cuisine A Journey Through the History of Food* New York: Doubleday

REYNOLDS, Ben 2009 "Feeding a World City: The London Food Strategy", International Planning Studies Special Issue: Feeding The City: The Challenge Of Urban Food Planning, Vol. 14, Issue 4, pages 417-424

RICHAIR (n.d.) *Porta 2030* [online] Available at: <http://richair.waag.org/porta2030/london/index.html>

ROBERTS, Peter & SYKES, Hugh (Eds) 2000 *Urban Regeneration A Handbook* London; Thousand Oaks. New Delhi: Sage

ROBBINS, Edward & EL-KHOURY, RODOLPH 2002 (Eds) *Shaping the City: Studies in History, Theory and Urban Design* London: Routledge

ROBSON, Garry & BUTLER, Tim 2001 "Coming to Terms with London: Middle-Class Communities in a Global City" International Journal of Urban and Regional Research, Vol. 25, No. 1, pages 70-86

ROSE, Gillian 2001 *Visual Methodologies: An Introduction to the Interpretation of Visual Materials* London. Thousand Oaks, Calif.: Sage

ROSENBAUM, Mark S 2006 "Exploring the Social Supportive Role of Third Places in Consumers' Lives" Journal of Service Research, Vol. 9, No. 1, pages 59-72

ROWE, Peter 1991 *Making a Middle Landscape* Cambridge Mass, London: MIT Press

—. 1997 *Civic Realism* Cambridge Mass, London: MIT Press

ROWLAND, Jon 1997 "Designing the Public" in *The Architects' Journal*, 4, pages 35-39

RUBIN, Guy; JATANA, Nina; & POTTS, Ruth 2006 "The World on a Plate: Queens Market, the Economic and Social Value of London's Most Ethnically Diverse Street Market" New Economics Foundation

RUDLIN, David & FALK, Nicholas 2001 *Building the 21st Century Home. The Sustainable Urban Neighbourhood* Oxford: Architectural Press

RUDOFSKY, Bernard 1964 *Architecture Without Architects: A Short Introduction to Non-Pedigreed Architecture* Albuquerque: University of New Mexico Press

—. 1980 *Now I Lay Me Down to Eat: Notes and Footnotes on the Lost Art of Living* Garden City N.Y: Anchor Press and Doubleday

SALAMAN, Redcliffe 1949 *The History and Social Influence of the Potato* Cambridge: Cambridge University Press

SASSEN, Saskia 1991 *The Global City, New York, London, Tokyo* Princeton: Princeton University Press

SAUSSURE, Ferdinand de 1983 *Course in General Linguistics* (Eds) Charles Bally and Albert Sechehaye with the collaboration of Albert Riedlinger; translated and annotated by Roy Harris, London: Duckworth

SAVAGE, Mike; WARDE Alan & WARD, Kevin 2003 *Urban Sociology, Capitalism and Modernity* 2nd Edition, Basingstoke; New York: Palgrave MacMillan

SAVAGE Mike; BAGNALL Gaynor & LONGHURST, Brian 2005 *Globalisation and Belonging* London: Sage

SCHLOSSER, Eric 2001 *Fast Food Nation, What the All-American Meal is Doing to the World* London: Allen Lane, The Penguin Press

SCHMIECHEN, James & CARLS, Kenneth 1999 *The British Market Hall. A Social and Architectural History* New Haven: Yale University Press

SCOTT, Alan 1997 *The Cultural Economy of Cities* Oxford: Blackwell

SELF, Peter 1982 *Planning the Urban Region. A Comparative Study of Policies and Organisations* London: Allen and Unwin

SENNETT, Richard 1991 *The Conscience of the Eye. The Design and Social Life of Cities* New York: Knopf

—. 1992 *The Uses of Disorder. Personal Identity and City Life* New York. London: Norton

—. 1994 *Flesh and Stone. The Body and the City in Western Civilization* London: Faber

—. 1995 "Something in the City; The Spectre of Uselessness and the Search for a Place in the World" TLS No 4825, 22 September, pages 13-17

SENNETT, Richard (Ed) 1969 *Classic Essays on the Culture of Cities*, Prentice-Hall

THE SHARD LONDON BRIDGE (n.d.) *Information* [online] Available at: http://www.shardlondonbridge.com/information/

—. (n.d.) *Vertical City* [online] Available at: <http://www.shardlondonbridge.com/vertical_city/location.php>

SHAW, Hillary J 2006 "Food Deserts: Towards the Development of a Classification" Human Geography, Vol. 88, pages 231–247

SHIRVANI, HAMID 1985 *The Urban Design Process* New York. Wokingham: Van Nostrand Reinhold
SHORT, Anne; GUTHMAN, Julie & RASKIN, Samuel 2007 "Food Deserts, Oases, or Mirages? Small Markets and Community Food Security in the San Francisco Bay Area" Journal of Planning Education and Research, Vol. 26, pages 352-364
SHUSTERMAN, Richard (Ed) 1999 *Bourdieu: A Critical Reader* Oxford: Blackwell
SIMMEL, Georg 1903 "The Metropolis and Mental Life" in Kurt H. Wolff, Ed. and translated *The Sociology of Georg Simmel*, 1964, New York: Simon and Schuster, pages 409-24
SIMMS, Andrew; KJELL, Petra & POTTS, Ruth 2005 "Clone Town Britain: The Survey Results on the Bland State of the Nation" London: New Economics Foundation
SIMMS, Andrew; ORAM, Julian; MACGILLIVRAY, Alex & DRURY, Joe 2002
"GHOST TOWN BRITAIN II. Death on the High Street. How Britain's local economies are losing ground *and* fighting back" London: New Economics Foundation
SITTE, Camillo 1965 *City Planning According to Artistic Principles*, translated by George R. Collins and Christiane Crasemann Collins, London: Phaidon Press
SKLAIR, Leslie 2006 "Iconic Architecture and Capitalist Globalization" City, Vol. 10, No. 1, pages 21-47
SMITH, Colin 2002 "The Wholesale and Retail Markets of London, 1660 – 1840" Economic History Review, LV, No 1, pages 31-50
SMITH, Darren & HOLT, Louise 2007 "Studentification and `Apprentice' Gentrifiers Within Britain's Provincial Towns and Cities: Extending the Meaning of Gentrification", Environment and Planning, Vol. 39, pages 142-161
SMITH, David M 2005 *On the Margins of Inclusion: Changing Labour Markets and Social Exclusion in London* Bristol: Policy Press
SMITH, Neil 1996 *The New Urban Frontier: Gentrification and the Revanchist City* London and New York: Routledge
SMITH, Neil & WILLIAMS, Peter 1986 *Gentrification of the City* Boston. London: Allen & Unwin
SOBAL, Jeffery & WANSINK, Brian 2007 "Kitchenscapes, Tablescapes, Platescapes, and Foodscapes Influences of Microscale Built Environments on Food Intake" Environment and Behavior, Vol. 39, No. 1, pages 124-142

SOJA, Edward 1989 *Post Modern Geographies. The Reassertion of Space on Critical Social Theory* London, New York: Verso
—. 1993 "Postmodern Geographies and the Critique of Historicism" in J. P. Jones et al (Eds) *Postmodern Contentions, Epochs, Politics, Space*, page 115
—. 2000 *Postmetropolis: Critical Studies of Cities and Regions* Oxford, Malden, MA: Blackwell
SONNINO, Roberta 2009 "Feeding the City: Towards a New Research and Planning Agenda", International Planning Studies, Special Issue: Feeding The City: The Challenge of Urban Food Planning, Vol. 14, Issue 4, pages 425-435
SORKIN, Michael 1991 *Exquisite Corpse. Writing on Buildings* London: Verso
SOUTHWORTH, Michael 1997 "Walkable Suburbs? An Evaluation of Neotraditional Communities at the Urban Edge" Journal of the American Planning Association, Vol. 63, No. 1, Winter, pages 28-44
SPRADLEY, James P 1980 *Participant Observation* New York: Van Rinehart and Winston
STAKE, Robert 1994, 1995 *The Art of Case Study Research* Thousand Oaks CA: Sage
STANCZAK, Gregory C. (Ed) 2007 *Visual Research Methods: Image, Society, and Representation* Thousand Oaks: Sage
STARK, Sheila & TORRANCE, Harry 2005 "Case Study", in B. Somekh, & C. Lewin (Eds) *Research Methods in the Social Sciences* London. Thousand Oaks. New Delhi: Sage, pages 33-40
STERNBERG, Ernest 2000 "An Integrative Theory of Urban Design" Journal of the American Planning Association, Vol. 66, No. 3, Summer, pages 265-278
STEUTEVILLE, Robert 2000 "The New Urbanism: An Alternative to Modern, Automobile-Oriented Planning and Development", New Urban News
STEVENSON, Deborah 2003 *Cities and Urban Cultures* Maidenhead: Open University Press
—. 2004 "'Civic Gold Rush: Cultural Planning and the Politics of the Third Way" International Journal of Cultural Policy, Vol. 10, pages 119–131
STRWBERRYDELIGHT 2nd February 2006 *Broadway Market* [online] Available at: http://www.urbanpath.com/london/food-markets/broadway-market.htm

STREN, Richard; WHITE, Rodney & WHITNEY, Joseph (Eds) 1992 *Sustainable Cities, Urbanisation and the Environment in International Perspective* Boulder, Colo.: Westview Press

STOUT, Frederic & LEGATES, Richard T 1996 *The City Reader* London, New York: Routledge

STURKEN, Marita & CARTWRIGHT, Lisa 2001 *Practices of Looking: An Introduction to Visual Culture* Oxford: Oxford University Press

SUDJIC, Deyan & SAYER, Phil 1992 *The 100 Mile City* Andre Deutsch: London

SUI, Daniel. Z 2003 "Musings on the Fatcity: Are Obesity and Urban Forms Linked?" Urban Geography, Vol. 24, No. 1, pages 75-84

SUSTAINABLE DEVELOPMENT COMMISSION 2008 *Green, Healthy and Fair. A review of government's role in supporting sustainable supermarket food* London: SDC 2008 [online] Available at: <http://www.sdcommission.org.uk/presslist.php?id=74>

—. 2011 *Looking Back, Looking Forward: Sustainability and UK Food Policy 2000-2011* London: SDC

SUSTAINWEB (n.d.) *Food and Planning* [online] Available at: <http://www.sustainweb.org/localactiononfood/food_and_planning/>

SWARTZ, David L & ZOLBERG, Vera L 2004 *After Bourdieu: Influence, Critique, Elaboration* Dordrecht, Kluwer Academic Publishers

SWINBURN, Boyd; EGGER Garry & RAZA, Fezeela 1999 "Dissecting Obesogenic Environments: The Development and Application of a Framework for Identifying and Prioritizing Environmental Interventions for Obesity" Preventive Medicine, Vol. 29, No. 6, pages 563–70

SYMONS, Michael 1982 *One Continuous Picnic. A History of Eating in Australia* Adelaide: Duck Press

—. 1998 *The Pudding That Took a Thousand Cooks. The Story of Cooking in Civilisation and Daily Life* Viking

TANSEY, Geoff & WORSLEY, Tony 1995 *The Food System: A Guide* London: Earthscan

TAYLOR, Nigel 1998 *Urban Planning Theory Since 1945* London: Sage

—. 1999 "The Elements of Townscape and the Art of Urban Design" Journal of Urban Design, Vol. 4, No. 2, pages 195-209

TAYLOR, John; MADRICK, Matina & COLLIN, Sam 2005 "Trading Places: The Local Economic Impact of Street Produce and Farmer's Markets" Research Report, New Economics Foundation: Mayor of London. London Food. London Development Agency

TD 26th April 2006 *Broadway Market* [online] Available at:

<http://www.urbanpath.com/london/food-markets/broadway-market.htm>
THOMAS, Randall (Ed) 2002 *Sustainable Urban Design* New York: Spon Press
THOMSON, Hilary; ATKINSON, Rowland; PETTICREW, Mark & KEARNS, Ade 2006 "Do Urban Regeneration Programmes Improve Public Health and Reduce Health Inequalities? A Synthesis of the Evidence from UK Policy and Practice Health 1980–2004", Journal of Epidemiology and Community Health, 60, pages 108-115
THRIFT, Nigel 1999 "Cities and Economic Change: Global Governance?" in John Allen, Doreen Massey and Michael Pryke (Eds) *Unsettling Cities* London and New York: Routledge in Association with The Open University, pages 271-319
THRIFT, Nigel & GLENNIE, Paul 1993 "Historical Geographies of Urban Life and Modern Consumption", in G. Kearns and C. Philo (Eds) *Selling Places: The City as Cultural Capital. Past and Present* Oxford: Pergamon, pages 33-48
TIBBALDS, Francis 1992 *Making People Friendly Towns. Improving the Public Environment in Towns and Cities* London: Longman
TIME OUT (n.d.) *Maltby Street* [online] Available at: <http://www.timeout.com/london/gallery/837/maltby-street>
TONKISS, Fran 2001 "Analysing Discourse" in C. Seale (Ed) 2001 *Researching Society and Culture* London, Thousand Oaks: Sage
TRANCIK, Roger 1986 *Finding Lost Space: Theories of Urban Design* New York: Van Nostrand Reinhold
TRAVERS, Tony 2004 *The Politics of London: Governing an Ungovernable City* New York: Palgrave Macmillan
TRENDHUNTER (n.d.) *Kitchenless Living* [online] Available at: <http://www.trendhunter.com/trends/kitchenless-living) [Accessed 13th March 2008]
TUNBRIDGE, John 2001 "Ottawa's Byward Market: a Festive Bone of Contention?" The Canadian Geographer, Vol. 45, No 3, pages 356-370
URBAN TASKFORCE 1999 "Towards an Urban Renaissance" London:
DETRURRY, John 1990 *The Tourist Gaze: Leisure and Travel in Contemporary Society* London, Thousand Oaks, New Delhi: Sage
—. 1995 *Consuming Places* London: Routledge
VILJOEN, André AND WISKERKE, Johannes 2012 *Sustainable Food Planning Evolving Theory and Practice* Wageningen Academic Publishers: The Netherlands

VALENTINE, Gill 1998 "Food and the Production of the Civilised Street" in Nicholas R. Fyfe (Ed) *Images of the Street: Planning, Identity, and Control in Public Space* London. New York: Routledge

VAN LEEUWEN, Theo & JEWITT, Carey (Eds) 2001 *Handbook of Visual Analysis* London. Thousand Oaks: SAGE

VISSER, Margaret 1987 *Much Depends on Dinner: The Extraordinary History and Mythology, Allure and Obsessions, Perils and Taboos, of an Ordinary Meal* Toronto: McClelland and Stewart

—. 1993 *The Rituals of Dinner: The Origins, Evolution, Eccentricities, and Meaning of Table Manners* London: Penguin

—. 1997 *The Way We Are* London: Penguin Books

WALDHEIM, Charles (Ed) 2006 *The Landscape Urbanism Reader* New York: Princeton Architectural Press

WALLERSTEIN, Immanuel 2004 *World Systems Analysis: An Introduction* Durham, N.C.: London: Duke University Press

WANSBOROUGH, Matthew & MAGEEAN, Andrea 2000 "The Role of Urban Design in Cultural Regeneration" Journal of Urban Design, Vol. 5, No. 2, pages 181-197

WARD, Graham (Ed) 2000 *The Certeau Reader* Oxford: Blackwell

WARDE, Alan 1991 "Gentrification as Consumption: Issues of Class and Gender" Environment and Planning D: Society and Space Vol. 9, No. 2, pages 223-232

—. 1997 *Consumption, Food and Taste: Culinary Antimonies and Commodity Culture* London, Thousand Oaks. California: Sage

—. 1999 "Convenience Food: Space and Timing" British Food Journal, Vol. 101, No. 7, pages 518-527

—. 2005 Consumption and Theories of Practice" Journal of Consumer Culture, Vol. 5, No. 2, pages 131-153

WARDE, Alan (Ed) 1990 "The Sociology of Consumption" Special Edition of Sociology, Vol. 24, No. 1

WARDE, Alan & MARTENS, Lydia 2000 *Eating Out: Social Differentiation, Consumption and Pleasure* Cambridge: Cambridge University Press

WARD, Paul; COVENEY, John & HENDERSON, Julie 2010 "A Sociology of Food and Eating: Why Now?" Editorial, Journal of Sociology, Vol. 46, No. 347

WARDE, Alan; MARTENS, Lydia & OLSEN, Wendy 1999 "Consumption and the Problem of Variety: Cultural Omnivorousness, Social Distinction and Dining Out" Sociology, Vol. 33, No. 1, pages 105–127

WARDE, Alan & MARTENS, Lydia 1998 "Eating Out and the Commercialisation of Mental Life" British Food Journal, Vol. 100, No.3, pages 147–153

WATSON, Anna 2002 "Hunger from the Inside: The Experience of Food Poverty in the UK" based on work done and material provided by Vicky Johnson and Clare Mills, London: Sustain

WATSON, Sophie & BRIDGE, Gary (Eds) 2000 *A Companion to the City* Oxford: Blackwell

WATSON, Sophie with STUDDERT David 2006 "Markets as Sites for Social Interaction: Spaces of Diversity" The Open University. Joseph Rowntree Foundation: Policy Press

WATSON, Sophie & WELLS, Karen 2005 "Spaces of Nostalgia: The Hollowing Out of a London Market" Journal of Social and Cultural Geography, Vol. 6, No. 1, pages 17-30

WEBBER, Melvin M 1964 "The Urban Place and the Non Place Urban Realm" in Webber, M.M et al (Eds) *Explorations into urban structure* Pennsylvania: University of Pennsylvania

WEBBER, Richard 2007 "The Metropolitan Habitus: Its Manifestations, Locations, and Consumption Profiles" Environment and Planning, Vol. 39, pages 182-207

WEBER, Christopher L. & MATTHEWS, Scott. 2008 "Food-Miles and the Relative Climate Impacts of Food Choices in the United States", Environmental Science and Technology, 2008, Vol. 42, No. 10, pages 3508–3513

WEBSTER, Jacqui, in consultation with the Food Poverty Working Party 1998 "Food Poverty: What are the Policy Options?" National Food Alliance Poverty Project, London: National Food Alliance

WHELAN, Amanda; WRIGLEY, Neil; WARM, Daniel & CANNINGS, Elizabeth 2002 "Life in a 'Food Desert'" Urban Studies, Vol. 39, No. 11, pages 2083-2100

WHITE, Jerry 2007 *London in the 19th Century* London: Jonathan Cape

WHITE, Martin; BUNTING, Jane; WILLIAMS, Liz; RAYBOULD, Simon; ADAMSON, Ashley & MATHERS, John 2004 "Do Food Deserts Exist? A Multi-Level, Geographical Analysis of the Relationship Between Retail Food Access, Socio-Economic Position and Dietary Intake" Final Report to the Food Standards Agency, London: FSA

WHITECROSS STREET (n.d.) [online] Available at: <http://www.whitecrossstreet.co.uk/>

WHITEHAND, Jeremy & LARKHAM, Peter 1992 *Urban Landscapes: International Perspectives* London. New York: Routledge

WHITELEGG, Drew 2002 "From Market Stalls to Restaurant Row: The Recent Transformation of Exmouth Market" London Journal Vol. 27, No. 2, pages 1-11

WHYTE, William. H 1980 *The Social Life of Small Urban Spaces* Washington DC: The Conservation Foundation

—. 1988 *City. Rediscovering the Centre* New York: Doubleday

WILKS-HEEG, Stuart. & NORTH, Peter 2004 "Cultural Policy and Urban Regeneration: a Special Edition of Local Economy" Local Economy, Vol. 19, No. 3, pages 305–311

WILLS, Wendy 2011 "Introduction to Food: Representations and Meanings" Sociological Research Online, 16 (2) 16

WILSON, Elizabeth 1991 *The Sphinx in the City: Urban Life, The Control of Disorder and Women* London: Virago

WRIGLEY, Neil 2002 "'Food Deserts' in British Cities: Policy Context and Research Priorities" Urban Studies, Vol. 39, No. 11, pages 2029–2040

WRIGLEY, Neil & LOWE, Michele (Eds) 1996 *Retailing, Consumption and Capital: Towards the New Retail Geography* London: Longman

WRIGLEY, Neil; WARM, Daniel & MARGETTS, Barrie 2003 "Deprivation, Diet, and Food-Retail Access: Findings from the Leeds 'Food Deserts' Study" Environment and Planning, Vol. 35, No. 1, pages 151-188

UNWIN, Raymond 1911 *Town Planning in Practice: An Introduction to the Art of Designing Cities and Suburbs* 2nd Edition, London: T. Fisher Unwin

YASMEEN, Gisèle 2006 *Bangkok's Foodscape: Public Eating, Gender Relations, and Urban Change* Bangkok: White Lotus Press

YIN, Robert K 1993 *Applications of Case Study Research* Newbury Park, Calif.; London: Sage

ZUCKER, Paul 1959 *Town and Square. From the Agora to the Village Green* New York: Columbia University Press

ZUKIN, Sharon 1982 *Loft Living: Culture and Capital in Urban Change* New Brunswick, NJ: Rutgers University Press

—. 1991: *Landscapes of Power: from Detroit to Disney World*. Berkeley, CA: University of California Press

—. 1992 "Postmodern Urban Landscapes: Mapping Culture and Power," in *Modernity and Identity* Lash, S. and Friedman, J. (Eds) London: Blackwell

—. 1995 *The Cultures of Cities* Cambridge, Mass. Oxford: Blackwell

—. 2004 *Point of Purchase: How Shopping Changed American Culture*, New York, London: Routledge

ZUKIN, Sharon & MAGUIRE, Jennifer S 2004 "Consumers and Consumption" Annual Review of Sociology, Vol. 30, pages 173-310

INDEX

alternative food geographies
   counterpointing dominant spatiality, 67
   present in gentrifying space, 57
alternative food spaces
   Broadway situated, 178
   development of quarters, 221
ambience
   'cool' at Broadway Market, 181
   aspect of habitus formation, 56
   food-centred at Borough, 134
   importance at Exmouth, 206
   property marketing at Borough, 127
   role of design at Borough, 153
   views at Borough, 142
architecture
   'exit ramp', 48
   'invisible', 115
   Borough's refurbishment, 122
   contribution to sociability, 262
   design in each quarter, 232
   Exmouth as hip location, 210
   experts interviewed, 20
   infilling on Borough High Street, 85
   markets' consumption design, 52
   player at Borough Market, 151
   regeneration tool at Borough, 232
   relevant discipline in research, 24
   revitalisation of Broadway, 154
   role at Exmouth, 111
   role of contextual approaches, 268
   strategy at Borough, 121
   style related to gentrification, 59
   stylish backdrop to consumption, 263
   undertheorised in food space, 46
area character
   coherence at each quarter, 115
   design at Borough, 133
   gastronomic over time, 224
   shared elements, 5
   traditional at Broadway, 96
   traditional at Exmouth, 108
art practice
   food quarters as sites, 59
   observed at Broadway, 174
artisanal producers
   aspirations of market proponents, 248
   food quarters supporting, 254
   modern food system, 43
   relationship to Borough, 131
   relationship to Broadway, 170
   relationship to Exmouth, 186
aspatiality
   in food research, 31
   in food sociology, 222
   sociological problem, 43
atmosphere
   'hidden gem' quality, 257
   contribution to food space, 192
   relating to authenticity, 147
authenticity
   in relation to food, 253
   traditional food shops as marker, 181
book's structure, 27
Borough Market, 3
   'global' food space, 143
   'indulgent' street, 152
   ambience, 134
   arguments about the future, 147

attraction for capital, 84
buyers' environmental
    consciousness, 131
catchment analysis, 88
commodification issues, 261
design and architecture for
    conviviality, 151
design and economic revival,
    121
designed renewal, 118
diversity of visitors, 242
food chain transparency, 129
food education, 129
food mapping, 136
food prices, 126
food renewal synergies, 233
food renewal trajectory, 28
future direction, 243
gentrification, 242
good governance, 61
governance structures, 125
head count process, 140
historical background, 78
importance of urban design, 266
leadership of charitable trust,
    231
local development 'anchor', 147
morphology and urban design,
    76
post war decline, 83
problems of success, 143
revitalisation strategy, 125
role of design and catchment
    growth, 264
role of external funds, 235
role of wholesalers, 233
shaping socio-spatial practices,
    151
shoppers' knowledgeability, 150
site map, 76
spatial development as market,
    82
structural issues in decline, 119
summary as food space, 90
support for food quality, 149
understood as social space, 134

visitor catchment, 126
Bourdieu, 35
    analysing food space, 222
    approaches to taste, 45
    development of social capital at
        each quarter, 249
    distinction at food quarters, 258
    habitus at Borough, 149
    habitus construction at
        Broadway, 171
    influence on food theory, 35
    notion of habitus, 37
    spatialising the habitus, 55
Broadway Market, 3
    accessibility, 101
    art processes, 60
    avoidance of clone town, 260
    community led renewal, 178
    comparisons with Exmouth
        Market, 193
    context of area regeneration, 243
    demolitions, 99
    design aspects of renewal, 182
    design facilitating social life, 172
    design for sociability, 257
    destruction as food space, 100
    development as food quarter,
        154
    food eating zones, 173
    food led regeneration, 155
    food mapping, 175
    food market decline, 97
    food morphology, 92
    food quality and diversity, 169
    food renewal trajectory, 29
    food-centred outdoor room, 173
    from desert to quarter, 180
    gastronomic entrepreneurs, 62
    gentrification, 57
    gentrification narratives, 160
    gentrification paradox, 244
    good governance, 231
    growth of food market, 158
    habitus and social space, 171
    hipness, 172
    issues of rapid success, 165

leadership, 63
local authority issues, 238
market shopping, 173
nature of food market, 163
ordinary place, 265
physical fabric changes, 99
political battles, 174
protecting diversity, 58
residential boom, 168
role of local leadership, 14
role of market manager, 155
role of physical shape, 232
site map, 91
socio-spatial practices, 173
stirrings of renewal, 98
structural implications for renewal, 179
sustainable food space, 169
urban design qualities, 101
urban village, 262
case studies
    approach to research, 19
    defining spatial boundaries, 115
    design and morphological investigations, 76
    fuzzy-edged area boundaries, 75
    interviews and observations, 20
    of spatiality, 50
    process of development, 21
    recent findings in London, 57
    research focus, 3
    research into socio-spatial practices, 59
catchment
    class diversity findings, 237
    design linkages, 264
    pedestrian range, 224
    variations in viablity, 249
    varying scales at each quarter, 226
    widening at Borough, 135
catchment analysis
    approach to, 25
    at Borough Market, 88
    at Broadway Market, 101
    at Exmouth Market, 113
    development of ped-sheds, 25
    mapping, 76
    results from each food quarter, 229
chain stores
    'moving in' on food quarters, 148
    'hub and spoke' tactics, 235
    association with gentrification, 59
    authenticity issues, 266
    avoidance at Exmouth, 198
    clone towns, 128
    conscious choice to avoid, 216
    food behaviour of incoming residents, 164
    inward spatial focus, 266
    relative absence at Broadway, 180
    strategies to keep out, 260
    strategy of colonisation, 180
character
    'rough and ready' at each quarter, 230
cheap rents
    appeal of new food spaces, 260
    attracting incomers to Broadway, 159
    historic situation at Exmouth, 198
città slow
    relevance to quarters' revival, 248
    slow cities movement, 13
civilising appetites
    changing relationship to food, 39
    framing element in research, 72
    insights from Elias, 31
    public food behaviour, 223
    role of habitus, 40
    table bound eating, 40
class
    'us and them' arguments, 243
    arguments at Exmouth, 210
    Borough's appeal transcending, 152
    catchment at Exmouth, 187

Market Place: Food Quarters, Design and Urban Renewal in London   313

conspicuous consumption, 263
contested role, 244
conviviality findings, 258
differences transcended, 254
discussed at Broadway, 155
food interests transcending at
   Broadway, 169
food-led regeneration, 242
gentrification at Broadway, 164
issues at Broadway, 157
issues in food space, 149
narratives at Broadway, 159
narratives at Exmouth, 196
oppositional views at Exmouth,
   210
renewal at Broadway, 179
reports about Broadway, 160
social mix at Exmouth, 213
climate change
   food related concern, 9
   food resilience concerns, 9
   food system issues, 42
   localising food consumption,
      267
   mitigation policies in food, 10
   quarters helping mitigate shocks,
      265
clone towns
   contrast to food quarters, 52
clusters
   noted at Broadway, 174
commodification
   effects at Borough, 147
   food led design improvements,
      147
   issues emerging at each quarter,
      249
   offsetting trends, 261
   property developers, 261
communities of interest
   'foodies' at each quarter, 254
   in food at Borough, 152
   in food at Broadway, 180
   in food at each quarter, 237, 249
   in food at Exmouth, 186
   role of physical space, 257

community leaders
   importance for developing new
      quarters, 265
   key role at Broadway, 178
   role in food led renewal, 62
   vision for the future, 62
community-based politics
   examples at Broadway Market,
      164
compact city design
   Borough an example, 145
   food quarters reflecting, 66
   informing everyday life, 3
   vernacular in support, 10
competition
   at Exmouth, 192
   avoidance of 'dog eat dog' at
      Broadway, 178
   food quarters as sites, 213
   food stalls at Broadway, 166
   food stalls versus fixed
      businesses, 212
   local authority management, 194
   other emergent food spaces, 193
   pull factors away from quarters,
      249
   tactics of food chains, 235
comprehensive renewal
   'municipal bulldozer', 226
   demolitions at Broadway, 155
connectivity
   analysis at Borough Market, 87
   analysis at Broadway Market, 99
   analysis at Exmouth, 113
   analysis elements, 76
   aspect of design based analysis,
      24
   improvements at each quarter,
      250
   in food quarter research, 20
   in planning food space, 267
   joined up urbanism, 68
   research findings from each
      quarter, 229
consumption
   'foodie' communities, 254

alternative socio-spatiality, 19
alternative to supermarkets, 170
car based patterns, 43
changing patterns at Borough, 134
conspicuous, 53, 259
conspicuous at Exmouth, 200
contrast to bland space, 143
decline of food markets, 226
decline of public space, 48
eating in public, 41
elite needs, 3
food, 5
food deserts, 65
food loci contexts, 45
food quarters, 50
food related, 8
food spaces as product, 146
food system, 3
food system loci, 223
gentrification, 54
habitus, 263
habitus formation, 150
history of markets, 52
household food, 9
identity formation, 34
local, small scale patterns, 43
localising, 266
mall based food, 48
mixed methods at Broadway, 183
nature at food quarters, 16
new gentrifying class, 58
new spatial forms, 6
performative at Borough, 152
quarters and supermarket based, 130
relationship to habitus, 38
relationship to obesity, 9
sociological analysis, 35
space at Broadway, 179
spaces, 7, 31, 32
spatial commodification, 214
stage in food system, 44
street eating, 40
structural changes, 236
structural forces at Broadway, 180
stylishness at Broadway, 183
stylishness in food, 217
suburban retailing models, 52
supermarket, 5
sustainability, 170
sustainable choices, 254
sustainable practices, 150
symbiosis with production, 151
theorised role, 16
underplayed spatial aspects, 45
urban scale, 8
urban sustainability, 253
walkable food spaces, 267
contextual design
  critical to food-led success, 268
  importance to renewal, 230
convivial cities, 10
  central food features, 11
  conclusions about, 223
  gastronomic strategies, 68
convivial ecology
  developing at food quarters, 12
  findings at each quarter, 257
conviviality
  aspect of everyday life, 4
  aspect of spatial design, 11
  cities, 10
  contribution to sustainability, 32
  design for gastronomic choices, 15
  food quarters as sites, 256
  food related opportunities, 268
  market spaces influencing, 153
  opportunities and threats, 265
  opportunities at Broadway, 183
  ordinary places, 13
  public realm, 15
  social mix at food quarters, 244
  supported at Broadway, 171
  underpinned at Borough, 146
cooking
  advice to buyers at Broadway, 170
  declining habit, 132

focus on in gentrifying areas, 57
  from produce at Borough, 126
  knowledge of market users, 256
  loss of skills, 132
  loss of spaces, 44
  skills of market food buyers, 123
  views of food traders, 133
core shoppers
  at Borough and Broadway, 165
  contrasted with tourists, 251
cultural capital
  'artiness' at Broadway, 159
  among incomers, 244
  aspect of gentrification, 55
  aspects at Exmouth, 211
  at Broadway, 181
  formation at Borough, 145
  formation at Exmouth, 188
demolition
  'comprehensive renewal', 226
  food market decline, 116
  housing at each quarter, 226
  in 1960s and 1970s, 229
  post war at Broadway, 98
  traditional housing at Borough, 90
  traditional terraces at Broadway, 99
design elements
  detailed street assessment, 230
  food quarter construction, 222
  present at Exmouth, 113
  sensuality of food, 134
destination dining
  views at Exmouth, 199
diversification
  food education and training at Borough, 123
  food quarter economic outcomes, 269
eating in the street
  civilised behaviour, 217
  culturally sanctioned at Borough, 152
  exemption from negative connotations, 174

opportunities for conviviality, 256
  practice at Broadway, 183
  practice at Exmouth, 206
  theoretical perspectives, 35
economic benefits
  città slow, 13
  identified at Broadway, 179
  returned to local area, 64
  ripple effects back along food chain, 242
  shorter food chain, 125
  theorised in food markets, 50
  theorised in food quarters, 4
  third sector approaches to food-led renewal, 147
economic revitalisation
  at Borough, 121
  at Broadway, 158
  at Exmouth, 189
  design aspects at each quarter, 231
enclosure
  apparent at Exmouth, 108
  at Broadway Market, 101
  at centre of Exmouth quarter, 115
  atmosphere at Broadway, 166
  design quality at each quarter, 145
  experience for pedestrians at Borough, 151
  figure-grounds to define, 75
  identified by place users at Exmouth, 201
  importance at each quarter, 227
  important to design of quarters, 25
  in Borough's public realm, 91
  level at Borough, 90
  outdoor rooms at food quarters, 228
  to create outdoor rooms, 69
European City Model, 3
  food quarter shaping, 71
  food spaces reflecting design, 18

principles underlying quarters,
    71
European food culture
    invoked at Borough, 150
    noted at Exmouth, 217
everyday life, 3, 4, 171, 222
    beyond economic exchange, 11
    community politics at Broadway,
        185
    expressed through food, 14
    food as central element, 33
    food practices at Borough, 151
    food quarters as richer sites, 256
    food scheduling, 151
    food's role, 132
    mystification, 16
    ordinary places, 14
    relating to food, 12
    renewed interest in, 7
    socio-spatial practices and
        design, 221
    theorising about, 15
    uncommodified encounters at
        Broadway, 183
Exmouth Market, 3
    'slow food' food court, 190
    'Little Italy', 107
    decline and renewal, 114
    design analysis, 112
    design aspects of renewal, 201
    food led renewal, 186
    gastronomic stakeholders, 62,
        103
    gentrification narratives, 196
    narrative of renewal, 30
    new industry clustering, 60
    street for eating, 207
farmers' markets, 3
    Bermondsey Square, 148
    Borough not defined as, 146
    brand commodification, 261
    Broadway favourably contrasted,
        167
    Broadway not defined as, 158
    inspiration at Exmouth, 191
    London Farmers' Markets, 155

revived markets differing, 247
    situating food quarters, 254
fashionability
    Broadway as hip place, 179
    Broadway site for, 172
    changing visitor catchments, 264
    commodification of food space,
        44
    food at Exmouth, 203
    restaurants at Exmouth, 251
fat cities
    connecting obesity and form, 5
    food quarters as elements, 221
    inflected design, 18
    theorised positively, 5
figure-ground analysis
    positive and negative space, 75
    public space at Borough, 84
    public space at Broadway, 99
    public space at Exmouth, 111
fine grain
    at each quarter, 229
    benefits at Exmouth, 204
    figure-grounds, 87
    frontages at each quarter, 261
    of theorised food quarter, 3
    reshaping space for food, 266
    urban design quality, 70
food and cities
    moving from margins, 5
    sustainable relationships, 240
food and design
    area commodification, 252
    connected study area, 6
    expert perspectives, 118
    longitudinal analysis, 224
    maps record connecting, 224
food and eating
    anthropological approaches, 33
    inadequate explanations, 34
    interdisciplinary concern, 35
    sociological perspectives, 35
    spatialised approaches, 44
    study within sociology, 6
food business clusters
    findings at Exmouth, 208

mapped at Borough Market, 138
food chain
 buyers interest in provenance, 131
 climate change, 9
 economic ripple effects, 242
 food standards, 255
 increased transparency at Borough, 150
 links to producers, 125
 patterns in food system, 42
 positive relationships, 254
 sustainability of food, 253
food consumers
 'fed up' with supermarket shopping, 128
 at Borough, 124
 avoiding supermarkets, 150
 consumer attitude, 50
 economic relationships with producers, 146
 education about food quality, 130
 education through market buying, 256
 gentrification patterns, 58
 increasing knowledge at Borough, 123
 interest in sustainability at Broadway, 183
 local food practices, 21
 reconnecting and relocalising, 67
 supporting artisanal production, 254
 sustainability awareness at Borough, 151
food deserts
 Broadway's previous status, 180
 complexity at Exmouth, 213
 continuum, 258
 Exmouth read as, 210
 findings at quarters, 223
 food quarters' complexity, 217
 nature of, 64
 quarters in contrast, 30
 retailing patterns, 256
reviving places at risk, 269
 spatial characteristics, 67
 theorised presence, 4
food entrepreneurs
 central role at each quarter, 209
 role at Exmouth, 63
 vision of food street at Exmouth, 238
food knowledge
 increasing value, 145
 lack of, 256
food led renewal
 area commodification, 179
 at Exmouth Market, 186
 design as key element, 232
 design strategy at Borough, 232
 positive views at Broadway, 179
 positive views at Exmouth, 197
 role of external funding, 235
food localism
 emphasis at Broadway, 170
 increasing concern, 6
food mapping
 adaption from gastronomic mapping, 26
 eating in the street, 217
 findings at Exmouth, 216
 in research process, 29
 results at Exmouth, 207
 use at Borough Market, 136
 use at Broadway, 175
 use at Exmouth, 206
food markets
 avoiding 'leftover' status, 267
 Broadway in broader movement, 169
 catchment issues at Exmouth, 193
 central to urbanism, 7
 coherent urban fabric, 115
 comparisons between Exmouth and Broadway, 192
 different trajectory at Exmouth, 217
 evolution of food spaces, 116

extension of destination dining at
Exmouth, 210
intentions at Exmouth, 191
interplay between spatial and
social aspects, 264
local development 'anchors', 127
long term history at each site,
225
loss, 49
moves toward urban
sustainability, 253
new food spaces, 148
new spatial and social forms, 19
public realm, 6
regeneration capacity, 127
residualisation, 239
revival of remnant markets, 221
spatiality of, 25
temporal aspects, 262
varying experiences of revival,
249
walkability findings, 229
food miles
complexities, 9
conceptualising food quarters, 44
concern in food quarters, 21
fair trade, 130
food quality, 253
prices and quality, 150
product sourcing, 170
sustainability questions, 255
food poverty
contrast to findings, 223
explored with interviewees, 21
relationship to food deserts, 64
food practices
anthropological exploration, 34
connecting to city form, 47
different discipline insights, 31
European food culture, 130
gentrification of space, 58
perspectives on city design, 27
physical space design, 224
shaping spatiality, 32
social differentiation, 36
urban design exploration, 32

food prices
findings from Borough, 149
justified environmentally, 150
perspectives at Broadway, 179
views at Borough, 126
food production
alienation from, 50
attitudes at Broadway, 170
food quarters' links, 253
geographic insights, 45
loss of food skills, 256
nature of food system, 41
new forms emerging, 6
spatial scales, 43
traditional links to markets, 225
undermining sustainability, 66
understood geographically and
culturally, 34
urban sustainability, 8
food quality
at Borough, 120
at Broadway Market, 169
behaviours reflecting concern,
256
buyers at Borough, 129
concerns at Borough, 149
concerns at each quarter, 253
design elements, 257
issues at Exmouth, 211
link to prices at Borough, 131
supermarket practices, 253
sustainability, 247
theme across each quarter, 234
food quarter
'gastronomic townscape', 6
attractive to art practitioners, 59
Borough most fully realised, 118
Broadway as developing quarter,
154
bucking spatial trends, 269
challenges to food system, 44
civilised eating, 40
combining social and spatial
methods, 27
community based leaders, 63
complex consumption site, 50

consumption space, 51
contrast to car based space, 10
contribution to sustainability, 4
convivial ecology, 12
conviviality and gentrification, 221
cultural commodification, 60
defining elements, 3
design characteristics, 68
designing for food, 7
European City Model, 32
Exmouth as different kind, 186
expression of urban sustainability, 253
focus on markets, 50
food-centred social life, 257
food-led trajectory, 242
gentrification issues, 4
governance issues, 61
habitus construction, 16
interplay with cultural quarters, 51
larger research field, 6
legacy of coherence, 224
local economic value, 64
manifestation of habitus, 55
narratives of gentrification, 58
new kind of place, 259
ordinary place for everyday life, 14
paradoxical qualities, 4
partnership issues, 62
place marketed sites, 53
positive interplay of urban design and economic renewal, 266
public realm primacy, 49
regenerating space, 53
relationship to gentrification, 54
research methods, 20
resistance to suburbanised retail models, 52
risks of commodification, 261
role of physical space, 223
scales of production, distribution and consumption, 43
sharing strategic vision, 233
site for conviviviality, 11
site for increased conviviality, 256
Slow Food and Slow Cities, 13
socio-spatial practices, 17
spatial design backdrop, 18
spatial design elements, 66
spatiality anaysis, 75
strong sense of place, 230
theorised, 31
traditional spatiality, 222
transformations in urban space, 47
unit of research and spatial construct, 67
urban design, 66
urban design connections, 63
walkable design, 10
food quarter viability
    'bottom up' at Broadway, 237
    design connections at Borough, 145
    food prices, 149
    issues with local authorities, 239
    land use mix at Exmouth, 198
    shorter food chains, 255
    visitor catchments, 249
food related land uses
    balance at Exmouth, 198
    centrality to each quarter, 225
    defining case study boundaries, 76
    diversity at Broadway, 178
    focus for community development, 186
    food markets, 115
    mapping, 136
    mapping at Exmouth, 208
    markets seen as marginal, 124
    mix at quarters, 70
    morphological research, 224
    part of mixed use areas, 181
    role in food quarters, 3
    semi prepared foods, 140
    study of physical evolution, 75

food resilience
  food quarters contribution, 255
  increasing concern, 6
  opportunities for food centred space, 267
food security
  food quarters supporting, 253
  increasing concerns, 9
food shopping
  catchment at Broadway, 157
  clone town expressions, 260
  comments at Broadway, 173
  inadequacies at food deserts, 64
  patterns at Borough, 135
  temporal issues, 140
  visitors buying at Borough, 152
  visitors versus core shoppers at Broadway, 165
food shops
  decline in individual, 65
  importance to social life, 173
  in Borough Market area, 87
  in theorised food quarter, 66
  issues of mix at Exmouth, 250
  mapped at Exmouth, 208
  role at Exmouth, 195
  social mix at Broadway, 163
  suitability of spatiality, 233
  synergy at Broadway, 180
  traditional mix at Exmouth, 114
  uniqueness at Exmouth, 189
food skills
  food quarters assisting revival, 254
  loss identified at Borough, 150
food stalls
  diversity at Broadway, 177
  focal points at Broadway, 100
  unique design at Borough, 84
food street
  at Exmouth Market, 215
  centre of food quarter, 185
  design qualities, 215
  habitus site, 258
  in contrast to clone town, 261
  subject of spatialised study, 6

food system loci
  at Broadway Market, 182
  quarters understood as, 223
  theorising about, 45
food tourists
  appeal of ordinary places, 13
  artful consumption spaces, 51
  Borough's experience, 149
  catchment at Borough, 141
  discussed at Borough, 135
  food-centred spectacle, 251
  future of Borough Market, 260
  gastro-tourism, 12
  in relation to 'real' shoppers, 259
  practices at Borough, 126
  subsidiary role, 252
food wholesaling
  basis for regeneration, 233
  Borough's background, 226
  importance at Borough, 147
  use of low rents, 234
food zones
  designed at Broadway, 176
food-centred spaces
  challenging food system, 43
  decay into remnant areas, 227
  dominant retailing models, 48
  food quarters as examples, 5
  individuality in design qualities, 257
  long term continuity in food quarters, 225
  sites for everyday consumption, 50
  sites for new forms of consumption, 51
  successful path to renewal, 247
  supporting sustainability, 64
  sustainability analysis, 8
  urban sustainability, 253
  visitor catchment key to revival, 230
food-led renewal
  context for community politics, 185
  future potential, 264

gentrification at Exmouth, 213
urban sustainability, 264
funding
    complexity at Borough, 121
    issues with local authorities, 236
    lack of recent external sources, 213
    last thoughts, 267
    partnership at Borough, 144
    regeneration at Borough, 119
    role of external sources, 235
gastronomic mapping
    previous use and adaption, 26
gastronomic possibilities
    food capacities of urban space, 5
    ways to extend, 15
gastronomic stakeholders
    approaches across quarters, 261
    importance at Exmouth, 231
    pivotal roles, 236
    role in food-led regeneration, 237
gastronomic townscape, 6
    character over time, 224
    development in food quarters, 221
    emergence near Borough, 148
    emergence at Exmouth, 189
gentrification
    aspects transcending, 237
    Borough challenging mainstream arguments, 147
    competing narratives, 241
    complexities at Broadway, 163
    conclusions about, 268
    considered in London, 48
    contested aspect of food renewal, 4
    different in each quarter, 243
    double sided quarters, 221
    effects in food quarters, 53
    expression at Borough Market, 146
    expression at Exmouth Market, 210
    gastronomy and urban renewal, 7

identity through food, 54
    in studied sites, 53
    less problematised at Exmouth, 214
    narratives at Broadway, 160
    notion of habitus, 16
    nuanced at each quarter, 245
    residential architecture at food quarters, 59
    stages reached at food quarters, 58
    subtext in food renewal, 242
governance
    arrangements at Exmouth, 209
    charitable trust, 62
    community based approach, 237
    community based structures, 237
    delivering wider food benefits, 261
    development 'from below', 4
    importance at Borough, 144
    informal leadership, 61
    local authority issues, 178
    partnerships, 62
    problems of formal capacity, 215
    public sector absence, 234
    role in viability of food market, 145
    trustee model at Borough, 124
    use of master planning, 237
habitus
    'mini habituses', 56
    analysis in quarters, 222
    behaviour in food quarters, 57
    Broadway as site, 179
    construction at Borough, 149, 152
    development at Broadway, 171
    expression at Exmouth, 210
    findings connected to food, 245
    food quarter design, 263
    food quarters as settings, 4
    gentrification, 32
    gentrification as a 'field' in habitus construction, 56
    individual food behaviours, 16

marks of distinction in relation to
   food, 17
metropolitan, 56
nature of quarters, 53
played out at Exmouth Market,
   204
spaces of consumption, 31
spatialised expression of food
   tastes, 54
studied in London context, 55
taste and food, 37
head counts
   comparing quarters, 259
   findings at Borough, 140
   use as method, 21
   use at Borough, 118
housing
   'yuppie' influx at Exmouth, 244
   demolition at each quarter, 226
   habitus 'field' in food quarters,
      245
   in food quarter development, 168
   increasing costs at Broadway,
      243
   localising consumption, 165
   mix near Exmouth Market, 214
   modernist renewal design, 226
   modernity fueling destruction,
      229
   prices and gentrification, 242
   role in quarter development, 246
   social capital formation, 263
human scale
   at Broadway Market, 100, 182
   at Exmouth Market, 202
   contributing to food renewal,
      229
   eating 'zones' at Broadway, 184
   findings at quarters, 230
   food quarter spatiality, 68
   getting close to food, 173
   importance at Exmouth, 204
   loss of at Borough, 87
   promoting conviviality, 14
   public space primacy, 4
   social space at Borough, 153

supporting convivial spatiality,
   248
supporting temporal shifts in
   food practices, 262
synergy with food market, 215
hybrid hospitality
   at food quarters, 15
   found at each quarter, 253
   theorised possibilities for
      conviviality, 12
infrastructure constraints and
   opportunities, 250
kitchens
   designed out, 44
   previous design research, 6
landmarks
   at food spaces, 19
   design element, 26
   findings, 228
   food businesses, 228
   food related at Borough, 86
   food related at Broadway, 100
   food related at Exmouth, 115
   urban design investigations, 76
lifestyle
   aspect of gentrification, 58
   constraints on food choices, 132
   effects on food choices, 256
   food and design issue, 24
   outdoor food focus, 217
   shaping food retail design, 48
local authorities
   approach at Broadway, 97
   approach to markets, 239
   conclusions from accounts, 240
   conflict over food markets, 62
   issues at Broadway, 155
   issues with food-led renewal, 61
   managing food market decline,
      62
   market management issues, 239
   partnership at Exmouth, 210
   problematic strategic partners,
      235
   recent shifts in food policy, 239
   seen as a barrier, 236

support for other food spaces,
  236
trading down approach, 234
local food
  'bottom up' regeneration, 178
  campaigning at food quarters, 65
  challenging status quo, 247
  explored through interviews, 21
  food resources disappearing, 64
  good quality at Borough, 146
  importance noted by place users,
    255
  loss of shops, 49
  needs of urban populations, 43
  proponents at Exmouth, 211
  provision at Broadway, 165
  sustainability at Exmouth, 216
  theorised in food system, 42
local leadership
  crucial to Broadway's revival,
    155
  exceptional at Broadway, 237
  in food led renewal, 14
London
  ''cultural' food quarters, 59
  authorities managing markets,
    238
  bicycle hire scheme, 250
  case studies of place marketing,
    61
  changing spatiality, 47
  choice of fieldwork sites, 19
  climate change effects, 10
  consumption space, 51
  context for habitus research, 55
  context of housing renewal, 243
  diversity of design influences, 71
  food history, 43
  food quarter development, 5
  food quarter lessons, 222
  food quarters as new element,
    247
  food related behaviour, 39
  Food Strategy, 63
  metropolitan policy shifts, 239

potential for food-led renewal,
  267
primary research, 13
quarters as convivial examples,
  264
quarters defying trends, 221
slow food and slow cities, 13
spatialised thinking about food,
  31
structural changes to food
  economy, 90
suburban food retailing design,
  52
London's larder
  Borough area, 120
  Borough Market in area, 85
lost space
  areas at Exmouth, 115
  at Broadway Market, 181
  identified at Borough, 85
  identified at Broadway, 100
  in Exmouth area, 109
  market decline, 116
  regeneration outcomes, 227
lunchtime
  'slow' fast food, 112
  food practices at Exmouth, 207
  liveliness at Exmouth, 114
  outdoor eating at Borough, 142
  place users at Exmouth, 212
  place users studied at Borough,
    140
market decline
  at all three quarters, 116
  of revived market at Exmouth,
    249
  reviewing history, 226
market management
  'bottom up' at Broadway, 155
  community based approach, 237
  comparisons with Broadway,
    195
  criticisms, 236
  issues with local authorities, 238
  local authority approaches, 61

local government at Exmouth, 194
Trustee based at Borough, 90
market stalls
   at Broadway Market, 164
   at Exmouth Market, 112
   retail strategy encompassing, 196
   shopping practices, 173
   synergies at Broadway, 195
   unique model at Borough, 232
master planning methods
   analysis of food space, 227
   use in research process, 75
methodological techniques
   range of areas, 21
   reflexivity, 27
modern food system
   challenged by Broadway, 182
   characteristics, 43
   consumption patterns, 50
   context for research, 41
   critique, 42
   cultural and social dimensions, 44
   definition, 41
   food quarter challenging, 44
   negative effects, 42
   placelessness, 144
   spatialised health effects, 9
   transition from traditional, 39
   unequal food relationships, 6
   unsustainable nature, 269
morphological analysis
   at Borough Market, 76
   at Broadway Market, 91
   considering urban structure, 227
   decline and renewal, 227
   in exploring food quarters, 75
   legacy of urban continuity, 224
   of Exmouth Market, 103
   results on urban structure, 257
   to understand food spaces, 18
   used with design approaches, 25
morphology
   atmosphere at Borough, 152
   shaping food quarters, 71
   use in interogating quarters, 222
nostalgia
   food centred space, 51
   food quarters transcending, 252
nutritional and socio-biological perspectives
   dominating research into food, 32
obesegenic environments
   Borough qualities in contrast, 144
   built form producing, 65
   design guidance to avoid, 71
   food quarters as challenging, 5
   food quarters avoiding, 223
   food-led regeneration, 266
   local food consumption, 216
   quarters challenging, 221
   walkability, 267
obesity
   links to design, 63
   neighbourhood scale of design, 67
   quarters helping combat, 266
   relationship to food deserts, 65
   relationship to food system, 42
   spatial form contribting, 5
observations
   about food knowledge, 256
   about trajectory at Borough, 146
   adjunct to head counts, 140
   comparing food behaviours, 251
   food behaviour at Broadway, 173
   narrative of regeneration, 231
   of food behaviours at Exmouth, 186
   of transformation at Broadway, 160
   practices at Exmouth, 206
   qualities of outdoor rooms, 173
   relating to food chain, 169
   relationship to practices, 19
   supporting morphological research, 75

unstructured at Borough, 90
use as research method, 21
use as visual method, 28
use in research process, 21
visitor numbers, 259
online food commentaries, 21
online food shopping
food consumption techniques, 3
in food quarter development, 66
inadequate in food deserts, 64
ordinary places
design in relation to, 19
food quarters developing, 265
sites for food-led revival, 265
organic food
box schemes, 66
findings at quarters, 255
food mix at Broadway, 170
mapped at Borough, 139
presence at Exmouth Market, 209
supported through quarters, 130
outdoor room
'enclosure', 69
at Exmouth, 258
design approaches, 69
design qualities at Broadway, 232
design supporting at Broadway, 101
each food market focused on, 228
elements at Exmouth, 113
linear version of at Broadway, 173
of food street, 6
passegiatta at Broadway, 184
postwar interventions, 227
public realm primacy at Borough, 145
qualities at Exmouth, 113
quarters centred on, 117
series at Borough, 90
supporting food-centred space, 269
passegiatta

at Broadway Market, 184
at each quarter, 259
characteristics at Exmouth, 206
walking at Broadway, 173
pedestrianisation
approach at Borough, 91
approaches at each quarter, 227
connectivity analysis, 25
design approaches, 229
issue at Exmouth, 201
priority at Exmouth, 206
segregating walkers, 229
permeability
at Borough, 88
Broadway's street grid, 100
findings at each quarter, 229
high degree at Exmouth, 115
high level at Exmouth, 113
street pattern at each quarter, 26
place marketing
approach at Broadway, 180
at each food quarter, 252
Borough transcending, 143
case study examples, 61
conviviality, 12
development at Exmouth, 212
retail space, 53
ubiquitous in regeneration, 60
productive city, 6
property market
'boosterism' at each quarter, 198
'overheating' at Broadway, 182
alongside food-led renewal, 242
at Exmouth Market, 111
public housing
development at Broadway, 100
renewal approach at Broadway, 103
Spa Green Estate at Exmouth, 109
urban structure at Exmouth, 114
public realm
context for urban life, 69
decline in relation to food, 47
design at Exmouth, 111
design in Borough area, 90

exploring detailed design of, 24
food and consumption, 48
food market as contributor, 201
human scale at Exmouth, 215
importance in food space, 6
lively at Broadway, 244
political activity in food space, 185
sense of place at Borough, 145
sense of place at Broadway, 181
public space
 'indulgent' at Borough, 152
 C20th decline at Borough, 145
 changing norms about eating, 40
 design supporting at Exmouth, 215
 enclosure at Borough, 91
 enclosure at Broadway, 96
 focus of book, 44
 food behaviour within, 39
 food market revival, 50
 food-centred public realm, 227
 in traditional city design, 68
 nostalgic simulacra, 51
 previous food research, 45
 primacy in food quarters, 40
 quarter design supporting, 262
 research into decline, 47
 shaping urban structure, 224
 spatiality at Broadway, 154
 well documented decline, 48
public transport
 Borough well connected, 144
 Borough's connectivity, 88
 Broadway well connected, 101
 element of European City Model, 71
 Exmouth well connected, 113
 focus in making food quarter, 70
 importance at each quarter, 229
 primacy for quarter visitors, 230
 strong linkages at Borough, 88
railway infrastructure
 factor at Borough, 226
 impinging on Borough, 81
 issue at Borough, 121

landmark at Borough, 86
severance effects at Broadway, 99
railway stations
 proximity findings, 230
ready meals
 competing with supermarkets, 151
 decline of domestic locus, 150
 design of houses responding, 44
 long working hours, 132
regeneration
 'sideways' at Exmouth, 211
 attempts at Exmouth, 187
 backdrop at Exmouth, 109
 built form assets, 85
 community based, 213
 community led partnerships, 237
 competition for Exmouth, 213
 cultural quarters, 59
 cycles at each quarter, 264
 design at Exmouth, 206
 dramatic at Borough, 143
 existing design in support, 231
 external funding, 235
 food as adjunct, 61
 food issues at Exmouth, 195
 food quarter spaces, 53
 food renewal success, 252
 food space and practices, 224
 food-centred, 61
 food-led at Broadway, 155
 food-led at Exmouth, 186
 food-led conviviality, 266
 funding at Exmouth, 189
 gastronomic tourism, 63
 gentrification at Exmouth, 217
 governance capacity, 238
 interventions at Broadway, 98
 local food leaders, 62
 mainstream models insufficient, 62
 management gap at Broadway, 156
 market schemes at Exmouth, 190

more satisfying consumption, 155
more work on food, 267
narrative of exclusion, 214
narratives at Broadway, 159
narratives at Exmouth, 196
new form of food based, 221
physical at Exmouth, 111
place marketing and inclusion, 146
place marketing focus, 53
problematised at quarters, 244
process at Borough, 119
restaurant led at Exmouth, 210
shared trajectory, 231
structural forces influencing, 236
sustainability at Broadway, 170
sustainability through food, 267
Trust at Borough, 144
urban design at Broadway, 166
renewal trajectory
 at each quarter, 116
 competing narratives, 241
 diversification at Borough, 123
 experienced at Broadway, 185
 nature at Borough, 124
 similarities across quarters, 233
 social and economic effects, 245
restaurant 'solution'
 strategy at Exmouth, 188
restoration
 Broadway's design context, 100
 programme at Borough Market, 83
semi-structured interviews
 findings at Exmouth, 206
 findings from Broadway, 169
 research method, 20
 results at Borough, 123
 use at Broadway, 169
 use at Exmouth, 186
sense of community
 attracting visitors to Exmouth, 199
 findings at Broadway, 184
 key to Exmouth's success, 193

mix of traditional and new food businesses, 245
 perceived at Exmouth, 189
 stressed at Broadway, 156
sense of place
 decline at Broadway, 99
 decline at each food quarter, 117
 evident at Borough, 85
 food as central, 19
 food role in, 60
 importance to market advocates at Broadway, 178
 interplay of design qualities, 70
 noted by visitors to Borough, 133
 reinforced by design elements, 216
 related to design at Exmouth, 113
 renewal interventions, 227
 street assessment confirming, 230
 strength at each food quarter, 229
 strongly marked at Exmouth, 112
 traditional space shaping, 69
 traditional urban structure, 257
 underpinning social life, 262
serial vision
 at Borough Market, 86
 at Broadway Market, 182
 at Exmouth Market, 228
 framing market views, 69
serious shoppers
 practices at Borough, 136
settlement pattern
 areas studied in terms of, 76
 food market as focal point, 115
 food market in each quarter, 225
 layers at Borough, 84
 rural to urban at Broadway, 94
Slow Cities (città slow)
 food quarters reflecting, 13
 movement, 7, 13
 relevance to quarters revival, 248

relevance to space shaping, 253
slow fast food
    'quick to prepare' products, 256
    at Exmouth, 206
    at Exmouth Market, 112
    element in new quarters, 265
    findings about Exmouth, 212
    food market changes, 251
    identified at quarters, 41
    role at each quarter, 252
Slow Food, 7
    'slow' fast street food, 41
    'courts' at food quarters, 50
    Exmouth as slow food court, 190
    food quarter parallels, 13
    market stalls, 12
    markets reflecting principles, 248
    sustainability at food quarters, 253
sociability
    at Broadway, 183
    at Exmouth, 231
    centrality of design, 262
    focus of research, 4
    food quarters as rich sites, 258
    food streets, 40
    physical space at Borough, 145
    place based nature, 5
social capital
    at Exmouth Market, 211
    construction at quarters, 267
    demonstrated through habitus, 39
    formation at Borough, 144
    spatialised through food, 263
    variations at each quarter, 249
social inclusion
    renewal at Borough, 126
social life
    design elements at Broadway, 173
    design influencing, 216
    food based at each quarter, 257
    food practices, 37

food space revival at Exmouth, 186
food-centred at Borough, 153
qualities of place, 265
quarters as new centrepieces, 260
richer at Broadway quarter, 171
role in conviviality, 11
temporal changes at quarters, 262
social mix
    attribute across quarters, 263
    Broadway's 'random' quality, 181
    food led renewal at Exmouth, 213
    views at Broadway, 158
    views at Exmouth, 193
social space
    at Exmouth Market, 200
    Borough as designed area, 264
    Borough's 'connector' role, 134
    focus on public realm, 233
    food quarters as, 17
    food related theory, 46
    morphological enquiry, 21
    outdoor rooms, 257
    relationship to physical space, 28
    understanding Broadway, 171
    urban design, food and health, 223
sociological approaches
    need to augment, 21
    relevance of urban design, 32
    strands explored, 222
    visual analysis, 22
sociology
    aspatial study of food, 44
    boundary crossing, 222
    food theories, 72
    study of food, 35
    use of visual methods, 22
socio-spatial practices
    as expressions of social capital, 39
    community politics, 174

convivial at Borough, 153
emerging forms of, 4
findings on urban design, 222
focused on food, 67
focused on food consumption, 183
food related at Exmouth, 206
form and behaviours, 259
impacts on physical space, 26
in relation to food, 17
new combinations, 30
new patterns, 256
physical shape of study areas, 19
positive at Borough, 146
range evident at Borough, 135
relationship to habitus, 222
spatial variations at Exmouth, 216
sustainability issues, 151
sustainable urbanism, 151
theories that inform, 16
theorised constructs, 31
urban design, 67
variations, 21
variations among place users, 17
spatial scale
  design based study of food, 45
  food systems, 43
  further food work, 46
  in food research, 31, 33
  in quarter development, 259
  issues at Broadway Market, 97
  issues at Exmouth, 112
  issues in Borough's morphology, 84
  nature of food system, 42
  neighbourhood design, 67
  notion of food deserts, 64
spatialised thinking
  applied to research, 31
  exploring primacy, 47
  results from research, 222
spatiality
  conclusions at Borough, 144
  conclusions at Broadway, 181

construction of food identities, 54
design for food, 18
economy of food places, 223
examining quarters, 75
food consumption, 5
food deserts, 64
food discussed, 44
food led regeneration, 53
food practices' contribution, 32
food-centred, 248, 250
interplay with new practices, 221
intertwining, 248
London's changing nature, 47
models for food retailing, 265
morphological results, 223
notion of habitus, 55
place-users views, 21
shifts relating to food, 50
techniques for capturing data, 23
work on conviviality, 7
sprawl
  food challenges, 8
  obesegenic environments, 65
  obesegenic space, 30
  potential for food retrofitting, 18
  retrofitting for food, 3
  shaping in contrast, 145
  urban context, 5
strategic food partnerships
  basis for renewal, 237
  community-based at Broadway, 233
  effective at Borough, 146
  possibilities for the future, 267
street assessment
  at Borough Market, 90
  at Broadway Market, 100
  at Exmouth Market, 113
  comparative results, 230
  overall conclusions, 231
streetscape
  analysis at Borough, 87
  analysis at Broadway, 101
  analysis at Exmouth, 115
  analysis of, 24

commodified approaches, 266
critique at Exmouth, 205
decline at each quarter, 228
previous focus at Exmouth, 200
role of improvements, 230
suburban retailing model
   Borough in contrast to, 143
   imposition, 52
   retrofitting traditional areas, 265
supermarkets
   attittudes to, 125
   car based model, 65
   competitors to Exmouth, 213
   consumers, 253
   decline of traditional markets, 166
   educated alternatives, 128
   food consumption, 5
   food deserts, 64
   growth, 49
   increasing scale of consumption, 65
   market traders competing, 256
   placelessness, 52
   preferences at Borough, 119
   prices at Broadway, 179
   public space, 266
   retailing strategies, 66
   spatial scale, 48
sustainability
   in food chain, 131
   increasing food consciousness, 151
sustainable cities
   design for food in support of, 4
   food-centred renewal, 264
   negative feedback loop in food, 8
taste
   as neighbourhood unifier, 57
   conviviality related to, 17
   dynamic nature, 33
   eating in the street, 40
   markets as expressions, 258
   markets as sites, 4
   nutritional approaches, 33

third places
   'hybrid' hospitality, 256
   importance at Exmouth, 212
   theorised importance, 11
trading 'out'
   design at Borough, 84
traditional food markets
   Borough prices in comparison, 126
   compared to farmers' markets, 3
   decline at Broadway, 180
   steep decline at Exmouth, 187
traditional food shops
   authenticity at Broadway, 181
   design of quarters, 263
   mix at Exmouth, 193
   part of food quarter mix, 12
   role at Broadway, 180
traditional urban form
   design qualities, 69
   food quarter development, 264
   larger scale food retailing, 49
   loss of coherence, 224
   setting for food quarters, 3
transforming role of food
   spatial scale, 6
transport
   accessibility at Borough, 91
   advances in food movement, 43
   changes at Broadway, 182
   design constraint, 229
   dramatic changes at Borough, 79
   infrastructure at Broadway, 96
   of food, 10
   proximity to hubs, 229
urban agriculture
   history at each quarter, 225
   increasing focus, 18
urban armature
   design methods to explore, 227
   elements at Exmouth, 112
   elements comprising, 24
urban blight
   at Broadway Market, 96
   Borough's resurgence, 85
   context at each quarter, 226

Market Place: Food Quarters, Design and Urban Renewal in London   331

legacy at Exmouth, 114
urban design
　analysis at Broadway, 100
　analysis at Exmouth, 111, 215
　analysis conclusions, 231
　applying methods, 23
　choices with food outcomes, 15
　comments at Exmouth, 201
　conclusions in food quarters, 268
　cultural quarters, 60
　economic revitalisation, 232
　elements relevant to food, 20
　European City Model, 32
　food-led at Broadway, 166
　in Broadway's revival, 182
　justification for use, 21
　links to food at Borough, 144
　master planning analysis, 75
　morphological research, 224
　nuanced renewal approach, 266
　qualities at Broadway, 232
　qualities for food-centred space, 69
　regeneration of Exmouth, 200
　relationship to principles, 65
　research questions, 4
　reviewing Borough area, 85
　reviewing Exmouth Market, 103
　revitalisation at Broadway, 181
　role in quarters, 19
　sense of place, 19
　shaping social use at Exmouth, 216
　socio-spatial practices, 18
　specifically for food, 68
　studying food and cities, 5
　sustainability at Borough, 122
　temporal aspects at Exmouth, 203
　theorists shaping analysis, 223
　theory and research methods, 18
　traditional city form, 186
urban design guidance
　greater focus on food, 266
urban food policy
　need to spatialise, 267

urban pioneers
　at each food quarter, 58
　creating value through food, 146
　first wave gentrifiers, 196
　narratives at Broadway Market, 164
urban structure
　compositional aspects, 75
　conclusions from quarters, 115
　design analysis at Borough, 86
　fine grained at Borough, 87
　historic analysis at Borough, 79
　historic analysis at Broadway, 99
　historic analysis at Exmouth, 111
　levels of enclosure, 228
　rich qualities at each quarter, 229
urban sustainability, 3
　central theme, 8
　food quarter development, 253
　food-led design contributing, 267
　impact of food quarters, 245
　new food spaces, 149
　paradigm for work on food, 223
　recent food focus in London, 239
　views about food at Exmouth, 216
urban village
　Broadway understood as, 165
　design theory context, 181
　Exmouth's historic status, 187
　liveability and sustainability, 244
　notion in food terms, 167
urbanisation
　context for research, 47
　morphology at Exmouth, 106
　predominant forms, 47
　transformations in London, 210
visitor catchment
　centrality of food, 252
　findings on spatiality, 250
　global at Borough, 76
　issues at Exmouth, 194
　nature at Exmouth, 197
　temporal aspects, 251
　use of mapping, 229

widening at Broadway, 154
wider spatial range, 230
visual methods
  comparative results, 225
  drawing research conclusions, 224
  to study design of quarters, 75
visual richness
  demonstrated at Borough, 90
  demonstrated at Broadway, 101
  demonstrated at Exmouth, 115
  design quality investigated, 20
  found at each quarter, 228
  theorised for food quarter, 70
walkable space
  'destination' dining, 234
  catchments, 25
  characteristic of food quarters, 3

combatting obesity, 266
defining spatial boundaries, 224
food catchment radius, 70
food quarter permeability, 229
food services focus, 66
growth at Exmouth, 203
growth of local catchment, 157
key to food quarters, 10
nature of Borough area, 88
nature of Broadway area, 101
nature of Exmouth area, 113
positive examples, 4
public realm for food, 262
radius for food quarters, 64
traditional urbanism, 67
Whitecross Street Market
  competitor for Exmouth, 211